Lecture Notes in Computer

Commenced Publication in 1973
Founding and Former Series Editors:
Gerhard Goos, Juris Hartmanis, and Jan van L

T0230293

Arend Rensink Jos Warmer (Eds.)

Model Driven Architecture – Foundations and Applications

Second European Conference, ECMDA-FA 2006
Bilbao, Spain, July 10-13, 2006
Proceedings

 Springer

Volume Editors

Arend Rensink
University of Twente
Department of Computer Science
P.O. Box 217, 7500 AE Enschede, The Netherlands
E-mail: rensink@cs.utwente.nl

Jos Warmer
Ordina
Chalonhof 153, 3762 CT Soest, The Netherlands
E-mail: jos.warmer@ordina.nl

Library of Congress Control Number: 2006928026

CR Subject Classification (1998): C.2, D.2, D.3, F.3, C.3, H.4

LNCS Sublibrary: SL 2 – Programming and Software Engineering

ISSN   0302-9743
ISBN-10   3-540-35909-5 Springer Berlin Heidelberg New York
ISBN-13   978-3-540-35909-8 Springer Berlin Heidelberg New York

Springer is a part of Springer Science+Business Media

springer.com

© Springer-Verlag Berlin Heidelberg 2006
Printed in Germany

Typesetting: Camera-ready by author, data conversion by Scientific Publishing Services, Chennai, India
Printed on acid-free paper   SPIN: 11787044   06/3142   5 4 3 2 1 0

Preface

Model-Driven Architecture, including model-driven approaches in general, holds the big promise of moving software development towards a higher level of abstraction. Given the challenges in the software industry of delivering more complex functionality with less effort, I am convinced that it isn't a question of *whether* model-driven development will succeed, but rather a question of *when* it will break through. However, before this can happen, we have many challenging problems to conquer. There are both theoretical and pragmatic problems to solve and therefore we need a close collaboration between industry and the academic world.

The goal of the European Conference on Model-Driven Architecture — Foundations and Applications (ECMDA-FA) is to bring together industry and academia to tackle the problems in model-driven development. This volume includes 18 foundation papers and 12 application papers, which is a fine balance between both worlds. ECMDA-FA 2006 also hosted six workshops on both theoretical and practical aspects of MDA. Furthermore, the keynote speakers, David Frankel and Bran Selic, from some of the world's largest IT companies proved that industry is very much involved in MDA.

This second ECMDA-FA conference is the result of the work of the authors who submitted a total of 78 papers, the Program Committee members who took the effort to review the papers, the people organizing the workshops, and of course the Steering Committee. All in all, several hundreds of people have worked hard to make this conference a success. I have the honor of speaking for all these people in this preface and I would like to thank each of them for their valuable contribution.

The ECMDA-FA 2006 conference was supported by the European Commission and the MODELWARE project under the "Information Society Technologies" Sixth Framework Programme, and by the Object Management Group (OMG).

July 2006

Jos Warmer
Program Chair
ECMDA-FA 2006

Organization

Organizing Committee

Programme and Conference Chair:	Jos Warmer (Ordina)
Local Arrangements Chair:	Asier Azaceta (ESI)
Workshop Chair:	David Akehurst (University of Kent)
Tools and Consultancy Chair:	Alan Hartman (IBM)
Webmaster:	David Kreische (imbus)
Public Relations Chair:	Robert Pastor (Thales)
Publications Chair:	Arend Rensink (University of Twente)

Steering Committee

Alan Hartman (IBM, General Chair)
David Akehurst (University of Kent)
Uwe Assman (TU Dresden)
Asier Azaceta (ESI)
David Kreische (imbus)
Arend Rensink (University of Twente)
Jos Warmer (Ordina)

Program Committee

Jan Aagedal
Mehmet Aksit
Mariano Belaunde
Antonia Bertolino
Jean Bézivin
Xavier Blanc
Manfred Broy
Krysztof Czarnecki
Miguel de Miguel
Jean-Luc Dekeyser
Serge Demeyer
Philippe Desfray
Jürgen Dingel
Gregor Engels
Tracy Gardner
Reiko Heckel
Simon Johnston
Gabor Karsai
Roger Kilian-Kehr
Anneke Kleppe
Tom Mens
Veronique Normand
Richard Paige
Yves-Marie Quemener
Chris Raistrick
Laurent Rioux
Bernhard Rumpe
Branislav Selic
Juha-Pekka Tolvanen
Andreas Ulrich
Marten van Sinderen
Gerd Wagner
James Willans
Clay Williams
Albert Zündorf

Additional Reviewers

Joao Paulo Almeida
Michal Antkiewicz
Terry Bailey
Aitor Bediaga
Laura Bocchi
Lossan Bond'e
Phil Brooke
Antonio Bucchiarone
Alessandro Campi
María Victoria Cengarle
Alexey Cherchago
Michelle Crane
Gregory Defombelle
Folker Den Braber
Zinovy Diskin
Cedric Dumoulin
Karsten Ehrig
Michael Fahrmair
Madeleine Faugere
Luis Ferreira Pires
Alexander Foerster
Leif Geiger
Rosemaria Giesecke
Adrian Giurca
Hans Grönniger
Renata Guizzardi
Baris Güldali
Antoine Honoré
Eshref Januzaj
Eric Jouenne
Dimitrios Kolovos
Holger Krahn
Ouassila Labbani

Georgios Lajios
Xabier Larrucea
Jérôme Le Noir
Marc Lohmann
Sergey Lukichev
Thomas Maier
Stefano Merenda
Raffaela Mirandola
Olaf Muliawan
Daniela Oldenburg-Oldenburger
Jon Oldevik
Fiona Polack
Carsten Reckord
Dirk Reiß
Erkuden Rios
Jochen Rode
Julia Rubin
Antonino Sabetta
Tim Schattkowsky
Stefan Scheidl
Martin Schindler
Hans Schippers
Christian Schneider
Maurice Schoenmakers
Boris Shishkov
Jeff Smith
Arnor Solberg
Bjørnar Solhaug
Prawee Sriplakich
Mark Stein
Pieter Van Gorp
Hendrik Voigt
Alexander Wisspeintner

Table of Contents

Model Consistency

Model Management

Transformation (1)

Ontologies

Reengineering

Tools and Profiles

Tool Generation

Constraints

Model Management and Transformations

Transformation (2)

A Model-Driven Architectural Framework for Integration-Capable Enterprise Application Product Lines

Vinay Kulkarni and Sreedhar Reddy

Tata Research Development and Design Centre, Pune, India
{vinay.vkulkarni, sreedhar.reddy}@tcs.com

Abstract. Enterprise business applications are critical to the smooth operation of modern businesses and need to quickly respond to changing business rules, processes and technologies. Also, the ever-increasing thrust on collaboration calls for these applications to smoothly integrate with each other. MDA enables an application to be specified in terms of platform independent models each addressing a concern of interest and then transforming them into a platform-specific implementation. Traditional organization of an enterprise, as a set of functionally distinct departments, results in a set of isolated applications providing point solutions each constructed for a specific purpose with context-specific built-in assumptions implicit in their specifications. These assumptions lead to conflicts or mismatches during integration calling for application integration to be addressed as an explicitly modeled concern. Typically, a business application needs to be specialized for the requirements of a specific enterprise. Product line architectures that organize systems into well-defined core and variable parts have been proposed to address this need. However, traditional code based development approaches lack suitable abstractions to support product lines. We propose a model driven architectural framework that enables a system to be specified in terms of composable units, along the required dimensions of variation, wherein the integration requirements are modeled explicitly. Component interface is augmented with data models, process models, constraints, assertions and pre/post-conditions. A set of properties that need to be satisfied for semantically correct integration are proposed along with a set of verification techniques. We propose a software factory that seamlessly addresses development and integration needs of enterprise product lines and describe our experience in building and using it.

1 Introduction

Modern businesses rely on enterprise business applications for their smooth operation that need to quickly respond to changes in business rules, business processes and technology platforms during their lifetime. Model-driven development approach addresses this problem by providing a set of modeling notations for specifying different layers of a system namely user interface, application functionality and database in a platform independent manner [18]. A set of code generators then

A. Rensink and J. Warmer (Eds.): ECMDA-FA 2006, LNCS 4066, pp. 1 – 12, 2006.
© Springer-Verlag Berlin Heidelberg 2006

transforms these models into platform-specific implementations. Models, being at a higher level of abstraction, are easier to understand and verify for properties of interest. Model based code generation incorporating proven design and architectural patterns results in significant gains in productivity and uniformly high quality [17].

The growing popularity of electronic business, use of Internet technology and the upcoming demand of globalization are escalating the demand for collaborative and extended enterprise application environments that span across the entire value chain providing value added services [8]. Future enterprise systems are unlikely to be developed from scratch. Instead, customized product lines will be integrated with off-the-shelf offerings and harvested legacy systems into a service oriented architecture. The ability to quickly customize such assets and integrate them into a vendor-specific variant of service oriented architecture will be a critical success factor in this emerging scenario [9, 10]. Typically, enterprise applications are designed to operate in a specific context with the context-specific built-in assumptions getting hard-coded in the implementation [19]. These assumptions lead to conflicts or mismatches during integration with other applications. Identification and mitigation of these conflicts are the principal challenges of application integration [16, 20]. For safe integration [3], it needs to be established whether an existing application fits into the context of the desired integrated application or not. In case of a mismatch, one would like to know if the existing application could be made to fit with some adaptation. The candidate applications, with or without adaptation, need to be integrated with assurance of completeness with respect to the desired integrated application. At present, we only have support for service adaptation that is limited to data transformation and service invocation across heterogeneous platforms with no guarantees for semantic correctness of integration.

As no two enterprises are exactly alike, a business application needs to be specialized for the requirements of a specific enterprise. Product line architectures that organize systems into well-defined core and variable parts have been proposed to address this need, the central idea being products within a product-line are differentiated by features [14, 7]. Producing a specific product variant can be seen as a stepwise refinement process wherein a common abstract model is refined to inject product-specific factors [5]. Feature commonalities can be captured as reusable patterns from which specific variants can be instantiated through suitable parameterization. A tool-driven software factory can provide the necessary machinery to assemble the instantiated patterns [11]. Multi-dimensional separation of concerns approach addresses this need through decomposition of a system along multiple dimensions of interest [25]. Aspect oriented programming provides support for this approach, but only at programming language level, where the same base language is used for specifying the different aspects of the system [15]. However, one would like to use purpose-specific languages to specify various aspects wherever possible. The richer abstractions provided by such higher-level domain specific languages lead to ease of understanding and analysis, and a possibility of code generation.

We propose a model driven architectural framework that enables a system to be specified in terms of composable units, along the required dimensions of variation of a product line, wherein integration requirements are explicitly modeled. The approach is based on an extended component abstraction wherein component interface is augmented with data models, process models, constraints, assertions and

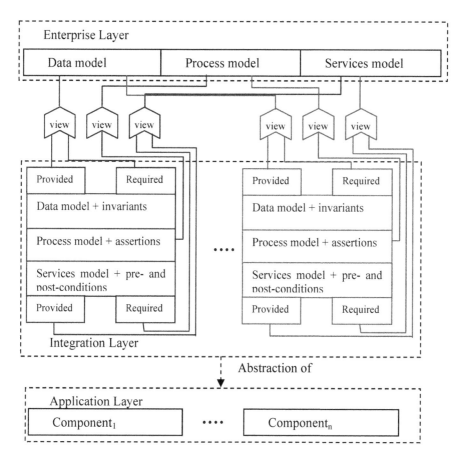

Fig. 1. Architecture for application integration

pre/post-conditions. A set of properties that need to be satisfied for semantically correct integration are proposed along with a set of verification techniques. We propose a software factory that seamlessly addresses development and integration needs of enterprise product lines and describe our experience in building and using it. Section 2 describes the proposed architectural framework to support semantically correct application integration. Section 3 describes a model-driven software factory to support enterprise application product lines. Section 4 discusses our experience in realizing and using the software factory. Section 5 discusses issues that need to be addressed for acceptance of the proposed approach. Section 6 provides a summary and outlines future work.

2   Architectural Framework for Application Integration

We propose a layered architecture wherein enterprise systems are modeled at three levels of abstraction, namely, Enterprise, Integration and Application as shown in figure 1. Enterprise layer specifies the desired integrated system in terms of its data model, process model and services supporting the data and process models. Enterprise layer is viewed in terms of a set of required components each providing a set of services that manage locally owned data. These services are responsible for supporting the process flows. Application layer specifies the existing applications using component abstraction. Typically, a component represents an existing application and specifies its interface in terms of a set of service signatures. Integration layer uses an extended component abstraction to specify what a component provides to the external world and what it needs from the external world. The abstraction specifies the data a component provides to and requires from the external world, the services it provides to and requires from, and its view of the business processes it participates in. The data part is specified in terms of an object model with constraints, the service part is specified in terms of pre- and post-conditions, and the process part is specified in terms of a process model annotated with assertions on data state. Essentially, the integration layer captures all the relevant information necessary for semantically correct integration of an existing application in a desired context. The integration layer can be viewed as an abstract specification of the application layer with all the built-in assumptions about its environment made explicit. The application layer can be viewed as a concrete realization of the *provided* parts of the specification given in the integration layer.

In a system development exercise, the enterprise layer specifies the desired integrated application; the integration layer specifies the integration requirements of the existing as well as new components if any, and a set of mappings that specify how each of these components is related to the desired integrated application. A mapping is specified in terms of three relationships, namely, data view, services view and process view. The architectural framework postulates that a set of participating components integrate correctly to produce the desired integrated application when the following properties hold:

- The data models provided by the integration layer are sufficient to meet the data model requirements of the enterprise layer
- The service models provided by the integration layer are sufficient to meet the service model requirements of the enterprise layer, i.e., the services provided by the integration layer are sufficient to realize the process requirements of the enterprise layer
- The process flows of the enterprise layer are safe [3] with respect to the process flow expectations of the participating components as specified in the integration layer
- The data state assertions of the process flows of the integration layer are satisfied by the process model of the enterprise layer
- The data that each participating component requires from its environment is provided by the data model of the desired integrated system as specified in the enterprise layer
- The data model constraints of participating components as specified in the integration layer are satisfied by the data model of the integrated system specified in the enterprise layer

– The services that each participating component requires from its environment are provided by the service model of the desired integrated application as specified in the enterprise layer

– The implementations of components in the application layer satisfy their specifications in the integration layer, and the integration layer is a complete specification of the integration requirements of the participating component implementations in the application layer.

The proposed architectural framework can be supported using the modeling notations prevalent in the industry. UML class diagrams can be used to specify data and service models [23]. Data constraints and service pre/post-conditions can be specified using OCL [24]. Process models can be specified using a UML profile for business process modeling [1]. The mappings between integration and enterprise layers can be specified using a model transformation language such as QVT [22]. The mappings are bi-directional and can be used to transform constraints and pre/post-conditions from one layer to the other. However, modeling notations such as BPEL4WS [12], UML profile [1] etc. used by industry practice to specify business processes do not have rich enough semantic underpinnings to verify integration properties. On the other hand, formal techniques like model checking and theorem proving require elaborate specifications and do not yet scale up to the sizes typical of industrial applications. There is a need for a pragmatic approach that bridges the gap between these high level modeling notations and formalisms that support various analyses.

The integration properties fall under two broad categories, namely, correctness and completeness. Correctness properties address whether existing applications can be safely integrated in the desired integration context. Completeness properties address whether all the requirements of the desired integrated system can be met by the applications being integrated. In the proposed architecture, correctness and complete-ness properties need to be verified for three models i.e. data, service and process models. Correctness of a participating application with respect to its data model can be modeled as a view definition problem. The participating application can be integrated correctly if its required data model can be expressed as a view over the data model of the integrated system specified in the enterprise layer. Completeness of the data model of the desired integrated system can be modeled as a view integration problem [6]. The data model of the desired application is complete if it can be realized as a composition of the provided data models of the participating applications. The service model has two parts namely, structural and behavioral. The behavioral part is addressed by correctness and completes of process models. Correctness of the structural part is essentially a type-checking problem wherein the signature in the integration layer is either an exact match of or is coercible to the signature in the enterprise layer with respect to the view definitions. Verifying the correctness of a participating application with respect to its process model has two parts to it. The process flows of the desired integrated system should be safe with respect to the expected process flows of individual participating applications, and the process model of the desired integrated system should satisfy the constraints, assertions and pre/post-conditions of the participating applications. The former can be verified by language inclusion techniques on process automata [3] and the latter can be addressed either by model checking or theorem proving or automated testing. The process model of the desired integrated system is complete with respect to the process models of the participating applications if all the process flows of the desired integrated system can be safely realized through the process flows supported by the participating applications. This can also be verified using language inclusion techniques on process automata [4]. We take recourse to automated testing through test-data and test-case generation where the verification techniques fail to scale. The proposed architectural framework caters only to the functional aspects of the application. Non-functional characteristics like architecture, technology platforms, design strategies etc are not addressed by this framework. We use a software factory approach discussed below to address these concerns.

3   Model-Driven Software Factory for Enterprise Product Lines

Typically, enterprise business applications tend to vary along five dimensions namely, functionality (F), business process (P), architecture (A), design strategies (D) and technology platform (T). Also, the integration requirements of an application change with the context in which it needs to operate. These requirements are modeled, as described earlier, along the Integration dimension of concern (I). A model based code generator encodes specific choices along A, D and T dimensions and generates suitable data and service adapters for integration. We propose a software factory for an enterprise business application product line wherein a set of product line variant specific model based code generators are generated from their specifications. Figure 2 shows the proposed model driven software factory for enterprise business application product lines.

A product line is organized as a repository of composable building blocks structured along the different dimensions of variation. A specific product line variant is derived as a composition of such building blocks of interest along these dimensions. The derivation process begins by matching the requirements of the desired variant against the repository to select closest matching building blocks. A gap analysis then identifies the necessary modifications and adaptations to the candidate building blocks, if any. It may also lead to development of new building blocks. A purpose-specific code generator is then generated from these modified building blocks along A, D, T and I dimensions. The component specifications verified for integration properties, as discussed in the previous section, essentially address functionality and process aspects of the desired application. The purpose-specific code generator translates these specifications into a platform-specific implementation incorporating the selected design and architectural patterns, and generates suitable data and service adapters if any required for integration.

In our approach, an application is specified as a hierarchical composition of building blocks of interest along the dimensions of variation. A building block encapsulates reusable functionality along a dimension of variation. A building block can be seen as a specification of an aspect expressed in terms of a language specified by an associated meta model. Figure 3 shows the meta model of a building block itself. On instantiation, a building block brings along a set of model elements that conforms to the meta model and associated constraints. Building blocks are of two

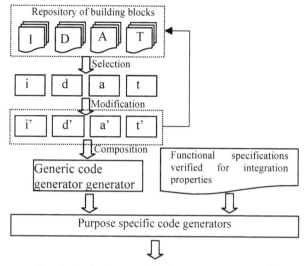

Fig. 2. A model driven software factory

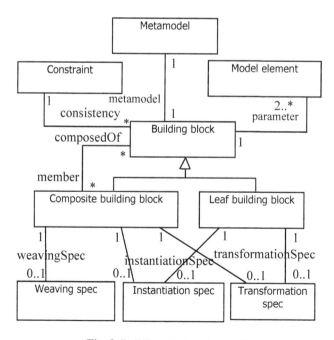

Fig. 3. Building block meta model

kinds: *leaf building block* and *composite building block*. The instantiation specification of a leaf building block specifies how to stamp out aspect-specific model elements. The transformation specification specifies how the model is transformed into code. The instantiation specification of a composite building block specifies how model elements constructed in member building blocks are merged (woven) together. We have found *merge by name* scheme of model merging sufficient for our purposes. Weaving specification of a composite building block specifies how the code generated by its member building blocks is woven together. We have found a code weaving specification language along the lines of Hyper/J [13] sufficient for our purposes. We have used a model-to-text transformation language called SpecL for model transformations [22].

The process of aspect composition is realized through a post-order traversal of the building block hierarchy in three sequential steps namely *Instantiation*, *Transformation* and *Weaving*. The instantiation step stamps out models and merges them. The transformation step transforms models into code and generates weaving specifications for composing the generated code. The weaving step composes the generated code fragments by processing the weaving specifications.

4   Experience

During the past 10 years we have developed several business-critical enterprise solutions for a variety of business verticals like banking, financial services and insurance [17]. We are in the process of organizing these purpose-specific enterprise solutions in the form of vertical-specific product lines. The proposed software factory provides infrastructure to address technology, process and integration concerns of product lines. We are in the process of defining the required domain specific languages to specify building blocks along the required dimensions for each product line.

The process of deriving a specific product variant begins by identifying the business process flows of interest. This leads to identification of functions required to implement these flows. A keyword based search identifies functionality, process and Integration building blocks available in the repository. A manual comparison of the desired business process flows and business functions with existing process flows and their implementations identifies the functionality gap. Non-functional requirements like performance, throughput, architecture and technology platform are the basis for identifying D, A and T building blocks. A simple keyword based search mechanism is provided for selecting suitable D, A and T building blocks. These building blocks are composed to generate an implementation of model based code generators that impart the desired non-functional characteristics to the business functionality under consideration. If found unsuitable, one goes back to select a different set of D, A and T building blocks from the repository or modifies the existing ones suitably.

We have realized the factory vision shown in figure 1 only in parts by being able to address the D, A and T dimensions of variation by aspect-oriented restructuring of our MDD toolset facilitating easy customization of the code generators. We decomposed the code generators into well-defined self-contained building blocks such as model to

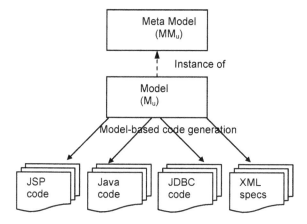

Fig. 4. Model driven development

java, object-relational map, auditing, concurrency management, error handling, message handling strategies like synchronous, asynchronous, queue-based etc.

Our MDD toolset [20] translates a model (M_u) that is an instance of a unified meta model (MM_u) to various software artifacts like Java code, JDBC code, JSP code and a variety of configuration specifications in XML as shown in figure 4. Limiting aspect weaving only to code level artifacts would necessitate specialized weavers for Java, JDBC, JSP, XML etc. each having separate join point models. Also, this approach would necessitate some commonality over these join point models so as to have an integrated Java application. With increased number of software artefacts to be produced the approach becomes increasingly complex as essentially it amounts to building aspect infrastructure for each such artifact. We address this problem by specifying aspect weaving at the unified meta model level and performing it at the model level whenever possible. Unified meta model enables specification of relationships between the various (sub) modeling languages. A reflexive meta modeling framework provides the necessary infrastructure to define and integrate the various modeling languages of interest and a meta model aware model transformation framework provides the necessary technology to address model weaving requirements. Performing aspect weaving at the model level also, whenever possible, results in simplification of model based code generators which are essentially model-to-text transformers.

We found that aspect-oriented restructuring of our MDD toolset has facilitated easy customization of the code generators and has resulted in increased reuse across their variants. Our MDD toolset has been used to develop several large enterprise class business applications for the past several years. These applications can be viewed as a set of vertical-specific product lines having toolset requirements that are *similar* but not exactly the same. Earlier, such a customization request meant opening up the implementation of the impacted tools that required expertise of all the tools to ensure the relevant changes are implemented in a consistent manner. Aspect-oriented restructuring has enabled us to organize the development team along two independent streams namely technology platform experts and design experts. A single design team can now service all the technology platform teams. Separation of design strategies has enabled leaner technology platform teams. Moreover, it has enabled our toolset itself to be organized as a product family wherein a tool variant can be composed from design strategy and technology platform aspects of choice. Containment of change impact due to localization and increased reuse due to composability have led to quick turn around times for delivering a tool variant. Use of a higher-level model-aware transformation language has made maintenance and evolution of our product line easy.

5 Issues

Several issues need to be addressed for widespread industrial acceptance of the proposed solution.

Regarding integration – For semantically correct integration, it is imperative that the terminology being used has the same standard meaning across all the applications being integrated. This calls for industry-wide standardization efforts to arrive at domain-specific ontologies [2]. Externalization of built-in assumptions encoded in implementations is central to the proposed architecture. This calls for tool support for sophisticated static and dynamic analysis of programs. System integration projects may involve use of 3rd party components from different vendors. These component interface definitions need to be extended along the lines mentioned earlier requiring an industry-wide standardization effort. It should be possible to take recourse to automated testing through test-data and test-case generation where the verification techniques fail to scale up. There is a need for tools capable of generating test-data and test-cases from the integration specifications. Results of formal analyses need to be translated back into the high level notations. This calls for a bi-directional bridge between high level notations used by industry practice and the formalisms supporting the desired analyses.

Regarding aspects – It is not clear which facets of a system deserve to be treated as aspects. There is a need to investigate how these aspects can be modeled and what the right kind of abstractions for modeling them are to satisfy the various 'ities' like maintainability, reusability etc. Aspects may overlap thus introducing a dependency on the order of their weaving. In such cases, how does one ensure that properties of all aspects hold after their weaving? An aspect specification may exist partly in model form and partly in code form. What's the right approach to integrate such aspects into the aspect modeling framework? How to trace an aspect to the final implementation? It is not clear how to compute the impact of a change in an aspect on the final implementation of the system. This information would be critical for 'what if analysis', estimating testing efforts, managing releases etc.

Regarding MDA tool support – Supporting separation of concerns for product lines using MDA raises several tooling issues. The modeling tool should be extensible to support new modeling languages so as to be able to define new aspect models and relate them to the existing component models through model transformation. The model transformation tool should have adequate support for pattern matching and composition, and should provide support for incremental reconciliation of models. The performance of the tool should scale up to cater to the demands of enterprise class applications. A bug detected at code level should be traceable back to the aspect specification. There should be support, preferably tool-aided, for aspect-based testing. Since aspects are independently specified, it should be possible to specify test cases for an aspect independently and compose the test cases to arrive at the system level test cases.

6 Summary

In this paper, we presented a model driven architectural framework to support integration-capable enterprise application product lines. We have discussed a set of properties that need to be verified to ensure semantically correct integration. A pragmatic approach has been proposed that combines the convenience of high level notations used by the industry practice and the rigour of formal verification techniques. We have implemented a proof-of-concept prototype for process integration validating the feasibility of the proposed approach. The proposed architectural framework can serve as foundation for a pragmatic application integration method. We have a partial realization of a model driven software factory that addresses Design strategies, Architecture and Technology platform concerns. We have also discussed several issues that still need to be addressed for the proposed approach to gain industrial acceptance.

References

[1] Jim Amsden, Tracy Gardner, Catherine Griffin and Sridhar Iyengar, "Draft UML 1.4 profile for automated Business process with a mapping to BPEL1.0", IBM
[2] A. Ankolekar et al. "DAML-S: Web Service Description for the Semantic Web", Proceedings of the International Semantic Web Conference (ISWC), 2002.
[3] Souvik Barat and Vinay Kulkarni, "Enterprise application Integration using Process Mediation", TRDDC Technical report, 2005.
[4] Souvik Barat, Vinay Kulkarni and D Janakiram, "A safety criterion for reusing a business process in the desired integrated process", submitted to SCC'06
[5] Don Batory, Jacob Neal Sarvela and Axel Rauschmayer, Scaling step-wise refinement, IEEE TSE, 2004
[6] M A Casanova and V M P Vidal, Towards a sound view integration methodology, Proceedings of the 2nd ACM SIGACT-SIGMOD symposium on Principles of database systems, pp 36-47, 1983
[7] K Czarnecki and U Eisenecker, Generative programming methods, tools and applications, Addison-Wesley, 2000.
[8] Gartner Research, ID Number: G00127586, 'Hype Cycle for IT Services, 2005'
[9] Gartner Research, ID Number: G00131143, 'Predicts 2006: The Strategic Impact of SOA Broadens'
[10] Gartner Research, ID Number: G00131254, 'Major Forces Changing the Software Industry, 2005 Update'
[11] Jack Greenfield and Keith Short, Software factories: Assembling applications with patterns, models, frameworks and tools, Wiley, 2004.

[12] IBM, "Specification: Business Process Execution Language for Web Services Version 1.1", July 2002, "http://www-128.ibm.com/developerworks/library/specification/ws-bpel/"

[13] IBM research. Hyper/J: Multi-dimensional separation of concerns for Java. http://www.research.ibm.com/hyperspace/HyperJ/HyperJ.htm

[14] K Kang, S Kohen, J Hess, W Novak and A Peterson, Feature-orientation domain analysis feasibility study, Technical Report, CMU/SEI-90TR-21, November 1990.

[15] Gregor Kiczales, John Lamping, Anurag Mendhekar, Chris Maeda, Cristina Videira Lopes, Jean-Marc Longtier and John Irwin. Aspect oriented programming. ECOOP'97 LNCS 1241, pp 220-242. Springer-Verlag. June 1997.

[16] P. Johannesson, B. Wangler, and P Jayaweera, "Application and Process Integration – Concepts, Issues, and Research Directions", Information Systems Engineering Symposium 2000, eds., Springer Verlag, 2000.

[17] Vinay Kulkarni, Sreedhar Reddy: Model-Driven Development of Enterprise Applications. UML Satellite Activities 2004: 118-128

[18] Vinay Kulkarni, R. Venkatesh and Sreedhar Reddy. Generating enterprise applications from models. OOIS'02, LNCS 2426, pp 270-279. 2002.

[19] Vinay Kulkarni and Sreedhar Reddy, "Integrating Aspects with Model Driven Software Development". Software Engineering Research and Practice 2003, pp 186-197.

[20] D Linthicum, Enterprise Application Integration, Addison-Wesley, 2000.

[21] MasterCraft – Component-based Development Environment. Technical Documents. Tata Research Development and Design Centre. http://www.tata-mastercraft.com

[22] MOF Query / View / Transformations http://www.omg.org/cgi-bin/doc?ad/05-09-01

[23] OMG, "UML Infrastructure 2.0 Draft Adopted Specification", 2003, www.omg.org/uml/.

[24] OMG, "UML 2.0 OCL specifications", www.omg.org/docs/ptc/03-10-14.pdf

[25] Peri Tarr, Harold Ossher, William Harrison and Stanley M. Suttom Jr. N Degrees of separation: Multi-dimensional separation of concerns. Proceedings of the International Conference on Software Engineering (ICSE'99) pp 107-119.

Systems Integration Methodology Based on MDA

Antonio Estévez[1], José D. García[1], Javier Padrón[1], Carlos López[1],
Marko Txopitea[2], Beatriz Alustiza[3], and José L. Roda[4]

[1] Open Canarias, SL, Elías Ramos González, 4, ofc. 304, S/C de Tenerife, 38001 España
info@opencanarias.com
[2] Open Norte, S.L., Madariaga Etorbidea, 1 – 4. Ezkerra, 48014 Bilbao, España
opennorte@opennorte.com
[3] IZFE, S.A., Pinares Plaza, 1 – 4. solairua, 20001 Donostia – San Sebastián, España
idazkari@gipuzkoa.net
[4] ULL, Escuela Técnica Superior de Ingeniería Informática
Universidad de La Laguna, La Laguna, España
jlroda@ull.es

Abstract. Business corporations use frameworks and heterogeneous tools in the running of their systems. Most of these systems require the interaction between heterogeneous architectures, technologies and platforms. This integration is usually a complex task, which Model-Driven Architecture (MDA) approach to Model-Driven Software Development (MDSD) has promised to facilitate. In this paper we present a MDA-based methodology to platforms integration and show how it is successfully applied to a real business environment. In particular, the integration of three technological platforms (a framework based on Struts and J2EE, the transactional system CICS and the document manager FileNet) into a single development environment was carried out. Using this development environment, application code is 100% generated from UML-based models.

1 Introduction

Business corporations use frameworks and heterogeneous tools in the running of their systems. Most of these systems require the interaction between heterogeneous architectures, technologies and information systems. At the moment, there are few consolidated solutions to solve these problems at a reasonable cost, which are also problem specific, proprietary and technology dependent.

Model-Driven Architecture (MDA) [14] approach to Model-Driven Software Development (MDSD) [15] has promised benefits to software development. However, MDA-based development is not an easy task, and tool support and methodologies are required. The goal of a MDA-based methodology must be to facilitate the implementation of applications using models as first class artifacts, i.e. the application code must be generated from these models. Among the benefits from using a higher level of abstraction when programming we can enumerate platforms integration and code correctness, maintenance and reusability. In this paper we propose an integration methodology to give support to those MDA functionalities,

A. Rensink and J. Warmer (Eds.): ECMDA-FA 2006, LNCS 4066, pp. 13 – 24, 2006.

and show its application to a real corporative environment. In particular, in this projects we aim at rising the productivity of J2EE [10] applications development, which can interoperate with transactional systems such as CICS [3] and with content managers such as FileNet [7].

In this paper we first describe the technological platforms to be integrated (Section 2). Section 3 describes the integration methodology and Section 4 shows its application to a specific problem. Sections 5 and 6 show some results and conclusions respectively. We close this article with the proposal for future work (Section 7).

2 Platforms Used in the Project

The Foral Society for Information Technology, belonging to the Foral Department of Gipuzkoa (IZFE) is responsible for maintaining an IT network with a wide range of machines: from an IBM mainframe to more than 130 Windows, Unix and GNU/Linuz servers. The network is used by staff member of the Foral Department itself---Tax Office, Transport Department, Culture and Youth, Social Services Department, Emergency Services, Innovation---as well as of all Town Councils of Guipuzcua. IZFE is responsible for more than 90 development projects each year and at the moment has more than 300 heterogeneous applications running in a state of permanent evolution. The number of persons working directly on these development projects has reached 165, without counting those collaborating within the closed environment of suppliers and providers. In this project we aim at integrating three of the heterogeneous platforms used within the IT network:

- The **IZFE framework** based on Struts [19] for J2EE web applications development. It incorporates a WebSphere Application Server for z/OS, version 5.1 [23] and a DB2 database server for z/OS, version 7.1.0 [6].
- The transactional manager **CICS** Transaction Server for z/OS, version 2.3 [4]. This platform is used to maintain inherited corporative processes and logic with a high strategic value.
- The file manager **FileNet**, version 3.0. This platform is used to maintain a great amount of high critical content.

This heterogeneous and complex set of platforms conforms to the ideal scenario to apply a MDA approach to carry out this project.

3 Integration Methodology

Given the variety and complexity of the platforms to be integrated, we decided to use a bottom-up methodology, beginning with the most specific aspects leading to generalizations and aspects in common. We thus planned a series of repeated tasks to be applied individually to each platform (Tasks1–4) and a final task (Task5) to proceed to their integration (see Figure 1).

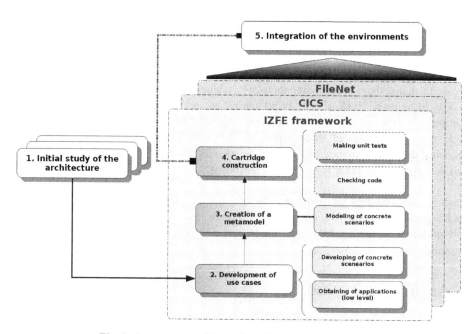

Fig. 1. Arrangement of the tasks with the methodology used

Task 1. Initial Study of the Technology and Architecture. At this stage all the available information is obtained and studied. The information is checked, validated and developed; we try to make the study as near as possible to real life circumstances.

Task 2. Development of Use Cases. At this stage, different previously developed platform-specific applications are obtained and analysed to define the functions required. As a result we establish a series of concrete scenarios to be developed. We then implemented a series of applications covering the most common work tasks and intrinsic necessities of the IZFE over that specific platform. The programes are analysed and verified at a trial stage with those technologies that already exist. We goal is to identify structures and components susceptible to be considered separately, along with abstractions and general concepts. In this process new patterns and templates were developed.

Task 3. Creation of a Metamodel. We have used UML Profiles [21] to define metamodels. UML profiles allow the customization and extension of the UML syntax and semantics to define specialized modelling languages for particular domains [8]. The basic principle for defining each profile is to obtain generalisations between different programming languages, platforms and technologies, as well as to incurporate other relevant aspects related to the integration of inherited systems and applications.

Task 4. Cartridge Construction. Having defined the functions and the metamodel, we can begin to construct the cartridge, whose function is to direct the working, compilation and packaging of the model exported in XMI [22]. In essence, a cartridge links the implementation of the UML profiles in a platform context with the programming language in which the code is generated, which in our case will be Java. This cartridge will contain a description where the profiles of each of the stereotypes are defined, and the corresponding template assigned.

We have used BOA [5] to build cartridges and platform-specific generation components. This tool allows the automatic generation of 100% of the application code through the use of three types of diagrams: class diagram (static model), sequence diagram (dynamic and interaction model) and state diagram (for integration and definition of the inner logic of class methods).

Task 5. Metamodels Unification. The creation of cartridges and metamodels for each specific domain should provide enough information to define a shared and unified metamodel. Likewise, an important work on cartridges integration is required.

4   Applying the Methodology

In order to carry out the integration we first perform Task1-4 to the different platforms. We started with the IZFE framework, as it was already identified as a key factor for the success of the project, as well as for its high level of complexity. The second platform considered was the transactional manager CICS, followed by the file manager FileNet. We finally perform Task5 to integrate all platforms in a common metamodel.

4.1   IZFE Framework

Task 1. Study of the Architecture. The IZFE framework is used for the creation of applications in a corporative business environment. It is based on the Struts framework version 1.1. The IZFE framework is divided into a series of subsystems, with the listener, control and presentation subsystems being of the first importance, as well as the business and the special security subsystems relevant in the corporative environment. Once guides and reference information had been studied, we replicate the IZFE framework into our own simulation framework to perform our studies.

Task 2. The Development of Use Cases. Two applications were selected for the administration of the framework. These applications were tested and run in our simulation framework. Having these applications as a reference, the requirements could be defined for a new application and reengineering techniques were used in its implementation. During this phase, unitary components were identified, which could be used as parametric components in the metamodel.

Task 3. Creating the Metamodel. The objective of the metamodel is to use a higher level of abstraction to describe the IZFE framework which retains the requirements of

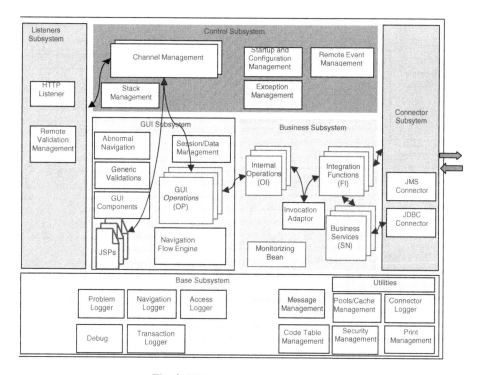

Fig. 2. IZFE Framework Architecture

the IZFE framework. We described the framewok following a MVC pattern [16], in which the domains are clearly defined and focussed on the functions of self contained web applications. With this simplification we gain in level of reuse and correctness in the applications development process, as well as a better distribution of the work to be done by separating between different domains or aspects of the project, i.e. initialisation, view, business logic, and persistence domains.

Task 4. Cartridge Construction. Our goal is to get 100% automatic code generation, which results in a considerable rise in the problem complexity, above all in the definition of the business logic. In order to reach this objective, state diagrams were used, incorporating into these states action semantics [1] which are described in the specifications 1.5 of the UML. To reach this approximation, Action Specification Language was employed (ASL) [2], and with certain modifications a grammar and a parser were developed, using a compiler from the SableCC [17] compiler. In this way a cartridge which generated 100% of the application code was built. Now the IZFE, instead of programming these applications directly, uses the metamodel defined in terms of a UML profile in order to represent their needs graphically. The system is capable of automatically generating applications from these diagrams.

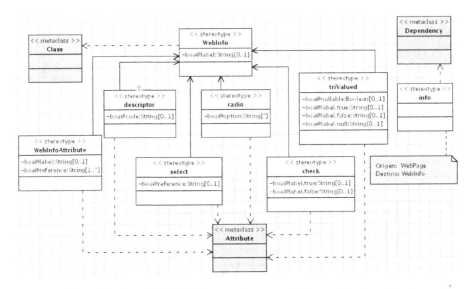

Fig. 3. Sample piece of the IZFE framework metamodel to model web applications

4.2   CICS Environment

Task 1. Architecture Study. The objective to be reached in the running of complex application components hosted in CICS through J2EE components. An exhaustive study of this area was needed as no similar development programs with these requirements have been developed before. Two key problems were identified: (1) the communication with the EIS (Enterprise Information system) and (2) the formatting of types between domains, i.e., J2EE and Cobol-based CISC applications.

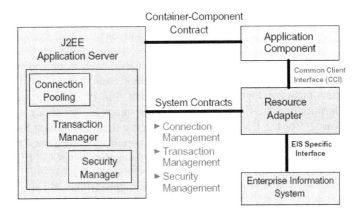

Fig. 4. EIS - JCA Diagram

Task 2. Development of Use Cases. JCA [11] was used to solve the communication problem (see Figure 4). Numerous references, documents and examples of use of JCA libraries were consulted. A CICS ECI Resource Adapter was implemented and set up on a CTG (IBM CICS Transaction Gateway). The second problem identified in Task 1 was solved using the JRIO [12] library. Although this second problem is equally critical few examples and documentation were available. Finally the minimum functions required were obtained through unitary tests in order to validate the solution.

Task 3. Creating the Metamodel. The metamodel was developed by identifying the general functional components (i.e. application components and resource adapter) and parameterizing the information which is needed to customize them for each application. Use cases developed in the previous task (Task2) were used as reference.

Task 4. Cartridge Construction. Finally, the cartridge was built. This cartridge contains a descriptor where the profiles are defined with each of the stereotypes assigned to the corresponding templates. Beforehand, the generated systems were checked. In this way, and using a generation motor, the IZFE can describe the model graphically through simple UML diagrams, and generate 100% of the code needed for the connection to CISC programs.

4.3 FileNet Framework

Task 1. Architecture Study. FileNet is a document manager and workflow tool with its own framework based on Struts. It has an API for J2EE which allows access to most of its functional components. IZFE has developed and maintains a simplified API which makes easier the running of the contents of the organisation's internal uses.

Task 2. Development of Use Cases. Two struts from two different applications were selected which made use of the API of IZFE. Based on the examples provided and using inverse reengineering, the common functions were extracted in real scenarios. Finally a series of unitary tests were made in the IZFE's environment.

Task 3. Creating the Metamodel. The metamodel was developed by identifying functional components that needed to be generalised, and then parameterizing the minimum information needed to customize them for every specific application. All this was carried out using past existing cases as a point of reference.

Task 4. Cartridge Creation. For the construction of the cartridge each one of the stereotypes were mapped out to the units of generation. A template was defined for each unit of generation, which allows for a generator motor for the creation of codes. The use of a cartridge allows, through the definition of UML diagrams, for the 100% generation of an access code of the resource contents defined in the corresponding document manager.

4.4 Metamodels Unification

The final task defined in Section 3 (Task5) corresponds to the integration of platforms using a single metamodel. We decided to conceive this metamodel as an extension of

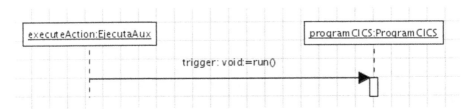

Fig. 5. Sequence diagram sample about CICS integration with IZFE framework in the view domain. In this interaction a web form triggers the execution of a CICS program.

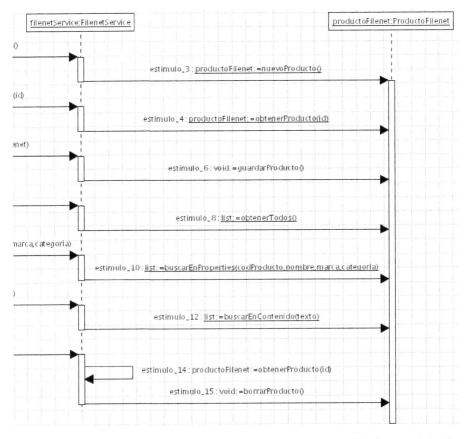

Fig. 6. Sequence diagram sample showing FileNet integration in IZFE framework in the business domain

the IZFE framework metamodel, as this one is the most complex and extent of them, and the rest of platform domains are complementary to this one.

We firstly carried out the integration of CICS with IZFE framework. In order to do so, CICS metamodel elements were incorporated into the IZFE framework meta-model, as well as new kinds of relations to allow the interaction with them. The resulting extended metamodel allows now the modelling of interaction between IZFE framework applications and CICS programs both in the presentation and business logic domain. In the first case, web forms are allowed to interact with CICS programs to retrieve information. In the second case, more complicated interactions between IZFE framework components and CICS business logic processes are allowed to be modelled using state diagrams.

The integration with FileNet was approached in a similar way. FileNet metamodel and cartridge were incorporated into the IZFE framework metamodel to be used along with it. This implies an enlargement of the target metamodel not only in the persistence domain (resource persistence) but also in the presentation domain. The integration was thought as a generic solution to maintain and manage resources, looking for a simply way of creating, editing and deleting resources from a content manager, in this case FileNet. A two-step strategy was followed. Firstly, we included in the IZFE framework metamodel components specific to FileNet characteristics. Secondly, we generalized the possible interactions that should be done against FileNet and we raised the level of abstraction in order to describe them with a single generic component. A new stereotype was defined, which simplified even more the modelling and integration of FileNet interactions. This strategy was successful due to the low variability of the requirements to access FileNet resources.

5 Results Obtained

The use of the proposed methodology has allowed us to build a development environment (a set of cartridges and a unified metamodel) with which a developer is able to built a complete application integrating IZFE framework, CICS and FileNet by simply creating a UML-based model. It is no longer necessary to have experts on J2EE, IZFE framework, CICS or FileNet to develop web-based applications that integrate all them; it is enough with having a basic knowledge of these platforms and UML profiles modelling.

Using a correct model as input, the engine on which this project is based is capable of generating all application code, entirely compatible with the corporative IZFE framework, able to communicate at the business layer with applications stored in the CICS systems, and in the persistence layer, with resources defined in the document FileNet database. All these complex interactions between heterogeneous platforms can now be programmed just by modelling through UML diagrams, without manually writing a single line of code or being an expert on those platforms (see Figure 7).

It is worth noting that working on a higher level of abstraction gives the opportunity to incorporate new functional components easily. For example, to allow the use of other databases within the IZFE framework rather than DB2 (see Section 2) we proposed the use of Hibernate [9] as a transparent and efficient solution for the

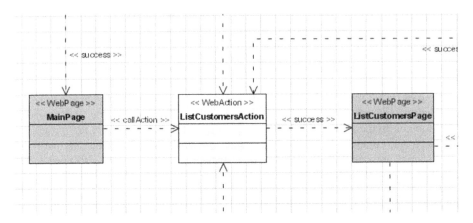

Fig. 7. Example of a model of an application in the presentation domain

persistence layer. This component was added as an element to the metamodel and the correspondent cartridge was created. Another example of the benefits from using a higher level of abstraction is the migration to other content managers: the metamodel had been sufficiently abstracted from FileNet characteristics as to be implemented using other content managers, by solely modifying the cartridge.

6 Conclusions

The goal of a MDA-based methodology must be to facilitate the implementation of applications using models as first class artefacts, i.e. the application code must be generated from these models. Among the benefits from using a higher level of abstraction when programming we can enumerate platforms integration and code correctness, maintenance and reusability. However, MDA-based development is not an easy task, and tool support and methodologies are required. In this paper we have shown how the methodology proposed and the tool used (BOA) are valid assets to give support to those MDA functionalities.

We have successfully defined and applied a methodology based on MDSD and MDA for heterogeneous platforms integration. This new methodology defines separate metamodels for each platform to finally integrate them in a single unified metamodel. With the resulting development environment, developers build their applications in terms of models whose elements represent functional components from the different platforms. Developers now do not have to introduce a single line of code as application code is 100% automatically generated. These methodologies have helped us to reduce risks within the development process of web applications in IZFE, such as delays and time uncertainty, code errors and maintenance problems.

On the other hand, the use of this methodology has represented a shift from the way of working of the development teams within IZFE. The new methodology was embedded as well as new work practices, along with the planning needed in the management of change to the rapid adaptation of the new paradigm. The modellers of the new systems should possess a high degree of knowledge of UML in order to work on the theory and creation of these applications.

Apart from the intrinsic advantages derived from a MDA-based development process, our methodology allows:

- The normalisation of the systems through UML models.
- The integration of heterogeneous systems, which hide the complexities of each of the technologies in question.
- The development of one system only based on the Web.
- A considerable rise in the quality of the systems to be developed, given that the generated code has been exhaustively tested.
- The possibility of a rapid development of prototypes, which could be easily converted into systems and final applications.
- An easier way of implementing the persistence of the models capturing the applications logic, independent from the continual technological change and evolution.

7 Future Proposals

We shall keep on working towards the adaptation and maintenance of the cartridge that has been made, according to the evolution of the platforms integrated. New cartridges might be generated for other programming languages apart from Java (.NET for example), as well as the incorporation of other tools (Spring [18]) into the corporative framework, or the interaction with other systems different from those integrated in this project.

There is also the possibility of integrating the technology into portlets [13], a challenge for the domain of our application. The portlet provided by Struts is recommended in order to avoid any compatibility problems with the IZFE framework controller.

Regarding MDA, it is worth noting the emergence and use of new engines for code generation. In this case, a "translational" method has been used, where, apart from the templates included in the corresponding cartridge we also managed to put the model designed into code. There also exist at the moment other methods known as "elaborational", where changes are made to models based on QVT [20]. This method has a great future within MDA architecture.

So far we have analysed the benefits that IZFE developers gain from the use of the new development framework in terms of qualitative indicators; we have now to perform a quantitative analysis of the benefits in terms of time, money, number of developers, etc.

References

1. Action Semantics Revised Final Submission. OMG document ad/01-08-04.SL
2. ASL – The Action Specification Language Reference Manual. http://www.kc.com
3. CICS – Customer Information Control System. http://www-306.ibm.com/ software/ htp/ cics/

4. CICS Transaction Server for z/OS http://www-306.ibm.com/software/htp/cics/tserver/
5. Estévez, A., García, F., Padrón, J., Roda, J.L.: An MDA-Based Framework to Achieve High Productivity in Software Development. Software Engineering and Applications, Track 436-218 (2004)
6. DB2 database server for z/OS http://www-306.ibm.com/software/data/db2/zos/index.html
7. FileNet http://www.filenet.com P8 3.0.0 Documentation
8. Fuentes-Fernández, L. and Vallecillo-Moreno, A. An Introduction to UML profiles. UPGRADE, The European Journal for the Informatics Professional, 5(2): pp 5-13. April 2004. ISSN: 1684-5285.
9. Hibernate: http://www.hibernate.org
10. J2EE – Java 2 Platform, Enterprise Edition. http://java.sun.com/javaee/index.jsp
11. JCA – J2EE Connector Architecture. http://java.sun.com/j2ee/connector/
12. JRIO – Java Record I/O. http://www 03.ibm.com/servers/ eserver/zseries/ software/ java/ jrio/overview.html
13. JSR 168, portlet specification. http://www.jcp.org/en/jsr/detail?id=168
14. MDA – Model Driven Architecture. http://www.omg.org/mda/
15. MDSD – Model-Driven Software Development. http://www.mdsd.info/
16. MVC –Model View Controller pattern. http://java.sun.com/blueprints/patterns/MVC-detailed.html
17. SableCC Parser generator. http://sablecc.org
18. Spring framework. http://www.springframework.org
19. Struts Framework http://struts.apache.org/
20. QVT –Query Views Transformations. http://www.omg.org/technology/ documents/ modeling _spec_catalog.htm#MOF_QVT
21. UML – Unified Modelling Language http://www.uml.org/
22. XMI – XML Metadata Interchange. http://www.omg.org/technology/ documents/ formal/ xmi.htm
23. WebSphere Application Server for z/OS http://www-306.ibm.com/software/ webservers/ appserv/zos_os390/

From Analysis Model to Software Architecture:
A PIM2PIM Mapping

Jorge Enrique Pérez-Martínez[1] and Almudena Sierra-Alonso[2]

[1] Departamento de Informática Aplicada, Universidad Politécnica de Madrid,
Crta. de Valencia, Km.7, 28031 Madrid Spain
jeperez@eui.upm.es
[2] Escuela Politécnica Superior, Universidad Autónoma de Madrid,
Crta. de Colmenar, Km. 15, 28049 Madrid Spain
Almudena.sierra@uam.es

Abstract. To our knowledge, no current software development methodology explicitly describes how to transit from the analysis model to the software architecture of the application. This paper presents a method to derive the software architecture of a system from its analysis model. To do this, we are going to use MDA. Both the analysis model and the architectural model are PIMs described with UML 2. The model type mapping designed consists of several rules (expressed using OCL and natural language) that, when applied to the analysis artifacts, generate the software architecture of the application. Specifically the rules act on elements of the UML 2 metamodel (metamodel mapping). We have developed a tool (using Smalltalk) that permits the automatic application of these rules to an analysis model defined in Rose[TM] to generate the application architecture expressed in the architectural style C2.

1 Introduction

It is well known that the development (and maintenance) of software applications is a very complex task. Software development methodologies ([1], [2], [3], [4], [7]) were proposed as tools to decrease complexity, by providing methods to elaborate each aspect involved in the application development. However, the weakest link in all those methodologies is the transition between phases: there are no established methods indicating what to do with the software artifacts generated in one step when moving to the next one. This deficiency is more evident in the transition from the analysis phase to the software architecture development [6].

With regard to the development paradigm based on model, in which MDA (Model Driven Architecture) is supported, permits to transform the software artifacts of a phase development defined in a source model, in other software artifacts that establish the target model. To do that transformation it is necessary to define a mapping; that is, a "specification of a mechanism for transforming the elements of a model conforming to a particular metamodel into elements of another model that conforms to another (possibly the same) metamodel" [10].

This work presents a proposal that enables the transition from the software artifacts generated by the analysis activity to the elements forming the resulting architecture.

A. Rensink and J. Warmer (Eds.): ECMDA-FA 2006, LNCS 4066, pp. 25–39, 2006.

To do so, we have designed a mapping that, when applied to the analysis model, generate the software architecture of the application. Both models (analysis and software architecture) are described in UML 2 ([11], [13], [14], [15]). The rules that define the mapping function operate over the UML 2 metamodel. To help this transition we have built a tool that, when given an analysis model (in Rational Rose™), and by the application of the rules of mapping, generates the software architecture of the application for the C2 architectural style [8].

The paper is organized as follows. Sections 2 and 3 characterize the elements that appear in the analysis model (source model) and in the software architecture (target model) respectively. Section 4 presents the mapping rules that permit to transform a PIM (the analysis model) into another PIM (software architecture). In Section 5 we present a tool to automate this mapping. Finally, in Section 6 we present the main conclusions of this work and some related future work.

2 Source Model: The Analysis Model

The set of artifacts generated in the analysis activity forms the analysis model. The analysis activity we are referring to is the use-case analysis as described in [7]. This analysis activity implies the analysis of the use-cases, the analysis of the classes and packages and the architectural analysis. We do not take into account this last aspect since this work proposes to obtain automatically the architecture from the analysis model. Therefore, this analysis activity is different from the analysis activity described, for example, in [20], where this activity focuses on: analyzing the consistency and completeness of requirements (defined in a software requirements document), negotiating the requirements (if there are conflicts), prioritizing the requirements, analyzing technical viability and costs to realize those requirements, etc. Therefore, the analysis activity is performed over the use case model obtaining the analysis model. Analysis artifacts include the analysis classes, use-case realization-analysis, analysis packages, and special requirements. Furthermore, we will use some stereotypes defined in Rational Unified Process, RUP (a specialization from [7]) to characterize analysis classes: <<boundary>>, <<control>> and <<entity>>. The set of artifacts generated in the analysis activity, and expressed in UML, is shown in Figure 1.

3 Target Model: An UML 2 Profile for C2 Architectural Style

In [19] we can read: "Abstractly, software architecture involves the description of elements from which systems are built, interactions among those elements, patterns that guide their composition, and constraints on these patterns." Now, we briefly describe the C2 architectural style. "The C2 architectural style can be informally summarized as a network of concurrent components hooked together by message routing devices" [8]. A fundamental aspect of this style is the principle of limited visibility or substrate independence, that is, a component only knows the components on top of it. Every component has its own control flow and no assumptions are made about the existence of a shared addressing space.

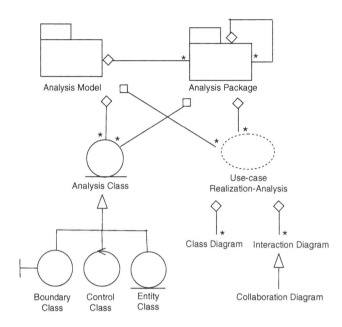

Fig. 1. Elements in the analysis model

The key elements of the C2 architecture are components and connectors. Components communicate through asynchronous message passing. Messages consist of a name and a set of associated typed arguments. There are two types of messages: notifications and requests. Notifications are announcements of changes in the state of the internal object of a component. Requests sent by a component indicate service requests to components on top of it. A notification is always sent downward through a C2 architecture while a request is always sent up. Both components and connectors must have top and bottom domains. The top domain of a component specifies the set of notifications to which the component responds and the set of requests that can be sent by the component. The bottom domain specifies the set of notifications that can be sent by the component and the set of requests to which it responds. The top domain of a component can only be connected to the bottom domain of a connector and its bottom domain can only be connected to the top domain of a connector. A connector can be connected to any number of components and/or connectors. Components can only communicate through connectors since direct communication between components is forbidden. Two connectors can only be connected from the bottom of one to the top of the other. Connectors are responsible for routing and, potentially, multicasting messages. A secondary responsibility of connectors is message filtering. Connectors can provide the following policies for filtering and delivery of messages: no filtering, notification filtering, message filtering, prioritized, and message sink.

As [17] says, UML 2 cannot represent some elements of a software architecture. For example, UML 2 cannot represent the software connector of the C2 style [18]. Because of this, in this work we have defined a UML 2 profile to represent the C2 architectural style (Figure 2).

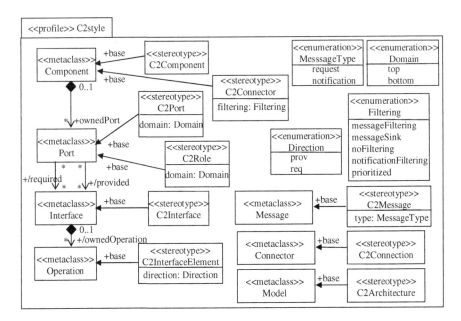

Fig. 2. UML 2 profile to describe the C2 architectural style

The stereotypes defined in the profile have associated constraints. Due to space constraint, we do not describe the stereotypes of Figure 2. As example, bellow we will show the constrains associated with the stereotype *C2Connection*.

3.1 C2Connection Stereotype

In C2, the component port may be linked to the role of a connector. On the other hand, the role of a connector can be linked to the role of another connector or to the port of a component. We have to remember that both *C2Port* and *C2Role* are stereotypes of *Port*. So, how could we state this relationship? It is necessary to define an association between *C2Port* and *C2Role*. However, an association between stereotypes is only possible if it is a subset of the existing associations in the reference metamodel between the base classes of those stereotypes. This means there must be an association between *Port* and *Port*. Here comes into play the metaclass *Connector*, establishing a link between two instances of type *ConnectableElement* (like instances of *Port* are). Then, to characterize the connection in C2 between a component port and the role of a connector, or between two roles of two different connectors, we will define a stereotype of the metaclass *Connector* called *C2Connection*.

To be able to access the stereotype from the metaclass it extends, we define in OCL [14] the function stereotype as follows:

```
stereotype (c: Class): Stereotype;
stereotype = c.extension.ownedEnd.type
```

In the context of this stereotype (*C2Connection*) we define the following constraints (also in OCL):

[1] A connection in C2 links two elements.
self.base.end -> size() = 2

[2] A connection in C2 links a component port with a connector role or two roles of two different connectors.
let ports: Set = self.base.end -> select (el| stereotype(el.role).name = 'C2Port')
let roles: Set = self base.end -> select (el| stereotype(el.role).name = 'C2Role') **in**
          ports -> size() = 1 **implies** roles -> size() = 1 **and**
          roles -> size() = 2 **implies** roles -> forAll (r1 r2| r1.end <> r2.end)

[3] A connection in C2 cannot link two ports.
let ports: Set = self.base.end -> select (el| stereotype(el.role).name = 'C2Port') **in**
not ports -> size() = 2

3.2 Relationships Constraints Among the Stereotypes Defined

Since the C2 style imposes certain topological constraints in relation with the connectivity between components and connectors, it is interesting to show the relationships among the different stereotypes defined and the constraints applicable to those relationships. Figure 3 shows those relationships. Due to space constraint we do not show that the all relationships between the stereotypes and the metaclasses are valid ones, meaning that they already exist between the stereotyped metaclasses in the reference metamodel. For instance, the relationship *connectP* between *C2Port* and *C2Connection* and the relationships *connectR* and *connectRR* between *C2Connection* and *C2Role* (Figure 3) imply that there must be a relationship between the metaclasses *Connector* and *Port*. The *Connector* metaclass is composed of *ConnectorEnd* and each *ConnectorEnd* is associated, through a relationship *role*, with a *ConnectableElement*. The metaclass *Port* is a type of *ConnectableElement*.

In this same sense, we will not detail all constrains that can be applied to the stereotypes and relationships indicated in Figure 3. Like example we detail the following constrains (expressed in OCL):

[1] One of the ports of a component in C2 belongs to the top domain of the component and the other one to the bottom domain.
context C2Component **inv:**
    self.ports -> one (p| p.domain = Domain::top) **and**
    self.ports -> one (p| p.domain = Domain::bottom)

[2] A component in C2 must be connected by at least one of its ports.
context C2Component **inv:**
    self.ports -> exists (p| p.c2Connection –> size() = 1)

[3] The roles of a connector cannot be connected among them.
context C2Connector **inv:**
    self.roles -> forAll (r1, r2| r1 <> r2 **implies** r1.c2Connection.connectRR <> r2)

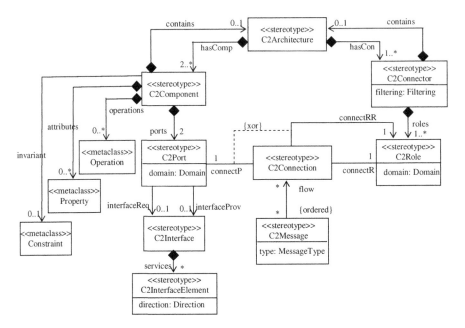

Fig. 3. Abstract syntax to represent the C2 architectural style

[4] If the port of the top domain of a component is connected, it must be with the role in the bottom domain of a connector.

context C2Port **inv:**
    self.domain = Domain::top **and** self.c2Connection.connectR -> size() = 1 **implies**
    self.c2Connection.connectR.domain = Domain::bottom

4 Mapping

Before describing the mapping rules we want to clarify why in this work we talk about a PIM to PIM transformation instead of PIM to PSM (as it is habitual). From our point of view, the architectural model expressed in the architectural style C2 is a PIM. This model will be transformed in a PSM when the implementation platform is selected. We think that the description of the software architecture of an application should be independent of the execution platform. Furthermore, to implement an architecture, heterogeneous platforms (software and hardware) are usually used. We only could consider that the architectural model in C2 is a PSM if it is supported by a platform that implements the C2 style (like ArchStudio 3.0). This platform [5] implements (among others) the component and the connector types specify in C2. In any case, as it is indicated in [10] "what counts as a platform is relative to the purpose of the modeller".

4.1 Characteristics of the Mapping

The transformation proposed in this work can be characterized from four orthogonal viewpoints:

- Degree of model transformation [10]: in this work we have developed a tool that transforms the models semiautomatically.
- Nature of mapping [10]: in this work the elements of the metamodel that describes the source PIM have been transformed into other elements of the metamodel that describe the target PIM. As both models are expressed in UML 2, the mapping has acted over elements of the UML 2 metamodel (described in MOF [12]).
- Scenario for mapping [9]: the mapping proposed is "refining mapping", because we are decreasing the abstraction level: from the source model (analysis) to the target model (architecture).
- Type of mapping function [9]: we express the rules of the mapping function in imperative mode. The problem of this approach is that the mapping is not reversible: we can not generate the PIM of analysis from the architectural PIM and the mapping rules.

Figure 4 illustrate the elements that take part in the proposed transformation. The mapping function indicated in Figure 4 has the following properties:

AM: set of elements of the UML 2 metamodel used to construct the analysis model (with the profile for RUP).

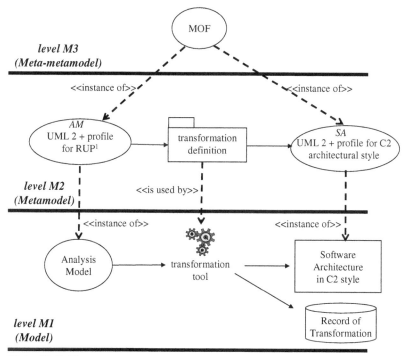

[1] Rational Unified Process

Fig. 4. Metamodel mapping function

SA: set of elements of the UML 2 metamodel extended (with the profile for C2) used to construct the architectural model.

$\exists f: AM \rightarrow SA \mid$

$$(f(x) = y \wedge f(x') = y) \Rightarrow x = x' . \tag{1}$$

$$\exists x \in AM \wedge \forall y \in SA \Rightarrow (x, y) \notin f . \tag{2}$$

$$\exists y \in SA \wedge \forall x \in AM \Rightarrow (x, y) \notin f . \tag{3}$$

Firstly we have to observe the function is unidirectional: from the analysis model to architectural model. This one involves that it is not possible obtain the analysis model from architectural model and the transformation rules. This constraint comes from the imperative nature of the mapping rules.

The expression (1) that indicates the function f is injective. The expression (2) indicates that not every element of the analysis model turns into an architectural model; that is, not every artifact generates during the analysis activity is significant to the architecture. For example: the association names or association roles. The expression (3) indicates that there are architectural elements that cannot associate with any analysis element; for example port and role. These elements are intrinsic to the architectural style.

4.2 Mapping Rules

We have designed 32 rules but, due to space constraint, we will only include here 9 of them. The rules have been expressed in natural language and OCL while waiting for MOF QVT [16] becomes an "Available Specification" (now is an "Adopted Specification"). The rules presented here deal with some aspects of the analysis classes, their attributes and operations, and some aspects of the collaboration diagrams. However, we have designed more rules to deal with different modelling aspects that can appear in the analysis, like inheritance, aggregations, compositions, abstract classes, class invariants, preconditions and postconditions on operations, analysis packages, association classes, class variables, etc.

To be able to define constraints on a stereotype that will apply to the metaclass that it extends or to any of its relations, we name *base* the association end (see Figure 2). From here we consider that:

let clas: Set (Class) = PIM_AM -> select (e | e.oclIsTypeOf (Class))
let comp: Set (Component) = PIM_SA -> select (e | e.oclIsTypeOf (C2Component))

PIM_AM is the analysis model and PIM_SA is the architectural model. The formal expression en every rule is described in OCL.

1) A concrete analysis class is transformed into a C2 component with the same name. This component is simple, which means that it does not contain other architectural elements. This transformation is based on the idea that both elements have similar abstraction levels: an analysis class represents an entity in the problem

domain while a component represents an independent element in the solution domain. However, when composition relationships exist among several analysis classes, these classes can be combined into a single component (see rule 9).

clas -> forAll (ca | comp -> one (co |
           ca.name = co.base.name **and** co.c2Architecture -> size() = 0))

2) The attributes of the analysis class become state variables of the component. All these variables are private, independently of the visibility of the attributes in the analysis class. Note that the value of the attributes defined in an analysis class shows the state of its instances, like the value of the state variables defined in a component shows the state of the component instances. Furthermore, since only the interfaces of a component are public, by definition its state variables are private.

clas -> forAll (ca | comp -> forAll (co | ca.name = co.base.name **implies**
    let cat: Set (Attribute) = ca.attribute
    let cot: Set (Attribute) = co.base.attribute **in**
    cat -> forAll (at1|
        if cot -> one (at2| at2.name = at1.name) **then**
           (at1.visibility = VisibilityKind::public **xor**
           at1.visibility = VisibilityKind::private **xor**
           at1.visibility = VisibilityKind::protected **xor**
           at1.visibility = VisibilityKind::package) **and**
           (cot -> any (at2| at2.name = at1.name)).visibility =
                                    VisibilityKind::private
    else
    endif)))

3) An operation declared as public in an analysis class becomes an operation assigned to the component interface. The component operation will have the value *prov* (provide) in the attribute *Direction*. This is a direct consequence of the object oriented paradigm, in which a class specifies what it offers to the rest of the world, but it does not specifies what it needs from it.

clas -> forAll (ca | comp -> one (co | ca.name = co.base.name **implies**
      ca.operation -> forAll (op| op.visibility = VisibilityKind::public **implies**
        co.bottomInterfaceProv -> exists (o| o.base.name = op.name **and**
                        o.direction = Direction::prov) **xor**
        co.topInterfaceProv -> exists (o| o.base.name = op.name **and**
                        o.direction = Direction::prov))))
  being:

context C2Component **def**
  let topPort: Port = self.ports -> select (p| p.domain = Domain::top)
  let bottomPort: Port = self.ports -> select (p| p.domain = Domain::bottom)
  let topInterfaceProv: Set(C2InterfaceElement) =
      topPort.interfaceProv.services -> select (e| e.direction = Direction::prov)
  let bottomInterfaceProv: Set(C2InterfaceElement) =
      bottomPort.interfaceProv.services -> select (e| e.direction = Direction::prov)

let topInterfaceReq: Set(C2InterfaceElement) =
    topPort.interfaceReq.services -> select (e| e.direction = Direction::req)
let bottomInterfaceReq: Set(C2InterfaceElement) =
    bottomPort.interfaceReq.services -> select (e| e.direction = Direction::req)

4) An analysis class with stereotype <<boundary>> is associated with a C2 component at the lowest level of the architecture, or at least without elements connected to its bottom domain (Figure 5). Recall that this kind of classes models the interaction between the system and the actors.

clas -> forAll (ca | comp -> one (co | ca.name = co.base.name **and**
                stereotype(ca).name = 'boundary' **implies**
                    co.bottomPort.connectP -> size () = 0

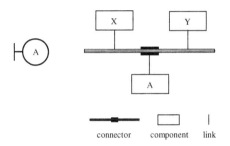

Fig. 5. Topology position of an analysis class boundary in the architecture

5) An analysis class with stereotype <<control>> is associated to a C2 component in the intermediate levels of the architecture. Recall that this type of component models the business logic and often (but not always) interacts with components in its top and bottom domains. Nevertheless, it is possible that it does not interact with elements in its top domain or with elements in its bottom domain.

clas -> forAll (ca | comp -> one (co | ca.name = co.base.name **and**
                stereotype(ca).name = 'control' **implies**
                    co.topPort. connectP -> empty() **implies**
                        co.bottomPort. connectP -> notEmpty() **and**
                    co.bottomPort. connectP -> empty() **implies**
                        co.topPort. connectP -> notEmpty()))

6) An analysis class with stereotype <<entity>> is associated to a C2 component in the top levels of the architecture, or that at least it always has elements connected to its bottom domain. Recall that this type of component models persistent data, repositories or abstract data types.

clas -> forAll (ca | comp -> one (co | ca.name = co.base.name **and**
                stereotype(ca).name = 'entity' **implies**
                    co.bottomPort.connectP -> size () = 1)

7) If in a collaboration diagram, an analysis class A does a request op to a class analysis B, then in the top domain of the component that represents the class A

there will be an operation op with direction *req* and in the bottom domain of the component that represents the class B there will be an operation op with direction *prov* (Figure 6).

let col: Set (Collaboration) = PIM_AM -> select (e |
                        e.oclIsTypeOf (Collaboration)) **in**
clas -> forAll (ca, cb |
    let compa: Component = comp -> one (col co.base.name = ca.name)
    let compb: Component = comp -> one (col co.base.name = cb.name) **in**
    ca.association -> exists (as | as.participant = cb) **and**
    col -> exists (cl c.interaction -> exists (il i.message -> exists (m |
            m.sender = ca **and**
            m.receiver = cb **and**
            m.callAction.operation.name = op))) **implies**
    compa.topInterfaceReq -> exists (e | e.base.name = op) **and**
    compb.bottomInterfaceProv -> exists (e | e.base.name = op)

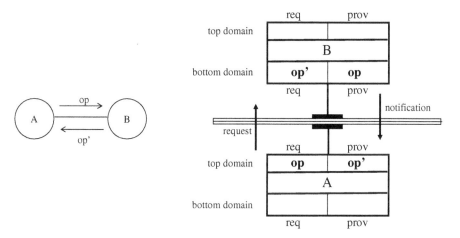

Fig. 6. Requests and notifications at the interfaces top and bottom

8) If in a collaboration diagram, an analysis class B invokes an operation op' (notification) in an analysis class A to indicates that it has finish a request and to return the result of that request, then in the top domain of the component that represents the class A there will be an operation op' with direction *prov* and in the bottom domain of the component that represents the class B there will be an operation op' with direction *req* (Figure 6).

let col: Set (Collaboration) = PIM_AM -> select (e |
                        e.oclIsTypeOf (Collaboration)) **in**
clas -> forAll (ca, cb |
    let compa: Component = comp -> one (col co.base.name = ca.name)
    let compb: Component = comp -> one (col co.base.name = cb.name) **in**
    cb.association -> exists (as | as.participant = ca) **and**
    col -> exists (cl c.interaction -> exists (il i.message -> exists (m |

m.predecessor -> exists (m| m.callAction.operation.name = op) **and**
m.sender = cb **and**
m.receiver = ca **and**
m.action.oclIsTypeOf(ActionReturn)))) **implies**
compa.topInterfaceProv -> exists (e | e.base.name = op') **and**
compb.bottomInterfaceReq -> exists (e | e.base.name = op'))

9) If in an analysis class diagram a class A is composition of another class B, then both classes are associated to a single component, whose name is the concatenation of the names of both classes. Furthermore, all the operations and attributes of class B are private to the component AB. Regarding this issue we must note that an element can only be part of a composition and that the composed element is the only one that can interact with the rest of the world (i.e., only the composed element can send/receive messages to/from the component). This restriction is introduced to preserve the encapsulation to follow Demeter's law.

clas -> forAll (ca, cb | ca.associationEnd -> exists (as |
        as.agregation = AgregationKind::composite **and** as.class = cb **implies**
            comp -> one (co| co.base.name = (ca.name).concat (cb.name) **and**
                        co.operation = ca.operation -> union (cb.operation) **and**
                        co.property = ca.attribute -> union (cb.attribute))))

5 Tool

As we have said, we have built a tool (in Smalltalk) that applies these rules automatically. In Figure 7 we illustrate the interface offered by the tool. To generate an architecture from an analysis model developed with Rational Rose™, we can use the tool executing the following two steps:

1. The user opens an analysis model of Rational Rose™ through the option *Open Model* from the menu *Actions*. After that, the tool invokes Rational Rose™, extracts the information of the corresponding model and places the set of analysis classes and analysis packages of the model in the single selection list of the left window. The tool analyzes the analysis model and applying the rules displays a description of the recommended topology indicating, for each component, the components that should appear in its top and bottom domains.
2. The user creates a new component and links an analysis class with the newly created component. To do so, she selects the analysis class, from the single selection list of the left window, places the mouse on top of the icon associated with the created component and clicks the right button. A menu with several options appears: *Remove*, *Assimilate class*, *Generate*, and *Change definition*. In the menu, she selects the option *Assimilate class*. The system extracts the information from the selected analysis class and, applying the rules, generates the characteristics of the component.

At any moment, the user can redefine/refine the information associated to a component (name, invariants, attributes, private operations, and top and bottom

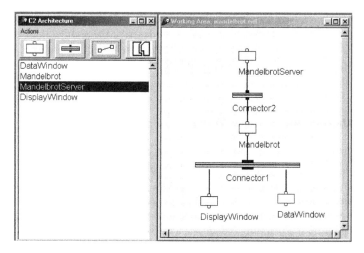

Fig. 7. Tool user interface

interfaces) by selecting the option *Change definition* from the menu corresponding to the component.

Figure 8 shows the architecture of the developed tool (using the C2 style).This architecture contains two packages:

1. The components in *C2Architecture* package support the graphical manipulation of architectural elements, allowing several operations: add, connect, remove, resize, move, check topological rules, etc. In this package there is also a component (Rose Extensibility Interface, REI) that supports collaboration with Rational Rose™, with the purpose of extracting information from the selected analysis model.

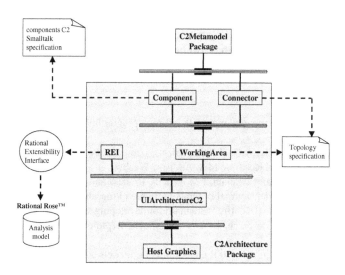

Fig. 8. Architecture of the tool

2. The *C2Metamodel* package contains a hierarchy of classes that implement the stereotypes defined on UML 2 metaclasses to describe the architectural elements of C2. Among these classes we can name *C2Component*, *C2Connector*, *C2Port*, and *C2Role* that support the concepts of component, connector, port, and role respectively.

6 Conclusions and Future Work

In this work we have presented a mapping from the software artifacts generated during the analysis activity (a PIM) to the architectural elements of style C2 (another PIM). The mapping consists of a set of rules that operate over the UML 2 metamodel extended with a profile (metamodel mapping). Also, we have developed a tool that extracts the analysis model from a file generated by Rational Rose™ (with extension .mdl) and, applying the mapping, generates a C2 style architecture.

This proposal has several benefits: (1) the software architecture of the system is directly derived by applying the mapping; (2) since the architecture is directly derived from the analysis artifacts, there is a direct trace relationship between these artifacts and the elements of the resulting architecture, which eases the system maintenance; (3) the current problem of transiting from coarse-grain abstractions in the problem domain (analysis) to fine-grain abstractions in the solution domain (design) is simplified. Furthermore, this work is an example of how can be generated the architectural model of an application from the analysis model and mapping rules.

The mapping proposed in this work generates an architecture in C2 style from an analysis model. With other mapping rules and other profiles for every architectural style, that analysis model can lead to the same architecture expressed in different styles. We want to elaborate other rules to generate other architectural styles (client-server, peer-to-peer, pipe&filter, etc.). On the other hand, the mapping defined is not reversible: one can't construct the source model from the target. To solve this problem we are going to express the rules using the declarative facilities of QVT. Lastly, we think it is interesting to generate a record of transformation that this work has not consider (which parts of the PIM have turned into which part of the PSM).

References

1. Beck, K. (1999). Embracing change with extreme programming. IEEE Computer, 32(10), 70-77.
2. D'Souza, D.F. and Wills, A.C. (1998). Objects, components, and frameworks with UML. The Catalysis approach. Reading, MA: Addison-Wesley.
3. Henderson-Sellers, B. and Graham, I.M. (2000). Process and product life cycles: OPEN's version 2 life cycle model. Journal of Object-Oriented Programming. 13(1), 23-26, 39.
4. IEEE (1997). IEEE Std. 1074-1997. Standard for developing software life cycle process.
5. Institute for Software Research. http://www.isr.uci.edu/projects/archstudio. University of California, Irvine.
6. Inverardi, P. and Muccini, H. (2001). Coordination models and software architectures in a unified software development process. [Internal Report 14/01. Universitá dell'Aquila, Italy].

7. Jacobson, I., Booch, G. and Rumbaugh, J. (1999). The unified software development process. MA: Addison-Wesley.
8. Medvidovic, N. (1999). Architecture-based specification-time software evolution. (Doctoral Dissertation, University of California, Irvine, 1999).
9. Mellor, S.J., Scott, K., Uhl, A. and Weise, D. (2004). MDA distilled: principles of model-driven architecture. Boston: Addison-Wesley
10. Object Management Group (2003). MDA guide V1.0.1. Document number omg/2003-06-01, Date: 12th June 2003.
11. Object Management Group (2004). Unified Modeling Language (UML) Specification: Infrastructure version 2.0. ptc/04-10-14. Finalized Convenience Document.
12. Object Management Group (2004). Meta Object Facility (MOF) 2.0 Core Specification. ptc/04-10-15. OMG Available Specification.
13. Object Management Group (2005). Unified Modeling Language: Diagram Interchange version 2.0. ptc/05-06-04. Convenience Document.
14. Object Management Group (2005). OCL 2.0 Specification version 2.0. ptc/2005-06-06.
15. Object Management Group (2005). Unified Modeling Language: Superstructure version 2.0. formal/05-07-04.
16. Object Management Group (2005). MOF QVT Final Adopted Specification. ptc/05-11-01.
17. Pérez-Martínez, J.E. and Sierra-Alonso, A. (2004). UML 1.4 versus UML 2.0 as Languages to Describe Software Architectures. First European Workshop on Software Architecture (EWSA 2004). St. Andrews – Scotland (UK).
18. Pérez-Martínez, J.E. and Sierra-Alonso, A. (2005). UML 2.0 can't represent architectural connectors. 3rd Nordic Workshop on UML Software Modeling. Tampere, Finland.
19. Shaw, M. and Garlan, D. (1996). Software architecture. Perspectives on an emerging discipline. Prentice-Hall.
20. Sommerville, I. (2004). Software Engineering, 7th ed. Addison-Wesley.

MDA Approach for Maintenance of Business Applications

Mila Keren[1], Andrei Kirshin[1], Julia Rubin[1], and Ahto Truu[2]

[1] IBM Haifa Research Lab, Mount Carmel, Haifa, Israel
{keren, kirshin, mjulia}@il.ibm.com
[2] WM-data, Tartu, Estonia
{ahto.truu@wmdata.ee}

Abstract. We present a case study that utilizes UML modeling methodology for typical business applications. Such applications generally contain a GUI front-end for manipulating database tables and are object-relational systems that deal with both relational databases and object-oriented technology. To model such applications, we use UML Profiles and metamodels based on a three-tiered application architecture for the different stages of the development lifecycles. The benefits of the model-driven approach include the possible use of the models for maintenance processes such as incremental code generation, updating test cases, and documentation. These models also enable developers to validate the application's flow by simulating its behavior through model execution.

1 Introduction

Today, more and more industry domains are beginning to understand the benefits of model-driven development for various products. The Model-Driven Architecture (MDA) was proposed by OMG as a radical move from object design to model transformation. The Unified Modeling Language (UML) was elected to play a key role in this architecture, being a general purpose modeling language. But being created for designing Object Oriented (OO) software applications, it often lacks the elements required to represent specific domains concepts. The solution proposed by OMG was to create profiles for certain application domains.

Our work focuses on a case study based on a UML profile and metamodel for business applications with a layered architecture. Our main goal is to support the application maintenance process through this modeling. The maintenance process includes requirements management for the customers changing needs and the subsequent updates of code and test procedures. At present, this is often done manually when changes in design and code documentation are made in an informal manner, where they are sometimes not even written down. In this situation it becomes difficult to maintain consistency between the requirement updates, code versions, and test sets. Making updates in the modeling environment with the possibility of automatically generated code and test cases may increase the efficiency of the maintenance process. In this way, the application model maintains the connectivity between the requirements, design elements, and the generated results.

A. Rensink and J. Warmer (Eds.): ECMDA-FA 2006, LNCS 4066, pp. 40–51, 2006.
© Springer-Verlag Berlin Heidelberg 2006

The paper is organized as follows. Section 2 provides an overview of the architecture for business applications and modeling practices. Section 3 describes the proposed metamodels and UML profiles for business application modeling. Section 4 describes an example of such an application model. Section 5 describes how the proposed model can be used for application maintenance. Finally, Section 6 contains conclusions and possible future directions.

2 Modeling of Business Applications

2.1 Business Application Architecture

"A Business, *an enterprise*, is a complex system that has a specific purpose or goal. All functions of the business interact to achieve this goal." [2]. Most business applications are designed to connect between end-user activities and different kinds of data repositories.

At the end of 90s there were many studies that looked for mapping solutions between Object Oriented (OO) and Relational Database (RDB) technologies [4]. The conceptual differences between RDB technology and OO technology make it difficult for the various parts of business applications to interact. To reduce the interaction and integration problems, the Business Object (BO) model was introduced for developing object-relational systems [1, 5]. In a BO solution, an application is divided into three tiers: the presentation tier, the RDB tier, and the business logic tier (also called the domain logic tier [1]). Typical three-tiered business architecture is characterized by loose coupling between the user interface and data repositories. The user interface has no direct interaction with the database, but instead, it interacts with the domain objects responsible for communication with the RDB. This separation allows each of the tiers to be developed independently, with a compact interface.

The upper, presentation layer handles the interaction between the user and the software implementing the business logic. It may be a rich client graphical user interface (GUI) application or the latest web-based clients. The software development practice of such applications is usually based on the Model-View-Controller paradigm (MVC) [1].

2.2 State-of-the-Art

Business application modeling took off in the late nineties with the increased usage of computer-aided tools. Since then, UML modeling has become a part of the development practices both for business process modeling and for system design [2, 5], together with the wider practice of EJB and J2EE patterns [3].

For modeling user interfaces, most of the existing work makes an effort to provide a means for modeling logical (abstract) views as well as concrete (physical) ones. Good modeling practices dictate that no interface details should be included in the early stages. The popular approach for designing GUI applications is based on the Model-View-Control (MVC) paradigm [1], which proposes separating between the view layout and its pieces of business logic. D.Anderson [6] describes this approach in a series of three papers; he also proposed using State Chart diagrams for interaction design. J.Conallen [8] proposed using UML for Web application modeling. He also suggested integrating UI development with UML and Rational Unified Process (RUP), with its iterative validation and testing. More papers define UML profiles for modeling Web applications [10, 11, 12]. They use stereotypes such as client page, navigation, Java script, applet, and so forth to express the web specifics. Other works concentrate on concrete view presentation design [7, 10, 13]. These works, which define the methodology of the UML modeling for GUI and Web applications can be useful for business application modeling. However, their approach deals primarily with navigation between views or layout presentation details and less on the composition of business objects, along with their structure and relations, derived from the customer requirements.

The use of UML for modeling relational database systems started later than modeling for software. The main rules of mapping OO to RDB are described in [1], together with detailed design patterns for enterprise systems (see also Sect. 3.2). In 2002, the UML profile for data modeling was proposed [5] and implemented as a Rational Rose add-in; it allows the generation of database scripts from Rose models and vice versa.

2.3   Current Development Process Pain Points

A significant problem with the existing development practices arises during application maintenance, when requirements may change and updates need to be made. Often the documentation is maintained in a text file or even on paper, and these are not kept up-to-date. Requirements changes are done informally and tests are both created and executed manually. This process can be improved using a model-driven approach, where the different artifacts, including documentation, code, and test cases, are automatically generated from the defined models.

3   UML Profiles and Metamodels for Business Applications

As noted above, there are several UML modeling directions for user interfaces and others for designing relational databases. Our intention is to combine them to provide a means for modeling the entire application as a business system, while paying attention to both its architecture tiers and the lifecycle phases of development.

To model business applications, we define metamodel and profiles implementing it while the described stereotypes follow the architecture described in Sect. 2.1. These profiles are used to create three models (see the figure on the right): analysis model, design model and domain data model. These models are tightly connected to 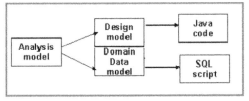 present the same business logic. The model transformations can be applied to them to create design and domain elements from the higher level analysis model. However, the designer can also make changes later to each of these models so they include specific details of the implementation. These lower level models can be used directly for generating code and SQL scripts or divided again into different levels to separate platform-specific features into additional models. In Sect. 4.2 on transformation and code generation, we describe how to combine manual and automated updates.

3.1 Analysis Model

The analysis model is a higher level abstraction of the application; it describes the customer view of the application, its requirements, use cases, the main flow, and the general structure of components and data objects. The goal of the analysis model is to help different stakeholders come to an understanding and agreement on how the application's high-level design corresponds to their requirements. The model can be used as basis for the generation of lower level models through transformations. The analysis model can also be used to create test cases for the views and behavior logic.

Figure 1 presents the classes of the analysis metamodel (a) and their relationships (b). The concrete classes are presented as stereotypes in the corresponding analysis profile. Requirement elements are included in this model, in keeping with the recently proposed SysML standard [14].

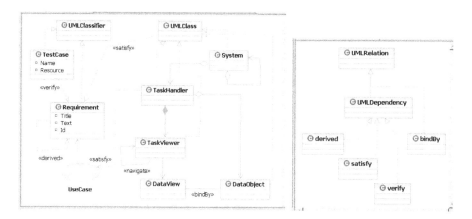

Fig. 1 (a, b). The metaclasses (a) and relations (b) of the analysis metamodel

The entire system is composed of smaller subsystems that contain data objects and handlers of tasks derived from the associated use cases. To model view aspects, we use stereotypes TaskViewer and DataView which are extensions of the general 'Viewer' metaclass in our metamodel. TaskViewer is analogous to a page or a window frame. One or several such viewers are associated with a class of stereotype TaskHandler; they are connected by naviation relashionships. In addition to view aspects, logic aspects are modeled by behavior diagrams that describe the control flow and navigation between viewers (see Sect. 4.2).

DataView stereotyped class is bound to DataObject class targeting to present its fields and actions. For business application modeling, we used two extensions of this metaclass: EditView presents a single instance of DataObject as a group of fields for editing its attributes; SelectView presents the same class as a set of instances in a table form. One or more of instances can be selected for the subsequent actions, like editing, deleting, etc. Other specific views can be added by the designer for their particular needs.

3.2 Design Model

The design model represents the same business logics captured in the analysis model, but includes implementation details; it is used for code generation through one or more transformation procedures. Some elements of the design profile and metamodel are taken from the analysis metamodel, e.g., DataObject, EditView, SelectView; however, in the design model these elements have more implementation details, like methods with typed parameters. The design model can be very flexible and extended by designers for their specific implementations. Its goal is to keep the implementation with the right architectural approach using best practices patterns [3], and make it easy to understand and update at a later stage.

Following the MVC pattern mentioned above (see Sect. 2.1), class stereotypes are defined as view-related classes, and the associated classes of control and model stereotypes (Fig. 2). In the design model, view classes involve concrete view elements (associated by aggregation relation or as attributes), and operations corresponding to the user actions in the viewer, such as the Button or Menu actions stereotypes.

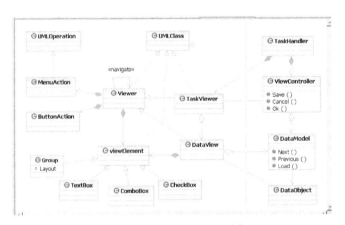

Fig. 2. The design metamodel

Elements stereotyped as 'Model' that are connectors to the data domain level, can be shared between views (Fig. 3, a) These elements are responsible for keeping a set of object instances retrieved from the relational tables by domain data model classes (see Sect. 3.3).

Navigation between views can be modeled by relationships with additional stereotypes (Fig. 3, b), where 'Page' navigation refers to the 'next-previous' navigation adopted by web pages. 'Child' creates a new view, keeping the old view for a later use when the child is closed. 'Tab' navigation is the notebook style where the user can switch views using several tabs.

Tagged values are additional attributes that are associated with the profile. For example, the stereotype 'Group' has attribute 'Layout' which is defined as a tagged

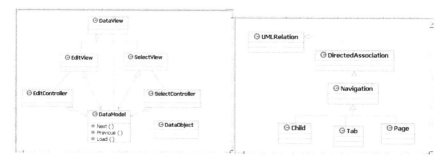

Fig. 3 (a, b). The hierarchy of view metaclasses (a) and navigation relations (b)

value set with two values, 'horizontal' and 'vertical'. Other tagged values can be added by designers who need to extend this profile.

3.3 Domain Data Model

The domain data model can be created by the transformation of Data Objects from either the analysis or design models. The main rules of mapping OO to RDB are briefly as follows [1, 4, 5]:

- Entities become tables
- Attributes become columns
- Identifiers become primary keys

For mapping object relations such as inheritance, aggregation, association into table relations, there are several patterns, like 'Embedded Foreign Key', 'Associated Lookup Table' and others [1]. If Data Objects can not be mapped into single tables having more complex structure, then classes with stereotype 'TableGateway' are used (Fig. 4) as table mappers.

The domain data model may then be reviewed and modified, or transformed into an additional platform specific model (PSM) that reflects specific implementation or performance requirements. The benefit of the domain data model is that it can be reused for implementation of the same business model on different database platforms.

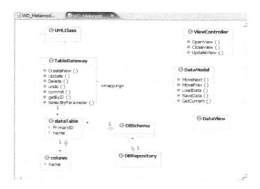

Fig. 4. The domain data metamodel

4   Example of a Business Application and Its Model

4.1   Application Overview

Our case study considers a typical business application called Verification Office Application. The company manages testing and the certification of various measurement devices – scales, speeds and distance meters, thermometers, and so forth. It also handles packaged goods and the quality of service at medical labs. Company employees need a comprehensive database system to manage the customers, their devices, test results, certificates and their validity, as well as billing and reporting. There are three kinds of application users: Regular worker, Secretary, and Administrator.

The application has a two-tiered architecture. The first tier contains the GUI front-end implemented in Java, designed following the MVC paradigm. Each use case has its handler class, with its own view and navigation between them supported by a specific mechanism. The second tier contains functions for database manipulations. These tiers communicate through the domain data objects included in the first tier.

Fig. 5 presents examples of use case (a) and class diagrams (b, c, d) related to the analysis model. Fig. 5, b shows the requirements associated with the corresponding

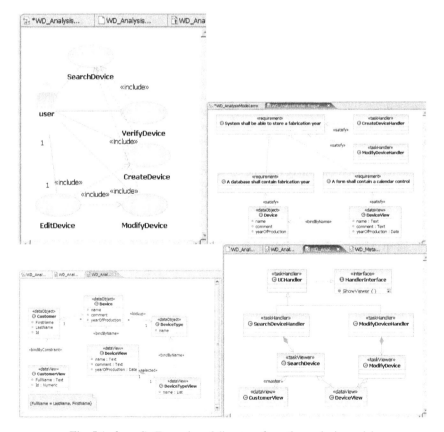

Fig. 5 (a, b, c, d). Examples of diagrams from the analysis model

design elements. Fig. 5, c shows relations between three data objects and their views. Fig. 5, d shows two use case handlers and the related view objects.

For behavior design we used UML activity diagrams. These activity diagrams (see Fig. 6) describe the task handlers' behavior as a specification of the detailed control flow, where the task handlers are responsible for fulfilling the functionality of the use cases. The following are examples of such diagrams where each lower level diagram contains details (Fig. 6, b) of an activity related to the higher level diagram (Fig. 6, a).

Fig. 7 presents an example of a class diagram from design model for the 'Create device' Task Handler, whose design follows the MVC pattern.

Fig. 8 shows an example of the domain model diagram presenting the relationship between the model and table elements.

Fig. 6 (a, b). Examples of activity diagrams for a task handler from the analysis model

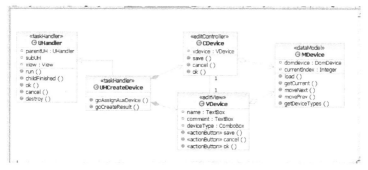

Fig. 7. Class diagram for a task handler from the application design model

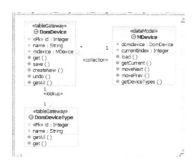

Fig. 8. The relationship between a model and table mappers

5 Using UML Modeling for Code Generation and Behavior Validation

Once the application models are created as a collection of structure and behavior elements, they can be used for several purposes for maintenance of the application. Our scenario for updating the application is taken from a real-life situation where some business object attributes are added or removed.

5.1 Model-to-Model Transformation

The reason for transforming a high-level model to a lower level model is to automate maintenance updates and to avoid manual changes whenever possible. The lower level model includes implementation-specific details of the application itself and of the middleware platform and hardware.

The transformation to domain data model is based on the OO-RDB mapping described in Sect. 2.3. The model contains table objects derived from the business objects and their relations. These table objects can be used directly in SQL scripts as single tables or grouped into more complex tables. In specific cases, additional lookup tables can be added to the model. This model can be derived from the data objects of either the analysis or design model.

In our study we use the specific mapping of the analysis model elements that reflects the existing application implementation design for the transformation to design model. The design model contains a set of classes related to the core of the framework, stereotyped as <<General>>; these classes are not changed during updates. Other stereotyped classes inherit from these core elements (see Fig. 9 a, b). This approach helps to support the code generation in a flexible way (see Sect. 4.2).

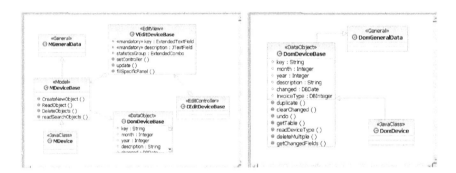

Fig. 9 (a, b). Class diagrams with stereotypes used for model-to-code transformation

The mapping of some of the profile elements is presented in Table 1. In addition to the stereotype mapping, a naming convention was used adding a prefix and a suffix to the original class names.

The model transformations were implemented using the Atlas Transformation Language (ATL) tool [15], which transforms an input model to another model using

Table 1. Part of the mapping between analysis and design model stereotypes

Analysis Model Stereotype	Design Model Stereotypes
<<dataObject>>	<<dataObject>>, <<model>>
<<editView>>	<<editView>>, <<editController>>
<<selectView>>	<<searchView>>, <<searchController>>
<<taskHandler>>	<<taskHandler>>,<<taskViewer>>, <<taskController>>

rules written in ATL and metamodels for both input and output models. In our study, the input and the output models have the same metamodel, which is the EMF/UML2 metamodel [16].

5.2 Model-to-Code Transformation

In our maintenance scenario the application code had already been implemented and some updates were carried out to the existing application design. To facilitate partial generation of the code, the design model needs to maintain consistency with the existing design and naming conventions.

During design model creation, each class that is a candidate for updates was divided into two: one of which is the target for code generation (named with a suffix) and the other is a subclass of the first for making manual code extensions and modifications. The stereotype "General" was used for the application classes that are in the stable part of the application and are not regenerated during model-to-code transformation.

In summary, we introduced three kinds of classes as input for the transformation: stable, automated and manual.

The code generation was implemented using the MOFScript tool [17]. The main transformation procedure was built from a set of libraries containing sub-procedures for specific stereotypes targeted for code generation, including for example: 'Data Object', 'Model', and 'Edit View'. The following is an example of this procedure:

```
uml.Class::mapClass() {
    var stereotype : string = ""
    stereotype = self.getStereotype();
    if (stereotype <> "General") {
        if (self.getStereotype() = data_stereotype )
            self.dataMapClass()
        else if (self.getStereotype() = view_stereotype )
            self.viewMapClass()
        else
            self.standardMapClass()
    }}
```

The body of these procedures includes parts of the real code, which is usually cut-pasted with manual updates while eventual programmer's mistakes can introduce bugs. Given class attributes and operations, the code is created by a loop procedure on each attribute as follows:

```
uml.Operation::generatePropertyLoopMethod () {
    self.standardMethodSignature()
    m_name = self.name
    names = self.owner.getPropertyNames()
    if (names != null) {
            names->forEach(n : String) {
                    a_name = n.firstToUpper()
            tab(1) a_name <%.%> m_name <%();%>
            nl(1) }}
    self.standardMethodEnd()
}
```

The following is the result of another generated method:

```
protected List getChangedFields () {
 // Generated body of getChangedFields method is here
    List var = new ArrayList();
    if (key.hasChanged()) var.add(key);
    if (month.hasChanged()) var.add(month);
    if (year.hasChanged()) var.add(year);
    if (description.hasChanged()) var.add(description);
    if (invoiceType.hasChanged()) var.add(invoiceType);
    return var;
}
```

The stereotype "JavaClass" was used for manual extensions, being a subclass of the automatically generated class. A template is generated for these classes; it includes only calls to the parent methods that are generated automatically. They may be used 'as is' or modified. This provides the flexibility for manually changing objects with specific needs. In addition, a library of utility procedures was created for the common use by other stereotype-specific libraries.

Analogous transformations may be created for other purposes, such as generating different kinds of documentation and test cases.

5.3 Behavior Simulation and Validation by Model Execution

The behavior diagrams presented in (3.3) can be used to validate the application logic. Presenting the logic in a graphical form enables developers to agree on the flow with analysts and stakeholders before starting the detailed design. A model execution tool was used to simulate and validate the specified behavior.

6 Conclusions

In this paper we describe the methodology and UML profiles for modeling business applications that access databases. The case study context was a business application with a specific maintenance scenario. This case study goal was to illustrate the benefits of modeling and code generation using a set of UML profiles. These benefits include: traceability between high-level design changes and the corresponding implementation updates; code generation for periodic updates; and behavior validation using model simulation.

We also introduced a technique for creating model-to-code transformation that supports the generation of code for maintenance updates.

Our future activities will focus on enhancing the current metamodel and profile with additional semantics. We are investigating ways to improve traceability between customer requirements, model entities, and the application code to allow broader lifecycle support through model-driven development.

References

1. M. Fouler: "Patterns of Enterprise Application Architecture", Addison-Wesley (2003)
2. H.E. Eriksson, M. Penker: "Business Modeling with UML: Business Patterns at work", Wiley & Sons, Fall 1999.
3. D. Alur, et al.: "Core J2EE Patterns: Best Practices and Design Strategies", (2001)
4. A.M. Keller, R. Jensen, S. Agarwal: "Persistence Software: Bridging Object-Oriented Programming and Relational Databases", SIGMOD, May, 1993
5. "Mapping Object to Data Models with the UML", Rational Software Whitepapers, October, 2002.
6. CT Arrington: "Enterprise Java with UML", Willey & Sons, 2001
7. P. Coad, E. LeFebvre, J. DeLuca: "Java Modeling in Color with UML", PH 1999
8. J. Conallen: "Building Web Applications with UML". Addison-Wesley (1999).
9. D. Anderson: "Using MVC Pattern in Web Interactions", UIDesign.net,2000 [weblink: http://www.uidesign.net/Articles/Papers/UsingMVCPatterninWebInter.html]
10. R. Hennicker, N. Koch: "Modeling the User Interface of Web Applications with UML", Practical UML-Based Rigorous Development Methods - Countering or Integrating the eXtremists, 2001
11. N. Guell, D. Schwabe, P. Vilain: "Modeling Interactions and Navigation in Web Applications", Lecture Notes In Computer Science; Vol. 1921, Pages: 115 – 127, 2000
12. R.S De Giorgis, M.Joui: "Towards a UML Profile for Modeling WAP Applications", Journal of Computer Science and Technology, Vol.5(4), December,2005
13. K. Blankenhorn, Mario Jeckle: "A UML Profile for GUI Layout", Lecture Notes in Computer Science, Net.ObjectDays 2004: 110-121
14. SysML Specification, 2005, [weblink: http://www.sysml.org/]
15. ATL tool [weblink: http://www.sciences.univ-nantes.fr/lina/atl/]
16. J. Oldevik, et al.: "Toward Standardized Model to Text Transformations", proc. ECMDA-FA 2005, Nuremberg, Nov, 2005
17. EMF/Eclipse UML2 metamodel [weblink: http://dev.eclipse.org/viewcvs/ indextools.cgi/ org.eclipse.uml2/plugins/org.eclipse.uml2/model/UML2.ecore]

Definition and Generation of Data Exchange Formats in AUTOSAR

Mike Pagel[1] and Mark Brörkens[2]

[1] BMW AG, Knorrstr. 147, 80788 München, Germany
`mike.pagel@bmw.de`
[2] Carmeq GmbH, Carnotstr. 4, 10587 Berlin, Germany
`mark.broerkens@carmeq.com`

Abstract. In this paper we present a methodology supporting the definition of data models on basis of a limited set of well-known UML features, thereby allowing these models to be created and discussed by a large group of domain experts. A transformation is then defined from such a platform independent UML model to XML schema, which exceeds the configuration possibilities of comparable approaches like XMI. This enables the generic reproduction of a wide range of existing XML languages and hence supports reverse-engineering legacy schemas and DTDs into well-structured UML models. The overview of an actual implementation of the generic methodology finally demonstrates the practical applicability or our approach. The work described in this paper is part of the AUTOSAR development partnership, an international effort to standardize automotive software infrastructure. The resulting XML schema is used today as the official AUTOSAR XML data exchange format.

1 Introduction

AUTOSAR (short for: automotive open system architecture) is an international development partnership [1] consisting of a multitude of car manufacturers, suppliers and tool vendors, defining concepts and workflows, how electronic automotive systems can be formally specified and processed. Currently, AUTOSAR is mainly focusing on software and addresses issues like hardware independence, design-by-contract, system scalability, reuse and so forth.

The definition of AUTOSAR concepts (which themselves are not in scope of this paper) in form of a metamodel leads to a domain specific language (DSL). While this language is specifically designed to describe distributed real-time software, it still is platform-independent in terms of processing platforms like XML, databases or a programming language. System descriptions written in this language must be interchangeable between various authoring, visualization and processing tools as well as the different organizational entities involved in an AUTOSAR-oriented project. One of the main goals of AUTOSAR is therefore the definition of an (automatically generated) XML-based data exchange format.

While generating XML schema from UML is not new, a number of problems were encountered with approaches and methods typically applied in the industry so far. For instance:

A. Rensink and J. Warmer (Eds.): ECMDA-FA 2006, LNCS 4066, pp. 52–65, 2006.
© Springer-Verlag Berlin Heidelberg 2006

- XMI [2][3], OMG's specification how to map UML models to XML schema, lacks certain configuration possibilities, thereby preventing the reproduction of already existing XML schemas from reverse engineered UML models. Furthermore, XMI uses particular schema features like xsi:type, which in the XML community are discussed as problematic [4][5].
- The MSR partnership [6] defined an XML DTD to describe automotive systems. The underlying data structures have not been formally modeled; but instead were designed directly at DTD level.
- The ASAM association introduced another modeling approach for the ASAM ODX standard [7], leading to an XML description for automotive diagnostic and programming systems. The corresponding schema is in fact generated from a UML model. However, the applied UML profile is highly specific for the XML domain and therefore alleviates the applicability of the metamodel as an MDA PIM, e.g. to produce a database schema.

Our transformation of the AUTOSAR metamodel to XML schema exceeds the configuration capabilities of current approaches. It is defined as a set of transformation patterns and model markings. The actual implementation of our tool-chain is based on the Eclipse Modeling Framework (EMF).

Outline of this Paper. The next section gives an overview of how our approach is aligned with general MDA concepts. The remaining sections then follow the logical order of applying our methodology. We begin with the description of our concepts to define a platform independent model. The following section explains our requirements for a new transformation from UML to XML schema and specifies the configuration capabilities of our approach. Next, we describe our implementation of the schema generator. The paper closes with a final summary of our results and an outlook of possible next steps.

2   Alignment with MDA Concepts

Fig. 1 gives an overview how our modeling and generation approach is aligned with the concepts defined by MDA, which are shown as stereotypes of our corresponding AUTOSAR artifacts.

The AUTOSAR metamodel is a PIM. Its definition is independent of the tooling and processing platforms (e.g. programming languages, databases, XML formats, ...) that eventually will be involved in creating, editing or persisting AUTOSAR models. This platform independence is strongly required to allow automotive domain experts to contribute efficiently without consideration of how modeled concepts eventually will be mapped to a certain platform.

Our primary platform is XML schema, i.e. that we are generating the AUTOSAR XML schema from the AUTOSAR metamodel.

The mapping is defined as a set of transformations, which are combinations of type and instance mappings. For each relevant PIM type a template is defining the default purely type-based mapping. If a certain element in the AUTOSAR metamodel requires different transformation, this is controlled by assigning values to platform specific marks which leads to the annotated metamodel, a marked PIM. A modeling guideline prescribes tagged values as the only UML feature allowed to express such PIM markings.

The target of our mapping is not a separate PSM. Instead, we follow the alternative path also mentioned in [8] by directly generating the actual XML schema file from the marked PIM, for two reasons: While research projects [9][10] start providing tools to perform model transformations, frequently as an implementation of the MOF QVT specification [11], we did not find sufficient transformation support as part of commercial UML tools available to AUTOSAR members. Having an explicit PSM does not seem to add much value to our methodology. Instead, performing the extra transformation step adds a potential error source, resulting from defects in the used tooling as well as problems introduced by improper usage.

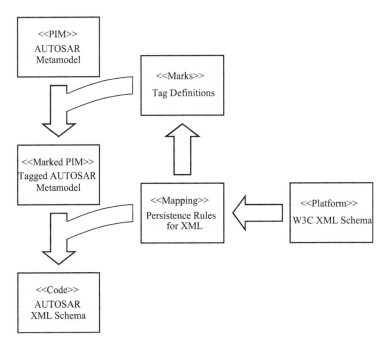

Fig. 1. The alignment between the MDA methodology and the AUTOSAR modeling and schema generation approach is shown in this figure. For each depicted AUTOSAR artifact the stereotype-like annotations indicate the corresponding MDA concept.

3   Definition of the AUTOSAR PIM

The language to describe AUTOSAR systems is a DSL enabling the definition of automotive software and hardware systems. It therefore contains specialized entities like certain types of software components that are responsible for handling hardware sensors or entities like communication protocols used on automotive bus systems. While the usage of UML to describe this metamodel was not disputed, a number of additional requirements had to be taken into account.

In the automotive industry the practical application of UML is not yet as widely adopted as in other, more traditional IT domains. To overcome this psychological barrier the AUTOSAR methodology had to limit itself in terms of used UML features. On the other hand, certain features required to describe AUTOSAR systems are not well supported in UML. In those cases, we had to extend the existing modeling capabilities. Finally, practical reasons like existing tool support forced us to sometimes deviate from pure MDA and UML approaches.

This section explains those limitations and extensions of UML.

3.1 Usage of a UML Subset

Even when using UML, still a number of alternative approaches can be considered for the definition of the AUTOSAR metamodel. First, the metalevel the AUTOSAR DSL is associated with or is build upon needs to be determined. Corresponding to OMG's four-layer metamodel hierarchy [12], AUTOSAR user models, e.g. the model of a concrete windshield wiper system, live on M1. Therefore, the underlying AUTOSAR metamodel that defines the language to express such M1 models is defined on M2.

To stay completely aligned with OMG's metalevel hierarchy, this suggests two well-known alternatives for the definition of the AUTOSAR metamodel: it can be defined as an instance of MOF [8], or as a UML profile. Unfortunately, both approaches have practical disadvantages.

The formal usage of MOF as modeling language was not well supported by tools when work on the AUTOSAR metamodel was started in the end of 2003. This means that limiting our modeling capabilities to the EMOF subset [8] was not possible through available tools. This is different today, as tools like IBM's RSM [13] and Sparx' Enterprise Architect [14] start providing metamodeling capabilities.

Creating a UML profile has the strong advantage that even standard UML tools are able to handle the corresponding UML instance models. However, tool support for creation and especially formal application of a UML profile was again too weak for us. While this also has been overcome by recent tools, the formal definition of such a profile is not trivial and naturally requires deep insight into UML's own metamodel. Such deep analysis of UML is typically not part of the daily business of automotive engineers and hence only sparsely available. Therefore, requiring the definition of a formal UML profile for the AUTOSAR metamodel was not possible.

As a consequence AUTOSAR is following a mixed approach. The original AUTOSAR metamodel is created as an instance of UML. From UML we only allow using basic class diagrams, essentially the concepts defined in EMOF or the UML infrastructure's Core::Basic package [12]. We further restrict the allowed set of modeling features, e.g. classes defined in the AUTOSAR model must not own any operations. These limited class-modeling capabilities are formally specified in form of its own UML profile. Since the AUTOSAR metamodel exists at M2, the underlying profile is defined at M3. Currently, the AUTOSAR metamodel itself is mapped to a formal UML profile by a small group of experts, who are involved in both, AUTOSAR development and UML inner workings. For simplicity and due to growing tool support the rest of the paper will assume the AUTOSAR metamodel residing at OMG's metalevel M2, i.e. either as direct MOF instance or in form of a UML profile, as shown in Fig. 2.

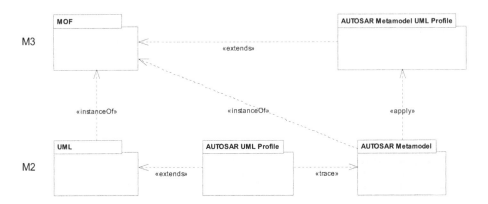

Fig. 2. The (AUTOSAR Metamodel) is effectively an instance of (MOF), which applies the (Metamodel UML Profile) to provide required extensions and enforce our limitations. Eventually, the (AUTOSAR Metamodel) is translated into its own (AUTOSAR UML Profile) to allow AUTOSAR modeling in standard UML tools.

3.2   Definition and Structure of PIM Markings

Platform-dependent information may be added to the model in form of tagged values only. Vice versa, tagged values are exclusively used to specify platform- dependent information. The names of the tag definitions are following a namespace scheme. E.g. a tag called xml.name specifies how a (platform-independent) model element will be called in a (platform-dependent) XML file, whereas a tag db.name could specify the same for a database platform. For an overview of available marks see table 1.

3.3   Stereotypes of the AUTOSAR Metamodel UML Profile

The AUTOSAR metamodel UML profile defines a handful of new stereotypes to either explicitly underline concepts already available in UML or to add modeling capabilities that are not part of standard UML. Those stereotypes are usually prefixed by 'atp' (AUTOSAR template profile; a synonym for AUTOSAR metamodel UML profile).

Types and Typed Elements.   UML supports types and typed elements as one of the most fundamental modeling concepts expressed in the Types diagram of the UML infrastructure's Core::Basic package [12]. While modeling of reusable types and their later use in form of roles and instances is typical in many IT domains, automotive software models are very often rather instance oriented. In those models, reuse is provided in form of creating copies and changing them if required.

One of the main goals of AUTOSAR in fact is the reuse of software and corresponding models. To make the distinction between types and typed elements more explicit, we enable this feature at M3, in the metamodel profile, in form of three new stereotypes:

– «atpType» is applied to classes in the AUTOSAR metamodel that are defining a type. This directly corresponds to classes being derived from UML's Type metaclass, in most cases those classes are refined forms of UML's StructuredClassifier.

- «atpPrototype» is applied to all typed classes. Again, this is a very explicit form of deriving a class from UML's TypedElement metaclass, in most cases these classes correspond to UML's Property. The name prototype was chosen because of compatibility concerns regarding MSRSW [6], an existing description format for automotive electronic systems. Additionally, since classes with stereotype «atpPrototype» are roles of a certain type, they in fact *are* prototypes for instances that are created at runtime.
- «isOfType» is finally applied to the relation between a prototype and a type. Every «atpPrototype» can reference at most one «atpType», just as in UML.

Through those stereotypes modelers are forced to explicitly distinguish types and typed elements. The following figure shows a small excerpt from the AUTOSAR metamodel where the aforementioned stereotypes are applied.

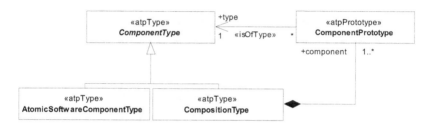

Fig. 3. The (AUTOSAR Metamodel Profile) defines new stereotypes for the explicit definition of types and the corresponding typed elements (called prototypes here for historical reasons). The figure shows a small example from the AUTOSAR metamodel demonstrating the stereotype application.

Deep References to Parts of Parts. The fact that AUTOSAR strongly supports the definition/usage dichotomy through its types and prototypes introduces a challenge in situations, where an element needs to be referenced that is deeply nested in a part-of-parts hierarchy as shown in Fig. 4. To ease understanding the chosen example is not a software problem but describes a bicycle; not just any bicycle, but yours! Your bike consists of two wheels of a certain type. Those wheel types in turn consist of their own parts like a tube and a tire of some kind. If you now take your bicycle out on a trip and blow the front tube you later will need to tell a mechanic what to fix. You can't just ask to repair a tube of type TubeX, because possibly every RacingWheel in the shop, and for sure the two wheels on your bike both have that tube. If you mention that the tube of a frontWheel needs to be fixed, there may still be multiple RacingBikes having this part. The work order is precise enough once you specify that the tube of the frontWheel of yourBike needs to be repaired as indicated in Fig. 5. In technical terms TubeX, TireY, RacingWheel and RacingBike are all types, while tube, tire, front- and rearWheel as well as yourBike are usages of those types. A type consisting of parts of certain other types, which in turn consist of more parts and so on is a typical pattern in object-oriented languages. The bike example shows that for an exact reference of a leaf (or intermediate) part in the hierarchy the containing parts must also be specified. In AUTOSAR

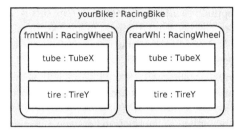

Fig. 4. Example for a typical part-of-parts hierarchy. A (RacingBike) is a type of bike that contains two wheels: (frontWheel) and (rearWheel). Those two wheels are usages of the same wheel type (RacingWheel). Some parts of that wheel type are a (tube) of tube type (TubeX) as well as a (tire) of tire type (TireY).

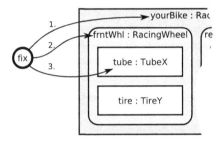

Fig. 5. To refer to a particular tube, the owning wheel as well as the bicycle must be specified. Complete references to parts-of-parts require the containing context. In AUTOSAR this is called in instance reference and consists of an ordered list of part references.

we find this requirement e.g. in case of a software component hierarchy. Composite components may consist of further composites and so on, which eventually consist of what in AUTOSAR is called an atomic software component. Only those leaf components contain actual code and use up resources like CPU time or memory, and exactly those leaf components must be deployed to the processing nodes (ECUs, electronic control units) of the system, i.e. they must be referable from a top level deployment element. UML 2 addresses this requirement only for exactly one hierarchy level in case of the UML connector connecting two ports of a structured classifier's parts: in addition to the port which is defined by its owning type the UML connector end also references the corresponding part through the attribute ConnectorEnd.partWithPort [15]. However, AUTOSAR requires this issue to be addressed for the general case of arbitrary depth. Therefore, we extended the UML 2 approach by not just specifying a single contextual part, but an ordered list of those, starting with the outermost and ending with the innermost part, just as shown in Fig. 5. A short form of this reference type is presented in Fig. 6 to once more allow our domain experts to express their concepts in a convenient and simple way. The corresponding stereotype «instanceRef» for the association got its name from the fact that the reference is indeed specifying an instance-like occurrence of the reference target instead of just a part in the context of its owning type. A

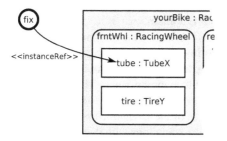

Fig. 6. AUTOSAR introduced an abbreviation for instance references in form of a regular association stereotyped («instanceRef»)

comparable motivation led to a similar concept in SysML in form of the SysML «Binding» stereotype, which also allows referencing a list of parts through the Binding.path attribute [16]. However, the SysML solution targets a different use-case.

4   Transformation of the PIM to XML Schema

This section describes our transformation of the AUTOSAR metamodel to an XML schema. Especially we motivate why and how our approach exceeds the possibilities provided by existing methods like XMI.

4.1   Design Patterns of the AUTOSAR XML Schema

Several approaches for translating UML or MOF based metamodels into XML Schema or XML DTD [3][2][17] have been evaluated. None of them fulfilled all requirements on the AUTOSAR data exchange format, the most important of which are listed below:

- unambiguous mapping between instances of the XML Schema and instances of the AUTOSAR metamodel,
- reuse of XML patterns well established in the automotive domain, and
- support of tools in the XML and the model domain.

The AUTOSAR XML schema fulfills these requirements by combining the strengths of several existing XML patterns: Our XML schema is a dialect of XMI 1.2 that is extended by legacy XML patterns, which are harmonized between several data exchange formats frequently used in the automotive industry.

The following sections describe the requirements and how they are fulfilled in more detail. After that the configuration possibilities and translation rules are explained.

Unambiguous Mapping.   The seamless exchange of data between tools requires unambiguous mapping of information stored in the model domain to the XML domain and vice versa. AUTOSAR follows the concept used in XMI: By default all navigable association ends, attributes and types in the model domain are explicitly represented by XML elements or attributes in the XML domain.

The default mapping rules used by AUTOSAR are inspired by XMI 1.2: navigable association ends, attributes and types in the metamodel are all represented as XML elements. Fig. 7 shows a typical metamodel fragment and an instance of the AUTOSAR XML schema created using the default mapping rules. The type information is required in order to manage inheritance: it must be possible to distinguish between ClassB and SubClassB. Additionally, the names of the navigable association ends (roleB1 and roleB2) are required in case of multiple associations with the same type. In case a model fragment doesn't make use of multiple association or inheritance it is allowed to overwrite the default mapping rules, as explained later in this section.

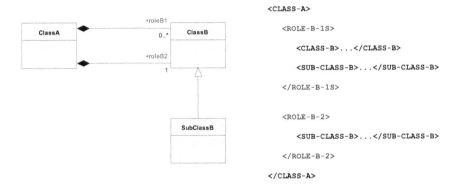

Fig. 7. A typical metamodel fragment, including classes, multiple composite associations, and a corresponding sample instance of the AUTOSAR XML schema created using the default mapping rules

Support for Tools in the XML and Model Domain. The AUTOSAR data exchange format will be used by a wide variety of different tools such as primitive XML editors, legacy tools and graphical tools explicitly optimized for the AUTOSAR methodology. Most tools internally implement their own data model with a structure different from the AUTOSAR metamodel. While XMI strives to satisfy the requirement to find a very simple transformation from a metamodel to its XML representation, we see no great advantage in pursuing this goal, as the resulting direct transformation is not possible for tools and their proprietary models. We therefore trade the straightforwardness of the XMI transformation against high configurability.

Additionally, we limit used XML schema features to a subset that is generally accepted within the XML community and is implemented by most off-the-shelf XML tools and libraries. E.g. we do not use XML schema inheritance because it is limited to single inheritance and makes use of features like xsi:type, the usefulness of which is debated among XML experts [4][5].

Inheritance in the AUTOSAR metamodel is mapped to the AUTOSAR XML schema using the copy-down-approach of XMI 1.2. However, instead of repeating inherited properties in the declaration of XML elements, (see e.g. the repetition of ModelElement.name in the XMI 1.2 MOF DTD [2]) we use element and attribute groups, which are referenced if needed. Polymorphism is made explicit in the schema by listing all concrete subtypes.

Support of Existing DTD Based XML Formats. Some concepts used in AUTOSAR are already well defined by existing XML formats used in the automotive industry. For selected contents the translation of the AUTOSAR metamodel to the XML Schema shall be flexible enough to reproduce such a standardized format. AUTOSAR addresses this requirement by providing the advanced configuration possibilities explained below.

Configuration of XML Schema Production Rules. The AUTOSAR XML schema production rules are configured by UML tagged values attached to the metaclasses and owned properties of the AUTOSAR metamodel. Default tagged values are implied in (the very typical) case, where no explicit values have been added to a model element. Tagged values on roles (references, composition and attributes) control which XML elements or attributes are generated for representing the given role. Additionally order and multiplicity is configurable.

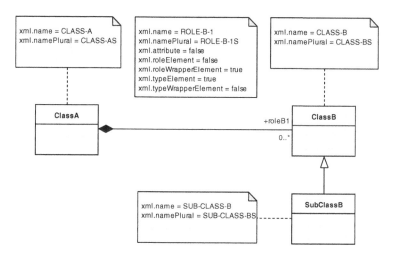

Fig. 8. The platform independent UML model is annotated with a set of predefined tagged values: our model marks. The tags specify how a model entity is translated to the XML schema platform, e.g. whether an XML element or XML attribute has to be generated, in which order XML elements have to appear, or whether wrapper elements for multiple classes need to be generated.

Fig. 8 shows the default configurations for a composition relationship with unbounded upper multiplicity. Table 1 lists the most important tagged values that are part of our schema production configuration.

Table 1. List of the most relevant tagged values used in our transformation from the AUTOSAR metamodel to XML schema. The values refer to roles as synonym for UML properties.

Tag name	Applicable to	Description
xml.name	role, class	Provides the name of a schema fragment representing the role or class.
xml.namePlural	role, class	Provides the plural name of a schema fragment.
xml.attribute	role	If set to true, the role is represented as attribute. This tag is only applicable for roles typed by a primitive datatype with an upper multiplicity of 1.
xml.roleElement	role	If set to true, the xml.name of the role shows up as XML element.
xml.roleWrapperElement	role	If set to true, the xml.namePlural of the role shows up as XML element. This XML element is typically generated in case the multiplicity of the role is greater than 1.
xml.typeElement	role	If set to true, the xml.name if the role's type shows up as XML element.
xml.typeWrapperElement	role	If set to true, the xml.namePlural of the role's type shows up as XML element.

The following listing shows how the aforementioned metamodel fragment is mapped to XML schema:

```
<xsd:element name="CLASS-A" type="CLASS-A"/>

<xsd:complexType name="CLASS-A" abstract="false" mixed="false">
  <xsd:sequence>
    <xsd:group ref="CLASS-A"/>
  </xsd:sequence>
 </xsd:complexType>

<xsd:group name="CLASS-A">
  <xsd:sequence>
    <xsd:element name="ROLE-B-1S" minOccurs="0">
      <xsd:complexType>
        <xsd:choice minOccurs="0" maxOccurs="unbounded">
          <xsd:element name="CLASS-B" type="CLASS-B"/>
          <xsd:element name="SUB-CLASS-B" type="SUB-CLASS-B"/>
        </xsd:choice>
      </xsd:complexType>
    </xsd:element>
  </xsd:sequence>
 </xsd:group>

<xsd:complexType name="CLASS-B" abstract="false" mixed="false">
  <xsd:sequence>
    <xsd:group ref="CLASS-B"/>
  </xsd:sequence>
 </xsd:complexType>

<xsd:complexType name="SUB-CLASS-B" abstract="false" mixed="false">
  <xsd:sequence>
    <xsd:group ref="CLASS-B"/>
    <xsd:group ref="SUB-CLASS-B"/>
```

```
      </xsd:sequence>
   </xsd:complexType>

   <xsd:group name="CLASS-B">
     <xsd:sequence>
       ...
     </xsd:sequence>
   </xsd:group>

    <xsd:group name="SUB-CLASS-B">
     <xsd:sequence>
       ...
     </xsd:sequence>
     </xsd:group>
```

5   Implementation of the Schema Generator

Our tool chain links a number of publicly available modeling and processing tools. The complete process is depicted in Fig. 9.

We have two important sources defining AUTOSAR concepts: (a) the AUTOSAR workgroups directly specifying particular content of the metamodel and (b) an existing standard for automotive software systems, the ASAM MSRSW harmonized objects [7]. The original AUTOSAR concepts were directly modeled utilizing our UML subset with Sparx System's Enterprise Architect. In order to incorporate the MSRSW models, which at that time did not exist in UML, but were available as DTD only, we realized a simple reverse-engineering script, which creates a model compliant with the AUTOSAR modeling guidelines from the MSRSW DTD. Explicit import statements starting at the original AUTOSAR metamodel specify, which parts of the complete MSRSW need to be available as part of the joint AUTOSAR metamodel.

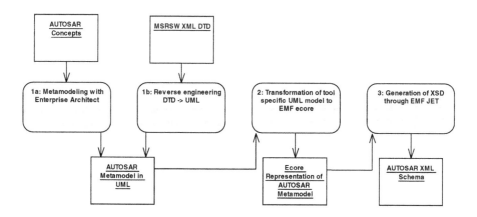

Fig. 9. Overview of the implemented AUTOSAR metamodel tool-chain. The applied process steps are numbered in their order of execution. (1a) and (1b) indicate the two possible sources for models: original AUTOSAR concepts as well as existing standard formats like the MSRSW DTD.

The second processing step transforms the modeling tool dependent metamodel into an independent Java representation. Here we found the Eclipse Modeling Framework (EMF) [18] most useful, with a very clean API and extremely good support for meta-modeling tasks through arbitrarily deep access to all metalevels of a model in a single application. The conversion step includes a number of mechanisms that allow for graceful degradation in case the model is not fully following the AUTOSAR metamodel rules. While the final model of course must be compliant, the sheer number of people contributing to it requires a resilient algorithm in order to create and verify results early in the process.

Finally, we use EMF's Java Emitter Templates (JET) to translate the EMF based metamodel into its final representation: the AUTOSAR XML schema.

6   Summary and Outlook

The Model Driven Architecture approach is well suited for defining the AUTOSAR domain specific language and the corresponding data exchange format. While using standard UML modeling techniques, we limit the expressive power of UML to a degree allowing automotive engineers to actively contribute to the metamodel. This is further supported by the strict platform independence of the model. No XML knowledge is required to work on the AUTOSAR metamodel and finally get new concepts into the exchange format.

The metamodel is optionally marked up with tagged values for configuring the translation to XML schema. The configuration possibilities allow for powerful adaptation of the resulting XML format. If the default XMI 1.2-like translation is not sufficient it may be customized to suite individual needs. This allows for reproduction of XML fragments out of the AUTOSAR metamodel, which are already established in the automotive domain as part of other standard data exchange formats. We proved the applicability of our approach by describing the Java implementation of our EMF-based schema generator. Future work may happen in the following areas:

– Additional transformations can be added. For instance, we are currently creating generators that realize persistence code to read and write the format defined by AUTOSAR. Since commercial tools typically will not be based directly on the AUTOSAR metamodel, but much rather will instantiate their own, tool- optimal model, such generators will therefore be specific for the target tool environment.
– Since many tools and projects start supporting formal model transformations as prescribed by the OMG QVT specification we will start evaluating available platforms and eventually switch over to begin using more formal methods instead of our handcrafted transformation code. This applies to both, the description of the transformations as well as the actual implementation.
– The AUTOSAR metamodel is annotated with OCL constraints [19] where required. But as of now, we are not automatically evaluating those. With the recent releases of more capable OCL processors we will start to implement automatic constraint checking in upcoming versions of our tool-chain.

References

1. AUTOSAR: Homepage http://www.autosar.org (2006)
2. OMG: XML Metadata Interchange (XMI) specification version 1.2 (2002)
3. OMG: XML Metadata Interchange (XMI) specification version 2.1 (2005)
4. Dubinko, M.: chapter 4. In: XForms Essential, XML Schema in XForms. Volume 1. O'Reilly Media Inc. (2003)
5. Walsh, N.: xsi:type train wreck. In: Norman Walsh Weblog. Volume 7. (2004) http://norman.walsh.name/2004/01/29/trainwreck.
6. Manufacturer Supplier Relationship (MSR): MSRSW V2.2.2, element and attribute documentation (2002)
7. Association for Standardization of Automation- and Measuring Systems (ASAM): ASAM MCD-2D (ODX) version 2.0, data model specification (2004)
8. OMG: Meta Object Facility (MOF) specification version 2.0 (2006)
9. IBM alphaWorks: Model transformation framework (2006) http://www.alphaworks.ibm.com/tech/mtf.
10. UMT-QVT: an open-source project targeting the QVT RFP (2006) http://umt-qvt.sourceforge.net/.
11. OMG: Meta Object Facility (MOF) query/view/transformation specification version 2.0 (2005)
12. OMG: UML Infrastructure specification version 2.0 (2004)
13. IBM Rational: Rational software modeler product page (2006) http://www-306.ibm.com/software/awdtools/modeler/swmodeler/.
14. Sparx Systems: Enterprise architect product page (2006) http://www.sparxsystems.com.au/.
15. OMG: UML Superstructure specification version 2.0 (2005)
16. SysML Partners: Systems modeling language specification version 1.0 alpha (2005)
17. Carlson, D.: Modeling XML Applications with UML, Practical e-Business Applications. Addison Wesley (2001)
18. Budinsky, F., Steinberg, D., Merks, E., Ellersick, R., Grose, T.: Eclipse Modeling Mramework, A Developer's Guide. Addison Wesley (2005)
19. OMG: UML OCL specification version 2.0 (2005)

A Model Driven Approach to Engineering of Flexible Manufacturing System Control Software

Christian Brecher[1], Tilman Buchner[1], Yong Cheng[2],
Matthias Jarke[2,3], and Dominik Schmitz[2]

[1] RWTH Aachen, Laboratory for Machine Tools and Production Engineering (WZL),
52056 Aachen, Germany
[2] RWTH Aachen, Informatik V, Ahornstr. 55, 52056 Aachen, Germany
[3] Fraunhofer FIT, Schloss Birlinghoven, 53754 Sankt Augustin, Germany
{C.Brecher, T.Buchner}@wzl.rwth-aachen.de, Yong.Cheng@rwth-aachen.de,
{jarke, schmitz}@cs.rwth-aachen.de

Abstract. Increasing the performance and flexibility of automated manufacturing systems is a key success factor for today's production companies. Flexible Manufacturing Systems (FMS) have proven to be particularly suitable in this regard since they support small lot sizes and high numbers of variants at the same time. The most important problems facing FMS are the huge expenditure of time and the high costs for "engineering" its control software. Engineering in this context refers to all aspects from planning the concrete production process, to assigning machines to control programs, to implementing software modules, and to testing the whole configuration. In this paper, we describe a model driven approach to support consistent engineering of FMS control software. It makes use of UML and customized UML metamodels for FMS-specific features, and includes a prototype implementation based on open source. We report on first experiences with a real FMS running *cosmos 4*, a distributed, agent-oriented FMS control software.

1 Introduction

Since the 90s, increasing the performance and flexibility of automated manufacturing systems has been a key success factor for today's production companies. Flexible Manufacturing Systems (FMS) have proven to be particularly suitable in this regard. A Flexible Manufacturing System is an arrangement of machines interconnected by a transportation system, which allows to build products in small lot sizes and high numbers of variants at the same time. In the different application domains such as milling and turning, sheet metal processing, and sawing of slug material, there exist manifold differences concerning the detailed modelling of the FMS, its workpieces and materials, as well as its manufacturing, handling, and transportation processes. To overcome this heterogeneity, a new automation solution, the *cosmos 4* platform, has been developed at Aachen University's Laboratory for Machine Tools and Production Engineering (WZL) [1]. It is a distributed, agent-oriented approach to universal and open control components for different types of FMSs.

A. Rensink and J. Warmer (Eds.): ECMDA-FA 2006, LNCS 4066, pp. 66–77, 2006.

However, a FMS control software like *cosmos 4* must be adapted and configured to control a concrete production process in a real manufacturing system. This kind of adaptation is called "engineering". Engineering here includes all aspects from planning the concrete production process, to assigning machines to control programs, to implementing new software modules, and to testing the whole configuration. One of the most important problems facing FMS is the huge expenditure of time for engineering its control software. This problem traces back to the lack of concept and proper tool support for engineering. In addition, the high complexity of the process itself requires extensive know how. Consequently, only few highly qualified and thus expensive employees are able to do this job. Furthermore, a largely manual implementation leads to high error quota. On the whole, this pushes costs and time of the implementation.

In this paper, we address these problems by proposing a model driven engineering concept and a corresponding tool, the *cosmos 4E* (E for Engineering). The solution is based on UML-related models together with corresponding transformations and thus enables engineering of FMS control software on a higher level of abstraction and in a more efficient way. In addition, this relaxes the dependence on expensive experts and reduces implementation errors.

The paper is organized as follows. In Section 2, we present the *cosmos 4* platform and the steps of engineering for a concrete production. Section 3 introduces the model driven engineering concept with a special focus on behaviour modelling by introducing a new metamodel in the style of Gantt charts. After presenting some implementation details (Sect. 4), we report on a first evaluation (Sect. 5) and conclude the paper with a brief discussion of our experiences (Sect. 6).

2   Foundational Issues

The *cosmos 4* platform addresses the heterogeneity of FMS by two major features. Firstly, it includes an independent reference model that holistically fits the static structure of FMS and its components as well as the dynamic behaviour of FMS operations. Secondly, it provides a new advanced concept for increased "programmability" of control components reflecting that the control logic is at the core of the FMS control system's software [1]. These two features ease also the adaptation to changing requirements. But due to its vast applicability and scalability, the profitability of *cosmos 4* depends predominantly on its engineering costs. Below you find the general process of engineering FMS control software, which follows the well-known waterfall software development model:

1. **Architecture Planning** establishes an overview of the manufacturing system. All components like machines, transportation systems, storage systems, and system places are listed and classified. Furthermore in a distributed, agent-oriented FMS setting, the assignment between machines and control components is not fixed. Thus, it has to be decided which machines will be combined to a cell and subsequently controlled by a single agent.

2. **Process Planning** defines the automated production process for the required workpiece. All necessary operations and their execution dependencies have to be identified. A Gantt chart is up to now the most popular mean to illustrate the production process, since people are accustomed to think chronologically.

3. **Data Collection** concerns recording the static structure of the FMS and its components as well as the dynamic behaviour of FMS operations and mapping it to a suitable data structure.

4. **Definition of Machine Interfaces** The machines are accessible via vendor specific device drivers. The resulting heterogeneity can be coped with by a universal, vendor-independent interface between the device control and FMS, which raises the level of abstraction and reduces the complexity.

5. **Definition of Control Logic** The dynamic behaviour of a control component is defined in its control logic. The control logic includes state variables and control rules. According to the current state, a matching control rule is identified and immediately executed. The separation of the control logic from other code is advisable since this part has to be modified frequently. Usually activity diagrams or Petri nets are used to illustrate the control logic.

6. **Implementation of Functional Modules** The operations called by agents are grouped into functional modules. There are three types: to process data, to execute operations, and to communicate with other agents.

7. **Testing and Optimization** reveal errors and weak points that can not be identified at implementation time. Nowadays, the testing is usually carried out in a virtual simulation environment to reduce the costs. Additionally, it is attempted to improve the overall performance of the whole system by reorganizing the production process, in order to minimize the waiting time of machines.

8. **Documentation** is especially important in this setting since processes and machines are often changed due to new pieces that have to be produced or machines that are replaced. It should accompany all of the steps mentioned above.

3   A Model Driven Engineering Concept

Two problems can be identified in the traditional engineering approach of FMS control software. Firstly, until now the above mentioned engineering steps are insufficiently connected to each other, thus, direct information flow from one phase to the next is prevented. Architecture planning and process planning, for example, deliver merely text and diagrams as output that can not be adopted directly during the implementation. Secondly, it is a tedious and error-prone job to write structurally rather similar code over and over again. To overcome these problems, our basic idea is to provide for each of the engineering steps a corresponding model and to support mostly automatic transformations between them. Consequently, as much code as possible should be generated automatically, fully or partially from the models. Thus, engineering is now considered as a process of refinement and concretion of models.

3.1   Overview

Above we described a vision of applying MDA to engineering FMS control software. It can only be realized through a proper interpretation. The key of the interpretation is to find an appropriate modelling language.

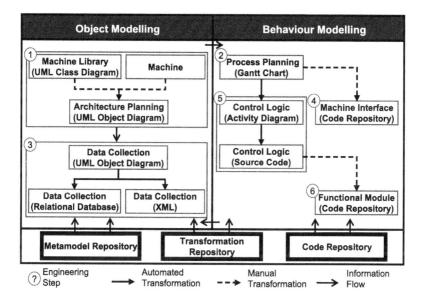

Fig. 1. A Model Driven Engineering Concept

Figure 1 gives an overview over the whole model driven engineering approach. The output of engineering can be divided into two categories: objects and behaviour. The objects represent all components within a FMS, while the behaviour describes the production process of machines. This separation makes sense since usually different modelling languages and methods are applied. In this paper, we focus on the behaviour modelling because changes to the production process are quite frequent due to the small lot sizes, while the object modelling for an FMS is rather static.

As a running example, we consider the adaptation of *cosmos 4* to control the integrated manufacturing and assembly system (IFMS) installed at WZL for producing a "Four Wins" game. The production includes sawing, milling, and assembling. For that, the sawing machine KASTO and the milling machine MAHO need to cooperate. In addition, a robotic palletiser and the transport system AGV are responsible for the material flow.

3.2   Object Modelling

As object modelling is not at the focus of this paper, we illustrate the idea only with a simple example. Figure 2 shows a pallet with fixture on a roller table. To

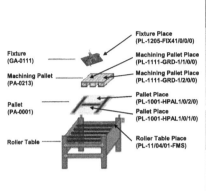

NO.	ENTITY_ID	DESCRIPTION
1	PA-0001	H-frame
2	PL-1001-HPAL1/0/1/0	place 1 on H-frame
3	PL-1001-HPAL1/0/2/0	place 2 on H-frame
4	PA-0213	MAHO grid machining pallet
5	PL-1111-GRD-1/1/0/0	place 1 on MAHO grid machining pallet
6	PL-1111-GRD-1/2/0/0	place 2 on MAHO grid machining pallet
7	GA-0111	fixture Four Wins, setting 1
8	PL-1205-FIX41/0/0/0	Workpiece place on Four Wins fixture 1

NO.	RELATION_A	RELATION_B	TYPE
1	PL-11/04/01-FMS	PA-0001	ASSIGN
2	PA-0001	PL-1001-HPAL1/0/1/0	HAS
3	PA-0001	PL-1001-HPAL1/0/2/0	HAS
4	PL-1001-HPAL1/0/1/0	PA-0213	ASSIGN
5	PA-0213	PL-1111-GRD-1/1/0/0	HAS
6	PA-0213	PL-1111-GRD-1/2/0/0	HAS
7	PL-1111-GRD-1/1/0/0	GA-0111	ASSIGN
8	GA-0111	PL-1205-FIX41/0/0/0	HAS

Fig. 2. Pallet Example

describe these objects and their relations, 16 entities in the relational database are needed, according to the data model in *cosmos 4*.

A more intuitive representation can be given by a UML object diagram (see Fig. 3 (a)). Furthermore, the object diagram can be based on a corresponding class diagram (see Fig. 3 (b)) to ensure consistent modelling for all objects. Thus, with a suitable library of FMS elements, architecture planning and the subsequent data collection can be alleviated.

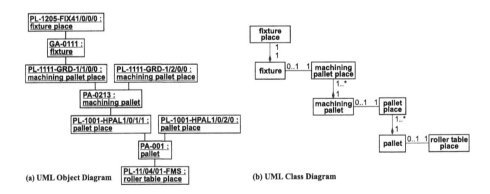

Fig. 3. UML Object Diagram and UML Class Diagram

In the last step of object modelling (see step 3 in Fig. 1) a decision has to be made as to how the data is stored e. g. as a relational database, as an XML file etc. But this is a purely technical decision and thus can be left to an appropriate transformation step. Due to efficiency, *cosmos 4* uses a relational database.

3.3   Behaviour Modelling

The desire for a consistent engineering environment promotes the use of the UML standard or at least UML-based modelling languages in all engineering phases. However, as mentioned above, the production process of machines is usually planned with Gantt charts, which unfortunately do not belong to the UML family. By comparing with all UML diagram types, it can be observed that Gantt charts are tightly related to UML activity diagrams. So UML activity diagrams are used as the basis for constructing Gantt charts.

There are two possibilities to establish a metamodel for Gantt charts: using UML's standard extension mechanism – UML profile – to extend the UML activity metamodel or building an own MOF-based metamodel using the UML activity metamodel as a reference. While UML with UML profile would be an ideal solution, we decided for the moment in favor of an own metamodel because it simplifies the implementation of our prototype and reduces in particular the complexity of transformations. Nonetheless, we still consider a corresponding UML profile as possible in the future, similar to the UML Profile for CORBA [6] that also follows this idea.

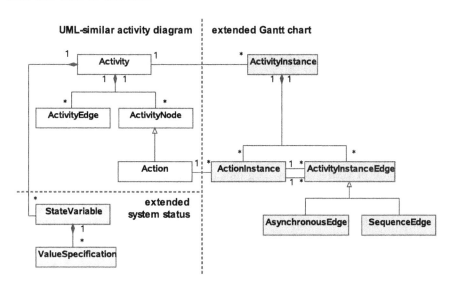

Fig. 4. Metamodel for Gantt Charts

Figure 4 shows the metamodel for Gantt charts. Compared to the UML activity metamodel, it is much more simplified. For example *ObjectNode* and *ObjectFlow* have been omitted. On the other hand some new elements are introduced. *ActionInstance*, for example, represents the execution of an action at runtime. Thus, *ActionInstance* has a n-to-1 relationship with *Action*. The edges that are used to connect *ActionInstances* show their dependence in time and have nothing to do with transitions. Therefore a new model element *ActivityInstanceEdge* is created, which is not related to *ActivityEdge*.

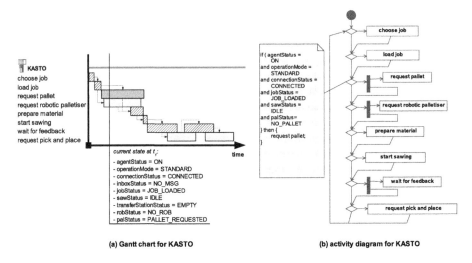

(a) Gantt chart for KASTO   (b) activity diagram for KASTO

Fig. 5. Gantt Chart and Activity Diagram Example for KASTO

Figure 5 (a) describes the process planning for the sawing machine KASTO. As we can observe from the figure, the agent controlling KASTO will request the transport system AGV to deliver the pallet and the robotic palletiser to be prepared for picking the sawed workpiece, before KASTO can start the sawing job. Since these are two independent operations, they can be executed simultaneously. As soon as the agent receives the commitments from AGV and the robotic palletiser, it will start the sawing process. It is not necessary to wait until they are in position.

Activity diagrams are used to model the machine control logic. Again we prefer our own metamodel shown in Fig. 6. We adopted as much elements from the metamodel of UML activity diagrams as possible. As to the conditions, we extended this concept to fit the special requirements of FMS control software.

The activity diagram for the sawing machine KASTO is shown in Fig. 5 (b). The control logic is executed in cycle and can only be terminated externally, so no final node is defined. Every action is accompanied by a decision node for checking the precondition. For example, only when the sawing job is loaded but no pallet is available, the KASTO will request the AGV to deliver an empty pallet. Since every action appears only once, the activity diagram provides a more technically suited view to the control logic than Gantt charts.

Machine drivers and functional modules belong to the individual parts of FMS control software. But nevertheless, some modelling support is possible. The difference is that only a code frame can be generated for machine drivers or functional modules. We omit details here due to the limit of space.

The steps for modelling of behaviour are illustrated on the right side of Fig. 1. The Gantt charts – representing process planning – and the activity diagrams – representing control logic – are connected by a fully automated model-to-model transformation. Since an official language for QVT has not yet been released, the model-to-model transformations are currently implemented in text,

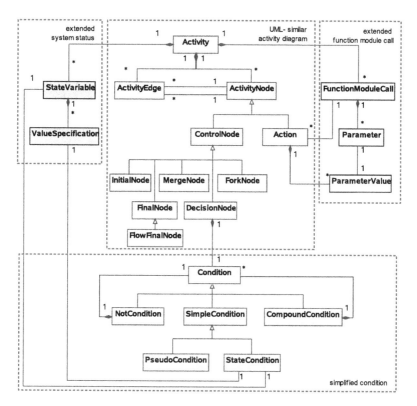

Fig. 6. Metamodel for Activity Diagrams

but encapsulated to ease their replacement. From the activity diagram, the implementation of the control logic can completely and automatically be generated.

4 Implementation

4.1 Technologies and Tools

Our prototype tool, named *cosmos 4E* (E for Engineering), focuses currently on the behaviour modelling, including process planning, definition of control logic, constructing functional modules, and testing. For this purpose a set of tools is needed that concern a model repository, a graphical model editor, a model transformation tool, a code transformation tool, and a runtime manager.

While in principle we should be able to choose any existing MDA tool with XMI support [7], the currently available tools on the market do not provide this ideal. Our implementation overcomes this problem by finding a platform first, in which each MDA tool for the prototype can be easily integrated. The choice of Eclipse is advantageous since it is primarily an integration platform through the concept of plug-in development environment (PDE). In addition, a lot of MDA-based tools are available as Eclipse plug-ins.

The commitment to a platform simplifies the choice of MDA tools. The Eclipse Modeling Framework [2] is an Eclipse plug-in, a modelling framework, and a code generation facility for building tools and other applications based on a structured data model. EMF provides mechanisms to view and edit the model and is able to import or export models from or into XMI. The Graphical Editing Framework [3], another Eclipse plug-in, allows developers to take an existing model and quickly create a rich graphical editor. As no suitable tool for model-to-model transformation is available yet, we implemented it directly in source code. Concerned with code generation, EMF contains two very powerful tools: Java Emitter Templates (JET) and Java Merge (JMerge). JET [8] is a generic template engine using a JSP-like syntax and can be used to generate any kind of output from templates. JMerge [9] is an extension to JET and allows code re-generation by ensuring that the customized code is not overwritten.

4.2 *cosmos 4E*

cosmos 4E is created as an Eclipse plug-in and integrated with the Eclipse platform and other plug-ins. The structural overview of *cosmos 4E* is shown in Fig. 7.

Figure 8 illustrates the use of the Gantt chart editor. In contrast to normal Gantt charts, this editor has some special features: The production process can be planned in minutes, seconds, and milliseconds instead of days and weeks. And each process can be assigned to a resource, which refers in this context to a functional module. With the aid of a tool palette, new elements can be created. The properties of these elements are accessible and editable through the property view.

After the process planning, the user can start the automated model-to-model transformation to create the activity diagram. The generation is preceded by a simple model verification that ensures that the model is valid. The generated activity diagram is shown in a read-only editor. After that the model-to-text transformation can be called. This generates the control logic in source code. As the user is supposed to provide the complete information in the Gantt chart editor, no modification in the source code is necessary. A re-generation always overwrites old data. A new functional module can be created via a dialog. Due to the complexity of functional modules, only an essential part of the Java code can be generated. Other methods must be manually implemented and it has been taken care that they will not be overridden by re-generation.

cosmos 4E	
model repository	activity diagram editor
Gantt chart editor	model transformation tool
code generator	runtime manager
Eclipse Modeling Framework (EMF)	Graphical Editing Framework (GEF)
Eclipse	

Fig. 7. Overview of *cosmos 4E*

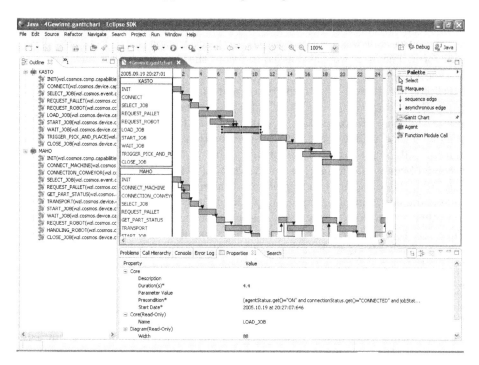

Fig. 8. Overview of Gantt Chart Editor

Furthermore, we implemented various views in Eclipse, which act as proxies to the source repository, for example, templates, functional modules, and control logic files. The functionality of a runtime manager is also integrated as a view. It allows a user to start an agent watcher, which reuses the model and logs the runtime activities of agents. The results can again be illustrated in the Gantt chart editor and compared with the planning data. This provides the users with a possibility to analyze the weak points in the planning and make an improvement.

5   Evaluation

To provide "useful feedback" to the prototype, we introduced a small evaluation. As mentioned in the introduction, the engineering process itself requires extensive know-how. Thus, we could only attract five users that already have a sufficient background knowledge about FMS and enough coding experience. They were divided into two groups and required to finish the same task. To complete the production process for the "Four Wins" game, a new agent for the milling machine MAHO had to be created. This includes the definition of the control logic, the preparation of all invoked functional modules, and other necessary agent configurations.

Group A was instructed to work with the prototype, while group B wrote the source code manually. Both groups were given corresponding material about a finished agent as an example. Models and source code were given to group A and merely source code was given to group B. User satisfaction was collected by a feedback form. The users were also asked to record the time needed for each step.

The prototype is evaluated as helpful. The feedback shows that group A, which got the models as introductional material, could learn much faster than group B working with source code only. On average, group A needed one third less of the time of group B. This confirms that the models are better understandable than source code. While the evaluation was not extensive enough to make a well-founded comparison of the quality of the engineering results, it has become obvious that group A's results contained fewer errors. This results not only from the automated code generation (about 500 lines that group B had to code manually), but also from a simple model checking that is provided by the prototype. It checks, for example, whether every needed parameter is specified. Enriching the model checking facilities, e.g. for including semantical checks, in the future is a strong wish of the users.

6   Discussion

We are aware of some other projects concerning efficient engineering of FMS control software that have been started in the academic field during the last years [12], [13], [4]. Most of them concentrate on single engineering steps, modules, repositories, or configuration files. Fewer approaches have been made by using models. Langen [5] tried to develop an engineering architecture covering various modellers and generators. Current research in this area mostly concerns the automobile industry. The project IMMOS[1] e.g. aims at an integrated methodology for model driven development of control devices [11]. Various modelling languages like Matlab, Stateflow are applied. Although the concepts and tools reported by IMMOS can not easily be adopted for the engineering of FMS control software, their experiences show that model driven engineering can cause improvements. Furthermore, it is reported that the available tools for model driven engineering are still insufficient [10].

The approach that we have presented here – consisting of a model driven concept and a set of MDA-based tools – allows an efficient and integrated engineering of FMS control software. The test trial of the prototype has proven that the engineering of FMS control software, driven by models, can make a profit. Meanwhile, we gathered a lot of experiences on developing MDA solutions.

Until now there is not a single tool that supports all features of MDA, thus, usually a set of tools is needed. To make the decision, as to which MDA tools are to be selected, designers have to look for different aspects or factors that are required by their particular project. We have made good experiences by starting from a platform that acts as a basis for MDA tools. Furthermore, based on long-term considerations, using standard metamodels like UML metamodel with specific extensions (e.g. UML profiles) is obviously advantageous. However, building own metamodels reduces development costs and implementation

---

[1] http://www.immos-projekt.de

complexity considerably, especially for model transformations. For our proto-type, we have thus chosen the latter way. Finally, MDA is still a new concept. Currently available open source MDA tools are not sufficiently mature to support all features of MDA. For example, there are few tools which can describe QVT or offer model-to-model transformation. Even so, it is important to be prepared for adopting new technologies or tools during the implementation. We packaged the source code for model-to-model transformation, for which we provide documentation and guidance, waiting for new MDA tools to replace it.

Future work will focus on extending the *cosmos 4E* engineering environment to object modelling and to elaborating the use of models during test and verification. Furthermore, we are looking forward to new MDA tools for better support, especially in the area of model-to-model transformation and model-checking. Eventually, our efforts might result in a new UML profile supporting consistently all phases of engineering FMS control software.

Acknowledgment. This work was supported in part by the Deutsche Forschungsgemeinschaft in its Graduate School 643 "Software for Mobile Communication Systems" and by the Federal Ministry of Education and Research (BMBF) in the project "Ramp-Up/2".

References

1. C. Brecher, F. Possel-Dölken, and C. Almeida. FMS control software with programmable control agents. In *CIRP Conference on Reconfigurable Manufacturing Systems*, 2005.
2. Eclipse Modeling Framework. http://www.eclipse.org/emf/.
3. Graphical Editing Framework. http://www.eclipse.org/gef/.
4. A. Kurth. *Entwicklung agentenorientierter Informationssysteme für die Fertiungsleittechnik.* PhD thesis, RWTH Aachen, 2002.
5. R. Langen. *Methoden und Werkzeuge zur Erstellung von Fertigungsleitsoftware.* PhD thesis, RWTH Aachen, 1998.
6. OMG. UML Profile for CORBA Specification. http://www.omg.org/docs/formal/ 02-04-01.pdf, April 2002.
7. OMG. MOF 2.0/XMI Mapping Specification, v2.1. http://www.omg.org/docs/ formal/ 05-09-01.pdf, September 2005.
8. A. Powell. Model with the Eclipse Modeling Framework, part 2. http://www-128.ibm.com/developerworks/library/os-ecemf2/, April 2004.
9. A. Powell. Model with the Eclipse Modeling Framework, part 3. http://www-128.ibm.com/developerworks/library/os-ecemf3/, May 2004.
10. H. Schlingloff, M. Conrad, H. Dörr, and C. Sühl. Modellbasierte Steuergerätesoftwareentwicklung für den Automobilbereich. In *Automotive Safety and Security 2004*, 2004.
11. H. Schlingloff, C. Sühl, H. Dörr, M. Conrad, J. Stroop, S. Sadeghipour, M. Kühl, F. Rammig, and G. Engels. Eine integrierte Methodik zur modellbasierten Steuergeräteentwicklung. In *BMBF-Workshop "Software Engineering 2006"*, 2004.
12. U. Siewert. *Systematische Erstellung adaptierbarer Leitsteuerungssoftware am Beispiel der Durchsetzungsplanung.* PhD thesis, Universität Stuttgart, 1994.
13. J. Uhl. *Entwurfssystematik für ein dezentral strukturiertes, objektorientiertes Fertigungsleitsystem.* PhD thesis, Universität Stuttgart, 1998.

MDD Maturity Model: A Roadmap for Introducing Model-Driven Development

Erkuden Rios[1], Teodora Bozheva[1],
Aitor Bediaga[1], and Nathalie Guilloreau[2]

[1] European Software Institute, Parque Tecnológico de Zamudio, #204
E-48170 Zamudio Spain
{Erkuden.Rios, Teodora.Bozheva, Aitor.Bediaga}@esi.es
http://www.esi.es
[2] Thales Research & Technology, RD128
E-91767 Palaiseau cedex France
nathalie.guilloreau@thalesgroup.com
http://www.thalesgroup.com

Abstract. Experience reports show that MDD reduces time-to-market and increases productivity by means of platform independent business logic modelling and automation. Achieving these two concepts in the organisation is not a one step process. This paper explains the MDD Maturity Model developed to drive this task in a structured way. The MDD Maturity Model establishes five capability levels towards the progressive adoption of MDD within an organisation. Each level describes a coherent set of engineering, management and support practices involved in the MDD approach, and characterizes the MDD artefacts, called MDD elements, used in or resulted from those practices. The paper presents also the validation process that the model will undergo in two large organisations and two SMEs.

1 Introduction

Several examples can be found of satisfactory MDD introduction in organisations, such as Interactive Objects' report on MDA experimentation in DainmlerChrysler TSS and M1 Global's own case study report, both available at Object Management Group's (OMG) MDA web site (www.omg.org/mda).

As seen in experiences of the like, successfully introducing MDD methods and tools in a project is not simple, and obviously deploying them throughout the organisation is much more complex because it implies serious changes in the organisation's culture and processes: start treating models as first class citizens (which means keeping them updated and on-track), adapt the roles, provide staff with the necessary tooling and methodological training, and so on.

Maximising the benefits of MDD for time-to-market reduction and productivity increment is achieved through two key factors: abstracting from platform specificities when modelling business logic and exploiting automation possibilities.

A. Rensink and J. Warmer (Eds.): ECMDA-FA 2006, LNCS 4066, pp. 78–89, 2006.

In this paper we explain the MDD Maturity Model developed within the MODEL-WARE project[1] aimed to help organisations in the MDD approach adoption, until the whole process automation is reached, and organisation acquires the sufficient capability for business knowledge capitalisation in reusable models.

The Model has been developed to be used as reference model for identifying and appraising the level of maturity of a given organisation with respect to MDD technology implementation. The validation of the model will be done through using the model in assessments of MDD implementations by different companies.

The remainder of this paper is organised as follows. The next section explains the concepts used in the MDD Maturity Model, and Section 3 explains the Model itself. Section 4 summarises its major contributions for the industry and Section 5 describes the validation process the model will undergo. In section 6 we deal with some related works and finally, we present our conclusions and future work.

2   The MDD Maturity Model Concepts

The MDD Maturity Model consists of five *maturity levels*. The maturity levels provide a general characterization of the organisations with respect to the degree of adoption and implementation of MDD; this means that each maturity level indicates a step forward in the MDD improvement path of the organisation. For each maturity level goals associated to both MDD practices and MDD elements status are defined.

2.1   MDD Practices

MDD practices describe only activities specific for the model-driven development and typical practices in traditional software development are deliberately excluded from this Model.

Three categories of MDD practices are defined in the MDD Maturity Model:

- *Engineering practices* (ENG) cover development activities in the model-driven software engineering discipline.
- *Project management practices* (PJM) address activities that are directly related to management decisions absolutely necessary to setup and manage an MDD project. The typical practices such as planning a project, milestone definition and resource assignment are not considered.
- *Support practices* (SUP) cover activities that support the implementation of the engineering and the project management practices.

2.2   MDD Elements

MDD elements are the basic artefacts used in the MDD technology such as models, transformations, MDD tools and so on. The following MDD elements are identified:

---

[1]   The work presented here has been developed within the MODELWARE project. MODELWARE is a project co-funded by the European Commission under the "Information Society Technologies" Sixth Framework Programme (2002-2006). Information included in this document reflects only the author's views. The European Community is not liable for any use that may be made of the information contained herein.

Table 1. MDD Elements and associated attributes

MDD Element:	Attribute:	Attribute description:
Models	Model purpose	The extent to which the model is defined according to established organisational policies and standards.
	Adherence to organisational policies and standards	The objective for which the model is defined.
	Scope of the model	The extent of the matters defined in the model.
	Integration degree	The extent to which the model is integrated in the development process, if the model is defined in isolation or it is linked to other MDD elements by means of formal and consistent relationships.
	Verification degree	To which extent the verification activities are focused on this model.
	Traceability depth	Extent of details addressing the traceability of the model to other MDD elements.
	Simulability	Ability of being simulated by means of a model simulator.
	Executability	Ability of being executed by means of a model executor or virtual machine.
Transformations and code generation mechanisms	Transformation type	Horizontal (generation of another model view at same level of abstraction) or Vertical (generation of another model or artefact at another level of abstraction).
	Round-trip engineering support	Degree of support for round-trip engineering (forward and backward transformation). The implementation of this aspect supports synchronisation among models.
	Platform dependency	Degree of dependency with the specific target platform of the system.
Tools	Integration facility	Capability of the tool to be integrated with other tools supporting the MDD process.
Documentation	Automation extent	Average ratio of automatically generated to manually written part in documentation.

- *Models*: A model represents an abstraction (simplification) of something in the real world and captures its essential characteristics. The following types of models are distinguished:
  - *Domain metamodel*: is the metamodel or language that captures the abstract structure of the business domain identifying fundamental domain entity types and the relationships between them.
  - *Architecture-centric metamodel*: is the metamodel that captures the concepts of the technical platform.

- *Domain model*: is the model that defines how a business works without reference to software systems, similarly to OMG's Computation Independent Model.
- *Business model*: is the model that resolves business requirements through purely problem-space terms and it does not include platform specific concepts, as the OMG's Platform Independent Model.
- *Technical model*: is a solution model that resolves both functional and non-functional requirements through the use of platform specific concepts. This model is equivalent to the OMG's Platform Specific Model.
- *Code*: is the final asset in the development, which can be considered as a model because it conforms to a specific metamodel, the programming language.
- *Model transformations and code generation mechanisms*: are mechanisms for converting a model to another model of the same system. Model to model, Model to text and Model to code transformations are examples of this MDD element type.
- *Modelling tools*: are tools that are used in modelling activities, e.g. model editors, model simulators, model executors, model repositories, transformation editors, transformation repositories, transformers...
- *Documentation*: is the set of text documents which describe all the development process and/or the assets generated and, thus, is linked to other MDD elements.

While MDD practices do not, MDD elements do have *MDD attributes* associated to them. Each attribute describes an essential characteristic of the MDD element. The next table summarizes the attributes identified in the Model.

The maturity level of an organisation is given by the assessment of two factors:

- whether the MDD practices and MDD elements corresponding to that maturity level exist or not and
- whether those MDD elements' attributes take the appropriate values corresponding to that maturity level.

3 The MDD Maturity Model

One of the major requirements of the MDD Maturity Model developed inside MODELWARE project is to be compliant with the Capability Maturity Model® Integration (CMMI®), which is a recognised and widely spread model, implemented in lots of software intensive organisations.

One approach to developing the MDD Maturity Model is to define how the MDD activities amplify the CMMI® specific practices. This approach could be useful for organisations that have experience and knowledge in applying CMMI®. However, organisations interested in adopting MDD without implementing CMMI® will get little benefit from an MDD Maturity Model represented as an amplification of CMMI®. Besides, lots of Small and Medium Size (SME) companies do not apply CMMI®, yet are interested in increasing the effectiveness of their software engineering processes by means of MDD. The MDD Maturity Model is developed as an independent model, which, however, complements CMMI.

Additionally, the MDD Maturity Model is aligned with the model developed within the FAMILIES (IP02009) project, with respect to the domain capitalization dimension, because the goals of the two upper levels in the MDD Maturity Model fit very well in it.

To define the MDD Maturity Model, literature and early adopters' MDD processes has been studied and the following approach was adopted:

• Analysis of the MDD practices and grouping them in levels representing different degree of profundity of the implementation of MDD
• Analysis of technical means: how they can be characterised, what are the different possible extents for using and deploying these means in a development process
• Study of the dependencies between the MDD practices and the technical means
• Identification of discrete levels of the MDD adoption that combine MDD practices and relevant technical means.

As shown in Figure 1, the MDD Maturity Model defines five maturity levels distributed bottom up, from less mature to more mature MDD adoption. The lower level MDD practices and elements are a basis for the implementation of the activities on the upper levels.

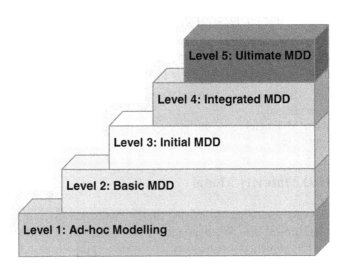

Fig. 1. MDD Maturity Model levels

3.1 Maturity Level 1: Ad-Hoc Modelling

The Ad-hoc modelling level corresponds to situations where modelling practices are sporadically used or not used at all in the organisation. This means that the organisation is performing traditional software development, and individuals may use some models for their own help, but no policy or common understanding applies to those scarce models. Obviously, the organization has no specific goals on modelling activities or artefacts.

3.2 Maturity Level 2: Basic MDD

In this level of maturity, the organisation is more mature in modelling and in each project developed in the organisation a Technical model is created with which the final code and system documentation have to be in line. In this level, the Technical model combines business and technical aspects of the system to be developed, with no distinction between them.

The final code and documentation shall comply with the system specification modelled. This alignment is done by means of basic automatic code generation and documentation generation mechanisms which generate (parts of) them from the Technical model.

In Level 2, the fact that models are used for guiding implementation and production of documentation is an organisational premise and not an individual initiative. In the projects, it is necessary to take decisions upon the modelling tools and techniques that will be used in the development, in accordance with project objectives.

The next table defines the goals in this level and the MDD practices aimed to achieve them.

Table 2. MDD Maturity Level 2 goals and practices

Goals:	
Goal 1	Develop technical model and use it to build up software
Goal 2	Include all business and technical requirements in models
Goal 3	Select MDD tools aligned to project objectives
MDD Practices:	
Engineering	ENG 1 Identify modelling techniques
	ENG 2 Define Technical model
	ENG 3 Generate code from the Technical model
	ENG 4 Generate documentation from the Technical model
	ENG 5 Complete code to comply with all req.
Project Management	PJM 1 Decide upon modelling tools
Support	N/A

Figure 2 shows the key elements in the MDD maturity level 2.

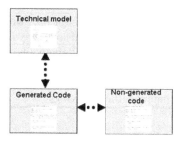

Fig. 2. MDD elements in MDD Maturity Level 2

Note that in all figures, a thick dashed arrow stands for "manual or automatic transformation", whereas a thick continue arrow means "automatic transformation".

3.3 Maturity Level 3: Initial MDD

The organisation starts developing systems in a more model-driven approach when, besides aligning the code and the models, it develops business models which address the business logic of the system separately from the technical models which cover the technical requirements. This is done for capitalising the business knowledge over all the projects.

Business models are then manually converted to technical models, but these technical models are represented by means of a tool and are converted to code automatically. The Business models can be directly converted to code also, which means that the Technical model with platform specifics resides implicit in this direct transformation.

In addition to business logic and platform specifics differentiation, in this level of maturity, the models are exchanged between different stakeholders for communication, which implies the need of models are checked with respect to well-formedness rules, and metrics on modelling activities are consistently defined, collected and analysed.

The next table defines the goals in this level and the MDD practices aimed to achieve them.

Table 3. MDD Maturity Level 3 goals and practices

Goals:	
Goal 1	Separate business and technical aspects in MDD elements
Goal 2	Define rules for modelling linked to organisation's strategy
Goal 3	Exchange system knowledge with other stakeholders through models
MDD Practices:	
Engineering	ENG 6 Define Business model
	ENG 7 Define transformations from Technical model to text
	ENG 8 Separate generated from non-generated code
	ENG 9 Check models
Project Management	PJM 2 Define MDD-project workflow
	PJM 3 Decide upon coverage of modelling activities
Support	SUP 1 Establish and maintain repositories for models and transformations
	SUP 2 Define, collect and analyze measures with respect to the modelling activities

The next figure depicts the MDD elements of the level 3 and their relationships.

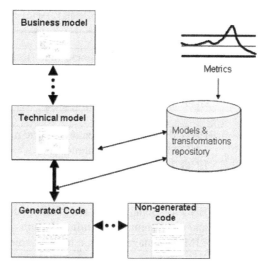

Fig. 3. MDD elements in MDD Maturity Level 3

3.4 Maturity Level 4: Integrated MDD

The organisation begins integrating the models when domain modelling is performed. This means that the domain concepts are represented by means of a domain model. Business models are derived from the domain models and are developed by means of a tool. Then, they are automatically transformed to technical models and these technical models into code. Domain, business and technical concepts are separated.

In this maturity level, two types of technical models are developed: the ones that model the core infrastructure shared by all products in a product family, and the technical models for a specific application development. This ensures reusability of infrastructure models.

At Level 4, the organisations are more mature in modelling and they simulate the models created with a tool, in order to verify them for early correcting possible design errors.

The next table defines the goals in this level and the MDD practices aimed to achieve them.

Figure 4 shows the MDD elements involved in the level 4 and the relationships among them.

3.5 Maturity Level 5: Ultimate MDD

To achieve a complete MDD adoption and reap its benefits, there is a need to have a system family engineering mindset, which means to have a common set of MDD assets (transformations, domain models, metamodels,...) that are reusable organisation-wide. Therefore, the ultimate maturity level is reached when the transformations between all the models are made automatically and models are fully integrated between them and with code. Executable models are developed so the focus of the organisation efforts is on the models and not on code programming. The whole life cycle becomes model-driven.

Table 4. MDD Maturity Level 4 goals and practices

Goals:	
Goal 1	Separate domain, business and technical aspects in MDD elements
Goal 2	Ensure efficient modelling performance
Goal 3	Share integrated development environment
MDD Practices:	
Engineering	ENG 10 Define architecture centric metamodel
	ENG 11 Define domain model
	ENG 12 Define transformations from Business model to Technical model
	ENG 13 Simulate models
	ENG 14 Separate the technical models of the product and the system family infrastructure
Project Management	PJM 4 Manage common infrastructure development.
Support	N/A

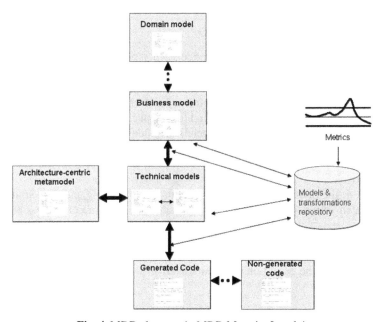

Fig. 4. MDD elements in MDD Maturity Level 4

Hence, the main characteristic of the ultimate MDD level is that the entire organisation's know-how is capitalised in models and transformations. The domain engineering practices are put in place and Domain Specific Languages (DSL) are created in order to make strategic assets reusable. Even the system verification and validation (V&V) knowledge is stored in models that are used for V&V of the implementation.

The next table defines the goals in this level and the MDD practices aimed to achieve them.

Table 5. MDD Maturity Level 5 goals and practices

Goals:	
Goal 1	Ensure complete model-centric development
Goal 2	Ensure organisation's knowledge is capitalised in models and transformations
MDD Practices:	
Engineering	ENG 15 Define domain specific languages
	ENG 16 Continuously improve and validate the meta-models
	ENG 17 Define transformations from Domain model to Business model
	ENG 18 Model-based V&V
Project Management	PJM 5 Establish and maintain strategic MDD elements
Support	N/A

Figure 5 shows the MDD elements involved in the level 5.

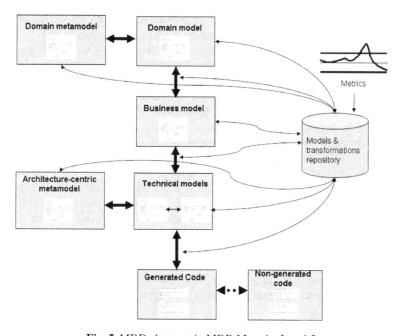

Fig. 5. MDD elements in MDD Maturity Level 5

4   MDD Maturity Model Benefits for the Industry

The main benefits that the MDD Maturity Model can offer to the industry are:

- Provides understanding of the steps towards a complete and efficient MDD adoption.

- Makes easier to further improve MDD practices and work products in the organisations.
- Establishes a common integrated vision of all MDD dimensions to improve in the organisation.
- Facilitates to accomplish the cultural and organisational changes that MDD implies simultaneously with the learning of a common language on modelling activities understood by all process participants.

The MDD Maturity Model complements other maturity models, such as the CMMI®, allowing the adoption of MDD specific practices within the CMMI® improvement initiative.

The MDD Maturity Model is the first step for building the standardized framework for categorizing the organisations' capabilities on MDD, for either internally identify or externally claim their maturity level.

5 Validation Process

The MDD Maturity Model described above is going to be used as the reference model for performing assessments of companies or project teams with respect to MDD. In particular, the model will be used to assess the MDD implementation by four leading companies: Thales ATM (France), France Telecom (France), WM-data (Estonia) and Enabler (Portugal). The first two are well known large businesses, WM-data is a SME branch of the leading supplier of design and IT services in the Nordic regions and Enabler is the SME branch of an international IT solution provider for retailing. These four companies are industrial partners in MODELWARE and the assessments' work is also part of the project results.

The assessment consists in rating the capability in each of the MDD practices and evaluating the status of the MDD elements in the Model, and therefore highlighting both strengths and areas candidate for improvement.

The MDD Maturity Model will be valid if it enables to distinctively characterize the maturity level of each organisation and if it helps organisations in effectively implementing MDD and improving its weak areas in MDD. Besides, the terminology used in the model shall be understandable for all these companies and it should embrace all the key modelling practices experimented by them.

After the validation process a refined version of the MDD Maturity Model will be issued. The improvement brought will mainly consist in refining the goals and practices in each of the levels and integrate them with appropriate MDD metrics to collect in each case.

6 Related Work

Assessing the capability of an organisation with regards to MDD technology is a relatively new subject, with limited material available and experimented in the MDD community.

Some partial attempts have been made in MDD maturity degrees definition, which focus on specific aspects of MDD. This is the case of Kleppe and Warmer's

Modelling Maturity Levels [2] or the IBM approach [3], which uses some form of a MDD technological capability model as commercial support for their proprietary tools. Whereas neither of these models has formal specification of the MDD practices and assets inside each maturity level, nor is validated by the industry yet, our Model makes a formal definition of both MDD practices and elements for unambiguously characterising the maturity levels. Besides, our model will undergo a validation process by the industry in near future.

7   Conclusion and Future Work

The MDD Maturity Model described has been developed inside the MODELWARE project to complement the existing models for quality and process improvements by putting the focus on how to execute software engineering activities applying the MDD technology.

The Model describes five maturity levels in the roadmap for improving MDD practices and MDD artefacts, from the lowest level (Ad-hoc modelling level) to the highest level-5 (Ultimate MDD level). Each level describes a consistent set of engineering, management and support practices within the MDD approach. Additionally, it provides a characterization of the MDD elements created or used at each level.

The MDD Maturity Model is the tool for organisations to establish the correct roadmap for the adoption of MDD. It provides them a means for identifying their strengths and weaknesses with respect to MDD. Therefore, the MDD Maturity Model serves to support industry in improving their MDD development processes, technology and organisation. A final, refined iteration of the model will follow after the model is validated in the industrial partners in MODELWARE in June 2006.

Acknowledgments

We would like to thank the contributions to the development and refinement of the MDD Maturity Model: as co-developers Veronique Normand (Thales Research & Technology) and Jason Xabier Mansell (European Software Institute); and as main reviewers Asier Azaceta (European Software Institute) and Robert Pastor (Thales Research & Technology).

References

1. Bettin Jorn, Patterns for Model Driven Software Development, (2004),
2. Kleppe, Aneke, Warmer, Jos: Getting started with Modeling Maturity Levels, (2004), http://www.devx.com/enterprise/Article/26664
3. A Roadmap for Agile MDA, http://www.agilemodeling.com/essays/agileMDA.htm
4. Family Evaluation Framework overview & introduction, Families project http://www.esi.es/en/ Projects/Families/
5. CMU/SEI-2002-TR-012 Capability Maturity Model Integration ver. 1.1
6. Kleppe, Aneke, Warmer, Jos, Bast, Wim: MDA Explained, ISBN 032119442X (2004)
7. Bézivin, Jean: In Search of a Basic Principle for Model Driven Engineering. Upgrade. Vol V, No. 2. (2004)

A Process Framework for the Successful Adoption of Model Driven Development[*]

Jason Mansell[1], Aitor Bediaga[1], Régis Vogel[2], and Keith Mantell[3]

[1] European Software Institute, Parque Tecnológico de Zamudio, #204
E-48170 Zamudio Spain
{Jason.Mansell, Aitor.Bediaga}@esi.es
[2] Enabler, Avenida da Boavista, 1223 4100-130 Porto, Portugal
Regis.vogel@enabler.com
[3] IBM UK Ltd, Hursley Park, Winchester, SO21 2JN, UK
keith.mantell@uk.ibm.com

Abstract. Organisations are always looking for better and faster ways of developing systems. One of the technologies that promise this is Model Driven Development (MDD), but there are still only a few organisations that have been capable of maximizing the benefits of MDD. The success of these few cases is based on the establishment of a clear system development process which encompasses both the activities that must be performed as well as the tools that need to be used within the organisation to adopt MDD. When an organisation considers adopting MDD, the first barrier it encounters is the lack of well-documented success stories which clearly state the process followed by these organisations. This paper presents a common repository of MDD processes/practices which have been extracted from successful MDD adoption stories, in the form of the MDD Process Framework.

1 Introduction

In today's more competitive environment, where higher productivity and quality make a difference, software intensive organisations need to introduce technology-specific processes within their current development process in a fast but controlled manner.

Software development organisations are focused on the return on their investments and on seeking higher process maturity levels, taking as reference maturity models such as CMMI®, SPICE and others. It is relevant to mention that organisations at a higher level of maturity in their process specification and execution will be at an advantage when adopting a new technology.

---

[*] The work presented here has been developed within the MODELWARE project. MODELWARE is a project co-funded by the European Commission under the "Information Society Technologies" Sixth Framework Programme (2002-2006). Information included in this document reflects only the author's views. The European Community is not liable for any use that may be made of the information contained herein.

A. Rensink and J. Warmer (Eds.): ECMDA-FA 2006, LNCS 4066, pp. 90–100, 2006.

This paper describes a solution that enables organisations to adopt MDD successfully, as well as standardise their system development process, by the use of the Software Process Engineering Metamodel [1] (SPEM). SPEM is a metamodel defined by the OMG [2] (Object Management Group) that offers an open standards-based approach to model development processes. This solution is the MDD Process Framework.

1.1 The MDD Process Framework

The MDD process framework is a process repository that contains reusable MDD process elements that describe MDD related processes and practices. To be more precise, the MDD Process Framework is a repository of MDD specific engineering and management process elements (MDD process elements) which have proven to be successful in the adoption of MDD within organisations in several contexts. These MDD process elements can be used to construct standardised project-specific or organisation development processes.

The MDD process elements have been defined in terms of the UML-based process modelling language SPEM v1.1 [1]. By using this standard as the basis of this work it makes the interchange of processes and the integration into existing processes easier. The MDD Process Framework contains MDD process elements that have been identified from real experimentation in adopting MDD. Some of the sources have been:

- MASTER project. "D3.2 - Process model to engineer and manage the MDA approach [3] "
- COMET Methodology Handbook. [4]
- SINTEF modelling methodology [5]
- "PIM Definition and Description" [6]
- "An introduction to UML Profiles" [7]
- Reflective Model Driven Engineering" [8]
- PLUTO, a simple test methodology for product families. [9]
- AGEDIS project [10]
- ENABLER software development process [13]

These MDD process elements are organised by means of phases such as Requirements, Analysis, Design, Development, Test and also Cross-phase process elements. The concept of phase used in the MDD Process Framework is basically a grouping issue to ease understanding, since, depending on the existing development life-cycle used, the MDD process elements can be integrated into different phases to those defined within the MDD Process Framework.

A MDD process element consists of a set of activities, roles and workproducts, and clearly specifies the MDD process/practice it defines.

1.2 The Environment of the MDD PF

Based on work done in "The Living Software Development Process" [15], where a new approach on building a development process is introduced, specific steps and roles have been identified as necessary to build a system development process using building blocks (process elements) from different process frameworks.

The MDD Process Framework and other process frameworks will be used mainly by the method engineer, manually or by means of a process modelling tool, to construct the organisational standard set of processes enriched with MDD-specific practices. The method engineer identifies and integrates the different process elements contained in different process frameworks, required to develop the system development process he/she needs to develop [14].

The method engineer needs to identify the modelling artefacts that should be produced during the project, and relate them appropriately. This selection will be based on the organisation's process needs and on the description provided within these MDD-specific practices that describe how to build an organisation system development process.

The method engineer uses pre- and post-conditions as well as the process descriptions in order to be able to adequately address the combination of MDD process elements with other process elements predefined by the organisation. The method engineer must ensure completeness of the defined system development process, for example, that roles adopted from the MDD process framework that he/she has integrated within the system development process are coherent with roles existing within the organisation. The method engineer is responsible for ensuring the correctness of the resulting system development process independently of the available tool support.

To do so, the MDD PF provides MDD tailoring guidelines which allow different MDD process elements to be joined with other process frameworks' elements in order to construct the resulting system development process. These MDD tailoring guidelines are used to aid the customisation of the MDD process elements in order to adequately adapt them to the organisation's context. The content of the MDD tailoring guidelines is provided by the users of specific MDD process elements, by capturing problems and solutions identified when integrating the MDD process elements together.

Once the method engineer has defined the system development process of the organisation, the project manager must make use of the defined system development process in the definition and execution of a specific project. The project manager must tailor the system development process to the project specific context.

Next, the application designer uses the project adapted system development process to build the final system. Finally, the method engineer, application designer and project manager should provide feedback to the knowledge engineer in order to modify, delete or add new process elements in the process frameworks with proved best practices. This final task allows an updated source of knowledge to be maintained within the organisational process framework.

Fig. 1 provides an overview of previously described steps as well as a detailed operational environment of the MDD PF. Note that actors identified in this section denote roles, so one person can perform many roles at the same time.

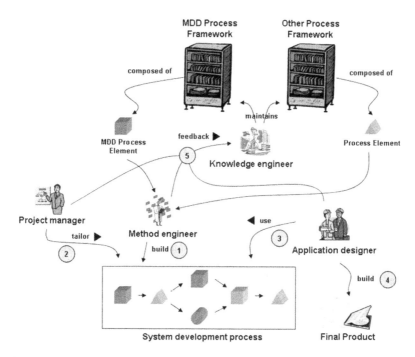

Fig. 1. Detailed operational environment for System development process construction

1.3 Making the MDD PF a Reality

The major drawback for the approach identified was the lack of tool support, therefore two prototypes were developed. Both prototypes were developed as plug-ins to Rational Software Modeller (RSM) from IBM. We implemented a SPEM v1.1 profile for RSM and used it to model all the MDD process elements. The other plug-in was implemented for the user, to select the MDD process elements which fit his/her needs from the MDD Process Framework.

2 Experimental Use of the MDD Process Framework in ENABLER

The first outline of this experimentation in a broader context was provided during the ECMDA-FA Conference within the Workshop "From code centric to model centric software engineering: Practices, Implications and ROI" in the paper "MDD process for SME: evolution, not revolution – Phase I" [13]. In this paper the major initial steps in the definition of the Enablers MDD Process were described.

Continuous work by Enabler, IBM UK and ESI, has identified MDD process elements which are for general purpose, such as developing profiles or transformations. At the same time the process structure is based on the traditional waterfall life cycle and for each of the phases there are a set of predefined MDD Process Elements.

As an initial exercise in browsing the MDD Process Framework, a set of MDD Process Elements were selected as having potential to be used. Once the MDD Process Elements had been selected, there was a need to identify the tailoring required to integrate the selected MDD Process Elements into the already defined MDD process.

One of the major issues was the correct mapping of roles and workproducts between the MDD PF and the organisation's MDD process; as is often the case, the roles that carry out activities or are responsible for producing specific workproducts are already related to the operational concepts of an organisation. Therefore the specified roles within the MDD process elements in many cases are renamed, while keeping responsibility, in order to integrate them into existing roles within the organisation.

Fig. 2 provides an overview of the construction of the Enabler MDD development process, using the MDD Process Framework as well as the SPEM v1.1 Rational Software Modeler plug-ins. The parties involved in the process specification were Enabler, IBM and ESI.

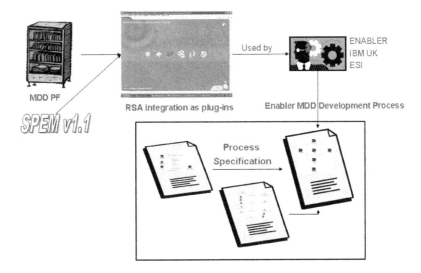

Fig. 2. Enabler's MDD development process: Construction overview

Fig. 3 provides an overview of the resultant Enabler MDD development process indicating the specific MDD Process Elements used in the different phases of MDD Process Framework in the Enablers industrial context.

In the following paragraphs we describe the different steps that were taken to describe Enabler's MDD development process. The first step is to identify the set of activities for each phase and describe the inputs and outputs for each of them. Next it is necessary to capture the roles involved in the defined activities, this is captured in a Role diagram, and finally there is a need to capture the relationships among the different input and outputs from the activities, also called workproducts.

In the following examples from the case of Enabler, two MDD Process Elements are shown as candidates for being reused in the requirements phase when addressing the customer needs and domain. They are: Define Domain Concept Model and Define Project Concept Model and presented in Fig. 4 which shows that they are to be used.

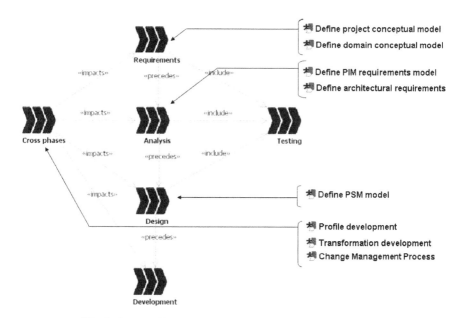

Fig. 3. Process Elements used in Enabler′s Development Phases

These two MDD Process Elements were tailored to Enabler's specific needs. In Enabler's case, where they customise an existing product family to particular customer situations, the overall domain model is well defined. This domain model is tailored to a particular project conceptual model to account for such things a customer specific terminology. As a result of a particular project, the overall Domain Conceptual Model may be enhanced with lessons learnt.

Fig. 5 shows the detail of the 2 example activities from the MDD PF with the resultant Enabler process description.

One of the main areas in which Enabler believes that MDD can help to improve ROI is in the Change Management Process, since this is a frequent activity in all Enabler projects. Actually one of the MDD experiments in the Modelware project is focussed on this as represented in Fig. 6 and is being harvested into the overall MDD PF. Notice the workproducts generated (for example SQL definitions). Change management is a fundamental process, and as such is represented in most existing

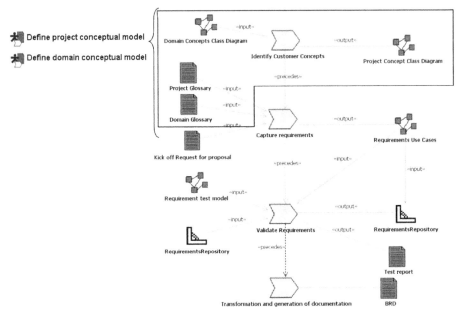

Fig. 4. Use of the Define Domain Concept Model and Define Project Concept Model MDD process elements in the requirement phase definition

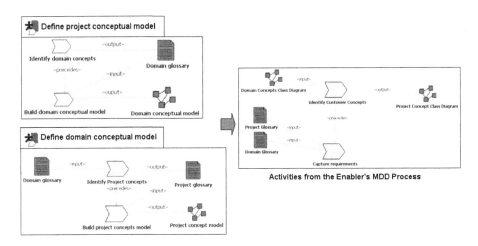

Fig. 5. MDD Process Elements in Enabler's requirements phase

Process Frameworks including RUP. Therefore it is essential to modify this standard process to apply to MDD techniques.

Fig. 7 shows how specific MDD techniques are added to the Enabler process, in this case the Requirements process; Object Constraint Language (OCL) statements are used to check that certain features of the Requirements have been fulfilled (for

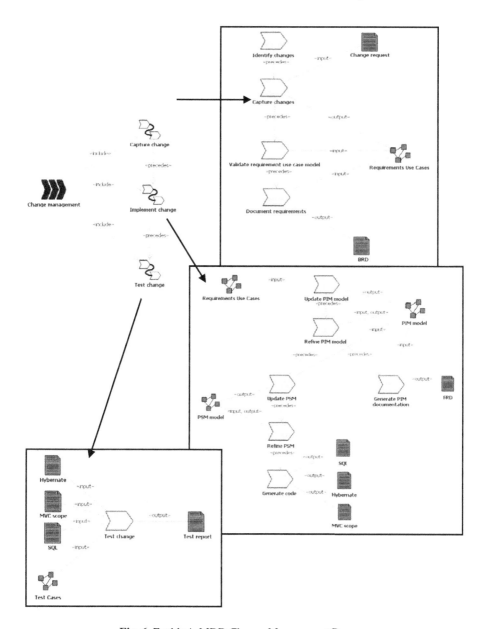

Fig. 6. Enabler's MDD Change Management Process

instance each requirement has at least one Stakeholder, has a priority etc.); these constraints should be satisfied before exiting the Requirements Phase. Likewise essential documentation is generated from models using transformations.

In fact there is a move to generate as much documentation as possible as shown in Fig. 8 where the Business Requirements Document (BRD) is generated from models.

Such documents are required by Enabler's customers, but producing them from models enhances their quality and brings greater productivity.

The MDD process has been instantiated within the Enabler experiment on the Modelware project. Fig. 9 presents this instantiation at the level of the specific tools used during that experiment. The objective is that by adding annotations to the components in the diagram we can then generate some of the configuration files for the tool set.

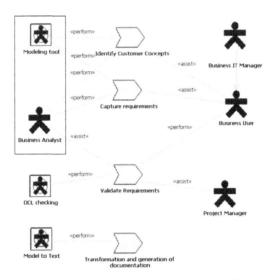

Fig. 7. Roles Used in Enabler´s Requirements Phase

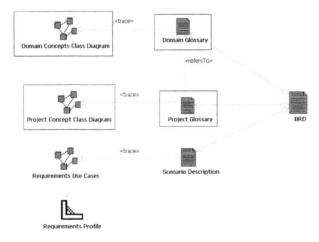

Fig. 8. Relationship between workproducts

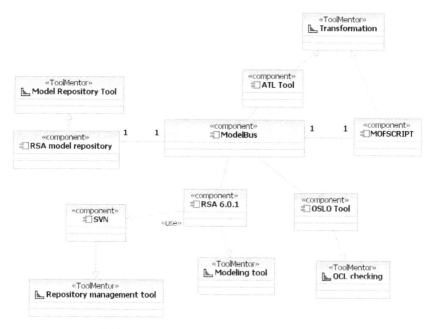

Fig. 9. Process instantiation in Enabler's experiment

3 Conclusion and Future Work

This paper presents an MDD process framework, which allows the reuse of existing knowledge of MDD which that can be used for standardising both the definition and execution of an organisation's system development processes. This MDD process knowledge has been extracted from many sources including the Modelware experiments.

The paper also provides a brief example of the use of the MDD Process Framework in an organisation, an example of the specification of an Organisation's standardised system development process.

The MDD Process Framework only covers MDD-specific engineering and management practices while organisations need a generic tool for all kind of practices (MDD specific, Agile-specific, etc.).

At the same the MDD PF is going to be used as the base MDD process repository for defining the telecom service creation process inside the W3GCreaTeS project (**Crea**tion Environment for **3G and WxAN Te**lecom **S**ervices) in which ESI is working together with Euskaltel Basque Country global operator. This project is being cofunded by the Spanish National Authorities inside the PROFIT programme.

The next step for the proposed MDD Process Framework is the integration of our MODELWARE work with the Eclipse Process Framework results, in order to provide an open solution for the adoption of not only MDD practices but of any kind of practices.

The Process Framework (EPF) Project <Beacon> [12] aims to provide an extendable framework for method and process authoring and provide exemplary and extendable process content for a range of software development and management processes. MODELWARE and WP2 partners will concentrate their efforts mainly on providing a set of MDD specific process elements to the EPF tool to create a system development process.

References

[1] Software Process Engineering Metamodel – SPEM Specification – January 2005 version 1.1 (http://www.omg.org/cgi-bin/doc?formal/2005-01-06)

[2] Object Management Group (http://www.omg.org)

[3] Master project (D3.2 - Process model to engineer and manage the MDA approach) http://modeldrivenarchitecture.esi.es/pdf/Deliverable-D32.zip

[4] COMET Methodology Handbook. (http://www.uio.no/studier/emner/matnat/ifi/INF5120/v05/undervisningsmateriale/COMET_Method_v2-4.pdf)

[5] SINTEF modelling methodology. (http://modeldrivenarchitecture.esi.es/pdf/Deliverable-D32.zip)

[6] Daniel Exertier, Benoit Langlois, Xavier Le Roux; "PIM Definition and Description" (http://modeldrivenarchitecture.esi.es/pdf/paper2-1.pdf)

[7] Lidia Fuentes-Fernández and Antonio Vallecillo-Moreno; "An introduction to UML Profiles" (http://www.upgrade-cepis.org/issues/2004/2/up5-2Fuentes.pdf)

[8] Jean Bézivin, Nicolas Farcet, Jean-Marc Jézéquel, Benoît Langlois, and Damien Pollet; "Reflective Model Driven Engineering" (http://www.irisa.fr/triskell/ publis/2003/Bezivin03 .pdf)

[9] PLUTO, a simple test methodology for product families. (http://fmt.isti.cnr.it/ WEB-PAPER/23-BertGnesi.pdf)

[10] AGEDIS project. (http://www.agedis.de/downloads.shtml)

[11] Software Process Engineering Metamodel (SPEM) 2.0 Request For Proposal (http://www omg .org/ cgi-bin/doc?ad/2004-11-4)

[12] Process Framework (EPF) project (BEACON project) (http://www.eclipse.org/ proposals/beacon/)

[13] Régis Vogel and Keith Mantell; "MDD process for an SME: evolution, not revolution – Phase I" (http://www.enabler.com/en/skills/ecmda/PAPER_Enabler.pdf)

[14] Jan Aagedal, Ida Solheim. "New Roles in Model-Driven Development" (2004)

[15] Michael Gnatz, Frank Marschall, Gerhard Popp, Andreas Rausch, Wolfgang Schwerin "The Living Software Development Process"

Finding a Path to Model Consistency

Gregory de Fombelle[1,2], Xavier Blanc[2], Laurent Rioux[1], and Marie-Pierre Gervais[2]

[1] Thales Research and Technology
RD 128 F-91767 Palaiseaux Cedex
{gregory.defombelle, laurent.rioux}@thalesgroup.com
[2] Laboratoire d'informatique de Paris 6, Université Paris 6
8 rue de Capitaine Scott – F75015 Paris
{fombelle, xavier.blanc, marie-pierre.gervais}@lip6.fr

Abstract. A core problem in Model Driven Engineering is model consistency achievement: all models must satisfy relationships constraining them. Active consistency techniques monitor and control models edition for preventing inconsistencies, e.g., using automatic errors correction. The main problem of these approaches is that strict enforcement of consistency narrows the modeler's possibilities for exploring conflicting or tradeoff solutions; this is just what temporaries inconsistencies enable. In this article, we propose a hybrid approach capitalizing on active consistency characteristics while allowing the user to edit inconsistent models in a managed mode: at any moment we are able to propose a sequence of modelling operations that, when executed, make the model consistent. The solution consists in defining a set of automatons capturing a sufficient part of the model state space for managing any inconsistent situation. We illustrate this approach on a consistency relationship implied by the application of a security design pattern impacting both class and sequence diagrams of a UML2 model.

1 Introduction

A core problem in Model Driven Engineering is model consistency: all models must satisfy relationships constraining them [2, 9]. This generic definition emphasizes the fact that consistency is a context specific definition, depending on used models, their relationships and their intended uses. An inconsistency is defined as a situation in which models break a consistency rule [3].

There are many consistency techniques. Those techniques often analyze models and report inconsistencies in a static way letting the user trigger checks and correct errors [18, 16, 17]. In this paper we focus on active consistency techniques, enacting at model edition time and interacting with models edition. These techniques aims to make consistency management more "user friendly", e.g., by automatically correcting some errors, forbidding operations or allowing consistency preserving operations.

In the first section we introduce such consistency techniques and raise issues narrowing their usage. Then we present an overview of our approach and illustrate it on a concrete scenario. After a few remarks we conclude the paper.

A. Rensink and J. Warmer (Eds.): ECMDA-FA 2006, LNCS 4066, pp. 101–112, 2006.
© Springer-Verlag Berlin Heidelberg 2006

2 Consistency Techniques

Consistency by monitoring outlined in [13] is an approach preventing inconsistencies thanks to a checking algorithm executed each time the user requests a model edition operation. Thus consistency rules encoded in the algorithm are impossible to be violated by the model editor. For example, the Objecteering modelling environment does not allow cross package references: each time the user edits a package referencing association, a check is performed and if this consistency rule is broken a dialog box informs the user that the requested operation is not allowed. It is then impossible to break this rule.

The problem with this approach is the strict enforcement of consistency rules. In some cases it would be necessary to relax it. For instance cross package references are allowed in Java and when the user imports Java source code to a Java model (retro-engineering) the user must inactivate consistency checks. In the opposite case the import will fail. But in such a situation, any kind of inconsistencies may be introduced in the model: there should be a balance between strict consistency enforcement and no consistency at all.

Another consistency technique called consistency by construction is also introduced in [13]. It enables automatic completion of models when specific operations are triggered by the user. For example when the user creates an "active class" the consistency engine automatically creates a default state machine and associates it to the class. These methodological consistency rules are often implemented in the model edition user interface. As a consequence, if the user edits a XMI[10] version of its model, he/she can easily break a consistency rule and reload the model into the environment, but without any inconsistency detected.

Constructive approaches can be more complex. In Fujaba, models can be automatically repaired. This works as follows: a background graph rewriting algorithm searches for negative patterns [15] (forbidden patterns) in the graph of objects representing the model. If there is a match (an inconsistency), then the rewriting engine replaces the negative pattern with another predefined correct pattern. This strategy automatically detects inconsistencies and then automatically corrects them. Once again, consistency is enforced, letting no places for inconsistencies, even temporarily. In this case detecting inconsistency and delaying its correction would enable the user to choose between different correct patterns. Furthermore this choice could be performed at his/her convenience, postponing inconsistency resolution at will.

Engels [6, 7] et al. introduce consistency preserving model evolution. Their solution consists in predefining a set of local model transformations rules that have been mathematically proven to preserve a consistency relationship, i.e., protocol consistency and deadlock freedom in this article. The main idea is to preserve consistency incrementally at model edition time, avoiding checking the whole model at each modification. In this approach, no inconsistencies can be introduced if transformation rules are applied correctly, e.g., by respecting a specific order.

The idea of consistency preserving model evolution is attractive since it claims that it is possible to build consistent models incrementally, without running global checks. Unfortunately, they do not describe any mechanisms for managing application order of local model transformations, depending on user awareness of this order. As a consequence, consistency is not guaranteed, likely resulting in incrementally introduced inconsistencies and requiring an unwanted global model check.

Furthermore enforcing consistency leads to overconstraining modelling activity, frustrating the modeler while he designs solutions, explores multiple alternatives, or does not model at a good precision degree. In [1] authors claim it is impossible, in general to maintain absolute consistency between all perspectives on the system (models) at all times. This position is adopted and reinforced in [5]. Spanoudakis et al. point out positive aspects of inconsistent models, like identification of parts of the system needing further analysis or assistance in specification of alternatives for the development. Finkelstein resumes this situation: "rather than thinking about removing inconsistencies, we need to think about managing inconsistency" [4].

It is clear that active consistency techniques lack such inconsistency management capabilities either by forbidding inconsistencies or by automatically correcting them. But inconsistency-driven correction and prevention reduces the amount of time the user spends in resolution activities. Furthermore, under certain circumstances the user might not have the skills for repairing complex errors. In such a situation those techniques become critical.

We propose to provide active consistency techniques with inconsistencies management capabilities. As a consequence, model edition monitoring and control should not only enable inconsistency prevention and automated correction but should also allow introducing inconsistencies in a managed mode. This implies that an inconsistency no more needs to be repaired synchronously, i.e., blocking user model edition until it is resolved. Instead when an inconsistency is introduced, it is automatically detected but models can still be edited, delaying the automated resolution at will.

3   Principles of Our Approach: Automata for Managing Inconsistencies

Model evolutions are caused by modelling operations triggered by the user or by automated means (i.e., patterns engines, model transformation engines, wizards etc.). While these modifications are performed, models go through a potentially infinite number of different states that are either consistent or inconsistent with regards to a consistency relationship. Before detailing our approach, we introduce model states' spaces and associated concepts.

3.1   Model State Space

We now introduce the theoretical concept of exhaustive model state space **M**, an infinite state transition systems [14] capturing all possible models and model evolutions. In **M,** a state is a model and a transition is a modelling operation.

The figure 1 illustrates the concept of model state space. As we can see it represents two complete (among multiple partial) potential model evolutions between an initial empty model and a model containing two classes linked by an association. Operation o1 means that the user creates a class named C1, operations o2 means that the user creates a class named C2 and operation o3 means that the user creates a

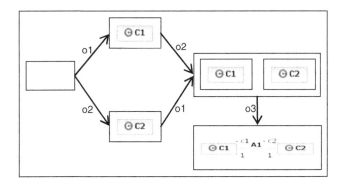

Fig. 1. A simple model state space representation

default association named A1 between C1 and C2. Example modelling operation sequences are <o1>, <o1,o2>, <o2,o1,o3> or <o1,o2,o3>.

The interest of model states lies in their property to validate or not a consistency relationship. The core thesis of our approach is that, given a consistency relationship we are able to specify the sufficient subset of **M** for automatically managing inconsistencies lifecycle. Notice that an inconsistency may exist inside a model (intra-model consistency) or between two or more models, i.e., inter-model consistency [12]. The first step of the solution is on-the-fly detection of transitions switching this model current state:

- from consistent to inconsistent: a new inconsistency is introduced
- from inconsistent to inconsistent: models evolve, but inconsistency remains
- from inconsistent to consistent: an inconsistency is resolved
- from consistent to consistent: models evolve but are consistent

This raises the **M** subset specification issue. Specifying a subpart of **M** implies a clear understanding of M states and transitions. On the first hand, states, i.e., models, are commonly represented as in-memory object data structures, each object being an instance of a meta class defined in the metamodel.

On the other hand transitions are defined as elementary operations on those objects, for instance instantiation of a metaclass, deletion of an object, linking of objects, setting values to object attributes. These operations are provided by the API metamodel repository and are fine grained, in opposition to the o1 operation presented in figure 1. The latter is actually a composite of three "low level" transitions: instanciation of the Class metaclass, setting the default "classname" attribute and linking the newly created object to the Model object.

3.2 Specifying a Subset of M

A direct specification of a subpart M is not conceivable. There are too many states and transitions. Thus it seems not feasible to directly represent a subpart of **M**. We propose three mechanisms for making such a specification feasible.

Transition abstractions save both transitions and states. We have explained that o1 replaces three low level elementary operations; o3 replaces about ten of them. Abstraction of transitions enables to avoid description of intermediate states and transitions.

State abstractions enable description of the sufficient state subpart which might impact the consistency condition. For example we will see in the example introduced in section 4.2 that class attribute descriptions are not necessary since they do not impact the consistency relationship. The language or technique for describing state content is out of the scope of this paper.

State partitioning: we exploit a property of model evolutions that we have observed. From a given state, it is possible to identify and isolate model parts evolving independently of each other. Thus independent model parts may be separated and each subpart evolutions be traced by one automaton. As a result we have a set of automata, each one being responsible for tracing evolution of an independent model part.

In the following abstract example, two automata illustrate such a situation:

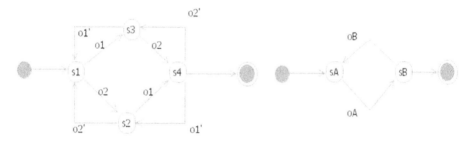

Fig. 2. Two automatons capturing model parts evolutions

Each automaton traces the evolution of a model state space part. For example, if the model is in a composite state given by the two automata states (sA,s1) and the user performs the sequence of model edition operation <o2, o1,o2',o'1>, then only the left automaton will be affected and it will go through states s2, s4, s3 to finally return to s1 state. But at any moment the model can evolve with an oA operation resulting in the appropriate composite model state. We will exemplify it in section 4.3.

3.3 Defining and Managing Inconsistencies with Automata

These automata enable to define consistency or inconsistency in term of relationships over the Cartesian products of automata states. Thus we can mathematically define consistency as a subset C of the Cartesian product of the sets of automata states $\{A1,...,AK\}$ where Ai is the set of states of Automaton number i. We will illustrate a concrete consistency relation in the section 4.3.

Once consistency defined, the second core idea of our approach is that these automata can be exploited by basic graph algorithms for managing consistent and inconsistent model editions:

- dynamically report to the user that he/she is entering or leaving consistent or inconsistent states.
- computing model edition operations sequences bringing models from inconsistent states to consistent ones. Once this sequence computed it is possible to automatically execute it or propose it to the user.

From an operational point of view our approach consists firstly in automated and incremental detection of inconsistent model states while the user edits models, i.e., on the fly. Secondly it provides users with automatable means for exiting such inconsistent model states. From a theoretical perspective the approach is based on the concept of consistent or inconsistent model state.

4 Running Example

For illustrating our approach, we consider a consistency relationship between two diagrams of a design model constrained by the application of a security design pattern.

4.1 A Security Design Pattern

This security pattern constrains both behavioral and structural properties of the software system. We choose the secure communication security design pattern published by the open security group in their technical guide [8]. The goal of this pattern is to ensure a security policy when two parties need to communicate over a channel that may be subject to security threats. When this pattern is correctly implemented it secures communications against threats by employing protection traffic mechanisms in the communication channel. The structure of this pattern involves three elements exposed in the following figure.

Fig. 3. The secure Communication Design Pattern Structure

The first element is a communication party, e.g., a client or a server. It is the source and/or the destination of messages that are delivered from the communication channel. The second element is the communication channel. It has a send method that, when invoked by parties, transports messages from the sender to the receiver.

Finally the last element is the communication protection proxy. It is responsible for protecting traffic over communication channels. It provides a protection method before sending the message on the channel and a verification method before delivering the message to the target communication party.

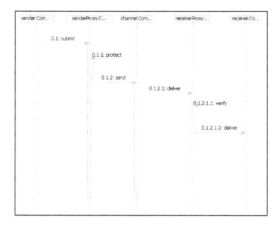

Fig. 4. The Secure Communication Design Pattern Collaboration version 1

This collaboration pattern describes a secured message exchange between a sender communication party and a receiver communication party. First the sender submits a message to its own proxy which protects the data by calling the `protect()` method. Then the proxy sends the message on the channel that delivers it to the receiver proxy. It checks the message by calling the `verify()` method and finally it delivers the message to the final recipient, i.e., the receiver.

4.2 Consistency Scenario

We define consistency of the two diagrams as a configuration in which security aspects of the system are both described in structural and behavioral diagrams. A contradiction may occur if one diagram represents security properties and not the other one. When no one of them represents security properties, then they are consistent because they do not contradict each other [1].

Now suppose we wish to manually secure the simple client server design model below.

Fig. 5. Unsecured Client Server Structure Diagram

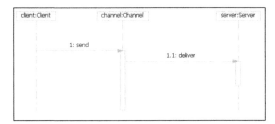

Fig. 6. Unsecured Client Server Sequence Diagram

We define two consistent model states. The first one is when the channel class is stereotyped with a "SecureComm" stereotype and the sequence diagram method calls are intercepted and secured by the proxies. The other one is when the channel class is not stereotyped and the communications are not secured, like in figures 5 and 6.

The user could start introducing a "SecureComm" stereotype on the Channel class. As explained above, both diagrams are consistent if they do not contradict each other. Thus at the moment the user stereotyped the channel class the model is inconsistent and it will remain in this state until the sequence diagram is secured in accordance with the behavioral pattern. We have illustrated a possible model evolution of the sequence diagram from its initial state to its final fully secured state.

Fig. 7. Initial state

Fig. 8. State 1 of the automaton (cf. fig12.)

Fig. 9. State 4 of the automaton (cf. fig12.)

Fig. 10. Secured State of the automaton (cf. fig12.)

From the initial state to the one of figure 8 the user has added the submit method call between the client and the proxy. Then from state of figure 8 to the one of figure 9 the user has added the protect method call. In the last step the user has added the send method call between the proxy and the communication channel.

4.3   Automata Supporting Scenario

In this section we define the automata supporting the scenario, and then we define the consistency relationship.

There are two automata, one responsible for monitoring the evolution of the class diagram and the other monitoring the evolution of the sequence diagram. The first automaton is given in the following figure.

Fig. 11. Automaton 1 for class diagram evolutions

Following the abstraction and partitioning mechanisms this automaton defines two abstract, partial model states respectively representing a "SecureComm" stereotyped channel class and a channel class without this stereotype. The transitions between the two states represent application or deletion of the "SecureComm" stereotype.

The following figure defines the automaton for tracing potential sequence diagram evolutions. Because the full automaton is huge, we have only represented the possible evolutions from the figure 7 to the figure 10. Its structure underlines multiple scenarios for securing these model parts. Each method call addition between two life lines (or one in the case of the protect method call) can be applied independently.

Now we define the consistency relationship. As previously explained the model has two consistent states: one before the application of the pattern and the other when the pattern has been completely applied in the two diagrams. It is possible to formulate this situation in terms of automata states. Indeed the model will be consistent if and only if both automata 1 and 2 are simultaneously in specific states.

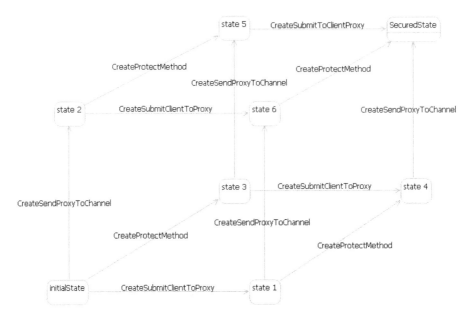

Fig. 12. Automaton 2 for sequence diagram evolutions

Thus we can mathematically define consistency as a subset C of the Cartesian product of automata A1 and A2 state sets ($C \subseteq A1 \times A2$).

A1={ $UnstereotypedChannelClass, StereotypedChannelClass$ }

A2={ $initialState, state1, state2, ..., state6, SecuredState$ }

C={ $(UnstereotypedChannelClass, initialState),$

$(StereotypedChannelClass, SecuredState)$ }

In the scenario we have illustrated a possible model evolution of the sequence diagram through different states. This scenario is only one of the possible sequences of modelling operations for building the model. The second automaton illustrates this point clearly: we see that for going from "initialState" to "SecuredState" there are many paths (6 exactly).

Imagine we are in the state where the class is stereotyped and the sequence diagram is in the state illustrated on figure 7. Then, the composite model state captured by our automata is given by the couple ($StereotypedChannelClass, InitialState$). This state is not consistent since it does not belong to the previously defined consistent set C. Thus it is possible to detect an inconsistent state while models evolve. Furthermore it is possible to compute a path in automata for reaching a consistent state; this path is a sequence of modeling operations. In our scenario such a path is for instance <CreateSubmitClientToProxy, CreateProtectMethod, CreateSendProxyToChannel>. If we execute this sequence of operations then it will switch the model to the consistent state ($StereotypedChannelClass, SecuredState$).

4.4 Remarks

A first remark is that there are multiple paths to consistency: it is possible to undo the first modelling operation that leads to an inconsistent state. Here when the model evolves to the state where the channel class is stereotyped, the trivial path to consistency is to undo the stereotyping action.

Some will notice that no inconsistencies will be raised if the user draws a method call between the client and the channel, resulting in an unsecured method call. This is not because our approach cannot deal with this situation. The simple reason is that it is not specified as an inconsistency. But it is possible to specify new automata or to modify existing ones for taking into account this constraint.

These automata have been manually produced following two main principles: abstraction and partitioning. But the complexity of this specification remains high. On this limited but concrete example there are still many states and transitions. We could then head toward automatic production of these automata from high level languages. For instance we believe feasible to generate these automata from simple QVT relation language[11] expressions.

5 Conclusion and Further Works

In this paper we have introduced active consistency techniques, an approach to model consistency enacting at model edition time, automatically correcting errors or preventing modelling operations when they break a consistency condition. Then we explained why their strict consistency enforcement policy should be relaxed. As a result we argued the need for a hybrid approach combining active consistency techniques and "live" inconsistency management capabilities. We detailed some issues of such an approach like how to determine inconsistent model states without running complete model checks.

Main contribution of our approach is to introduce the concept of model state space and to define mechanisms for producing automata tracing all model evolutions which might impact a consistency relationship. These automata enable on-the-fly detection of inconsistencies, specified as a subset of the Cartesian product of their states. Furthermore at each current model state, it is possible to compute paths to consistent states. A path is a sequence of modelling operations and may be automatically executed. But this execution may also be delayed enabling to edit the model while it is inconsistent. To the best of our knowledge this is the first time such an approach is proposed. However in this article this model of model evolution is not formally presented.

Our future works can be divided into theoretical and experimental aspects. At the theoretical level we firstly plan to provide a formalization of this model, a precise definition of modelling operations and model states. Based on these core concepts, we wish to explore the relationships between the automata and the state space of models. At the experimental level we designed an initial architecture and implemented a basic model listener for tracing model evolutions. The latter detects events modifying the model data structure. In the next step we will be able to specify composite modelling operations from atomic ones and detect them while the user edits models.

References

[1]   Anthony Finkelstein, Dov Gabbay, Anthony Hunter, Jeff Kramer and Bashar Nuseibeh, *Inconsistency Handling in Multiperspective Specifications* IEEE Transactions on Software Engineering, 20 (1994), pp. 569-577.

[2]   Bashar Nuseibeh, Jeff Kramer and Anthony Finkelstein, *A framework for expressing the relationships between multiple views in requirements specification*, IEEE Transactions on Software Engineering, 20 (1994).

[3]   Gregor Engels, Jochen M.Küster, *Consistency Management Within Model-Based Object-Oriented Development of Components*, FMCO 2003 proc., LNCS 3188 (2003), pp. 157-176.

[4]   Anthony Finkelstein, *A Foolish consistency: Technical challenges in Consistency Management, 11th International Conference on Database and Expert Systems Applications DEXA 2000*, LNCS, London, UK, 2000, pp. 1-5.

[5]   George Spanoudakis, Andre Zisman, *Inconsistency Management in Software Engineering: Survey and Open Research Issues*, in W. S. P. C. Chang S. K., ed., *Handbook of Software Engineering and Knowledge Engineering*, 2001.

[6]   Gregor Engels, Jochen Kuster and Reiko Heckel, *Toward Consistency preserving model evolution*, in ACM, ed., *IWPSE* Orlando, 2002.

[7]   Gregory Engels, Reiko Heckel, Jochen Kuster and Luuk Groenewegen, *Consistency-Preserving Model Evolution through Transformations*, *UML 2002*, 2002.

[8]   Heath, Bob Blakley, *Security Design Patterns*, 2004.

[9]   Jean-Louis Sourrouille, Guy Caplat., *Checking UML Model Consistency*, *Workshop on Consistency Problems in UML based software development I*, Dresden, Germany, 2002.

[10]   OMG, *MOF 2.0 / XMI Mapping Specification, v2.1*, (2005).

[11]   OMG, *MOF 2.0 Query/View/Transformation*, 2005.

[12]   Ragnhild Van Der Straeten, Tom Mens, Jocelyn Simmonds, *Maintaining Consistency between UML models using description logics*, *Workshop on Consistency Problems in UML based software development II*, San Francisco, USA, 2003.

[13]   Snoeck M, Michiels C and Dedene G, *Consistency by construction: the case of MERODE*, Workshops ECOMO, OWCMQ, AOIS and aXSD, 2814 (2003), pp. 105-117.

[14]   Tel, Gerard, *Introduction to Distributed Algorithms*, Cambridge University Press, 2001.

[15]   Wagner, Robert, *A Plug-in for flexible and incremental consistency management*, *Workshop on Consistency Problems in UML based software development II*, San Francisco, USA, 2003.

[16]   Zbigniew Huzar, Ludwik Kuzniarz, Gianna Regio, Jean Louis Sourrouille, *Consistency Problems in UML-based Software Development - Workshop proceedings*, *Fifth International Conderence on the Unified Modeling Language and its applications - UML 2002*, 2002.

[17]   Zbigniew Huzar, Ludwik Kuzniarz, Gianna Regio, Jean Louis Sourrouille, *Consistency problems in UML-based Software Development II - Workshop proceedings*, *Sixth International Conference on the Unified Modelling Language - the Language and its applications UML 2003*, 2003.

[18]   Zbigniew Huzar, Ludwik Kuzniarz, Gianna Regio, Jean Louis Sourrouille, *Consistency Problems in UML-based Software Development III - Understanding and Usage of Dependency Relationships - Workshop proceedings*, *Seventh International Confoerence on UML Modeling Languages and Applications - UML 2004*, Lisbon, Portugal, 2004.

Dynamic Logic Semantics for UML Consistency

Greg O'Keefe

Research School of Information Science and Engineering,
Australian National University, Canberra, ACT 0200, Australia
greg.okeefe@anu.edu.au

Abstract. The Unified Modelling Language (UML) is intended to describe systems, but it is not clear what systems satisfy a given collection of UML diagrams. Stephen Mellor has described a small collection of diagrams which appear to be inconsistent, yet are "cool" according to UML. We describe an approach to defining semantics for UML diagrams using dynamic logic, and show that Mellor's example is inconsistent, given a reasonable assumption. Our approach interprets all diagrams, static and dynamic, in a single semantic space. The modeller specifies how the meaning of a model is made up from the meanings of its diagrams, thus the "viewpoint" taken by each diagram is made explicit. This composition is achieved through formation of the dynamic logic formulae. It is therefore very flexible, and we propose it as a means for defining semantics for domain specific languages, and for specifying "bridges" or "weaving" model transformations used in aspect oriented modelling.

One approach to modelling is to begin with use-cases, and aim to reproduce them as sequence diagrams executed by the model being developed. Whether or not a model can execute a sequence diagram is therefore a question which will be asked frequently when working this way. We want the question to have a definite answer, and we want our tools to give us that answer.

Any multi-view approach to modelling will have similar questions about the relative consistency of its parts. The way to make these questions precise and amenable to automatic solution is by defining formal semantics for our language. Formal semantics are usually associated with formal verification for safety critical, or other trusted systems. Formal semantics are also usually associated with incomprehensible symbolic mumbo-jumbo.

The ability to formally certify the products of model driven development would certainly be beneficial. However, if the semantics could be understood by at least some modelling practitioners, the result would be clearer thinking and greater consensus in the modelling community. Modelling of problem domains would produce better understanding, and hence better solutions.

Although endowing parts of UML with formal semantics has become quite an industry, we do not know of any work that gives uniform semantics for class, state machine and sequence diagrams, as well as UML actions. Reggio and coworkers suggest an analogy between UML diagrams and logical axioms [13]. We promote the idea from analogy to practice, translating the diagrams and actions into formulae of dynamic logic [7]. Object diagrams can also be formalised, and adding OCL to the repetoire would be straightforward, following [3].

A. Rensink and J. Warmer (Eds.): ECMDA-FA 2006, LNCS 4066, pp. 113–127, 2006.

Some would argue that UML 2.0 is already well enough defined to resolve the kind of consistency question we study here. From this point of view, dynamic logic or any other rigorous mathematics are a complicated waste of time, since OCL and the UML action semantics provide all that is needed. Far from being the solution, we consider OCL and the action semantics to be a part of the problem. We believe that the current official definition is not adequate to unequivocally demonstrate the inconsistency of apparently inconsistent collections of diagrams. Attempting to do this would be an interesting test, but it is beyond our present scope. Here, we take UML model consistency to be a mathematical question, and tackle it using mathematical techniques.

By translating into a well studied formalism like dynamic-logic, we obtain precise semantics, along with a wealth of metatheory. Our example model attaches actions to states, and state diagrams to classes. We achieve this by making an action a subformula of a state machine diagram axiom, which is in turn a subformula of a class axiom. This suggests a general approach to specifying "weaving" of diagrams and models, by defining how their translations are combined to form model axioms. The idea of a "semantic variation point" used throughout the UML definition [11] can also be made precise in this way. One would simply use some parts of the translation output and not others, according to the required interpretation of the diagrams.

In [8], Stephen Mellor gives an example where UML blindly accepts an intuitively erroneous model. We use this example to demonstrate the style of semantics we propose, and their application to model consistency problems.

The first section briefly introduces dynamic logic, and then we introduce a version of Mellor's example inconsistent model, using the conventions of the Executable UML method [10]. In the following section we systematically translate each diagram into dynamic logic formulae. A system specification is then formed using these diagram formulae as subterms. We then search for a trace which satisfies this specification and establish that none exists. The conclusion compares this approach with related work, and considers the next steps towards a useful formal semantics for UML.

1 Dynamic Logic

In this section we briefly introduce logic, beginning with simple propositional logic. Then we consider two different extentions: modal logics and first order logic. Finally, we combine these extentions and obtain the form of dynamic logic we need to complete our formalisation.

A logic consists of syntax, semantics and a deductive calculus. The syntax defines a set of formulae, which we call the language of the logic. The formulae are just symbolised statements. The semantics defines a range of possible situations, each of which assigns either *true* or *false* to each formula of the language. A deductive calculus defines proofs, each of which derives a formula from some set of formulae. We will not say much more about deduction.

Propositional logic has atomic formulae $P, Q, R, \ldots$ and if φ and ψ are formulae, then so are $\neg\varphi$, $\varphi \vee \psi$, $\varphi \wedge \psi$ and $\varphi \longrightarrow \psi$. These symbols stand for not, or, and, and if ... then ... respectively. The possible situations of propositional semantics are functions from the atomic formulae to the truth values $\{true, false\}$. We will call these functions propositional interpretations. These are extended to the whole language by assigning each of the connectives $\neg, \vee, \wedge$, $\longrightarrow$ the obvious truth function. We write $\top$ as a formula that is always true, and $\bot$ for one which is always false.

Propositional modal logics add some one-place connectives. Typically we add to the above syntactic rules that if φ is a formula, then so are $\Box\varphi$ and $\Diamond\varphi$. Some intuitive interpretations of these connectives are: necessarily and possibly, always and sometimes, obligitory and permissible. We are interested in temporal interpretations, where $\Box\varphi$ means that φ is true at all possible future situations, and $\Diamond\varphi$ is true in some possible future situation. Semantics for a propositional modal logic are given by introducing a binary relation R between the propositional interpretations. Then $\Box\varphi$ is true at w if φ is true at every situation R-related to w, and $\Diamond\varphi$ is true at w if φ is true at some situation R-related to w.

This is already a useful formal language, because if R captures the possible evolution of a system, and we have formulae $Init$ and Bad which represent the acceptable initial states of the system, and undesirable situations respectively, then the formula $Init \longrightarrow \neg\Diamond Bad$ is true if and only if it is impossible for the system to evolve from an acceptable initial state into an undesirable situation.

Propositional dynamic logic **PDL** has a pair of modal operators for each program in a simple programming language. There are atomic programs, $\alpha, \beta, \gamma, \ldots$ and if ρ and σ are programs then so are $\rho; \sigma$, $\rho \cup \sigma$ and ρ^*. These are the regular expressions over the atomic programs. Also, if φ is a formula, then $\varphi?$ is a program. Each atomic program denotes a relation over the situations, $\rho \cup \sigma$ denotes the union of the two relations (non-deterministic choice) and ρ^* denotes the reflexive transitive closure of the relation denoted by ρ (non-deterministic repetition). The program $\varphi?$ relates a situation to itself when φ is true there. This can be used to place guards on programs, and to write conditionals, such as $(\varphi?; \alpha) \cup (\neg\varphi?; \beta)$ for if φ then α else β. In propositional modal logic, the semantics for the modal operators $\Box$ and $\Diamond$ were given using a binary relation. In propositional dynamic logic, each program ρ corresponds to a binary relation, and the semantics of the modal operators $[\rho]$ and $\langle\rho\rangle$ depend on this relation.

We can write for example $\langle\alpha\rangle\top$, to mean that the program α runs successfully (terminates), or $\langle\alpha\rangle\top \longrightarrow \varphi$ to mean that α only runs successfuly in situations satisfying φ.

First order logic also extends propositional logic. Where the basic formulae of propositional logic are unanalysed propositions P, Q etc, first order logic formulae assert properties of individuals or assert relationships between individuals. For example, a two place relation symbol L might be interpreted as "... loves ..." the name a might mean "Aaron" and b "Belinda" then Lab would be read as "Aaron loves Belinda." The logic includes equality, so we may write $a = b$

meaning "Aaron is Belinda." Names are one kind of *term*, that is expressions which refer to an individual. Variables $x, y, z, \ldots$ are another kind of term, and terms can be formed by applying n-place function symbols, $f, g, \ldots$ to n terms, for $n = 1, 2, \ldots$. For example if the 1-place function symbol f is read as "the father of ...," then $Lxf(b)$ should be read as "x loves Belinda's father." First order logic also has *quantifiers* $\forall$ and $\exists$ so that $\forall x, Lxf(b)$ means everybody loves Belinda's father, and $\exists x, Lxf(b)$ that somebody does.

The semantic situations for first order logic (which logicians call "*models*") consist of a set of individuals, called the semantic *domain*, and an *interpretation* which takes each name to an individual and each n-place relation/function symbol to a n-place relation/function. To evaluate variables and quantifiers, we also need a *valuation*. This takes each variable to an individual in the semantic domain. The formal definition of truth of a formula in an interpretation just says that, in the interpretation, things are as the formula says they are. The frightening notation required to state this precisely is unhelpful in the current context.

The semantics of quantified formulae are defined using the idea of *variants* of the valuation. An x variant of w is a valuation that is the same as w for all inputs except for x. This is worth explaining, because we will use these ideas again soon. We introduce some notation for a function the same as w, except that it takes x to q. Define $w \oplus x \mapsto q$ by

$$(w \oplus x \mapsto q)(y) = \begin{cases} q & \text{if } x = y \\ w(y) & \text{otherwise} \end{cases}$$

Then $\exists x, \varphi(x)$ is satisfied by the model and valuation $\mathcal{M}, w$ iff $\varphi(x)$ is satisfied by $\mathcal{M}, (w \oplus x \mapsto q)$ for some q. And similarly for $\forall$ formulae.

The language of dynamic logic includes that of first order logic plus modal operators similar to those of PDL. The atomic programs of DL are assignments of the form $x := t$ for some variable x and some term t. For each interpretation $\mathcal{M}$, the atomic program $x := t$ relates each valuation w to $w \oplus x \mapsto t^{\mathcal{M}, w}$, where $t^{\mathcal{M}, w}$ is the value of the term t under the interpretation $\mathcal{M}$ and valuation w. For example, the formula $a = 5 \longrightarrow \langle x := a \rangle x = 5$, says that if $a = 5$ then after you set x to a, you get $x = 5$. This is always true, because if $a = 5$ in $\mathcal{M}, w$, that is $a^{\mathcal{M}, w} = 5$, then $x = 5$ in $\mathcal{M}, (w \oplus x \mapsto a^{\mathcal{M}, w})$.

Our objective is to reason about object oriented systems, where objects retain their identity over time, but have attributes whose values may change. To achieve this, we have object identifiers as individuals, and object attributes as functions, so that the familiar $o.a$ notation becomes short-hand for $a(o)$. Then what we want is the ability to update these functions. An extension of dynamic logic studied in [7] allows such updateable functions, called array variables. Indeed, a similar system has been used to formalise parts of UML 1.1 in [17].

The syntax of DL is extended by n-place array variables for each $n = 1, 2, \ldots$. These can occur wherever an n-place function symbol can occur, but also on the left hand side of an assignment statement. The semantics are adapted so that now the valuations also assign an n-place function to each n-place array variable. For a fixed model $\mathcal{M}$, this assignment denotes a relation that relates each valuation

w to $w \oplus h \mapsto (h^w \oplus t^{\mathcal{M},w} \mapsto s^{\mathcal{M},w})$. That is, w is related to an updated form of w, which maps the array variable h to the same function w maps it to, except updated so that it sends the value of t to the value of s.

This is the form of dynamic logic that we use to precisely express our interpretations of the UML diagrams and actions.

2   The Problem Model

We begin this section with Mellor's description of the problem which we aim to a resolve.

> Consider this. We have two state chart diagrams, one of which sends a single signal X to the other. In the same system, we have a sequence diagram that shows lifelines for two objects whose behaviour is captured by the state chart diagrams, one of which sends a single signal Y to the other. Both diagrams are intended to describe the same behaviour; that is, a single message being sent between them. Which of these two - contradictory - models is correct? Astonishingly, UML's answer is Yes. So long as the syntax of each of the two diagrams is correct, UML is cool.

-Stephen Mellor in [8]

There should be some definite meaning attached to UML diagrams, so that tools can detect that no system can satisfy all the diagrams in Mellors' example.

We could formulate the problem as Mellor has, using two state machine diagrams one sequence diagram and no class diagram, but this would require more "weaving" logic (Section 4, Page 122) than the Executable UML [10] style of model we present here.

A class diagram (Fig. 1, Page 117) declares the two classes. The association between them will be used to target the signal.

Fig. 1. Class Diagram

We only give one state machine diagram (Fig. 2, Page 118), which describes the behaviour of class A. Since the other state machine is completely arbitrary, there is no point in specifying it. The join between the state machine and class A will be made explicit in Section 4.

The only actions which we consider are signal send and receive. These are only approximations of the official actions described in [11, §11.3.44 and §11.3.2], since we do not attempt to capture ideas such as values travelling across "pins," and we use a stricter message queueing policy. The entry action for state s' is

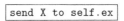

Fig. 2. State Machine for Class A

Fig. 3. Entry Action for State s'

given in an action language of our own devising in Figure 3. Again, the join will be given formally in Section 4.

Finally, the sequence diagram (Fig. 4, Page 118) shows an object of class A accepting a W signal from an external entity, enterning state s' and (erroneously?) sending a Y signal to a B object (presumably its ex).

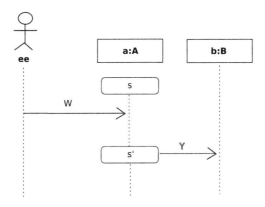

Fig. 4. Sequence Diagram

3   The Model as Dynamic Logic Formulae

How can we represent this model using formulae of dynamic logic? We begin this section with some general considerations about the relationship between dynamic logic and the small UML subset used for this model. In each of the following subsections, we will discuss one of the diagrams, and give its meaning as a dynamic logic formula. These meanings are influenced by the use made of the diagrams in the Executable UML [10] method. In the next section we will combine the class diagram, state machine diagram and action formulae to specify the system, and then show that this specification is inconsistent with the sequence diagram formula.

We give rather weak interpretations of each diagram, for example, assuming that there might be objects in the system that do not belong to any class on the class diagram. These interpretations are debatable, indeed it is possible that the weak interpretations are more appropriate in an analysis phase, whilst stronger ones might serve the design phase better. Indeed, we may want to keep several interpretations available to cater for UML's numerous "semantic variation points." The particular interpretations are not the main point though. Rather we aim to demonstate that dynamic logic provides a simple and useful way of giving the meanings of the diagrams. The reader should not overlook another important virtue of the weak interpretations: they are shorter!

3.1   System Snapshots and Evolution

In Section 1 we said that the possible situations of the semantics of dynamic logic consist of an interpretation and a valuation. We will consider all model specific vocabulary to be variables, evaluated by the valuation, while the interpretation takes care of the global UML vocabulary such as OCL library functions. Hence, a system snapshot is a valuation, and the interpretation can be largely ignored, because it is fixed.

Each DL program relates pairs of these snapshots, but not every DL program corresponds to a legal evolution of the system. What we need is a formal definition of legal evolution. So, what can happen in a system defined by our subset of UML? Only two things really: objects can send messages, and they can accept them. There are conditions though, an object can only send a message if that action is at the head of its todo list, although an external entity can send whatever it wants whenever it wants. An object can only accept a message if it has a message to accept, and it is not currently activated. The non-deterministic DL program ε which describes how these systems can evolve is defined as follows.

$$\varepsilon \equiv ((sendCond(x, M, y)?; \ x.\mathsf{send}\ M\ \mathsf{to}\ y) \cup (acceptCond(x)?; \ x.\mathsf{accept}))^*$$

where $sendCond(x, M, y)$ is a formula, defined below, stating the conditions under which it is OK for x to send an M message to y, send M to y is a DL program, also defined below, which does what the send action is meant to do, and similarly for $acceptCond$ and accept.

$$sendCond(x, M, y) \equiv class(x) = EE \lor (head(todo(x)) = \mathsf{send}\ M\ \mathsf{to}\ y)$$
$$acceptCond(x) \equiv todo(x) = () \ \land \ size(intray(x)) > 0$$

where $head$ and $size$ are library functions with the obvious meaning, and $todo$ and $intray$ are array variables used to represent an objects outstanding actions and messages respectively. The special class name EE is introduced so that external entities can be treated as objects having this class.

Note that $todo$ takes objects to programs, which on the face of it is a category error, because programs are part of the syntax, not individuals in the semantic domain. By adding function symbols corresponding to $*, :=, \cup$ and ;, we can copy the program language into the semantic domain. Whenever you see a program on the right hand side of an equals sign, it is shorthand for a term formed using this vocabulary.

Now we define the actions `send` and `accept`. When an object x sends a message M to the object y, the message is placed in y's *intray*, and the `send` action is removed from x's *todo* list.

$$x.\texttt{send } M \texttt{ to } y \equiv$$
$$intray(y) \ := \ append(intray(y), M);$$
$$todo(x) \ := \ tail(todo(x))$$

where *append* and *tail* are library functions.

When an object accepts a message, it makes the state transition specified in its state machine, loads the entry procedure of the new state, and removes the message from its *intray*.

$$x.\texttt{accept } \equiv$$
$$state(x) \ := \ nextState(state(x), head(intray(x)));$$
$$todo(x) \ := \ entryProc(state(x));$$
$$intray(x) \ := \ tail(intray(x))$$

Where *state* is an array variable used to record an objects state. This definition depends on the functions *nextState* and *entryProc*, which in turn depend on the state machine diagrams of the model. The definitions of these functions will turn out to be a consequence of the formulae we extract from the state machine diagram. We will consider them to be array variables in order to keep the interpretation general, but any attempt to assign them values that do not agree with the state machine diagram(s) would result in an inconsistency.

This program ε allows us to say things about model dynamics. Adapting the example in Section 1, we can say that nothing bad will happen so long as the model starts within acceptable initial conditions: $Init \longrightarrow \neg\langle\varepsilon\rangle Bad$. Note ε is a $*$ program, so the program under the $*$ can run 0 times. This means that for $[\varepsilon]\varphi$ to be true in some situation w, φ has to be true there and in every situation reachable by legal model evolution. Therefore, if we want to say that in our model, φ is always true (an invariant), we can assert $[\varepsilon]\varphi$.

This sets the general framework for systems defined by models of our tiny UML subset. Now we are ready to look at the diagrams that define Mellor's example model.

3.2   Class Diagram

This class diagram (Fig. 1, Page 117) does not tell us a lot. The association however, does tell us something. It says that each object of class A, has exactly one ex which is an object of class B. Since this is all the information we can obtain from the class diagram, we will name the formula CD.

$$CD \equiv [\varepsilon](\forall x, class(x) = A \longrightarrow$$
$$size(x.ex) = 1 \ \wedge \ (\forall y, \ y \in x.ex \longrightarrow class(y) = B))$$

Notice that we have taken some vocabulary from the class diagram. The class names A and B are variables, ex and *class* are array variables.

3.3   State Machine Diagram

The state machine diagram (Fig. 2, Page 118) does not specify which objects it applies to, so the state machine diagram formulae contain a free variable. In Section 4 we will use this variable to connect the state machine diagram to the class A.

For an object to conform to this state machine, it must be in one of the diagrams' states.

$$SM_s(x) \equiv [\varepsilon](state(x) = s \vee state(x) = s')$$

The transition in the state machine says that if an object x is in state s and it has a W message at the top of its *intray*, then after it does an **accept**, it will be in state s'.

$$SM_t(x) \equiv [\varepsilon](state(x) = s \wedge head(intray(x)) = W$$
$$\longrightarrow [x.\textsf{accept}]\ state(x) = s')$$

We will not combine the state and transition formulae yet, but will combine them with the entry procedure for state s' and the class A in Section 4.

3.4   Sequence Diagram

The sequence diagram (Fig. 4, Page 118) partly specifies an initial model state, and lists some occurrences in the order that they are meant to happen. It is satisfied by model execution traces that begin in a state that satisfies the diagrams intitial conditions, and in which all the occurrences happen legally, in the given order.

Note that other things are allowed to happen in between the occurrences given in the diagram. Read, write, link and unlink actions are not shown in sequence diagrams. An object or external entity not shown in the diagram might send one of the participants a message. Indeed, we might allow participants of the sequence to exchange messages not shown on the diagram. If the diagram is intended as a high-level summary, we might choose to omit some of these details.

The following formula captures our interpretation of the sequence diagram. It says that ee is an external entity, a has class A, b has class B, and that it is possible for some stuff to happen, and then for ee to legally **send** a W to a, and then for some more stuff to happen followed by a legally doing an **accept** (activation) after which some stuff can happen and then a can legally **send** a Y message to b.

$$
\begin{aligned}
SEQ \equiv\ & class(ee) = EE \ \wedge\ class(a) = A \ \wedge\ class(b) = B \ \wedge \\
& \langle\varepsilon\rangle(\ sendCond(ee, W, a) \ \wedge\ \langle ee.\textsf{send}\ W\ \textsf{to}\ a\rangle \\
& \langle\varepsilon\rangle(\ acceptCond(a) \ \wedge\ \langle a.\textsf{accept}\rangle \\
& \langle\varepsilon\rangle(\ sendCond(a, Y, b) \ \wedge\ \langle a.\textsf{send}\ Y\ \textsf{to}\ b\rangle \ \top)))
\end{aligned}
$$

As usual, we use variables for all the model specific vocabulary.

4   Weaving and Consistency

Having specified the meaning of each of the parts of the model, we now turn to the task of connecting these parts to specify the required system. Because we have interpreted the diagrams using logical formulae, we can join them using logical connectives.

We want to make the send action the entry action of state s'. That is, if an object is in state s', then immediately after it does an accept, we want its *todo* list to contain only this action.

$$SM_p(x) \equiv [\varepsilon][x.\texttt{accept}](state(x) = s' \longrightarrow todo(x) = \texttt{send } X \texttt{ to } x.\texttt{ex})$$

Putting $x.\texttt{ex}$ rather than $\texttt{self.ex}$ saves us the trouble of evaluating $\texttt{self}$.

Recall that in Section 3.3 we defined two formulae from the state machine diagram, $SM_s(x)$ for the states and $SM_t(x)$ for the transitions. Now, we attach the state machine diagram augmented by the entry procedures, to the class A.

$$SM \equiv [\varepsilon](\forall x,\ class(x) = A \longrightarrow SM_s(x) \wedge SM_t(x) \wedge SM_p(x))$$

We are now in a position to ask whether our model is consistent. In other words, is there an execution trace which can satisfy CD, SM and SEQ?

Semantic tableaux deductive calculi [4] do a systematic search for an interpretation which satisfies their input formulae. Their purpose is to show that an argument is valid, that is, that it is impossible for the premises of the argument to all be true in the same situation where the conclusion is false. To test this, the conclusion is negated, and together with the premises, input to the search procedure. If a situation that satisfies these inputs is found, it is a counter-example to the argument, because it makes the premises and the negated conclusion all true, hence it makes the premises true and the conclusion false. It is important that the search procedure is exhaustive, because then if no counter-example is found, we may conclude that the argument is valid. Some logics, such as first order logic and DL are undecidable, so for some inputs, the procedure will not terminate. However, when it does terminate without finding a counter-example, we still know that the argument is valid.

Our goal is different: we want to show that a collection of formulae are consistent. We can therefore simply enter our formuale into the search procedure. If it finds an interpretation which satisfies the inputs, our model is consistent. If it terminates without finding one, it is inconsistent. Since the required execution traces are unlikely to be difficult to find, if the process runs for a long time without terminating, this would be a fair indication that the model has problems.

For now, we will outline a manual search. We will assume that there is a situation which satisfies SEQ, CD and SM, and we will call it w_0. Recall that these situations are valuations, which take variables to individuals, and array variables to functions. Recall also that programs denote relations between these valuations. So our search will consist in breaking down the formulae until we have a collection of explicitly specified valuations, related as required by DL programs.

The three formulae, and some harmless assumptions tell us that w_0 satisfies: $class(ee) = EE, class(a) = A, class(b) = B, a.ex = \{b\}, state(a) = s, intray(a) = (), intray(b) = ()$ and also the dynamic part of SEQ

$$\langle \varepsilon \rangle (sendCond(ee, W, a) \wedge \langle ee.\text{send } W \text{ to } a \rangle \dots \top) \text{ at } w_0 \qquad (1)$$

But ee is an external entity which can send as it pleases, and ε can run 0 times, so it is sufficient to have

$$\langle ee.\text{send } W \text{ to } a \rangle \dots \top \text{ at } w_0 \qquad (2)$$

For this to be true, we need the send action to relate w_0 to another valuation which we will call w_1. We write $w_0 \xrightarrow{\text{send } W \text{ to } a} w_1$ to express this. Satisfaction of (2) now reduces to

$$\langle \varepsilon \rangle (acceptCond(a) \wedge \langle a.\text{accept} \rangle \dots \top) \text{ at } w_1 \qquad (3)$$

Nothing needs to happen before a accepts this message, so we turn our attention to w_2 where $w_1 \xrightarrow{a.\text{accept}} w_2$. Now the definition of accept, on Page 120, depends on the array variables $nextState$ and $entryProc$, so its not immediately obvious what the situation will be in w_2. A little reasoning, for which we do not have space, shows that the state machine formula SM determines that these variables behave as we expect, and so we require w_2 to satisfy $state(a) = s', todo(a) = \text{send } X \text{ to } b$ and

$$\langle \varepsilon \rangle (sendCond(a, Y, b) \wedge \langle a.\text{send } Y \text{ to } b \rangle \top) \text{ at } w_2 \qquad (4)$$

and now, it would appear that we are stuck, because it seems nothing that can possibly happen is going to put $\text{send } Y \text{ to } b$ into a's todo list, which we need in order to satisfy $sendCond(a, Y, b)$. But recall that X and Y are variables. Hence each valuation maps them both to individuals in the semantic domain. If w_2 maps X and Y to the *same* individual, then $sendCond$ is satisfied, the send can proceed and the sequence successfully completes, showing that it is consistent with the model defined by the class and state machine diagrams.

This is clearly not how the story is supposed to end. We are developing a formal theory of our intuitive understanding of the diagrams, and our intuition says they are inconsistent, because X is X, Y is Y, and they can not be the same thing. That is "X" is not just a label we stick on that message from outside the system, but rather something essential to its identity. We can capture this idea formally by retrospectively asserting the following naming invariant

$$NAMES \equiv [\varepsilon](name(X) = \text{``}X\text{''} \wedge name(Y) = \text{``}Y\text{''} \wedge \cdots \wedge name(s') = \text{``}s'\text{''})$$

which makes $X = Y$ impossible. It also prevents the classes A and B from being the same, and also weird possibilities like $A = s$, identifying a class and a state. (Although Mellor [9] has made suggestions that are almost this strange when discussing how domain models might be woven together.)

So now there really is no way to find a situation with $\text{send } Y \text{ to } b$ on a's todo list, so the sequence diagram is inconsistent with the model. This could be proven by induction on the definition of ε.

5   Related Work, Future Work, Conclusions

Our work is influenced by that of Roel Weiringa and collaborators. Executable UML's predecessor, the Shlaer-Mellor method [15] is studied in [16]. Another shorter paper [17] studies a subset of UML 1.1, but the work is so similar that we focus on the earlier contribution. The visual modelling language of the Shlaer-Mellor method is given formal semantics using their own language LCM, which is based on dynamic logic. This logic is first order, but the programs are not explicit assignments, but rather unanalysed atomic programs like those of PDL. To ensure that these programs have the desired effect, guard axioms $\langle \alpha \rangle \top \longrightarrow \varphi$ and effect axioms $\varphi \longrightarrow [\alpha]\psi$ are employed, but assumptions not expressible as axioms are also required.

Shlaer-Mellor is subjected to a "methodological analysis" resulting in many suggested revisions, some of which appear in Mellor's newer method, Executable UML [10]. Some of the revisions though, seem too extreme.

> Our methodological analysis has led to a system transaction concept that is simple to formalize: Each system transaction is a synchronous execution of a non-empty finite set of local object transactions. Because each object transaction has a local effect only, this composition is harmless and we can simply conjoin the local effects.

Thus tracing a timeline of object interactions, as we have done with our sequence diagram formalisation, would be impossible. Weiringa's goal is requirements engineering, which is not concerned with the internal behaviour of a system, only its interaction with its environment. Model driven development asks more than this of its models. We require the ability to fully describe a system, including its internal operations.

Another body of work using a type of dynamic logic to formalise parts of UML is that of the KeY project [1], led by Peter Schmitt and Bernhard Beckert. Their KeY tool verifies programs written in a subset of the Java programming language against OCL constraints and their contextual class diagram, using a specialised dynamic logic [2] with over 250 rules. This tool is tightly integrated with a commercial CASE/modelling tool. This combination of UML class diagrams, OCL and Java which they have formalised [2,3], can be seen as an executable modelling language like UML, or various executable subsets of it. The difference is that the Java code is much more complex and less flexible than UML actions, but can stand alone as an implementation. To formalise such a system and build a practical tool from it is a remarkable accomplishment, which we find encouraging for our own project. Java, although complex, is according to Beckert [2, §4] quite well defined. Almost everybody, except for Bran Selic [14], would argue that this is not the case with UML.

Algebraic specification extended with "generalised labelled transition systems," is used by Gianna Reggio, Maura Cerioli and Egidio Astesiano to formalise parts of UML in [13] and earlier papers by the same authors. They do this by translating UML diagrams into the language Casl-LTL, though they emphasise that the particular language is immaterial. This work, like our own, explicitly aims for a way of giving useful formal semantics to the whole of UML, and as the title suggests, they take seriously the idea that the different diagrams combine to specify a single system. Our translation seems, to us at least, to more closely resemble the original model, although the Casl-LTL specifications are perhaps more readable for software developers. We agree with Reggio and her coauthors that

> It is worth noting that to state the behavioural axioms we need some temporal logic combinators available in Casl-Ltl that we have no space to illustrate here. The expressive power of such temporal logic will also be crucial for the translation of sequence diagrams.

A small executable subset of UML suitable for real-time systems is defined in [5], and given formal semantics using symbolic transition systems. These are due to Amir Pnueli, who is one of the papers authors. While we and Reggio's group translate diagrams into an existing language with semantics of its own, this work starts with a "blank slate." The metamodel abstract syntax of the official definition is ignored, and a traditional formal syntax is given for the selected UML subset. For tools based on this language definition to interoperate with metamodel based tools, a translation will be required. Also, in order to do verification, one needs to express ones proof goals. Ideally, OCL should be used for this, since it is the official constraint language of UML. However, even if you can not use OCL, if you translate the diagrams into some other language, you can use that to express your constraints. This work has neither semantics for OCL nor any alternative constraint language, so more work must be done before they can state what they want to prove. Much of the complexity of this work comes from the need to model hard real-time systems. It may be best to spare the general UML semantics from this complexity, and save it for specialised efforts like this one.

Finally, for something completely different, [6] uses UML collaboration diagrams as graph transformation rules which specify the semantics for object and state machine diagrams. The state of a UML specified system is actually an object diagram, and its evolution is determined by these rules. This is certainly a very direct kind of formal semantics which would have great advantages if it can be applied to more of the language.

How is one to compare these different approaches? None yet comes close to covering a convincing selection of UML's huge repetoire. None can demonstrate an actual proof of a plausible model requirement. Without careful presentation, only the graph rewriting approach is likely to be understood by practitioners. Only KeY is implemented in a form useable by practicing developers. It seems to us that it is more urgent to find justifiable and testable criteria for UML formal semantics proposals, than it is to find more proposals.

Our formalisation has its weaknesses. Dynamic logic lacks types and specialisation. The DL variant used in [16,17] has ordered sorts for this purpose. We have no concurrency, though concurrent dynamic logics have been studied [12]. We consider only a tiny fragment of UML, with less than perfect fidelity.

Readability must also count as a serious weakness of dynamic logic formulae. An attractive possible solution is to obtain a dynamic logic from a graph-based logic, rather than from the usual text-based logics. The atomic programs of such a logic would be graph transformations.

On the positive side, we have shown that our approach can solve a practically motivated problem that no previous effort can manage. The translation into dynamic logic has made the meaning of each diagram quite precise, and made explicit the role they play in the meaning of the model. We have tackled the problem of consistency in UML using the much better developed theory and techniques from logic. Expressing models as logical formulae has the additional benefit that they are ready for use in formal proofs.

A suitable variant of dynamic logic, perhaps graphical, could we believe, serve as the foundation for UML. A definitive translation from the UML metamodel to the syntax of this language would make it absolutely clear what any given model means. By applying tools and techniques from logic, model consistency could then be checked automatically.

References

1. Wolfgang Ahrendt, Thomas Baar, Bernhard Beckert, Richard Bubel, Martin Giese, Reiner Hähnle, Wolfram Menzel, Wojciech Mostowski, Andreas Roth, Steffen Schlager, and Peter H. Schmitt. The KeY tool. *Software and System Modeling*, 4(1):32–54, 2005.
2. Bernhard Beckert. A dynamic logic for the formal verification of java card programs. In *Java on Smart Cards: Programming and Security*, number 2041 in LNCS, pages 6–24. Springer, 2001.
3. Bernhard Beckert, Uwe Keller, and Peter H. Schmitt. Translating the object constraint language into first-order predicate logic. In *Proceedings of VERIFY, Workshop at Federated Logic conferences (FLoC)*, 2002.
4. M D'Agostino, D Gabbay, R Haehnle, and J Posegga, editors. *Handbook of Tableau Methods*, chapter Tableau methods for modal and temporal logics, by Rajeev Goré. Kluwer, 1999. http://rsise.anu.edu.au/~rpg/Publications/Handbook-Tableau-Methods/TR-ARP-15-95.ps.gz.
5. Werner Damm, Bernhard Josko, Amir Pnueli, and Angelika Votintseva. Understanding UML: A formal semantics of concurrency and communication in real-time UML. In *Formal Methods for Components and Objects, Proceedings 2002*, volume 2852 of *LNCS*. Springer, 2003.
6. Gregor Engels, Jan Hendrik Hausmann, Reiko Heckel, and Stefan Sauer. Dynamic meta modeling: A graphical approach to the operational semantics of behavioural diagrams in UML. In *Proceedings of UML*, volume 1939. LNCS, 2000.
7. David Harel, Dexter Kozen, and Jerzy Tiuryn. *Dynamic Logic*. MIT Press, 2000.
8. Brian Henderson-Sellers. UML - the good, the bad or the ugly? perspectives from a panel of experts. *Software and System Modeling*, 4(1):4–13, 2005.
9. Stephen J. Mellor. A framework for aspect-oriented modelling. In *The 4th AOSD Modeling With UML Workshop*, 2003.
10. Stephen J. Mellor and Marc J. Balcer. *Executable UML, A Foundation for Model-Driven Architecture*. Object Technology Series. Addison-Wesley, 2002.

11. Object Management Group. Unified modeling language: Superstructure. Technical report, Object Management Group, August 2005. `http://www.omg.org/docs/formal/05-07-04.pdf`.

12. David Peleg. Concurrent dynamic logic. *Journal of the ACM*, 34(2):450–479, April 1987.

13. Gianna Reggio, Maura Cerioli, and Egidio Astesiano. Towards a rigourous semantics of UML supporting its multiview approach. In H. Hussmann, editor, *FASE 2001*, volume 2029 of *LNCS*, pages 171–186. Springer, 2001.

14. Bran V. Selic. On the semantic foundations of standard UML 2.0. In Marco Bernardo and Flavio Corradini, editors, *Formal Methods for the Design of Real-Time Systems: International School on Formal Methods for the Design of Computer, Communication, and Software Systems*, number 3185 in LNCS, 2004.

15. Sally Shlaer and Stephen J. Mellor. *Object Lifecycles: Modeling the World in States*. Yourdon Press, 1992.

16. R.J. Wieringa and G. Saake. A formal analysis of the Shlaer-Mellor method: Towards a toolkit of formal and informal requirements specification techniques. *Requirements Engineering*, pages 106–131, 1996.

17. Roel Wieringa and Jan Broerson. Minimal transition system semantics for lightweight class and behaviour diagrams. In Manfred Broy, Derek Coleman, Tom S. E. Maibaum, and Bernhard Rumpe, editors, *Proceedings PSMT'98 Workshop on Precise Semantics for Modeling Techniques*. Technische Universitaet Muenchen, TUM-I9803, April 1997.

The Epsilon Object Language (EOL)

Dimitrios S. Kolovos, Richard F. Paige, and Fiona A.C. Polack

Department of Computer Science, University of York,
Heslington, York, YO10 5DD, UK
{dkolovos, paige, fiona}@cs.york.ac.uk

Abstract. Model-Driven Development requires *model management* languages and tools for supporting model operations such as editing, consistency checking, and transformation. At the core of these model management techniques is a set of facilities for model *navigation* and *modification*. A subset of the Object Constraint Language can be used for some of these tasks, but it has limitations as a general-purpose language to be used in a variety of model management tasks. We present the metamodel independent Epsilon Object Language (EOL) which builds on OCL. EOL can be used both as a standalone generic model management language or as infrastructure on which task-specific languages can be built. We describe how it has been used to construct a selection of languages, such as model merging, comparison, and text generation languages.

1 Introduction

Increasingly, software-intensive systems are constructed using Model-Driven Development (MDD). For MDD approaches, such as the Model-Driven Architecture (MDA) [25], to be used successfully, two key technologies are required.

- Standardised modelling and metamodelling languages, which are rich and expressive enough to capture domain-independent and domain-specific concerns. MDA relies on languages that are based on the Meta-Object Facility (MOF) [24].
- *Model management features*. Effective model management requires a set of languages and tools for manipulating models in *automated* ways [2]. A toolset for model management might include model editors (e.g., UML diagram tools, or tools for domain-specific languages such as Microsoft's domain-specific language tools for Visual Studio [7]), transformation engines (e.g., ATL [3]), model version control, consistency checking engines, and model merging engines.

In this paper, we present a new model management language, with prototype tool support: the Epsilon Object Language (EOL). EOL has evolved from careful analysis of existing model management frameworks and languages (discussed in the next section), particularly the Object Constraint Language (OCL). The novelties with EOL are its technology agnosticism, as it can be used to manage models from diverse technologies such as MOF, EMF and XML, its metamodel independence, since it is not bound to a specific metamodel, and the fact that it can be used as both a generic model management language and as the basis for defining task-specific model management languages. We describe how EOL has been used for the latter purpose in Section 4.

A. Rensink and J. Warmer (Eds.): ECMDA-FA 2006, LNCS 4066, pp. 128–142, 2006.

The paper is organised as follows. We establish terminology and review related work on model management, and identify the need for a common infrastructure language for core model management operations, namely model navigation, modification and multiple model access. We argue that OCL is insufficient as such an infrastructure language, and then present EOL. We show how EOL can be used as a standalone language for model navigation and modification, and then describe how EOL has been used to derive a selection of model management languages, e.g., a model comparison, a model merging and a text generation language.

2 Background and Motivation

We take a very general view of MDD in this paper: a *model* is a description of phenomena of interest; thus, a model is represented using textual or graphical languages. Examples of models include UML models, XML schemas, or web documents.

A variety of *operations* on models can be provided by model management systems. These operations can be classified in the same way as database management system operations:

- *create* new models and model elements that conform to a metamodel;
- *read* or *query* models, e.g., to project out information of interest to specific stakeholders. Specific examples of queries include boolean queries to determine whether two or more models are mutually consistent, and queries to select a subset of modelling elements satisfying a particular property.
- *update* models, e.g., changing the properties of a model, adding elements to a model. A specific example of an update operation is *model merging*.
- *delete* models and model elements.

2.1 Model Management Frameworks and Languages

The Meta-Object Facility is a standard model management framework from the OMG [24]. It is a metamodelling language that provides core facilities for defining modelling languages. There is limited tool support for MOF 2.0 at present, though there are tools for earlier versions, e.g., UML2MOF and the MetaData repository under NetBeans for MOF 1.4 [21].

Possibly the most well-known and widely used framework for implementing model management is the Eclipse Modelling Framework (EMF) [17]. EMF is a model engineering extension for Eclipse, and enriches it with model manipulation capabilities via a model handling API. EMF provides support for operations such as creation and deletion of model elements, property assignment, and navigation.

An exemplar of a model management framework mainly built atop EMF is the Atlas Model Management Architecture (AMMA) [2]. AMMA is a general-purpose framework for model management, and is based on ATL. AMMA provides a virtual machine and infrastructural tool support for combining model transformations, model compositions, resource management into an open model management framework.

XMF-Mosaic is a standalone meta-programming environment from Xactium [32] that can be used for model management. It is based on a dialect of MOF and an

executable dialect of OCL, and provides built-in support for defining model transformations. It is not yet clear whether the infrastructure in XMF-Mosaic is sufficiently flexible
and extensible to define other model management operations, e.g., model composition.
These operations are not yet supported in the tool, to the best of our knowledge.

Perhaps of greatest similarity to the framework proposed in this paper is the work on
Kermeta [18]. Kermeta is a metamodelling language, compliant with the EMOF component of MOF 2.0, which provides an action language for specifying behaviour. Kermeta
is intended to be an imperative language for implementing *executable* metamodels; as
such, it is general-purpose and can be used directly for implementing metamodels for
transformation languages, action languages, etc.

2.2 Transformations and Compositions

Transformations are sets of rules describing how models that conform to a metamodel
are to be expressed in models that conform to a second (not necessarily different) metamodel. Specialised transformation tools are beginning to become available. Of note is
ATL, which is inspired by (but does not entirely conform to) the MOF 2.0 QVT standard
for transformations on MOF-defined languages [11]. The XMF-Mosaic environment
can be used to implement (much of) the QVT standard, and bases its transformation
rules on an executable language called XMap. Since XMF-Mosaic is a general-purpose
meta-programming environment, the transformations are not dependent on any metamodel. Patrascoiu has proposed the YATL transformation language as part of the Kent
Modelling Framework (KMF) [28], and uses a subset of OCL for model navigation.

Model *compositions* involve merging or integrating two or more models to produce a
consistent single model. Model composition is founded on theory from database schema
integration [29]. One of the first prototypes of a model composition framework is the Atlas Model Weaver (AMW), which is part of the AMMA model management framework
[20]. The intent of AMW is to allow compositions of two models or two metamodels
via *weaving* sessions, which are based on specific weaving metamodels. AMW has been
shown to have general applicability to data management and software engineering [20].

2.3 Model Consistency Checking

An essential model management operation is *model consistency checking*, which involves determining whether information contained in two or more models contains
contradictions. Model consistency is recognised as one of the most important quali-
ties sought in model management [12,14]. Two types of consistency are intra-model
and inter-model consistency [12]. To achieve intra-model consistency, a model must
comply with its meta-model. Moreover, in multi-view modelling languages (such as
UML [27]), views of a model must not contradict each other [33]. Inter-model consistency, on the other hand, is about maintaining a set of models in a state where they
are consistent with each other. Substantial work has been carried out on checking intra-
model consistency, e.g., based on evaluating OCL constraints [9,10]. However, OCL is
inherently limited to specifying constraints in the context of a single model and cannot
be used as-is for expressing consistency rules across different models. This is of importance when checking consistency between different versions of a model. Intra-model
consistency has been achieved via construction [23], and by analysis [23,31]. Generic

consistency checking approaches, e.g., based on XML [13] may be at the inappropriate level of abstraction for defining meaningful consistency constraints on models.

2.4   Common Requirements

Among the generic and specific model management tools and frameworks discussed above (e.g., OCL [26] for inter-model consistency checking, QVT [11], Kermeta, YATL [28], ATL [3]), we can clearly identify a need for a *common infrastructure* for model management that provides three key facilities in languages and tools, as illustrated in Figure 1.

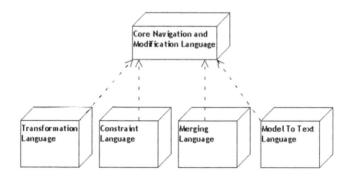

Fig. 1. Model Management Languages Requirements

The first characteristic is the ability to *navigate* models to extract elements of interest. The second characteristic is the ability to *modify* models to implement model management operations for change, e.g., to add, update and delete elements. Finally, multiple models must be concurrently accessible to support cross-model operations such as transformation, merging and inter-model consistency checking.

2.5   Limitations of OCL for Model Management

OCL provides model navigation facilities for UML and MOF models, and it is an OMG standard. The majority of contemporary model management languages and tools use a subset of OCL for navigation and expressing constraints. However, there are a number of limitations with using OCL as the basis for model management:

- The subset of OCL used for navigation and expression varies among different model management frameworks; incompatibilities can easily arise between, e.g., a transformation language using a subset of OCL, and a model-to-text language using a slightly different subset of OCL. There is *no standard OCL core* that can be reused for model navigation and building new task-specific languages.
- By design, OCL does not support model modification capabilities. In particular, it cannot be used to create, update, or delete model elements, nor can it update attribute or reference values. However model modification features are essential to

most model management tasks. Consequently, each new model management language has to implement its own model modification features, adding unnecessary diversity between languages and duplicating effort.

- OCL does not support statement sequencing; this must be encoded using nested and quantified expressions, leading to complex statements which are difficult to understand and maintain. This makes it difficult to use a model management framework in batch mode, and to express complex navigations.
- OCL can only refer to a single model at a time. This is particularly problematic for tasks such as inter-model consistency checking, transformation, and merging. It is particularly challenging in the case where some models have been constructed manually and others automatically. OCL needs to be supplemented with other languages and tools for inter-model consistency checking [22].
- OCL provides two operators for model navigation (the '.' and $\rightarrow$ operators). This adds unnecessary diversity to navigation expressions [19].

However, OCL has a significant user base and its navigation mechanisms are efficient, platform independent, and allow expression of complex queries. What is needed is a flexible, metamodel-independent model navigation language that builds on OCL but also addresses the aforementioned limitations. Such a language could play the role of a common infrastructure language for model management tasks and is essential to provide integrated support for diverse (domain specific) modelling languages.

In the next section we introduce the Epsilon Object Language as a language that contributes to filling this gap.

3   The Epsilon Object Language

The *Epsilon Object Language* (EOL) is the result of efforts to reuse the navigational mechanisms of OCL while adding support for other language features like multiple model access, statement sequencing, simple programming idioms and model modification capabilities. We are using EOL as a core language upon which we are developing a family of task-specific model management languages such as transformation, code generation, merging/integration and consistency checking languages. We call this family of languages the *Extensible Platform for Specification of Integrated Languages for mOdel maNagement* (Epsilon).

We now present an overview of EOL focusing on its differences from OCL, its abstract and concrete syntax, and some examples. In the next section we briefly describe the use of EOL in deriving task-specific model management languages.

3.1   Features

EOL reuses a significant part of OCL, including model querying operations such as the `select()`, `collect()` and `iterate()`. Moreover, it uses a similar syntax for defining variables: `def <name>:<type>;` and has an identical type system. In the sequel we describe the additional features of EOL in relation to OCL.

3.1.1 Access to Multiple Models. To support multiple model access in EOL, each model has a unique identifier (name). Access to a specific meta-class of a model is performed via the ! operator. For example, if UML is a UML 1.4 model, UML!Class will return the Class meta-class reference and UML!Class. allInstances() will return all the instances of the Class meta-class that are contained in UML. If there are conflicting meta-class names, the full path, e.g., UML!Foundation::Core::Class can be used. The ! operator is inspired by ATL [3]. However, in ATL, instead of the model name, the name of the metamodel is used as identifier. This is not appropriate for EOL, which must accommodate multiple models of a metamodel.

3.1.2 Statement Sequencing and Grouping. Sequencing and grouping statements allow developers to disentangle complicated, nested queries, potentially making them easier to read and debug. Statements in EOL can be sequenced using the ; and grouped using the { and } delimiters.

3.1.3 Uniformity of Invocation. Providing two operators for invoking operations and accessing model element features (› and '.') adds unnecessary diversity to OCL expressions. In EOL, we use the dot operator as a uniform navigation and invocation operator. The arrow operator can still be used to facilitate compatibility with the syntax that OCL developers are familiar with, or to resolve potential conflicts with built-in EOL operations. For instance, EOL provides a built-in print() operation that displays a String representation of the object to which it is applied. However, a meta-class may itself define a print() operation. In that case, the arrow operator will invoke the built-in operation while the dot operator will invoke the metamodel-defined operation.

3.1.4 Model Modification. A core requirement of OCL as a constraint language is to preserve the state of models by performing read-only operations [26]. Therefore, OCL expressions cannot create, update or delete model elements. While such operations are not required for expressing constraints, for most model management languages this feature is essential. Therefore, in EOL we have introduced the := operator, which performs assignments of values to variables and model element features: e.g., class.name := 'SomeClass'. Moreover, EOL extends the built-in collection types (Bag, $Sequence$, Set, $OrderedSet$) with operations (such as the $add(Any)$ and $remove(Any)$ operations) that can modify the contents of the collection to which they are applied. Regarding element creation and deletion, EOL supports the new keyword and the $newInstance()$ operation for creating new model elements as well as the $delete()$ operation for deleting model elements from a model.

3.1.5 Debugging and Error Reporting. For debugging and error reporting, it is essential that the user can send text to predefined output streams. While nearly all programming languages support this feature, OCL currently lacks such a mechanism. In EOL we have introduced the print() and err() built-in operations that send a $String$ representation of the object that they apply to, to the standard output and error stream respectively. Reporting operations return the object to which they are applied, to facilitate integration of debugging messages without changing the structure of a program. For instance the statement `a.owner := b.owner.print();` prints a *String* representation of `b.owner` and returns `b.owner` so that it can be assigned to `a.owner`. To facilitate meaningful messages, the EOL engine supports pluggable *pretty printers* that can print *String* representations of model elements in a readable way.

3.1.6   Reusability. EOL allows users to define operations that apply to elements of a specific meta-class (similar to OCL helpers). Such operations can be used not only from EOL programs but also from any EOL-derived languages programs as well. Moreover, operations can be grouped in different physical files and be imported on demand through the `import` statements. An operation that checks if a `UML!ModelElement` has a specific stereotype is displayed in Listing 1.1.

Listing 1.1. EOL Operation example

```
operation UML!ModelElement hasStereotype(name : String) : Boolean
{
    return self . stereotype . exists ( st : UML!Stereotype|st.name = name);
}
```

Having outlined the basic features of EOL, we now present its abstract syntax and a short worked example that demonstrates its concrete syntax.

3.2   EOL Abstract Syntax

Figure 2 presents a snapshot of the core part of the abstract syntax of the language. The example that follows, demonstrating parts of the concrete syntax of EOL, clarifies the missing parts of the abstract syntax (e.g., the syntax for logical expressions).

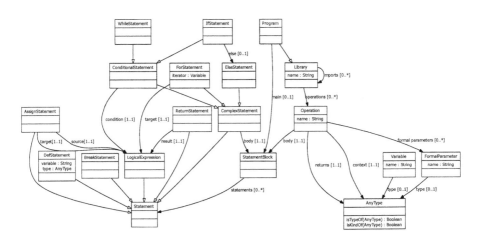

Fig. 2. Snapshot of EOL Abstract Syntax

3.3   EOL Concrete Syntax Example

In this section, we demonstrate a scenario and a working solution using EOL as a stand-alone model management language.

3.3.1   Scenario. When designing class diagrams in UML, it is common practice to mark attributes as private and to provide public getter and setter operations. A common naming convention commonly is that for an attribute named `attr` of type `AttrType` the setter and getter operations should have signatures `getAttr():AttrType` and `setAttr(attr:AttrType)` respectively.

Adding getter and setter operations is mechanical and can benefit from automation. In fact, some UML tools provide built-in wizards for converting public attributes into triplets of private attributes, setters and getters. However, those wizards are tool-specific and often pertain only to a particular extent. EOL allows a generic, tool-independent (requiring only that the modelling tool can serialise models, e.g., in XMI) solution to be defined.

3.3.2   Solution. In Listing 1.2, we demonstrate a user-defined EOL program that runs on any UML 1.4 model and performs the desired addition of getters and setters.

Listing 1.2. EOL Program

```
1   for ( attribute  in UML!Attribute. allInstances ()) {
2     if ( attribute . visibility  = UML!VisibilityKind#vk_public){
3        attribute . visibility  := UML!VisibilityKind#vk_private ;
4        attribute . createGetter ();
5        if ( attribute . changeability =
6        UML!ChangeableKind#ck_changeable){
7          attribute . createSetter ();
8        }
9      }
10  }
11
12  operation UML!Attribute createSetter () {
13    def setter  : new UML!Operation;
14    setter .name := ' set ' + self .name.firstToUpperCase ();
15    setter . visibility  := UML!VisibilityKind#vk_public;
16    setter .concurrency := UML!CallConcurrencyKind#cck_sequential;
17
18    def valueParam : new UML!Parameter;
19    valueParam.name := self .name;
20    valueParam.type := self .type ;
21    valueParam.kind := UML!ParameterDirectionKind#pdk_in;
22    setter . parameter . add(valueParam);
23
24    self .owner. feature . add( setter );
25  }
26
```

```
27   operation UML!Attribute createGetter () {
28     def getter  :  new UML!Operation;
29     getter .name := 'get' + self .name.firstToUpperCase ();
30     getter . visibility  := UML!VisibilityKind#vk_public;
31     getter .concurrency := UML!CallConcurrencyKind#cck_sequential;
32
33     def returnParam  :  new UML!Parameter;
34     returnParam. type  := self . type ;
35     returnParam. kind  := UML!ParameterDirectionKind#pdk_return;
36     getter . parameter .add(returnParam );
37
38     self .owner. feature .add( getter );
39   }
```

Lines 1-10 constitute the body of the EOL program. It iterates over each attribute of the UML model, changing its visibility to private. If the attribute is changeable, both setter and getter operations are created, otherwise only a getter operation is created.

Lines 12-25 define the `createSetter` EOL operation. Line 12 declares that the operation applies to elements of the type `UML!Attribute`. In lines 13-16, a new `UML!Operation` is created using the new keyword with its name set according to the naming convention discussed above. Its visibility and concurrency are set. In lines 18-22, the parameter of the operation is defined, its type and kind are set and it is added to the formal parameters of the operation. Finally, in line 24, the setter is added to the features of the class that owns the attribute.

Lines 27-39 define the `createGetter` operation that creates a getter `UML!Operation` for an attribute, in a similar way to the `createSetter` discussed above.

As proof of concept, we execute this EOL program using the model displayed in Figure 3 (left) as input. In this model, all of the attributes are public and changeable except for the `registrationNumber` of class `Student` that is read-only (*frozen* according to UML terminology). The target, refactored model is shown in Figure 3 (right).

All public attributes of the source model have been converted to private in the target, and setters and getters have been added for all except for `registrationNumber`, for which only a getter has been added.

This example demonstrates using EOL as a standalone language, showing key parts of EOL's concrete syntax. The program of Listing 1.2 shows a minimal functionality. A more complete program would include looking for existing setters and getters before creating, as well as handling static, derived and multi-valued attributes.

3.4   EOL Tool Support

We have implemented an EOL engine using a modular architecture that allows us to plug-in virtually any type of structured model. In its current implementation, we have

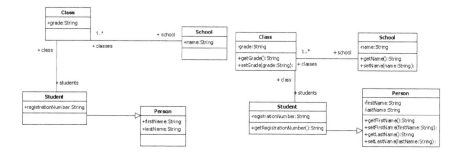

Fig. 3. UML models for EOL example

developed full support for Meta-Object Facility (MOF) models using the MetaData Repository [30], EMF models and XML documents using JDOM [6]. We are also experimenting with models from the Microsoft DSL Toolkit [7]. Since the EOL engine treats all models identically through a layer of abstraction we call `EolModel`, it is feasible to access and manage models from different platforms in the same program. For instance, we have developed EOL programs that check XML documents against MOF models and vice versa.

We have developed a set of plug-ins for Eclipse [4] (editor, perspectives, wizards, and launching configuration) that allow developers to use the language in real problems. The plug-ins and the source for the examples can be found at [15].

For EOL-based languages, the architecture of both the execution engine and the Eclipse plug-ins is designed to facilitate reusability, as described in the next section.

4   Building Task-Specific Model Management Languages

In Section 3.3 we presented EOL as a standalone language. However, a primary motivation for developing EOL is to embed it in a family of task-specific languages for model management. In this section, we briefly describe several task-specific languages we have constructed: the Epsilon Merging Language (EML), the Epsilon Comparison Language (ECL), and the Epsilon Generation Language (EGL) for generating text (e.g. code and documentation) from models.

4.1   Epsilon Comparison Language (ECL)

ECL is a metamodel-independent model comparison language built atop EOL. It is used to express rules that compare a pair of models. The results of comparisons can then be used in, e.g., a merging process. An ECL specification consists of match rules that apply to the elements of the models; these rules include compare and conform parts. The matching process classifies elements into those that match and conform, those that do not, those that match *or* conform, and those to which no match rule has applied. Further discussion about the rationale of this classification approach is presented in [16]. The results can then be processed in a variety of ways. The classification is made accessible through the API of the ECL engine that executed the specification; it can be processed according to the needs and capabilities of the environment. For example, it can be used to visually highlight the elements in the source models, or to provide text messages to the user pointing at the sources of inconsistencies; the type of post-processing depends on the application domain and the needs of the users of ECL.

A very simple and partial ECL example allows us to illustrate both ECL and its relationship to EOL. Listing 1.3 contains an ECL program containing rules for comparing elements from two models: the first of a simplified class diagram metamodel, and the second a simplified relational database metamodel (we omit the metamodels themselves, but they are typical).

Listing 1.3. ECL Specification

```
−− Match classes against  tables  rule  Class2Table
  match class:CD!Class
  with  table :DB!Table {

  compare {
    return  class .name = table .name;
  }
  conform {
    return  table .columns. exists (
      c:DB!PrimaryKey|c.name = class.name + 'ID ');
  }
}
```

The Class2Table rule is executed for each pair of instances of CD!Class and DB!Table in the source models. In its compare part, it checks that the class has the same name as its comparable table. When this condition is met, the two entities are considered to be semantically equivalent and the match rule can proceed to executing its conform part. There, it checks if the table has a primary key named after the name of the class suffixed with ID. Thus, the compare part of a rule identifies a small amount of contextual information necessary to carry out deeper semantic checking in the conform part. In general, whether to check constraints in the compare or the conform part of a rule is application dependent. A similar rule can be written to match attributes against database columns, but we omit this due to space restrictions.

4.2   Epsilon Merging Language (EML)

EML is a metamodel-independent language for expressing model merging operations. It is built atop EOL: model navigation expressions and model modification operations used within the merging process are written directly in EOL.

EML is rule based. It allows specification of different kinds of rules for expressing model merges. Rules in EML are either *match* rules (identical to those of ECL), *merge* rules, or *transform* rules. In the example presented in Listing 1.4, the match rule on Classes returns true iff two classes (the left and right class) are both abstract or both concrete, and their names and namespaces match. The merge rule on Classes produces, in the merged model, a class which has the name and namespace of the left class, and all features of both left and right.

Listing 1.4. Match and merge rules in EML based on EOL

```
rule MatchClasses {
    match l: Left!Class  with r: Right!Class

    compare {
      return l.name = r.name and
              l.namespace.matches(r.namespace);
    }
    conform { return l.isAbstract = r.isAbstract ; }
}

  rule MergeClasses {
    merge l: Left!Class  with r: Right!Class
    into  m: Merged!Class

    m.name := l.name;
    m.namespace := l.namespace.equivalent ();
    m.feature := l.feature.includeAll (r.feature).equivalent ();
  }
```

EML provides more features than we can describe here. It includes rule inheritance, exception handling, and transformation capabilities. An EML development tool, which builds on the EOL tool, has been developed and is available at [15].

4.3   Epsilon Generation Language (EGL)

A third task-specific language that we have recently been developing is the Epsilon Generation Language (EGL), which targets the problem of model-to-text mapping, similar to MOFScript[8]. Unlike MOFScript, EGL is once again built on top of EOL, and uses EOL to provide model navigation and modification facilities. An example EGL specification is in Listing 1.5. The delimeters [% and %] separate EOL code from static text (similar to what is done in MOFScript).

Listing 1.5. Example EGL specification built atop EOL

```
[%for ( class in UML!Class.allInstances ())  { %]
public class [%=class.name%] {
  [%for ( att in class.feature.select (a:UML!Attribute|true )){ %]
    private [%=att.type.name%] [%=att.name%];
  [%}%]
}
[%}%]
```

In the example, an EGL program iterates across all UML classes and outputs target Java code, wherein each UML class is mapped to a Java class, and each UML attribute is mapped to a private Java attribute. The EGL development tool transforms this specification into a pure EOL program, which can then be executed against a UML model.

4.3.1   Reuse of EOL Tools in Task-Specific Languages.   The details of the implementation process of ECL exemplifies the effort that is saved by using EOL as an infrastructure language for the development of task-specific model management languages.

The abstract syntax (grammar) of ECL contains only a small number of task-specific elements (*MatchRule*, *Conform* and *Compare*), and depends substantially on EOL (*Statement Block*, *Formal Parameter*, *Library*) for its navigational and computational characteristics. This, together with the flexible architecture of the EOL engine, makes the implementation of the ECL engine straightforward. More specifically, the ECL parser required 121 lines of ANTLR [1] grammar specification and 6910 lines of Java code, with 4883 of them being generated automatically from the ANTLR grammar, leaving only 2027 lines of hand-written code.

5   Conclusions and Further Work

In this paper we have presented the Epsilon Object Language, a metamodel independent model management language. Its novelties include its support for model modification, additional conventional programming constructs, and the ability to access multiple models, e.g., for model comparison. While EOL can be used as a standalone language for model management, its primary purpose is to be embedded into higher-level task-specific languages of the Epsilon platform. The architecture of the EOL execution engine helps to achieves this. As proof of concept, we have designed and implemented three task-specific languages built on EOL: a merging language, comparison language, and model-to-text language. Implementing these languages and reusing the EOL infrastructure was predominantly straightforward.

We are in a continual process of attempting to align with the OCL 2.0 standard in those aspects of EOL that are not characterized by fundamentally different design decisions (such as the ability to modify models).

Our plans for the near future include releasing the EOL execution engine and plug-ins as part of the Eclipse GMT [5] project, and to develop comprehensive documentation of the internals of the architecture of the EOL execution engine. This will allow external developers to use the EOL infrastructure to build custom task-specific languages. As well, we are aligning the merging language with the approach taken by Atlas Model Weaver, to produce weaving models, enabling reuse.

Acknowledgements

The work in this paper was supported by the European Commission via the MODELWARE project. The MODELWARE project is co-funded by the European Commission under the "Information Society Technologies" Sixth Framework Programme (2002-2006). Information included in this document reflects only the authors views. The European Commission is not liable for any use that may be made of the information contained herein. We thank the Atlas and AMMA teams at INRIA for their help.

References

1. ANTLR: ANother Tool For Language Recognition, Official Web-Site. http://www.antlr.org.
2. Atlas Model Management Architecture. http://www.sciences.univ-nantes.fr/lina/ atl/AM-MAROOT/.
3. Atlas Transformation Language, official web-site. http://www.sciences.univ-nantes.fr/lina/atl/.
4. Eclipse Foundation, Official Web-Site. http://www.eclipse.org.
5. Eclipse GMT - Generative Model Transformer, Official Web-Site. http://www.eclipse.org/gmt.
6. JDOM Official Web-Site. http://www.jdom.org.
7. Microsoft Domain Specific Languages Framework, Official Web-Site. http://msdn.microsoft.com/ vstudio/ teamsystem/ workshop/ DSLTools/ default.aspx.
8. MOFScript. Official Web-Site: http://www.modelbased.net/mofscript/.
9. OCLE: Object Constraint Language Environment, official web-site. http://lci.cs.ubbcluj.ro/ocle/.
10. Octopus: OCL Tool for Precise Uml Specifications, official web-site. http://www.klasse.nl/ocl/octopus-intro.html.
11. QVT Partners Official Web-Site. http://qvtp.org/.
12. Bogumila Hnatkowska, Zbigniew Huzar, Ludwik Kuzniarz and Lech Tuzinkiewicz. A systematic approach to consistency within UML based software development process. In *Consistency Problems in UML-based Software Development Workshop*, pages 16–29, 2002.
13. Christian Nentwich, Wolfgang Emmerich, Anthony Finkelstein and Erns Ellmer. Flexible Consistency Checking. *ACM Transactions on Software Engineering and Methodology*, 12(1):28–63, 2003.
14. Dan Chiorean, Mihai Pasca, Adrian Carcu, Christian Botiza, Sorin Moldovan. Ensuring UML models consistency using the OCL Environment. In *Sixth International Conference on the Unified Modelling Language - the Language and its applications*, 2003.
15. Dimitrios S. Kolovos. Extensible Platform for Specification of Integrated Languages for mOdel maNagement (Epsilon), Official Web-Site. http://www.cs.york.ac.uk/~dkolovos/ epsilon.
16. Dimitrios S. Kolovos, Richard F. Paige, Fiona A.C. Polack. Model Comparison: A Foundation for Model Composition and Model Transformation Testing. In *Proc. 1st International Workshop on Global Integrated Model Management (GaMMa)*, 2006. http://www.cs.york.ac.uk/~dkolovos/publications/GaMMa02-kolovos.pdf.
17. Eclipse.org. Eclipse Modelling Framework. http://www.eclipse.org/emf.
18. F. Chauvel and F. Fleurey. Kermeta Language Overview. http://www.kermeta.org.
19. Mandana Vaziri and Daniel Jackson. Some Shortcomings of OCL, the Object Constraint Language of UML. Response to Object Management Group's Request for Information on UML 2.0 , December 1999. http://www.omg.org/docs/ad/99-12-05.pdf.
20. Marcos Didonet Del Fabro, Jean Bezivin, Frederic Jouault, Erwan Breton, Guillaume Gueltas. AMW: A Generic Model Weaver. *Proceedings of IDM05*, 2005.
21. Martin Matula. NetBeans UML Profile for MOF. http://mdr.netbeans.org/uml2mof/.
22. MODELWARE Partners. D1.5: Model Consistency Rules, 2005. http://www.modelware-ist.org.
23. Monique Snoeck, Cindy Michiels and Guido Dedene. Consistency by Construction: The Case of MERODE. In *International Workshop on Conceptual Modeling Quality*, 2003.
24. Object Management Group. Meta Object Facility (MOF) 2.0 Core Specification. http://www.omg.org/cgi-bin/doc?ptc/03-10-04.
25. Object Management Group. Model Driven Architecture, official web-site.

26. Object Management Group. UML 2.0 OCL Specification. http://www.omg.org/docs/ptc/03-10-14.pdf.
27. Object Management Group. UML official web-site. http://www.uml.org.
28. Octavian Patrascoiu. YATL:Yet Another Transformation Language. In *Proceedings of the 1st European MDA Workshop, MDA-IA*, pages 83–90. University of Twente, the Nederlands, January 2004.
29. Rachel A. Pottinger and Philip A. Bernstein. Merging Models Based on Given Correspondences. Technical Report UW-CSE-03-02-03, University of Washington, 2003.
30. Sun Microsystems. Meta Data Repository. http://mdr.netbeans.org.
31. Tom Mens, Ragnhild Van Der Straeten, and Jocelyn Simmonds. Maintaining Consistency between UML Models with Description Logic Tools. In *Sixth International Conference on the Unified Modelling Language - the Language and its applications, Workshop on Consistency Problems in UML-based Software Development II*, 2003.
32. Xactium. XMF-Mosaic. http://www.xactium.com.
33. Zhiming Liu, He Jifeng, Xiaoshan Li, Yifeng Chen. Consistency and Refinement of UML Models. In *Consistency Problems in UML-based Software Development Workshop III*, 2004.

Using a Model Merging Language for Reconciling Model Versions

Klaus-D. Engel[1], Richard F. Paige[2], and Dimitrios S. Kolovos[2]

[1] Fraunhofer FOKUS
engel@fokus.fraunhofer.de
[2] Department of Computer Science, University of York, UK
{paige, dkolovos}@cs.york.ac.uk

Abstract. A difficult challenge in the industrialisation of Model-Driven Development is managing different *versions* of models. Different versions may arise at any time during the development process, due to different individuals or teams working on different parts of the overall model. To manage these versions it is necessary to be able to identify differences and *reconcile* these differences in a single, integrated model. We describe the use of *model merging* technology for managing different versions of a model in an industrial software development process. The use of automated model merging technology is contrasted with an alternative, semi-automated approach. The contributions of model merging to helping to solve this problem are outlined.

1 Introduction

Industrial applications of Model-Driven Development (MDD) require facilities for managing models. In particular, such facilities need to offer support for creating, updating (e.g., transforming or merging models), analysing (e.g., consistency checking) and deleting a variety of models, manipulated by different stakeholders. Model management platforms are beginning to become available – such as the AMMA [6] and Epsilon [7] platforms.

A key problem faced by developers of model management platforms is the ability to manage and manipulate different *versions* [11] of the same model. This is particularly relevant in an industrial application of MDD where different developers work on the same model at different times: differences and similarities between different model versions need to be *identified*, *reconciled*, and finally *integrated* into a unified single model. This is a difficult problem in itself, given the complexity of industrial MDD models, and the variety of changes that can be made to them, in a typical MDD process. The problem is exacerbated in the case where a solution to model version management needs to be introduced, *without* changing the existing development process, e.g., by replacing a predominantly manual solution with an automated or semi-automated one.

In this paper, we sketch an approach to managing model versions based on use of a model merging language – the Epsilon Merging Language (EML). In order to properly assess the value and utility of applying model merging in this context, we

A. Rensink and J. Warmer (Eds.): ECMDA-FA 2006, LNCS 4066, pp. 143–157, 2006.

aim to compare the use of EML with an alternative, semi-automated solution – developed in-house – that did not use model merging facilities.

The remainder of this paper is as follows. We first briefly define the problem of managing model versions, and touch on related work. We introduce the Epsilon Merging Language, and then provide context by explaining the development process into which model version management is to be introduced. Two solutions to managing model versions are presented: the first not based on model merging, and the second using model merging via EML. The two approaches are then compared, and lessons learnt identified.

2 Background and Related Work

We start with a brief overview of the characteristics of a version control/management system, and then discuss model version control. We then give a short overview of the Epsilon Merging Language (EML), focusing on its characteristics that can help with model versioning.

2.1 Version Control and Model Versioning

A version control system (also called a *revision control system*) [14] is a software system that manages multiple revisions of the same unit of information. Conceptually, any serialisable information can be managed by a version control system (VCS). In practice, a VCS is typically applied to source code and textual documentation. Other applications include managing versions of CAD files. Some modelling tools, e.g., Enterprise Architect [8], include built-in support for managing versions of diagrams, but do not offer all of the facilities of a fully-fledged VCS.

The fundamental characteristics of a VCS as applied in software engineering are as follows [14]:

- the ability to return to any earlier state in the design (e.g., rollback to a previous version of a source file because of the introduction of a bug).
- to allow multiple versions of a software system to be executed independently (e.g., to identify in which version a bug arose).
- to allow multiple developers to work on a system simultaneously.
- to allow documentation of changes and revisions (e.g., the changes that were made in moving from one version to the next).
- to allow identification of differences between versions.
- to allow developers to merge different versions.

There are both centralised repository and distributed variants of VCSs, which mainly differ in terms of the approaches taken to avoiding conflicts (e.g., locking mechanisms).

A key difficulty in using traditional version control systems for managing versions of models [11] is that the traditional approaches are based on linear, text-based files.

Models, however, are structured graphs presented visually. Traditional VCSs are not designed to operate with hierarchical data.

The key issues in resolving this abstraction mismatch are identified by Lin, Zhang and Gray [10], who clarify the need for efficient and precise definitions of *model comparison*, needed for supporting model version control. Alanen and Porres [12] formalise a definition of union and difference of models which can form the basis of an implementation of model version control, perhaps based on XML or XMI serialisation [3] of models. One challenge to overcome is the problem of visualising model differences. Ohst et al [9] make use of colours to highlight differences and redundancies, but it is unclear whether this is sufficient to cover all the potential differences (e.g., between elements and between hierarchies), and whether a colour-based approach scales.

2.2 Epsilon Merging Language

The Epsilon Merging Language (EML) is a metamodel-independent language for expressing model composition operations. It is built atop a generic model management language called the Epsilon Object Language (EOL) [5], which is inspired by OCL. EML is a general-purpose model composition language, and is rule based. It allows specification of three different kinds of rules and fulfills the general requirements for a model comparison solution identified in [9]. EML also supports model transformations, by building atop the EOL. EML supports model transformations by *transform rules*. EOL provides only model navigation and generic management of models.

An EML specification consists of a set of rules describing how model compositions should be carried out. Rules in EML are of three types:

- Match rules
- Merge rules
- Transform rules

Match rules can be further subdivided into comparison and conformance rules (examples to follow). EML also provides support for a *pre* block and a *post* block, which are actions that are executed prior to and after the compositions have taken place. These blocks are used to perform tasks that are not pattern based (e.g., initialisation and post-processing; an example will follow).

Each match rule has a unique name and two metaclass names as parameters. The rule itself is composed of a *compare* part and a *conform* part . The rule is executed for all pairs of instances of the specified metaclasses that appear in the source models.

The compare part of a match rule determines whether two instances match, using a minimum set of (syntactic) criteria. The conform part applies only to instances that satisfy the compare part of a rule; the conformance rule set refines this match. If the conformance part of the rule fails, then an exception is raised (work is ongoing on improving EML's exception handling capabilities).

An example is shown in Figure 1.

```
abstract rule ModelElements
    match l: Left!ModelElement
    with r: Right!ModelElement
    extends Elements {

    compare {
            return l.name = r.name
            and l.namespace.matches(r.namespace);
    }
}

rule Classes
    match l: Left!Class
    with r: Right!Class
    extends ModelElements {

    conform { return l.isAbstract = r.isAbstract; }
}
```

Fig. 1. Matching rules in EML

The rule ModelElements is abstract; it is not instantiated and is not used to carry out any matches. It provides basic behaviour used by rules that *extend* it. The basic behaviour of this abstract rule is to match model elements that have identical names (l.name=r.name) and matching namespaces. A similar match rule is used for classes. However, the Classes rule is concrete and will be executed by the EML virtual machine. Classes match when they obey the rules declared in their parent, the rules they extend (in our case the ModelElements rule), and when the additional *conform* part of the rule holds, i.e., when classes are either both abstract or both not abstract.

2.2.1 EML Model Element Categorisation

After the execution of all match rules in an EML specification, four types of model elements can be identified with respect to a particular pair of models (which we designate as *left* and *right* models, respectively)

1. Elements that *match and conform* to elements of the opposite model (i.e., elements of the left model that match and conform to elements of the right model, and vice versa).
2. Elements that *match but do not conform* to elements of the opposite model. Elements in this category trigger cancellation of the composition process.
3. Elements that *do not match* with any elements in the opposite model.
4. Elements on which no matching rule has applied; elements in this category may suggest that the specification is incomplete and thus trigger warnings.

After the matching rules have been applied, the following results are obtained.

- Elements that match and conform will be merged with their identified opposites. The specification of merging is captured in a *merge rule*.
- Elements in categories 3 and 4 (that do not match) will be *transformed* into model elements compatible with the target metamodel. The specification of transformation is defined in a transformation rule. We do not go into further details regarding transformation rules in this paper.

- Elements in category 2 either generate or an exception, or are handled by a *fix* block (similar to *try-catch* in Java), which we discuss further in Section 3.

2.2.2 EML Merge Rules

Merge rules in EML are used to specify the behaviour necessary to compose two instances of model elements that match and conform. Each merge rule consists of a unique name, two metaclass names as input parameters, and the metaclass of the model element that the rule creates in the target model.

For all pairs of matching instances of the two metaclasses, the rule is executed and an empty model element is created in the target model. The content of the newly created model element is defined by the body of the merge rule. Two examples of merge rules are shown in Figure 2.

```
rule ModelElements {                     rule Classes {
    merge l: Left!ModelElement               merge l: Left!Class
    with r: Right!ModelElement               with r: Right!Class
    into m: Merged!ModelElement              into m: Merged!Class
                                             extends ModelElements {

    m.name := l.name;                        m.feature := l.feature.
    m.namespace:=l.namespace.equivalent()      includeAll(r.feature).
}                                              equivalent();
                                         } }
```

Fig. 2. EML Merge Rule

Figure 2 presents two merge rules, one for merging ModelElements and a second for merging UML classes ("Classes"). The first rule applies to all Model Elements and produces a new, merged ModelElement whose name is that of the left original model, and whose namespace is that of the left original model. In the second rule, the two metaclasses, *left* and *right*, are declared; the merge rule is also declared to produce an instance of Class metaclass. The result of applying a merging rule is referred to via the merge result, declared by the *into clause*. The "Classes" rule creates a new instance of the Class metaclass, carries out all mergings declared in its parent (ModelElements), and sets the feature list of the new class to be the union of all features from the left and right arguments.

There is a slight twist to the merging rule that takes the union of all features from the left and right model elements: the use of the *equivalent()* operator. This operator returns the *equivalent of the model elements to which it is applied* in the target model. The equivalent of an element is the result of a merge rule if the element has a matching element in the opposite model; otherwise it is the result of a transform rule. In short, this operator is necessary because the target and source metamodels may differ. This operator ensures that model elements from the source metamodel are expressed in the target metamodel before revealing the result of the composition.

Additional details on EML, including its merging strategies, and its support for different metamodels (e.g., MOF [1], EMF) can be found at [7].

3 Application of Model Merging

We now describe an application of model merging for managing model versions. The aim of this application was to develop MDA [2] support for an established and intensively used approach to software development process without changing it. This work was done as a joint effort between Fraunhofer FOKUS and an industrial partner. The focus here is to contrast previously gathered experience on managing model versions *without* the use of automated model merging, with a model merging-based approach, making use of EML.

In the following sections a short overview of the specific software development process will be given, and an example will be used to illustrate the approach used for merging model versions. This example will comprise only a fragment of the overall process but will be sufficient to illustrate the complete model merging approach used. The approaches to managing model versions will then be described: first, a semi-automated model difference analysis and merge facility will be described; and then our attempt at using EML rules to obtain similar results will be presented.

The first (semi-automated) approach has tool support; this model difference analysis and merge facility, implemented and used in an industrial project, is predominantly confidential. Presentations about the tool have been made [13]. For reasons of confidentiality, in this paper we describe a separate implementation of a similar merge approach in the Eclipse/EMF environment.

3.1 Context: The Software Development Process

We now describe the software development process that was to be extended and further developed to support MDA. The original software construction process supports all phases from planning through design and realization of the construction of enterprise information systems in an integrated environment. In the first phase the business rules and their relations are specified. The second phase allows the definition of Use Cases and their interrelations. In the third phase the flow of screens has to be specified, i.e., anticipated screens and the flow of control from screen to screen. This has to been done for each screen flow / use case; this description of screen flow can be seen as a behavioural description for the use cases.

For each screen flow, diagrams are derived in the fourth phase, which describe system boundary objects to the user, server control objects and the data entities linked to the screens. This derivation is done using transformations starting with the objects from phase three. The resulting diagrams will be manually augmented increasing the description of control and data flow in the system.

After this step a transformation can be used to generate a detailed class design for each of the diagrams received in phase four. These are still on a design level and not code, but are comparable to the code generation which is done in the next step.

All objects created or modified within the different phases are stored in a MOF repository. Passing from phase to phase is supported by transformations. Relationships between objects that are derived from other objects by these transformations are kept as traces within the repository.

To limit the degree of detail in this paper, we will restrict our example to the use case phase and design of screen flow section since the requirements for versioning and model merge are similar for all phases.

3.2   The Model Difference Analysis and Merge Facility

We now briefly describe the initial approach to providing model merge and differencing tool support for the development process presented in Section 3.1. We go into sufficient detail so as to be able to precisely understand what needs to be implemented using EML rules.

The existing tool offers team support facilities. It allows users to model different system aspects in parallel, to store them in model versions, and consolidate the results of parallel development. Consolidation is complex and time consuming. Within this environment a semi-automated approach is used. The person utilizing the diff/merge facility (model integrator) controls which model artefacts get transferred from the source to the target or are to be removed from the target.

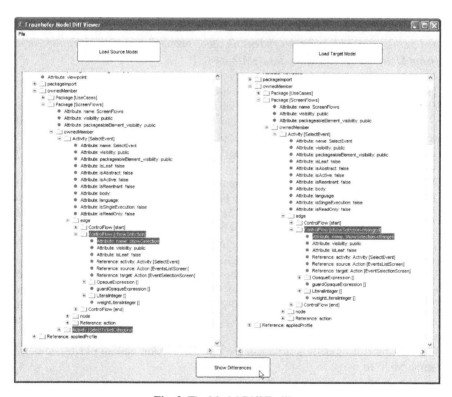

Fig. 3. The Model Diff Facility

The diff/merge process consists of three phases:

- Load the two versions of the model to be merged and determine the differences (the two versions are displayed in two sub windows).

- Navigate the artefact differences in the source and target window and decide whether to copy them from source to the target or delete them within the target window. In this phase this is done by only marking the artefacts as "to be" copied or deleted.
- After the above decisions have been made the resulting model is to be saved as a new version. This is the actual execution of the merge process.

3.2.1 Phase 1: Loading the Versions and Identifying the Differences

Only versions of complete models, and not parts of models, are supported. So the two versions of a model must have had a common subset of artefacts - at least the root element - before they evolved into separate versions.

The development environment is based on a MOF Repository [1]. Every MOF object obtains, at the time it is created, a unique identifier within the model which cannot be changed for the lifetime of the object. This MOF Id can be used to definitively establish an object's identity.

Instance typed objects have full object identity; that is, it is always possible to reliably distinguish one instance (object) from another. Object identity is intrinsic and permanent, and is not dependent on other properties such as attribute values. [from MOF 1.4 specification formal/02-04-03]

The first step during loading therefore uses those modelling artefact identities to identify elements that have been dropped or created in between the creation of those two versions. Objects with MOF Ids in the older version that do not appear in the newer one have been dropped, those that appear in the newer but not the older version have been created. Changes will be marked and highlighted in the Diff/Merge browser (Figure 3).

Having two modelling artefacts representing the same object (i.e., with the same MOF Id) does not mean that they cannot be different. Their attributes or references may have changed, e.g., new ones may have been added, deleted or changed. We therefore have to elaborate how to discover a difference in more detail.

To determine differences, we can make use of the reflective module of MOF. This has the advantage that the difference algorithm can be used for other metamodels too without changes. The reflective module allows working on the model and metamodel level without using metamodel specific interfaces that means without having knowledge of the metamodel in advance. For example, we can start with a modelling object, find its attribute names and values, its references, multiplicities of attributes and references and so on.

For each pair of modelling artefacts (i.e., a new version and an old version) with the same MOF Id we

- Check whether the attributes (names and values respecting the multiplicity) are different.
    For primitive types we directly compare the values. For complex types we have to recursively compare the objects pointed to for differences.
- Check whether the references (referenced objects) are different. This is also done recursively.

If we have found differences, we mark them and also mark the objects we started with as different. We have to be aware of cycles during the recursive search. If we are not interested in highlighting all differences in the browser, we could abort the search for differences after the first difference found for an object. To identify all changes we have to look from version A to version B for differences and vice versa.

As a result we will have a list of all modelling artefacts in version A that have changed or added to version B and all those in version B which have changed or are added to version A. This holds for all attributes and references in the model artefacts.

This reflective approach has the advantage that we do not need to know anything specific about the metamodel. Its disadvantage is that we perhaps compare too many objects that haven't changed. If we have knowledge about the metamodel and more specifics about the way changes could have taken place within the model, we could restrict the number of objects we have to look at. For example, only modelling artefacts that are visible in the modellers GUI could have been changed by the modeller.

3.2.2   Interpreting the Differences and Identifying the Elements to Merge

Within the merge phase we have a directed operation, i.e., one specific version of the model is the source and the other the target. The source elements may be added/merged from the source to the target but not vice versa. Elements may be deleted from the target that are not present in the source. This phase is normally done with support by a human being, who decides which differences should take part in the merge in which way and marks them as to be added from the source to the target or deleted from the target etc. The following kinds of objects can be identified:

- Objects (identified by their MOF Id) that are present in the source but not in the target may be added to the target (marked as *add*).
- Objects (identified by their MOF Id) that are present in the target but not in the source may be deleted from the target (marked as *delete*).
- Attributes present in a modelling artefact in the source but not in the corresponding target can be created in the corresponding target artefact (mark as *add*).
- Attributes present in a modelling artefact in the target but not in the corresponding source can be created in the corresponding target artefact (mark as *delete*).
- References or links between objects to be added or deleted
- Changes in modelling artefacts that are present in both versions but which have changed their values

3.2.3   Merge Phase

This phase executes the identifications and decisions made in phase 2 and creates a new target model in the repository. It takes the following steps:

1. Delete all references to objects that are marked to be deleted
2. Delete all the objects marked to be deleted
3. Add all objects marked to be added (without their attributes and references, because they may reference objects not present)

4. Add all attributes to be added
5. Add all references to be added

Since it is not guaranteed that the decisions made in phase 2 lead to a consistent metamodel instance, we have to make a constraint check to validate the resulting model.

3.2.4   The Metamodel

The metamodel used within the industrial project is proprietary. Within the OMG presentation [13] a single slide gives an overview of the package structure used within the metamodel. This structure is shown in Figure 4.

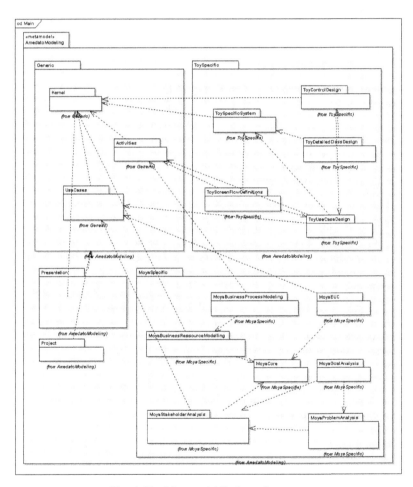

Fig. 4. The Metamodel Package Structure

The metamodel is based on parts of UML 2.0, specifically UseCases, Activities and Kernel elements. These elements are specialized for their usage in the different development phases in the specific packages. These specific modelling elements are offered through a graphical modelling tool to the user. The models are stored within a MOF repository generated from the metamodel. Additional metamodel packages are defined for project metadata and the graphical representation data of the model. Within our examples we will concentrate on the use case screen flows.

For use case design the modeller will offer the following (specific) elements: actors, use cases, association, generalization, include and extend dependencies. At model creation time the user has to enter an identifier (e.g. for use cases) that will be unique within the model. These identifiers are not as secure as the MOF ids assigned automatically, but can also be used to identify objects in the merge process.

For the specification of screen flows we will have a screen (derived from activity), transitions between screens, initial and final nodes. These elements will also have specific identifiers assigned by the user during creation.

3.3 Model Merge with the Epsilon Merging Language

In this section we briefly outline how we use EML to manipulate the models, identify matches, and carry out the kinds of merges discussed in the preceding. In this sense, we are demonstrating the value and applicability of generic model composition technology for helping to solve a specific model management task, namely model differencing and merging of different model versions.

With EML, the developer defines a set of rules which will be applied to two metamodel instances (one, for example, called the *left* instance, and the other the *right*). Applying the rules will partition the modelling elements into the four categories noted earlier, in Section 2.2.1, i.e., elements that do not match, elements that match and conform, etc. This partitioning of model elements will be used to separate the newly added, deleted and changed from the unchanged elements within the two versions.

For the matching model elements, and hence writing the matching rules in EML, a combination of attributes/elements will be used that have the capability of uniquely identifying the element. For example, for use cases, the use case name suffices, and for screen flows the activity name will suffice. For associations we need a more complex construct of source and target, e.g., their role names, to identify it. A better approach would be to use the MOF identifier or the corresponding EMF identifier and a comparison function that checks two objects for identity, as we did with the approach previously described. Support for use of MOF identifiers was not available in the version of EML trialed for this experiment, but has since been added. In the case that a modelling tool preserves unique MOF identifies, an identity-based *matching strategy* (currently implemented for both MOF and EMF) can be used to identify matches based solely on element identity. We use EML conformance rules to identify changes in other characteristics of an element (e.g. changes in an element's visibility, multiplicity, direction for navigation, etc.). Applying the matching to two model versions will lead to the partitioning mentioned earlier. We discuss the information provided in each case with respect to the problem at hand.

Category 4 elements are a hint that we have forgotten to define a match rule needed for the model versions. In this case we infer that our rule set is incomplete and must augment it.

Category 1 elements are those that are contained in both model versions. However, the partitioning and inclusion of elements in this category does not say anything about them being different since contained elements like attributes or references may have changed. Elements of category 1 match and conform with their opposites. This means that even if some attribute values are different, the designer of the EML specification has decided that they are not important enough to raise a conformance issue – then they would belong to category 2.

Category 3 elements are those elements that lead to changes. These may be elements that have been deleted or added in one model version.

Elements of Category 2 have a corresponding partner but an expression that was checked in the conformance part of an EML rule has changed (e.g., the type of the attribute, the visibility of the element, direction of an association etc.).

A sample of the EML matching rules used for such an application is presented in Figure 5. We present an example of a merge rule thereafter.

```
abstract rule Elements
    match l : V1!Element
    with r : V2!Element {

    compare { return l.owner.matches(r.owner); }
}

abstract rule NamedElements
    match l : V1!NamedElement
    with r : V2!NamedElement
    extends Elements {

    compare { return l.name = r.name; }
}


rule UseCases %% matches only on names
    match l : V1!UseCase
    with r : V2!UseCase
    extends NamedElements {
}

rule Properties
    match l : V1!Property
    with r : V2!Property
    extends NamedElements {

    compare {
      return l.type.matches(r.type) and
        l.association.matches(r.association);
    }
}
```

Fig. 5. Example EML match rules to support model version management

The manual decision process used in the earlier approach, where a person responsible for the merge decides which elements should be added or deleted within or to the target model, cannot be fully used with EML since the merge and transformation rules will applied automatically. However, such a process could be supported with EML if *traceability information* (e.g., sources of elements in a merged model) can be recorded. [15] presents an approach to recording traceability information in EML. In general, if it is desired to be able to apply a manual decision-making process in concert with automated merging tools, a less strict set of rules should be written (e.g., leading to more elements in categories 2 and 4), which should lead to more exceptions during the automated merging process (in the case of increased elements in category 2) or more diagnostics suggesting model elements to which no rule applied (in the case of increased elements in category 4). Within match blocks an exception handling-like mechanism can be used. In practice, we attach a *fix* block to a *compare* rule; these fix blocks can be executed during a matching process. Their purpose is to allow modular conflict resolution and reporting. To add support for manual decision making we intend to split the matching/merging process into two distinct processes. The output of the match process will be a model (trace model) that will store the identified match-relationships (and the category in which each belongs) thus giving the opportunity to revise/correct/enhance the trace model before feeding it back into the merging process.

The merging process for model versions can be done (in the simplest case) automatically; however, this depends on the policy followed for team coordination and synchronisation. This in turn will dictate whether we will have more or less conflicts during the merge. A merge rule for this process is shown in Figure 6.

```
auto rule ModelWithModel
  merge l : V1!Model
  with r : V2!Model
  into m : Vm!Model {

    if (l.name <> r.name){
        m.name := l.name + ' merged with ' + r.name;
    }
}
```

Fig. 6. Example EML Merge Rule

3.4 Comparison of Both Approaches

The MOF reflective approach described in Sections 3.1-3.2 is independent of the metamodel; EML is also metamodel independent. In general, in both approaches a person is needed to resolve the conflicts appearing during the merge and to determine the merge strategy. The merging afterwards is done automatically. With EML this may require some experimentation with the matching and merging rules in order to determine where and when human feedback can best be injected. We found this not difficult to do with EML, particularly because the rule structure inherent in any EML program is helpful in determining exactly what kind of feedback is needed from a human operator due to a failed rule. Including traceability information, as in [15], would also help with this process.

For complex metamodels like the UML 2.0 metamodel the efforts for obtaining a complete set of matching rules needed for the EML approach will not be negligible; for this reason, the developers of EML are exploring matching strategies, e.g., based on the ideal of a weaving model. With the strategies currently implemented within EML, this is straightforward. Another issue is dealing with the frame of rules, i.e., their domain of applicability. Frames for the rules may be generated from the metamodel using an Epsilon helper utility [5].

In general, MOF identifiers may not be available for determining the identity of objects since some tools do not persist such identifiers (e.g., Rational Studio Architect). While this is not a problem that a model composition tool such as EML can overcome, the user of automated composition tools must be aware of these limitations, as they will impact on the human intervention needed to deal with failed composition rules.

With EML, it is currently not possible to support the conflict decision process as it currently exists. The process of deciding how to resolve conflicts must be done in advance and coded within the merge and transform rules set. The whole process afterwards can be executed predominantly automatically, but human intervention will be needed to deal with conflicts that have been overlooked.

4 Conclusions

We have discussed the problem of model versioning, and explored its use in an industrial software development process in which a human-intensive approach was used to identify and reconcile differences. This approach was compared with that offered by an automated model composition solution based on EML. The automated approach was found to be appropriate for dealing with many of the problems of model differencing and model version management, though it is by its nature incomplete. A particular challenge with using an automated rule-based solution like EML for model versioning will arise in terms of producing a complete set of rules for large metamodels. EML supports a notion of a *merging strategy* which provides a default set of rules for compositions involving models from the same metamodel, and this may help in providing default rules for comparison and differencing for managing model versions. There are also issues in terms of using a model composition tool with other modelling tools, e.g., for maintaining visual presentations.

By using EML to merge model versions we identified two key limitations: limited support for exception handling and support for managing MOF identifiers. Support for both features has been added to EML as a result of this experiment.. Technical limitations (e.g., the need to support additional modelling technologies, and the utility of a separate model comparison language) have also been identified, and this will guide our future work. We also plan an additional experiment to demonstrate that EML is sufficient to carry out all key tasks of model versioning, as identified in Section 2.

Acknowledgement

The work in this paper was supported by the European Commission via the MODELWARE project. The MODELWARE project is co-funded by the European Commission under the "Information Society Technologies" Sixth Framework

Programme (2002-2006). Information included in this document reflects only the authors' views. The European Commission is not liable for any use that may be made of the information contained herein.

References

1. Object Management Group. Meta Object Facility official web-site. Internet resource. http://www.omg.org/mof/.
2. Object Management Group. Model Driven Architecture official web-site. Internet resource. http://www.omg.org/mda/.
3. Object Management Group. XMI specification. Internet resource. http://www.omg.org/technology/documents/formal/xmi.htm.
4. Modelware IST Project. Internet resource. http://www.modelware-ist.org.
5. D. Kolovos, R.F. Paige, and F.A.C. Polack. The Epsilon Object Language (EOL), to appear in *Proc. EC-MDA 2006*, LNCS, Springer-Verlag, July 2006.
6. Atlas Model Management Architecture, available at http://www.sciences.univ-nantes.fr/lina/atl/AMMAROOT/, last accessed February 2006.
7. Epsilon Model Management Platform, available at http://www.cs.york.ac.uk/~dkolovos/epsilon, last accessed February 2006.
8. Enterprise Architect. http://www.sparksystems.com.au, last accessed January 2006.
9. D. Ohst, M. Welle and U. Kelter. Differences between Versions of UML Diagrams. In *9th European Software Engineering Conference*, pages 227–236. ACM Press, 2003.
10. Y. Lin, J. Zhang, and J. Gray. Model Comparison: A Key Challenge for Transformation Testing and Version Control in Model Driven Software Development. In *OOPSLA Workshop on Best Practices for Model-Driven Software Development*, 2004.
11. M. Alanen and I. Porres. Version Control of Software Models In *Advances in UML and XML-Based Software Evolution*, Idea Group Publishing, 2005.
12. M. Alanen and I. Porres. Difference and Union of Models. In *Proc. UML 2003 - The Unified Modeling Language*, LNCS 2863: 2-17, Springer-Verlag, Oct. 2003.
13. O. Kath, The AMEDATO Solution - A Success Story For Model Driven Technologies, Burlingame, CA, U.S.A. December 5-9, 2005 (AMEDATO Presentation: mda-user/05-12-01)
14. Revision Control Wikipedia Entry, http://en.wikipedia.org/wiki/Revision_control, last accessed February 2006.
15. D.S. Kolovos, R.F. Paige, and F.A.C. Polack. On-Demand Merging of Traceability Links with Models, submitted April 2006. http://www.cs.york.ac.uk/~dkolovos.

RubyTL: A Practical, Extensible Transformation Language

Jesús Sánchez Cuadrado[1], Jesús García Molina[2],
and Marcos Menarguez Tortosa[3]

[1] University of Murcia, Spain
jesusc@um.es
[2] University of Murcia, Spain
jmolina@um.es
http://dis.um.es/~jmolina
[3] University of Murcia, Spain
marcos@um.es

Abstract. Model transformation is a key technology of model driven development approaches. A lot of research therefore is being carried out to understand the nature of model transformations and find out desirable characteristics of transformation languages. In recent years, several transformation languages have been proposed.

We present the RubyTL transformation language which has been designed as an extensible language–a set of core features along with an extension mechanism. RubyTL provides a framework for experimenting with features of hybrid transformation languages. In addition, RubyTL has been created as a domain specific language embedded in the Ruby programming language. In this paper we show the core features of the language through a simple example and explain how the language can be extended to provide more features.

1 Introduction

The model-driven development (MDD) promotes an intensive use of models in the software life cycle. Software models are used to guide the construction of the application, and an automatic generation of source code from models is possible. At the end of 2000, OMG launched its initiative on the Model Driven Architecture^{TM} (MDA) [1], an MDD approach to address the integration challenges and the continuous changes in technology. Since then other approaches have been proposed [2][3][4], and MDD has become the new software paradigm that promises to improve software productivity and quality.

Model-to-model transformations are a key technology of the MDA approach. Most MDA research has been focused on understanding the nature of transformations and discovering desirable characteristics of model transformation languages and tools. In recent years, several transformation languages have been defined [5][6][7]. among them the QVT [8] standard proposed by the OMG. Today the success of QVT is not clear, and an alternative of a set of languages providing different styles makes sense [9].

A. Rensink and J. Warmer (Eds.): ECMDA-FA 2006, LNCS 4066, pp. 158–172, 2006.

In this paper we present RubyTL, a hybrid transformation language which has been designed with three main requirements in mind: i) rapid implementation, ii) it should allow us to experiment easily with different sets of features, iii) it should provide enough functionality for writing complex transformation definitions. Three design decisions have allowed us to satisfy these requirements: the technique of embedding a domain specific language (DSL) in a programming language such as Ruby facilitates the implementation; a plugin mechanism provides a way of adding extensions, so that the language may be configured to experiment with different sets of features; finally, Ruby constructs could be used to write some kinds of complex transformations, in which a declarative style is not the most suitable. In short, RubyTL is an extensible language which provides a set of core features and an extension mechanism to add new features.

The paper is organized as follows. Section 2 describes the basic features of RubyTL transformation language, while Section 3 shows the extension mechanism. In Section 4 the transformation process is discussed. Section 5 compares RubyTL with other proposed languages. Finally, in the last section we present our conclusions and outline future work.

2   Language Description

In this section we explain the RubyTL core features, and use a transformation definition example between two simple models to illustrate the syntax and semantics of the language. These features are the basic ones for a usable transformation language, but they can be extended, as explained in Section 3.

Ruby [10] is an object-oriented programming language which is gaining constantly acceptance, especially over the last year because of the success of Ruby on Rails, a web application framework. Ruby is dynamically typed and provides an expressive power similar to Smalltalk through constructs such as code blocks and metaclasses. Because of these characteristics, Ruby is very suitable to define internal DSLs [3].

Thus, RubyTL is a model transformation language defined as a Ruby internal DSL. RubyTL is a hybrid language since it provides both declarative and imperative constructs to write transformation definitions. Like ATL [6][9], a binding construct is used to express rules in a declarative way.

The RubyTL abstract syntax, expressed as a metamodel, is shown in Figure 1. As can be seen, a transformation definition is a set of transformation rules packaged in a transformation module, and each rule has a name and four parts:

- A *from* part, where the source element metaclass is specified.
- A *to* part, where the target element metaclass (or metaclasses) is specified.
- A *filter* part, where a condition over the source element is specified, such that the rule will only be triggered if the condition is satisfied; this part is optional and if a rule has no filter it will always be triggered.

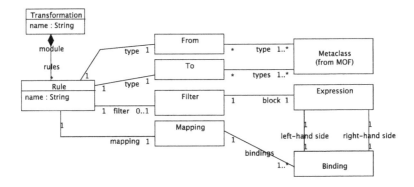

Fig. 1. Abstract syntax of RubyTL

- The *mapping* specifies relationships between source and target model elements. These relationships can be expressed either in a declarative style through of a set of *bindings* or in an imperative style using Ruby constructs. As we will explain below, a binding is a special kind of assignment that makes it possible to write *what needs to be transformed into what* instead of *how the transformation must be performed.* The declarative style is recommended, and Ruby imperative code should only be used when it is difficult to express declaratively some part of a transformation.

The concrete syntax of a RubyTL transformation definition is shown in Figure 2. It is determined by the fact that the language is implemented as a Ruby internal DSL (e.g. notice the use of do - end to write a code block and | | to set the block parameters). We have used a well-known technique to implement Ruby internal DSLs, that is, every keyword in the language is mapped to a method call and nested structures are mapped to parametrized code blocks. A discussion about the definition of Ruby internal DSLs can be found in [3].

A rule is defined by the **rule** method which expects two parameters: the rule name as a string and a code block which must have a structure conforming the concrete syntax of the rule element. The *from* and *to* parts of a rule are defined by the **from** and **to** methods, which expect as parameter a class belonging to source and target metamodels, respectively. The *filter* part of a rule is defined by the **filter** method which expects as parameter a block receiving an element of the source metaclass. The filter evaluates true if the attached block returns true, otherwise false[1]. The *mapping* part of a rule is defined by the **mapping** method which expects as parameter a block receiving the source element and one or more target elements. This block consists of either a set of *bindings* if a declarative style is adopted to implement the rule, or any other Ruby code if an imperative style is adopted. Bindings, which establish a mapping between source and target elements, have been implemented by overloading the Ruby

---

[1] In Ruby, the result of the last expression evaluated in a block is taken as the return value of such a block.

```
module <module-name> do

  rule <rule-name> do
    from <source-metaclass>
    to   {target-metaclass}

    filter do |source_element|
      <expression>
    end

    mapping do |<source_element>, {target_element}|
      {bindings}
      # bindings has the form:
      #     target_element.property = source_element.property
    end
  end

  # one or more rules
end
```

Fig. 2. Concrete syntax of RubyTL. In this notation <> means one ocurrence and {} means one or more ocurrences.

assignment operator. It is worth noting that RubyTL is easy to learn and, since a new notation has been built on top of Ruby, only a little knowledge of the Ruby language is required.

2.1 Example

Once we have outlined the structure of the language, we show an example of transformation definition and explain some language features. The example is a simple transformation from a class model to a Java model, such that i) each class is transformed to a Java class, ii) each public attribute of a class is transformed to a pair of get/set methods plus a private field in the Java class, and iii) each private attribute of a class is transformed to a private field in the Java class.

Figure 3 shows the source (Class) and target (Java) metamodels [11]. Class metamodel is defined inside a package named SimpleClass. According to this metamodel, a class is composed of attributes; an attribute has a name and a visibility and the type of an attribute can be a class or a primitive type. Java metamodel is defined inside a package named SimpleJava. According to this metamodel a Java class is composed of features which can be fields or methods; a method can have zero or more parameters; both features and parameters are typed, therefore they inherit from TypedElement, which gives them a type and a name.

The following transformation definition expresses the transformation from class model to Java model, as explained above. In *http://gts.inf.um.es/downloads*

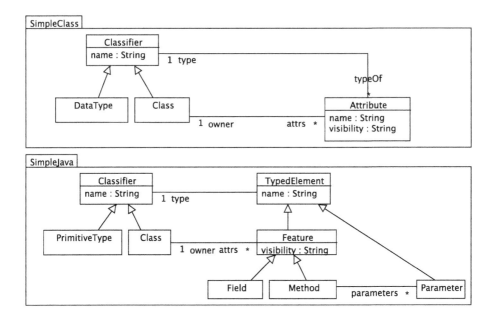

Fig. 3. Class metamodel and Java metamodel

a more complex version of this transfomation example, in which operations are introduced in the source metamodel, can be found.

```
module Transformation

    rule 'klass2javaclass' do
        from    SimpleClass::Class
        to      SimpleJava::Class
        mapping do |klass, javaclass|
            javaclass.name = klass.name
            javaclass.features = klass.attrs
        end
    end

    rule 'attribute2features' do
    from SimpleClass::Attribute
    to   SimpleJava::Field, SimpleJava::Method, SimpleJava::Method
        filter   do |attr|
            attr.visibility == 'public'
        end
        mapping do |attr, field, get, set|
            field.name = attr.name
            field.type = attr.type
```

```
                field.visibility = 'private'
                get.name = 'get'  + attr.name
                get.type = attr.type
                get.visibility = 'public'
                set.name = 'set' + attr.name
                set.visibility = 'public'
                set.parameters = attr.type
            end
        end

    rule 'attribute2field' do
        from    SimpleClass::Attribute
        to      SimpleJava::Field
        filter  do |attr|
            attr.visibility == 'private'
        end
        mapping do |attr, field|
            field.name = attr.name
            field.type = attr.type
            field.visibility = 'private'
        end
    end

    rule 'type2parameter' do
        from    SimpleClass::Classifier
        to      SimpleJava::Parameter
        mapping do |classifier, parameter|
            parameter.name = 'value'
            parameter.type = classifier
        end
    end

    rule 'datatype2primitive' do
        from    SimpleClass::DataType
        to      SimpleJava::PrimitiveType
        mapping do |src, target|
            target.name = src.name
        end
    end
end
```

A key point of the example is the binding construct. For instance, the binding `javaclass.features = klass.attrs` establishes a mapping from class attributes to Java features and yields to the execution of a rule that specifies such mapping. In this case both `attribute2features` and `attribute2field` rules are valid choices, but the filter of these rules allows the selection of only one, depending on the attribute visibility. If there are more than one possible choice, the decision of which rule will be selected depend on which plugins are installed. The default plugin simply raises an error if this occur, but a more complex plugin could provide the developer a mechanism to resolve such situation.

Note that bindings established between primitive types (e.g. `field.name = attr.name`) do not involve any rule invocation since they belong to the same underlying meta-metamodel.

It is worth mentioning how clear and legible the transformation shown above is. The non-intrusive Ruby syntax and the combination of code blocks and methods have allowed us to design a very clean language. An important feature of RubyTL, which makes it a clean language, is the implicit rule application driven by the bindings established between model elements. The order in which the rules are written in the transformation definition is irrelevant. Below, we discuss some features of the language, and use the example to explain them.

2.2 Naming Metaclasses

In the rules of the example, notice how the metamodel classes (metaclasses) are named in the *from* and *to* parts: the name of the metaclass is prefixed by the name of the package in which that metaclass is enclosed plus two colons. This usual notation can be used because the metaclasses organization in packages is replicated in Ruby as classes enclosed in modules (the name of a class is prefixed by the name of its module). For example, in RubyTL the `Attribute` metaclass enclosed in the `SimpleClass` package can be named as `SimpleClass::Attribute` because of a class named `Attribute` has been created within a module named `SimpleClass`.

2.3 Expressions

Ruby expressions are used to write filters and bindings. For example, in the `attribute2features` rule a simple example of filter expression can be seen: `attr.visibility == 'public'` checks if the attribute visibility is public.

It is very usual among transformation languages to use OCL as a query language to navigate source metamodels and to express conditions. RubyTL does not use any OCL-like query language since Ruby provides a powerful library for managing collections. This library offers great expressive power for writing expressions, due mainly to the existence of internal iterators. For example, `klass.attrs.select {|attr| attr.visibility == 'public'}` collects all the public attributes of a class.

2.4 Bindings and Rule Conformance

As we have noted, the mapping of a rule is composed of a set of bindings. The purpose of a binding is to specify a relationship between source and target elements and it is written as an assignment in the form `target.property = source-expression`, where:

- **source-expression** is a Ruby expression whose result is an element, or a collection of elements, belonging to the source model. Therefore, the type of the right-hand side of the assignment is given by the type (metaclass) of source-expression.
- **target** is a parameter of the mapping code block; this parameter denotes a target element to be created and its type is given in the *to* part of the rule.
- **property** must be a property of the previously created target element. The type of the left-hand side of the assignment is given by the type of the metamodel feature to which the property corresponds.

The definition of binding semantics is based on the "conforming rule" concept: "A rule conforms to a binding if the type in its *from* part conforms to the type in the right part of the binding assignment and the type in its *to* part conforms to the type in the left part of the binding assignment". The semantics of a binding can be defined as "there exists a conforming rule which transforms the type of the right-hand side of the binding assignment into the type of the left-hand side of the binding assignment".

In the example, the binding `javaclass.features = klass.attrs` in the `klass2javaclass` rule means that there exists a rule whose *from* part conforms to `SimpleClass::Attribute` and its *to* part conforms to `SimpleJava::Feature`. It is important to note that conformance between types must take into consideration inheritance between metaclasses, that is, a subtype conforms to its parent type. For example, the `attribute2features` rule conforms to the previous binding: its *from* part is `SimpleClass::Attribute` and its *to* part conforms to `SimpleJava::Feature` as both `SimpleJava::Field` and `SimpleJava::Method` are subtypes of `SimpleJava::Feature`.

A transformation definition is well-formed if for each binding involving two non-primitive types, as left-hand and right-hand side types, there exist one or more conforming rules but there is one and only one applicable rule. This means that if two or more conforming rules exist, their filter conditions must be exclusive, since only one of them can be applied. Since RubyTL is an embedded DSL, checking if a transformation definition is well-formed must be done at runtime.

2.5 Rule Evaluation

The evaluation of a transformation definition is driven by the bindings established between source and target elements. Assignment operator has been overloaded in such a way as to look for the correct rule to transform the right part of the binding assignment into the left part. Whenever a conforming rule is found it is applied using the element in the right part of the binding as the source element. If the type of the right-hand side element is a collection then it will be flattened and the rule will be applied once for every single element.

Every transformation must have an entry point in order to start the evaluation. The entry point is the first rule which is applied to all existing elements of the metamodel class specified in its *from* part (in the example it is applied to all instances of `SimpleClass::Class`). In Section 3 the language is modified to allow different entry points.

Applying a rule is simply executing the code block of its mapping part. Just before a rule is applied, new target elements are created–one element for each metaclass specified in the *to* part of the rule. While the first parameter of the mapping code block receives the source element, the rest of parameters receive the target elements created as a result of the rule execution. In the example, the mapping code block of the rule `attribute2features` has four parameters: `attribute` whose type is `SimpleClass::Attribute`, `field` whose type is `SimpleJava::Field`, and `get` and `set` whose type is `SimpleJava::Method`. We refer to the first parameter as *source parameter* and the rest as *target parameters*.

Execution of a rule returns one or more target elements which are assigned to the target feature related to the binding which triggers the rule. An important consideration is that a source element is never transformed twice by the same rule, that is, if a source element has been already transformed by a rule the previous result is returned. In the example, when the `attribute2features` rule is applied, the result of the binding `field.type = attribute.type` is stored and it is returned as the result of `get.type = attribute.type` when that rule is applied to resolve such binding.

This way of evaluating rules is applied when the rules are written in a declarative style based on bindings. Since the evaluation algorithm simply executes the Ruby code written in the mapping code blocks (notice bindings are a Ruby construct), it is also possible to write any Ruby construct inside the mapping part of a rule, thus yielding an imperative style.

2.6   Reflection

Another property of RubyTL is that it can be used in a reflective way. Just like reflective languages such as Java or Ruby, the main concepts of the language (transformation, rule, mapping and metaclass in this case), except binding, can be manipulated in runtime since they are Ruby objects. Therefore, they can be handled by RubyTL rules, making it possible to write a RubyTL transformation that takes another RubyTL transformation as input and generates a modified RubyTL transformation as output.The main limitation is that reflectivity cannot deal with bindings, since they are actually Ruby code. This makes that the output transformation cannot be serialized, but only used in runtime.

To sum up, RubyTL is an unidirectional hybrid language, which relies on the concepts of rule and binding to specify a transformation. Rules are resolved implicitily and in a deterministic way. Figure 4 shows the core features of RubyTL through a feature diagram according to [12].

3   Extension Mechanism

RubyTL is an extensible language, that is, the language has been designed as a set of core features with an extension mechanism. In the previous section we have explained the core features, and in this section we will present the extension mechanism based on the use of plugins.

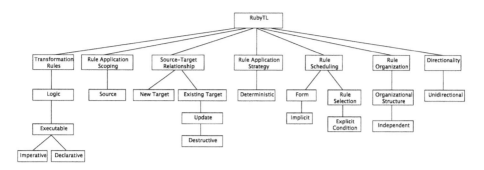

Fig. 4. Feature diagram showing the core features of RubyTL according to [12]

A plugin is a piece of Ruby code which modifies the runtime behaviour of the language by acting on the language syntax, the evaluation engine or even the model repository. The language can be considered a framework with a set of extension points that plugins can implement to add functionality. Some examples of additional features are the following: definition of new kinds of rules with a different behaviour, adding or removing syntax elements, renaming existing keywords, and modifying the transformation algorithm. Adding a new language feature is as simple as creating a plugin which implements a few extensions points. Obviously, a new feature can only be added if the necessary extension points have been planned.

The underlying idea behind this plugin mechanism is to have an extensible language intended to experiment with transformation languages features. Given a transformation problem, different combinations of features could be tried out in order to decide which is the most appropiate. Before the evaluation of a transformation, the developer should select the set of suitable plugins so that the language is properly configured. Each time a set of plugings is installed it is as if a new instance of the language were created.

Next we outline some advanced features implemented as plugins. In addition to implicit rule execution (expressed through bindings), it is possible to call rules explicitly by their name. A plugin traverses all rules in the transformation and creates a method with the same name of the rule which can be explicitly invoked. This plugin allows to call rules when mappings are written in an imperative style.

As mentioned before, the entry point of a transformation is the first rule. This behaviour is generalized by a plugin which implements a new kind of rules, named *top rules*. A top rule is always applied to all instances of the type specified in its *from* part, thus a transformation definition could have more than one entry point.

A rule never transforms a source element twice, and this is the behaviour that is usually expected. However, it may be necessary for a rule to be evaluated more than once for a particular source element (in ATL this is the default behaviour of rules). In order to provide this behaviour, we have implemented a plugin by adding a new kind of rule, named *creator*.

Another plugin allows mappings not to be restricted to one-to-one mappings, but it is possible to perform one-to-many and many-to-one mappings. At this moment, we are exploring different ways of writing such mappings in a declarative and readable manner. Finally, adding traceability support has been quite easy with a plugin.

In [12] several variation points in transformation languages are identified. Some of these variation points could be extensions to RubyTL, and they are summarized in Figure 5. For instance, the language can be modified to perform a transformation in several phases, where each phase has a specific purpose and only certain rules can be invoked in a given phase. It would allow us to think about a transformation as a set of refinement steps o phases, where each phase rely on the job accomplished by previous phases to complete its job.

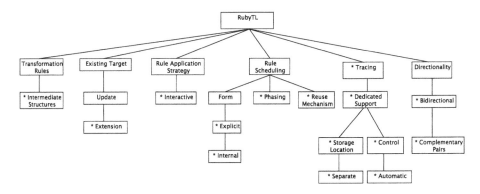

Fig. 5. Feature diagram showing possible language extensions according to [12]. Features marked * are suitable to be implemented as plugins.

There are several advantages of this extensible language approach. First, we have an environment in which to experiment mixing transformation languages features and where new features can be implemented if required. Second, implementation and maintenance are easier due to the modular design. Finally, both experimenting with features and even implementing new features does not require any knowledge about language internals. In addition, the fact that RubyTL is an internal DSL makes the plugin mechanism easy (e.g. modifying the language syntax in runtime).

4   Transformation Process

RubyTL has been implemented as a Ruby internal DSL. This key design choice means we are relying on the Ruby interpreter to parse and evaluate the transformation definition. The transformation engine and the XMI parser has also been implemented in Ruby.

Figure 6 is a process diagram which shows the components and the data involved in the whole transformation process. The steps are the following:

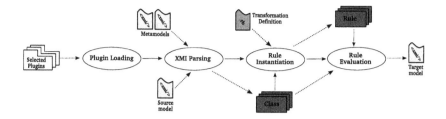

Fig. 6. Execution of RubyTL transformation engine

1. Since RubyTL has a pluggable design, the first step is to load the suitable plugins to configure the language with certain features. The user should select the plugins to be loaded, and the plugin mechanism check dependencies between them.
2. Source metamodel, target metamodel and source model are *xmi* files. A parser written in Ruby reads these input files and a set of Ruby classes are generated and loaded in the Ruby interpreter. These classes correspond to the classes defined in the source and target metamodels.
3. Once metamodels have been loaded, the transformation definition (it is in effect Ruby code) is read by the Ruby interpreter itself, which leads to the creation of a set of rule objects. These rules will be used by the transformation engine to perform the transformation.
4. As explained above, the transformation execution is driven by the bindings established in the mapping part of the rules. As the rule evaluation is being performed plugins implementing extension points could be called. For instance, if a plugin implements a strategy to choose between two or more applicable rules, it will be called when more than one rule can be applied.
5. The output of the transformation process is an *xmi* file containing a target model conforming to the target metamodel.

5   Related Work

Several classifications of model transformation approaches have been developed [12][13][14]. According to these classifications, the different model-model approaches can be grouped into three major categories: imperative, declarative and hybrid approaches. Imperative approaches are focused on *how* the transformation is done; the direct model manipulation approach is the most common mechanism which uses programming languages such as Java and procedural APIs. Declarative approaches, such as relational, functional or graph-based approaches, are focused on *what* the transformation does. Finally, hybrid approaches combine declarative and imperative constructs.

Some of the latest research efforts in model transformation languages are ATL, Tefkat, MTL and Kermeta. MTL and Kermeta [5][15] are imperative executable metalanguages not specifically intended to model-model transformation, but they are used because the versatility of their constructs provides great expressive power. However, the verbosity and the imperative style of these languages make writing complex transformations difficult because they are very large and not readable.

ATL is a hybrid language with a very clear syntax [6][9]. It includes several kinds of rules that facilitate writing transformations in a declarative style. However, the complete implementation of the language is not finished yet, and at the moment only one kind of rule can be used. Therefore it may be difficult to write some transformations declaratively. ATL and RubyTL share the same main abstractions, i.e. rule and binding, but ATL is statically typed while RubyTL uses dynamic typing. Static typing allows ATL to perform compile time checks, for instance to do optimizations. On the other hand, dynamic typing is less restrictive and offers more flexibility, which is very important for an extensible language such as RubyTL.

Tefkat is a very expressive relational language which is completely usable [7]. As noted in [16], writing complex transformations in a fully declarative style is not straightforward, and the imperative style may be more appropriate. That is why supporting a hybrid approach is a desirable characteristic for a transformation language, to help in writing practical transformation definitions. Tefkat only supports the declarative style, which could be an important limitation.

In [16], a set of quality requirements for a transformation language is presented. If RubyTL is evaluated against these requirements the following are found. Usability is facilitated providing a clear syntax and a style of writing transformation definitions appropriate to the usual background of the developers. Furthermore there is a good trade-off between conciseness and verbosity because it is a hybrid language–a declarative style allows rules to be written in a concise way and a more verbose imperative style can be used when is needed. Regarding scalability, the use of a native EMOF[2] repository provides a good performance, and it can cope with large transformations without loss of performance due to the nature of the language itself.

6   Conclusions and Future Work

In June 2005 we started a project for the creation of a framework intended to experiment with ATL-like transformation languages features, that is, features of hybrid languages in which the declarative style is expressed by a binding construct. The result of this project have been RubyTL, an extensible transformation language. We have gone through the following steps.

1. We observed that the technique of embedding a DSL in a programming language such as Ruby provided three important advantanges: i) a fast implementation, ii) changes in the language could be easily made, and iii) Ruby constructs can be used to write complex transformations.

---

[2] http://rmof.rubyforge.org/

2. We also realized that Ruby facilitates the creation of a plugin mechanism, so that RubyTL could be designed as an extensible language. We established the core features and the extension points, and we implement a set of plugins.
3. Finally, we have experimented with the language by writing transformation definitions.

In this paper we have presented RubyTL core features and the plugin mechanism. We have used a classical example for describing the language. This example has illustrated that RubyTL transformation definitions are readable and easy to understand because of the declarative style of the language. An imperative style could be adopted for complex transformations by writing Ruby code. Therefore, RubyTL is a fully usable language to write transformations of any level of complexity. But the main novelty of RubyTL is to provide a framework in which to experiment with features of hybrid transformation languages and to extend the language without taking into account its internals.

The fact that RubyTL is implemented as a Ruby internal DSL causes some limitations. The main drawback is that there is not a static type checking, due to Ruby being a dynamically typed language and it may make a good tool support difficult. In any case, we are currently working on the integration of our transformation engine inside the Eclipse platform by using RDT[3]. At this moment, an editor with syntax highlighting, a launcher for transformation definitions, and a configuration tool for plugins is available[4]. As future work, we expect to be able to provide a debugger to RubyTL, and we are exploring the possibility of using RubyTL to refactor Ruby code.

We will continue writing transformation definitions in the context of real applications to find problems which require new constructs in order to be declaratively specified.

Acknowledgments

This work has been partially supported by Fundación Seneca (Murcia, Spain), grant 00648/PI/04, and Consejera de Educación y Cultura (CARM, Spain), grant 2I05SU0018. Jesús Sánchez enjoys a doctoral grant from the Spanish Ministry of Education and Science.

References

1. Object Management Group. MDA Guide version 1.0.1. omg/2003-06-01, 2003. OMG document.
2. Jack Greenfield, Keith Short, Steve Cook, and Stuart Kent. *Software Factories: Assembling Applications with Patterns, Models, Frameworks, and Tools*. Wiley, 2004.

---

[3] http://rubyeclipse.sourceforge.net/
[4] http://gts.inf.um.es/downloads

3. Martin Fowler. Language workbenches: The killer-app for domain specific languages?, June 2005. http://www.martinfowler.com/articles/languageWorkbench.html.

4. Tony Clark, Andy Evans, Paul Sammut, and James Willans. *Applied Metamodelling, A Foundation for Language Driven Development*. Xactium, 2004.

5. Pierre-Alain Muller, Franck Fleurey, Didier Vojtisek, Zoé Drey, Damien Pollet, Frédéric Fondement, Philippe Studer, and Jean-Marc Jézéquel. On executable meta-languages applied to model transformations. In *Model Transformations In Practice Workshop*, Montego Bay, Jamaica, 2005.

6. Jean Bézivin, Grégoire Dupé, Frédéric Jouault, Gilles Pitette, and Jamal Eddine Rougui. First experiments with the ATL model transformation language: Transforming XSLT into XQuery. In *OOPSLA 2003 Workshop*, Anaheim, California, 2003.

7. Michael Lawley and Jim Steel. Practical declarative model transformation with Tefkat. In *Model Transformations In Practice Workshop*, Montego Bay, Jamaica, 2005.

8. OMG. Revised submission for MOF 2.0 Query/View/Transformation, 2005. http://www.omg.org/cgi-bin/apps/doc?ad/2005-03-02.

9. Frédric Jouault and Ivan Kurtev. Transforming models with ATL. In *Proceedings of the Model Transformations in Practice Workshop at MoDELS 2005*, Montego Bay, Jamaica, 2005.

10. D. Thomas. *Programming Ruby. The Pragmatic Programmers' Guide*. Pragmatic Bookshelf, 2004.

11. Anneke Kleppe, Jos Warmer, and Wim Bast. *MDA Explained. The Model Driven Architecture: Practice and Promise*. Addison-Wesley, 2003.

12. Krzysztof Czarnecki and Simon Helsen. Classification of model transformation approaches. In *Proceedings of the 2nd OOPSLA Workshop on Generative Technique in the Context of the Model Driven Architecture*, Anaheim, October 2003.

13. Tracy Gardner, Catherine Griffin, Jana Koehler, and Rainer Hauser. Review of OMG MOF 2.0 Query/Views/Transformations submissions and recommendations towards final standard, 2003.

14. Shane Sendall and Wojtek Kozaczynski. Model transformation: The heart and soul of model-driven software development. *IEEE Software*, 20(5):42–45, September/October 2003.

15. Pierre-Alain Muller, Franck Fleurey, and Jean-Marc Jézéquel. Weaving executability into object-oriented meta-languages. In Lionel C. Briand and Clay Williams, editors, *MoDELS*, volume 3713 of *Lecture Notes in Computer Science*, pages 264–278. Springer, 2005.

16. Tom Mens and Pieter Van Gorp. A taxonomy of model transformation. In *International Workshop on Graph and Model Transformation (GraMoT). A satellite event of the Fourth International Conference on Generative Programming and Component Engineering (GPCE)*, Tallinn, Estonia, September 2005.

MCC: A Model Transformation Environment

Anneke Kleppe

University Twente, Netherlands
a.kleppe@utwente.nl

Abstract. In the model driven software development process, software is built by constructing one or more models and transforming these into other models. In turn these output models may be transformed into another set of models until finally the output consists of program code that can be executed. Ultimately, software is developed by triggering an intricate network of transformation executions.

An open issue in this process is how to combine different transformation tools in a flexible and reliable manner in order to produce the required output. This paper presents a model transformation environment in which new transformation tools can be plugged in and used together with other available transformation tools. We describe how transformations can be composed. Furthermore, in the cause of answering the question where and how transformations can be successfully applied, we created a language-based taxonomy of model transformation applications.

Keywords: MDA, QVT, model driven development, model transformation, transformation taxonomy.

1 Introduction

Model Driven Architecture (MDA) [1, 2, 3] and Model Driven Engineering (MDE) [4] propose a software development process in which the key notions are models and model transformations. In this process, software is build by constructing one or more models, and transforming these into other models. The common view on this process is that the input models are platform independent and the output models are platform specific, and that the platform specific models can be easily transformed into a format that is executable. In other words, the model driven process is commonly viewed as a code generation process.

There is also a more generic view on model driven development [1, 5, 6], in which the difference between platform independent and platform specific is not dominant. The key to this more generic view is that the software development process is implemented by an intricate network of transformation executions, combined in various ways. This makes model driven development much more open and flexible.

For example, in figure 1 at the start there are two models, one that describes the functionality of the system (M_1) and one that describes the security aspects of the system (M_2). Because we require code that has a certain package structure, consisting of interfaces for each class in the main package and a subpackage containing the implementations, the first transformation we apply is one that changes M_1 into the

A. Rensink and J. Warmer (Eds.): ECMDA-FA 2006, LNCS 4066, pp. 173–187, 2006.

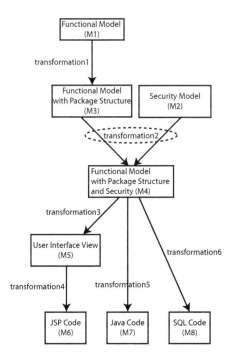

Fig. 1. Example of a combination of transformations

required structure. The resulting model is M_3. The second transformation merges M_3 with M_2, thus creating a model M_4 that has the right package structure and the required security aspects. Next we generate a model M_5 that contains all classes from M_4 that are directly visible to a certain actor named in the use cases in M_1. From this model we generate a platform specific model of the user interface (M_6). Meanwhile, we take M_4 as input to a transformation that generates a database model for the system (M_7), and we use M_4 again as input to a transformation to generates the middle tier of our system (M_8). Even in this fairly simply example, we can recognise six separate transformations.

In this paper we describe an open environment for model transformations in which users may combine the available tools that implement transformations, at will and apply them to models in various languages. Transformation tools may be added or removed, and are thereby available (or not) for composition. Language definitions may be added or removed thus enabling/disabling transformation of certain categories of models. The inclusion of separate language definitions also enables us to formalise and check the types of transformation tools, and the compositions of transformations that are allowed in the environment. We are working towards a model of MDA that makes the input/output relationship of transformations more explicit, and doing so makes transformation scripting look like expressions in functional languages.

We will often use a comparison with compiler technology to explain our ideas, because this comparison helps to illuminate the similarities and differences between traditional compilers and transformers, which are sometimes called *model compilers.*

Please note however, that not all knowledge of compiler construction can be transposed onto the field of model transformation directly. This is due to the fact that the languages in which the models are written are often visual and therefore multidimensional. (See [7]). Another difference is that transformers must be able to handle models in multiple languages. Whereas compilers work with multiple representations of the same program, from parse tree through several stages of abstract syntax tree, transformers work with multiple representations of multiple programs or models.

The paper is structured as follows. Section 2 explains why we have set out to implement an open model driven development environment. Section 3 gives a linguistically based taxonomy of transformations that is used in Section 4, which describes the formalisation of the units that are recognised in our environment. In section 5 the implementation of the environment is outlined. Section 6 contains references to related work and Section 7 concludes the paper with a short summary.

2 Rationale

This section explains the reasons for our approach to transformation composition. Key is the difference between internal and external composition. The environment that we describe in this paper is focused on external composition.

2.1 Internal Versus External Composition of Transformations

There are various approaches for model transformation that offer forms of compositionality, either based on sceduling, reuse, or logical composition of transformation rules. (See [6] for an overview.) For instance, the upcoming QVT standard [8] specifies a language in which one is able to express transformation definitions that consist of a number of mapping rules. The mapping rules may be combined by *calling*, or by using the *refines or extends* mechanisms.

We call this the *internal* composition of transformations, whereas the combination of transformation tools is called the *external* composition of transformations. The latter must tackle tool interoperability as well as the logical composition of transformation rules. In the following, the set of transformation rules that is implemented by a single execution of a single transformation tool will be called a *transformation definition*.

A special concern with interoperability of transformation tools is that not all transformation tools are ready to execute any transformation definition. Some are what we call *specialized transformation* tools, in which the transformation definition is hardcoded, in contrast to the *general transformation* tools, which are able to execute any transformation definition written in a given transformation language.

We focus on external composition of transformations, because it offers the user more flexibility, such as enabling the user to combine transformation tools from different sources. For example, open source transformation tools could be combined with vendor specific tools, and specialized transformation tools could be combined with general transformation tools.

2.2 Towards an Open Model Driven Development Environment

In our view there is ample reason for creating tool support for external composition of transformations. The user of transformation tools could very much benefit from a tool chain of transformation engines, each executing small parts of the transformation execution network. This gives the user full control over the process, thus enabling her or him to be most productive.

An open environment for model driven development should offer multiple transformation tools, multiple transformation definitions in various transformation languages, and multiple tools for other model-related services, such as model creation, or even model checking tools like SPIN [9]. The environment should take care of the concrete interoperability between the tools, and it must provide a means to specify the network of transformation executions that is necessary to produce the required outcome. To prove the feasibility of this approach we have build an open tool environment for transformation execution, which will be described in section 5.

3 Taxonomy of Model Transformation Applications

In this section we present a taxonomy of model transformations based on a linguistic approach. This taxonomy is needed for the formalisation of transformation composition in section 4. The transformations are categorised according to the part of its source and target language definition it addresses. In order to clearly define this taxonomy we first need to formalise our notion of language.

3.1 Language Definitions

Because a model transformation always relates the language of its source model with the language of its target model, one has to be aware of the structure of the definition of these languages in order to understand the different applications of model transformations. The formalisation of language given by Chen e.a. in [10] is a simple and elegant one. They define a language to be a 5-tuple $L = <A, C, S, M_S, M_C>$ consisting of abstract syntax (A), concrete syntax (C), syntax mapping (M_C), semantic domain (S), and semantic mapping (M_S).

However, for our purposes this formalism is too simple. We need to take into account languages that have multiple concrete syntaxes. For instance, one could argue that the visual diagrams of an UML model and the textual XMI format of that model are representations of the same abstract syntax graph[1] in two different concrete syntaxes. (The latter is called the serialization syntax in [11].) Another example is OCL, for which we have defined a second concrete syntax that resembles SQL [12]. Therefore, we extend the given formalism into the following.

---

1 Instead of using the more common term abstract syntax tree, we use the term abstract syntax graph to stress the fact that such a representation can be made for also languages that are context-free or type 0 in the Chomsky hierarchy.

Definition 1: *(Language) A language is a 5-tuple L = < A, SC, S, M$_S$, SM$_C$> consisting of an abstract syntax (A), a set of concrete syntaxes (SC), a set of syntax mappings (SM$_C$), a semantic domain (S), and a semantic mapping (M$_S$). For each element C$_n$ in SC, there is an element M$_{Cn}$ in SM$_C$, which is a mapping between C$_n$ and the abstract syntax A.*

Most of the times the mapping between a concrete syntax and the abstract syntax will be bi-directional, but this is not necessarily so. Sometimes a concrete syntax is used only to visualize a model, not to edit it or create it. The syntax mapping may be defined in either way; from abstract to concrete syntax, or from concrete to abstract syntax, or bi-directional. In section 4.1 we will look into this in more detail.

Another observation that needs to be made is that the semantics of some languages are not defined by giving a direct mapping of the abstract syntax to the semantic domain, instead they are defined by mapping the abstract syntax to the abstract syntax of another language of which the semantics are known. This type of semantics is known as translational semantics. We formalise this as follows.

Definition 2: *(Translational semantic mapping) A translational semantic mapping for language L$_i$ with the use of language L$_j$ is a semantic mapping TransM$_{Si}$ = M$_{Aij}$ ° M$_{sj}$, where M$_{Aij}$ is a mapping of the abstract syntax A$_i$ of L$_i$ to the abstract syntax A$_j$ of L$_j$.*

3.2 Types of Transformations

In this section we present our taxonomy of transformations based on the formalisation of language in the previous section. An overview of the various types of transformations can be found in table 1, an overview of the relation between the transformation types and elements of the source and target language definition can be found in figure 2. Note that although the arrows in the figure indicate a bi-directionality, not all transformations need to be defined bi-directionally. The arrows indicate that transformations in both directions are possible.

Table 1. A taxonomy of transformations

Name	Category	Maps .. to ..
Syntax transformation	*Intra-language*	$A_i \rightarrow C_i$ and/or $C_i \rightarrow A_i$
Semantic definition	*Intra-language*	$A_i \rightarrow S_i$
Refactoring	*Intra-model*	$A_i \rightarrow A_i$
View transformation	*Intra-model*	$A_i \rightarrow A_i$
Structure transformation	*Inter-model*	$A_{i*} \rightarrow A_{j*}$
Stream-based transformation	*Inter-model*	$C_i \rightarrow C_j$
Hybrid syntax transformation	*Inter-model*	$A_i \rightarrow C_j$

Intra-language transformations. The first category of transformations is formed by the *intra-language transformations*. Transformations in this category are used to

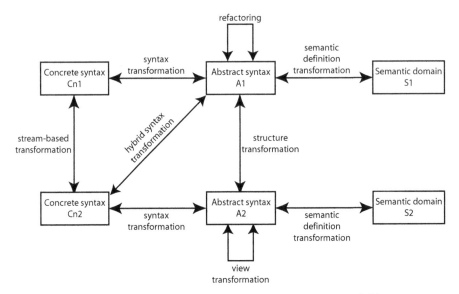

Fig. 2. The relation between transformations and language definition

define a language. They either specify one of the syntax mappings (M_{Cn}), or the semantic mapping (M_S). A transformation that implements a syntax mapping is called *syntax transformation*. An example of a syntax transformation is the MOF to text standard [13]. A transformation that implements a semantic mapping is called *semantic definition transformation*[2]. An example can be found in [14]. Note that in the case of a translational semantic mapping, either or both of the constituting mappings may be defined by an automated transformation.

Intra-model transformations. The second category of transformations is formed by the *intra-model transformations*. In this case the transformation is applied to a single model. Logically, the source and target model of the transformation are one and the same, and therefore the source and target language are the same as well. Again, we can recognise two subtypes in this category. The first subtype consists of the transformations that change the source model, which are also called *refactorings*, or *in-place transformations*. A refactoring is a mapping from the abstract syntax A_i of language L_i to the same abstract syntax A_i.

The second type of intra-model transformations are transformations that generate views. *View transformations*, like refactorings are mappings from abstract syntax A_i of language L_i to the same abstract syntax A_i, but they serve a different purpose. View transformations will never make changes in the source model, which is the purpose of a refactoring. Views present the same system from a different viewpoint, using different criteria. Views are always dependent upon their source model. If the source model changes the view should change. If the source model is removed, the view

---

[2] The word 'definition' is added here in order to avoid confusion with the term *semantic transformation*, which is often being used to indicate a transformation that is semantics preserving.

should be removed. We therefore consider the view to be part of the original source model, hence its category. The close link between source model and view also makes traceability a key issue to view transformations.

Inter-model transformations. The last category contains the transformations that are commonly considered to be the essence of model driven development: the *inter-model transformations*. Here, one model is transformed into another model, where the output model is often written in another language. Again, we can recognise a number of subtypes of this category. The first is very well-known in practise, namely the change of a textual representation of a model (or program) into another textual format. This is a mapping of a concrete syntax to another concrete syntax. We call this type of transformations *stream-based transformations*. The name indicates that these transformations are focused on textual, i.e. one-dimensional languages, which are handled sequentially, i.e. one token after another. Examples of this type of transformation are templates written in languages like AWK.

The second type of inter-model transformations maps an abstract syntax graph into a different abstract syntax graph. We call them *structure transformations*. Note that there is a difference between refactorings and structure transformations, even when the language of the source and target models are the same. A refactoring makes in-place changes in a model, therefore the input and output model is the same. A structure transformation produces a new model; the source and target model are two separate models. This might seem a minor difference from a theoretical viewpoint, but from the point of tool interoperability it is important.

What is making matters more complex is that structure transformations may take multiple input models and produce multiple output models. We describe in more detail how we handle this in section 4.3. In essence, the latest version of the QVT standard [15] focuses on structure transformations, although - as its name suggests - it should also provide a solution for defining views.

A third, very special case of inter-model transformations are the transformations that take an abstract syntax graph in one language as source and produce text in another language as output. Examples are transformations implemented in Velocity [16] templates. In this case the structure of the source model is available in the form of an abstract syntax graph, but the output is a character stream. We call this type of transformations *hybrid syntax transformations*. These transformations map the abstract syntax of one language upon the concrete syntax of another.

4   Elements in a Transformation Environment Architecture

This section describes the elements that constitute an open model driven development transformation environment.

4.1   Executable Units: Creators, Transformers, and Finishers

Because we focus on automation, the basic building blocks in our MDA environment are the tools that are able to execute transformations. The environment defines three tool types: the creator, the transformer, and the finisher, which are defined as follows.

Definition 3: *(Creator) A creator is a tool that implements for some language L a mapping M_{Cn} in the direction from the concrete syntax to the abstract syntax.*

A creator is able to produce the abstract syntax graph of a model based on some concrete syntax, in other words, it implements a unidirectional syntax transformation. In traditional compiler terminology the creator would encompass the lexical analysis (scanning), syntax analysis (parsing), and semantic analysis (type checking, amongst other things). However, the creator concept is broader than the traditional parser concept. Because it is well-known that the complexity of parsing visual languages is in general NP-complete (see [7] for an overview of approaches to parsing visual languages), the creation of an abstract syntax graph is often automated using a syntax-directed editor. Such an editor is also considered to be a creator. Multiple creators may be defined for one language.

Definition 4: *(Finisher) A finisher is a tool that implements for some language L a mapping M_{Cn} in the direction from the abstract syntax to the concrete syntax.*

A finisher is able to take an abstract syntax graph of a model and to create some concrete syntax representation of this model. It could, for instance, write the model to file. Finishers, like creators, implement syntax transformations, but they may also implement hybrid syntax transformations. In traditional compiler terminology the finisher would be called a deparser. Again, the concept finisher is broader than the concept deparser. For instance, a syntax directed editor could provide a diagram generating option that implements the finisher functionality. Multiple finishers may be defined for the same language. Although in general the mapping M_{Cn} will be bi-directional, there is no need in the MDA environment to have a corresponding finisher for each creator, or vice versa.

Definition 5: *(Transformer) A transformer is a tool that implements the mapping $A_{i^*} \rightarrow A_{j^*}$.*

A transformer is able to take one or more abstract syntax graphs and to transform them into different abstract syntax graphs. It implements either a refactoring, a view transformation, or a structure transformation, in other words, it implements a model-to-model transformation.

4.2 Non-executable Units: ModelTypes or Languages

The fourth building block in our MDA environment specifies the type of the models to be transformed. This is an essential unit though it is not executable. It is defined as follows.

Definition 6: *(ModelType) The type A_m of a model m is the abstract syntax of the lan-guage in which M is written.*

We use the term *ModelType* instead of language to distinguish between the specification of a language and a certain implementation of this language. The relation between a model and its *ModelType* is called the *instanceOf relationship* in [17], whereas the relation between a model and its language is called the *modelOf* relationship.

Because transformations may take multiple input models and produce multiple output models, we define the following.

Definition 7: *(Input types). Each executable unit (creator, transformer, or finisher) T defines an m-tuple of its input types* $T_{inTypes} = \{A_i .. A_m\}$.

Definition 8: *(Output types). Each executable unit T defines an m-tuple of its output types* $T_{outTypes} = \{A_i .. A_m\}$.

Note that in the above definitions we focus on the abstract syntax, therefore $C_{inTypes}$ of creator C will be the empty sequence, and likewise, for finisher F, $F_{outTypes}$ will be the empty sequence.

Not present in the model driven development environment are semantic definition transformations or stream-based transformations. The reason to exclude the latter is that model driven development focuses on structure instead of streams. Semantic definition transformations are excluded because their nature does not permit their use in a chain of transformation executions.

4.3 Combinations of Executable Units

Using the definitions from the previous section, it is easy to see that the functionality provided by a traditional compiler would be represented by a simple creator-transformer-finisher combination. The challenge of model driven development, how-ever, is not to rebuild compilers in a different fashion, but to use a network of trans-formers and (intermediate) models to produce the desired output. Therefore, in this section we present a means to define this network.

We propose to use the following three commonly known combinatorial operators which have proven to be successful in the history of computing.

- **Sequence:** a combination of two executable units; one is executed before the other, and the output of the first is the input of the second.
- **Parallel:** a combination of many executable units; the input to all of them is the same (set of) input model(s), the output is the combination of all the outputs of all of them.
- **Choice:** a combination of an ordered list of executable units; the first unit is executed if the conditions posed by this unit are met by its input, else the next unit is tried, until finally one of them is executed, or it is clear that the input does not meet the conditions of any of the units.

In order to formalise these operators, we need to introduce the following definitions.

Definition 9: *(Transformer type) The type of transformer T is the type of the function* $FUN_T: T_{inTypes} \rightarrow T_{outTypes}$

Definition 10: *(Creator type) The type of a creator C is the type of the function* $FUN_C: S_{empty} \rightarrow C_{outTypes}$, *where S_{empty} represents the empty sequence.*

Definition 11: *(Finisher type) The type of a finisher F is the type of the function* FUN_F: $F_{inTypes}$ -> S_{empty}.

Definition 12: *(Transformer condition) The condition $COND_T$ of transformer T is the type of the function $COND_T$: $T_{inTypes}$ -> Boolean.*

Using the types of the basic elements and the combinatorial operators, we define a language of transformation expressions, according to the following rules.

1. The application of transformer T, denoted by $T(m_1, .., m_n)$, is allowed when every m_i represents a model, and the n-tuple of types of these models $\{A_{m1}, .., A_{mn}\}$ is equal to $T_{inTypes}$.

2. The conditional application of a transformer T, denoted by $T_{cond}(m_1, .., m_n)$, is allowed when the application of T is allowed and $COND_T(m_1, .., m_n)$ = true.

3. The sequence of unit T_1 followed by unit T_2, denoted by $[T_1 ; T_2]$, is allowed when $T_{1.outTypes}$ is equal to $T_{2.inTypes}$. Each unit can be either a creator, transformer, or finisher. The type of the combination is $FUN_{T1} \circ FUN_{T2}$: $T_{1.inTypes}$ -> $T_{2.outTypes}$

4. Unit T_1 and unit T_2 may always be combined in parallel, denoted by $[T_1 \| T_2]$. The type of the combination is $T_{1.inTypes} \Delta T_{2.inTypes}$ -> $T_{2.outTypes} + T_{2.out-Types}$, where + denotes the concatenation of both tuples, and Δdenotes a right tuple overwrite. A right tuple overwrite creates a tuple with the union of all the elements of the two tuples. Whenever both tuples have a given element, the value of the leftmost argument tuple is taken. Note that the output models of both participating units are separate; T_1 and T_2 do not generate parts of the same model, both produce their own output models.

5. A 'choice' combination of transformer T_1 and transformer T_2, denoted by $[T_1$ or $T_2]$, is always allowed. The type of the combination is $T_{1.inTypes} \Delta T_{2.inTypes}$ -> $T_{2.outTypes} + T_{2.outTypes}$, where + denotes the concatenation of both tuples, and Δdenotes a right tuple overwrite. The difference with the parallel operator is that both participating transformations will be applied conditional, as define in rule 2.

Compositions of transformers can be regarded as transformers themselves, thus allowing compositions to be used as part of another combination. The combinatorial operators defined above are higher order functions known amongst others from functional programming languages like Haskell [18].

5   The MDA Control Center Implementation

In section 2.1 we explained why a model driven development environment should be open to the addition of new transformation tools and why it should provide a means to combine the execution of transformation tools in a tool execution chain. In sections 3 and 4 we described the types of elements that can be part of such a development environment. In this section we describe how we have implemented such an environment.

5.1 The MCC Eclipse Plug-In

To implement our MDA environment we have created an Eclipse plug-in called *MDA Control Center (MCC)*. This environment uses the Eclipse extension point mechanism [19] to recognise the available units. It defines four extension points, each of which specifies a certain type of (Eclipse) plug-in.

5.2 Extension Points for the Executable Units

Three MCC extension points specify the three types of executable units defined in section 4.1: *Creator, Transformer*, and *Finisher*. Note that from the point of view of the MCC a transformer, creator, or finisher does not represent the actual tool, instead it represents the service offered by the tool. This also means that it is possible that a single plug-in implements multiple extension points. For example, the same plug-in may function both as a creator and as a transformer. In fact, one could build a plug-in that implements all extension points. In the following we will use the term *MCC service* to indicate either a creator, transformer, or a finisher.

An example of the declaration of a plug-in that implements both the transformer and the creator extensions points can be found in figure 3. In this example the creator reads resources of type "file" that have ".alan" as file extension, and produces models of type "IAlanModel", whereas the transformer takes as input an "IAlanModel" and produces as output an "OJPackage". (Alan is one of the languages for which we have defined a number of MCC services, see for more information [20], and "OJPackage" is part of our implementation of the Java metamodel, which is part of the Octopus tool [21].)

Note that each transformer may define multiple inputs and multiple outputs. In that case the order in which the outputs appear in the declaration determines the order of the elements of the tuples $T_{inTypes}$ and $T_{outTypes}$, as defined in section 4.3.

5.3 Extension Point for the Non-executable Unit

The fourth extension point specifies the type of the models to be transformed as defined in section 4.2: the *ModelType*. The fact that the MCC deals with in-memory representations of models, i.e the abstract syntax graphs, means that resources like files are not considered to be models. Another consequence of the focus on abstract syntax graphs, is that it is necessary to handle implementations of languages. *A ModelType* plug-in defines an implementation of the metamodel of a language.

For instance, it is not enough to claim that a certain model is a UML model as specified by the UML 2.0 superstructure [17], instead we need to know from which set of classes that implement the UML 2.0 superstructure, this model is an instantiation. There can be large differences between a model that is an instantiation of one UML implementation and another. For example, the Eclipse UML2 project [22] defines an implementation in Java based on EMF [23], but many other implementations —in other languages— are possible.

```
<plugin
  id="com.klasse.alan.alan2java"
  ....
  <extension
      point="com.klasse.mdacontrolcenter.creator">
    <creator
        resource="file"
        filter=".alan"
        output="com.klasse.alan.abstractsyntax.IAlanModel"
        label="Alan Model Creator"
        class="com.klasse.alan.MCCCreator">
    </creator>
  </extension>
  <extension
      point="com.klasse.mdacontrolcenter.transformer">
    <transformer
        output="com.klasse.javametamodel.OJPackage"
        input="com.klasse.alan.abstractsyntax.IAlanModel"
        label="Alan to Java Transformer"
        class="com.klasse.alan.javagen.MCCTransformer">
    </transformer>
  </extension>
</plugin>
```

Fig. 3. Example extension point implementations

5.4 Executing Transformations

The MCC offers its users the possibility to run simple Creator-Transformer-Finisher combinations without using any complex composition facilities. Each resource is associated with certain extra properties. Using these properties the user can indicate for each resource separately which creator should be used, and which transformer and/or finisher should be used to work on the thus created in-memory representation. Next to the properties view the MCC offers a button and a resource menu item called *Run Transformer*. By clicking this button or selecting the menu, the user can initiate a run of the service combination given by the properties of the given resource.

In order to make the combinations of executable units as defined in section 4.3 available to MCC users, we have created a small scripting language for transformation combinations. Each script itself defines a new transformer, which is available for use in another script or in a creator-transformer-finisher combination as defined by the resource properties. An example of an MCC script can be found in figure 4. It implements the example given in figure 1 in section 1.

```
transformer kleppe.myFirstScript (in m1: FuncModel,
                                     m2: Security)
{
    m4 := T2( T1( m1 ), m2 )->first();
    T4 ( T3(m4) ) || T5(m4) || T6(m4)
}
```

Fig. 4. An example transformer script

5.5 Type Checking

The interoperability between the executable units in MCC is taken care of by the Eclipse environment. However, MCC performs extra type checks on (the composition of) the executable units. A first type check that is performed by the MCC, is a check on the plug-in declarations. For each plug-in that declares input and output types, the types are matched against the types known in the MCC.

Additional type checking in MCC is implemented by dedicated operations that compare the type of each element in the list of inputs of the transformation with the required inputs ($T_{inTypes}$). If the types do not match, the user is issued an error message.

6 Related Work

We have found that the work of Xavier Blanc e.a. [24, 25] is closely related to the work described in this paper. Their Model Bus tackles the same problems in the manner of OMG's CORBA. There are however, a few differences, the most important one being that the MCC offers a scripting language to define new services.

Other work that has resemblance to our work is [26]. The differences between their ToolBus approach and MCC are that the ToolBus uses a common data representation whereas MCC offers more generality and flexibility because it uses several data representations, which are determined by the ModelTypes that are available in the environment. Furthermore, the ToolBus enables communication between processes other than data exchange, using messages or notes. The MCC does not offer this possibility.

The UMLAUT transformation toolkit [27] is build with the same intension as MCC: to provide the model designer with a freedom of choice with regard to combinations of transformations to be executed. The differences are that UMLAUT is limited to transforming UML models whereas MCC is able to handle models written in various languages. Furthermore, although UMLAUT provides a transformation library and a pluggable architecture, the composition of transformations in UMLAUT is internal rather than external.

7 Summary and Future Work

In this paper we have defined the elements that should be present in an open model driven development environment. In the process we have established the difference between internal and external composition of transformations, and we have developed a linguistically based taxonomy of transformations. Furthermore, we have described an implementation of the open model driven development environment, which includes a scripting language that enables the user to define his own transformations based on the transformation tools that are available.

To support the interoperability of transformation tools, every unit must be defined as Eclipse plug-in, but no further restrictions apply. This makes the MCC one of the most generic MDA environments. What is new in our approach is the application of knowlegde from the fields of compiler construction and functional programming to the area of model transformations. Our research has shown that the well-known concepts from the area of compiler construction have a limited application in the area of model transformation. In this paper we have extended these concepts to fit them to the new challenges of model driven development. In the future, our work will focus on taking into account performance or optimization (i.e., not model) parameters to transformations.

References

[1] Anneke G. Kleppe, Jos Warmer, and Wim Bast. *MDA Explained: The Model Driven Architecture: Practice and Promise.* Addison-Wesley Longman Publishing Co., Inc., Boston, MA, USA, 2003.

[2] Stephen J. Mellor, Kendall Scott, Axel Uhl, and Dirk Weise. *MDA Distilled, Principles of Model_Driven Architecture.* Addison-Wesley, 2004.

[3] David Frankel. *Model Driven Architecture: Applying MDA to Enterprise Computing.* John Wiley & Sons, 2003.

[4] Stuart Kent. Model driven engineering. In *Proceedings of IFM2002*, volume 2335 of LNCS. Springer-Verlag, 2002.

[5] Colin Atkinson and Thomas Kühne. A generalized notion of platforms for model-driven development. *Model-driven Software Development - Volume II of Research and Practice in Software Engineering,* pages 139–178, 2005.

[6] Krzysztof Czarnecki and Simon Helsen. Classification of model transformation approaches. In Jorn Bettin, Ghica van Emde Boas, Aditya Agrawal, Ed Willink, and Jean Bezivin, editors, *Proceedings of the 2nd OOPSLA Workshop on Generative Technique in the Context of the Model Driven Architecture,* Anaheim, October 2003. ACM Press.

[7] R. Bardohl, M. Minas, A. Schurr, and G. Taentzer. Application of graph transformation to visual languages, 1999.

[8] Revised submission for MOF 2.0 Query/Views/Transformations RFP. Technical Report ad/2005-03-02, OMG, March 2005.

[9] Gerard J. Holzmann. The model checker SPIN. *IEEE Transactions on Software Engineering,* 23(5):279–295, 1997.

[10] Kai Chen, Janos Sztipanovits, Sherif Abdelwalhed, and Ethan Jackson. Semantic anchoring with model transformations. In Alan Hartman and David Kreische, editors, *Model Driven Architecture – Foundations and Applications,* volume 3748 of LNCS. Springer-Verlag, November 2005.

[11] Jack Greenfield, Keith Short, Steve Cook, and Stuart Kent. *Software Factories, Assembling Applications with Patterns, Models, Frameworks, and Tools.* John Wiley & Sons, 2004.

[12] Jos Warmer and Anneke Kleppe. *The Object Constraint Language: Getting Your Models Ready for MDA.* Addison-Wesley Longman Publishing Co., Inc., Boston, MA, USA, 2003.

[13] MOF Model to Text Transformation Language RFP. Technical Report ad/04-0407, OMG, 2004.

[14] H. Kastenberg, A. Kleppe, and A. Rensink. Engineering objectoriented semantics using graph transformations. Technical Report, University of Twente, December 2005. Pre-final version available at http://www.cs.utwente.nl/rensink/papers/taaldraft.pdf.

[15] MOF QVT final adopted specification. Technical Report ptc/05-11-01, OMG, 2005.

[16] Velocity. http://jakarta.apache.org/velocity/.

[17] Ivan Kurtev Ivanov. *Adaptability of Model Transformations*. PhD thesis, University Twente, Enschede, The Netherlands, May 2005.

[18] Simon Peyton Jones and John Hughes (editors). Haskell 98: A non-strict, purely functional language. Technical report, February 1999.

[19] Erich Gamma and Kent Beck. *Contributing to Eclipse, Principles, Patterns, and Plug-Ins*. Addison-Wesley, 2004.

[20] Anneke Kleppe. Towards general purpose high level software languages. In Alan Hartman and David Kreische, editors, *Model Driven Architecture – Foundations and Applications,* volume 3748 of *LNCS*. Springer-Verlag, November 2005.

[21] Octopus: Ocl tool for precise UML specifications. http://www.klasse.nl/octopus.

[22] Eclipse uml 2 project. http://www.eclipse.org/uml2.

[23] The eclipse modeling framework. http://www.eclipse.org/emf.

[24] Xavier Blanc, Marie-Pierre Gervais, and Prawee Sriplakich. Model bus: Towards the interoperability of modelling tools. In *Proceeding of the Workshop on Model Driven Architecture - Foundations and Applications 2004,* Linkping, Sweden, June 2004. Linkping University.

[25] Xavier Blanc, Marie-Pierre Gervais, Maher Lamari, and Prawee Sriplakich. Towards an integrated transformation environment (ITE) for model driven development (MDD). In *Proceedings of the Invited Session "Model Driven Development", 8th World Multi-Conference on Systemics, Cybernetics and Informatics (SCI'2004),* Orlando, USA, July 2004.

[26] J.A. Bergstra and P. Klint. The discrete time toolbus – a software coordination architecture. *Science of Computer Programming,* 31:205–229, 1998.

[27] Jean-Marc Jézéquel, Wai-Ming Ho, Alain Le Guennec, and Franccois Pennaneac'h. UMLAUT: an extendible UML transformation framework. In Robert J. Hall and Ernst Tyugu, editors, *Proc. of the 14th IEEE International Conference on Automated Software Engineering, ASE'99*. IEEE, 1999.

A Model Driven Integration Architecture for Ontology-Based Context Modelling and Context-Aware Application Development

Shumao Ou[1,2], Nektarios Georgalas[1], Manooch Azmoodeh[1],
Kun Yang[2], and Xiantang Sun[3]

[1] British Telecom Group, Ipswich, UK
{shumao.ou, nektarios.georgalas, manooch.azmoodeh}@bt.com
[2] University of Essex, Colchester, UK
{smou, kunyang}@essex.ac.uk
[3] University of Aberdeen, Aberdeen, UK
xsun@csd.abdn.ac.uk

Abstract. Context-awareness is a very important feature for pervasive services to enhance their flexibility and adaptability to changing conditions and dynamic environments. Using ontologies to model context information and to reason about context at a semantic level has attracted a lot of interest in the research community. However, most of the proposed solutions are ad hoc or proprietary. Therefore, employing standard approaches to formulate the development process becomes of importance. In this paper we examine how OMG's Model Driven Architecture (MDA) can be applied to tackle the issues of context modelling and Context-Aware Application (CAA) modelling and development. A Context Ontology Model (COM) is presented to model context information at two levels: upper-level and extended specific level. A Model Driven Integration Architecture (MDIA) is then proposed to integrate rigorous model specifications and generate CAA implementations either semi-automatically or automatically.

1 Introduction

In order to flexibly adapt to changing conditions and dynamic environments, pervasive services need to become more context-aware. A pervasive service can be a simple service such as helping a user on a mobile device (such as a PDA or a smartphone) to find their favourite restaurant in the immediate vicinity around their current location. The challenges of context semantic representation, inference and interoperation in pervasive computing environments are well recognised. Earlier research work focused on context information gathering and integration aiming to achieve reusability for higher level pervasive applications [1, 2]. Other work studied the modelling of information from types of context in a platform independent way in order to support context management and interoperation [3, 9]. More recently, the notion of *ontology*, which is often used by Artificial Intelligence practitioners for knowledge representation, has emerged as a new approach to context modelling. Ontologies can model context at a semantic level establishing a common understanding of terms and meaning and enabling context *sharing*, *reasoning* and *reuse* in pervasive environments [9, 10, 11, 15].

A. Rensink and J. Warmer (Eds.): ECMDA-FA 2006, LNCS 4066, pp. 188–197, 2006.

Languages such as W3C's OWL [13] or RDF Schema can be used to specify ontologies in a machine-interpretable way. Without loss of generality, we consider both of them in this paper. An ontology includes definitions of commonly understood vocabularies and of logic statements that specify what each term in the vocabularies mean and how they relate to each other. An ontology removes ambiguity and is semantically independent to context. Ontology is, therefore, useful in bridging terminology differences thus enhancing interoperability. The concepts and logic expressed by ontologies are commonly accepted and can be communicated between human users and computer programs from different vendors. These features make ontologies the right mechanism for modelling context information in support of Context-Aware Application (CAA) development for pervasive computing environments, as they tackle heterogeneity introduced by diverse device technologies, the multiplicity of vendors developing CAAs and various operating systems that CAAs run on.

The use of ontologies to model context augments the development process of pervasive services with additional complexity introduced by the work required for ontology specification and management. Therefore, to make the use of ontologies viable, development approaches need to be applied those are capable of tackling this complexity. Such an approach cannot be ad-hoc and proprietary but rather it must allow for rigorous/precise modelling of context ontology and for automatic development of ontology-based context-aware applications. To this end, we have been investigating the use of Model Driven Architecture (MDA) [12], the emerging standard by the Object Management Group (OMG) for software systems design and development in order to evaluate benefits of this approach in ontology development.

MDA aims at providing clear separation between technology-neutral and technology-specific concerns involved in the different stages of a system's development process. MDA [12] consists of a set of standards, namely, MOF, OCL, XMI and QVT [18] that enable the definition of Domain Specific Languages (DSLs) used to specify a system's structure and behaviour. DSLs are represented as meta-models based on the Meta-Object Facility (MOF) and can be precisely defined using the Object Constraint Language (OCL). OCL allows the definition of constraints over meta-models as well as actual models for a specific system.

We have applied MDA in a number of case-studies that demonstrated the advantages the approach offers in the development process of systems and services [3, 4, 5]. In [3] and [4] we discussed the use of MDA for context-aware pervasive service modelling, provisioning and service composition. In [5] we presented how MDA is used for the design, development and integration of telecommunications Operations Support Systems (OSS) and the benefits gained in terms of improved quality, rapid delivery and lower development costs.

The above experiences lead to the conclusion that MDA can be a beneficial paradigm for capturing context ontologies with a number of advantages. Modelling ontologies as Platform Independent Models (PIMs) can be a one-off activity as these PIMs (models of roles, devices, and tasks) can be re-used in the development of other CAAs. Heterogeneity is also catered for since ontology and CAA PIMs can be transformed into implementations suitable for the platforms and devices at hand. MDA can facilitate the semi-automatic or automatic generation of ontology-based CAAs with significant reductions in time and costs during the development and maintenance phases.

This paper presents an MDA-based approach for context ontology modelling towards the development of context-aware applications for pervasive systems. To the best of our knowledge, no previous work has made use of MDA in this field. The primary contributions of our work are: 1) a context ontology model (COM) for pervasive services based on the RDFS and OWL meta-models; 2) a model driven integration architecture (MDIA) for ontology-based CAA development.

The rest of the paper is organized as follows. The next section presents related work in ontology based context modelling for pervasive services. Section 3 describes the context ontology models developed using MDA. Section 4 illustrates our Model Driven Integration Architecture (MDIA) for ontology-based CAA development. Section 5 provides some concluding remarks and plans for future work.

2   Related Work

Related research has dealt with the issue of ontology-based context modelling and reasoning in a number of perspectives. Wang et al [9] proposed an OWL-encoded ontology (CONON) for modelling and reasoning about context in pervasive computing environments. Chen et al [10] proposed an architecture called Context Broker Architecture (CoBra) that uses OWL to define ontology in intelligent environments. Furthermore, they proposed a Standard Ontology for Ubiquitous and Pervasive Computing Applications (SOUPA) [15]. Henricksen et al [11] proposed a hybrid approach for context modelling, reasoning and interoperation between object-oriented context models and ontology-based context models. All the above referenced research illustrated the advantages of handling context at a semantic level by using different solutions. However, no evidence was found of any solutions trying to model ontology in the context of MDA.

Other research work focuses on ontology-based CAA development. Biegel and Cahill proposed a framework to develop CAAs based on their sentient object model. They focus on fusing data from disparate sensors to ease context-aware application development by simple coding [16]. McFadden et al [17] proposed a model driven approach to develop CAA based on their object-oriented Context Modelling Language (CML). These practices are aiming to reduce the development effort or to automate the CAA development process through specific and proprietary mechanisms.

In our work, a pure MDA-based approach has been applied for context ontology modelling that is based on well-recognized OMG standards, such as MOF, OCL, and XMI and on OMG's recent efforts regarding ontology modelling, the Ontology Definition Meta-Model (ODM) [8], which deals with modelling and engineering of context information in the pervasive services domain.

3   Context Ontology Modelling

This section presents how ontologies are captured using the four layers of abstraction that MDA adopts. In the MDA paradigm, ontology languages need to be abstracted and expressed using MOF in the form of meta-models. Based on these meta-models, we then construct our Context Ontology Model (COM). COM consists of the

Upper-Level Context Ontology Model (ULCOM) and the Extended Specific Context Ontology Model (ESCOM) and is used to model context information. We employed an MDA tool, XMF, from Xactium[1] in our modelling work.

3.1 Ontology Meta-modelling

MDA is based on four layers of abstraction, M0 through M3. M0 contains application run-time data; M1 contains application models designed for a specific problem domain; M2 contains meta-models that capture domain specific languages (DSLs) used in the application designs of M1; M3 hosts the Meta-Object Facility (MOF), which serves as a language to specify DSLs.

Fig. 1 shows how the ontology models and meta-models are positioned around the above four layers. M2 hosts the MOF-based Ontology Definition Meta-model (ODM) and the UML profile for Ontology. Domain Ontology Models are situated on M1 and are instances of ODM representing models of domain-specific ontologies. An example of a domain ontology model is the Context Ontology Model (COM) introduced in the next section. M0 contains models that are instances of M1 domain-specific ontologies.

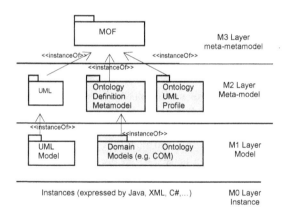

Fig. 1. Ontology Modelling in MDA Four-layer Architecture

To enable ontologies become machine-interpretable, they need to be represented as software artifacts. To achieve this in MDA, the primary elements of ontology need to be abstracted out and be represented as a meta-model using MOF.

Several efforts have already been made towards ontology meta-modelling in the MDA paradigm. Fuchs et al proposed a meta-model specification for OWL DL [6]; Duric et al proposed a meta-model for Semantic Web ontology [7]. OMG launched a request for proposals (RFP) regarding an Ontology Definition Meta-model (ODM). The latest adopted submission of ODM proposal is available on [8]. All this work aims to use MDA standards for ontology engineering. Our ontology meta-modelling work presented in this section is compliant to [8].

---

[1] Xactium: www.xactium.com

Based on RDF, RDFS, OWL and ODM, we constructed the RDFS Meta-Model and OWL Meta-Model; both are MOF-based meta-models that allow users to define ontology models using the same terminology and concepts as those are defined in RDFS and OWL, respectively.

One challenge that characterizes the definition of MOF-based ontology meta-models is how to make these meta-models precise enough so that ontology model definitions on M1 are unambiguous. We tackle this by means of the Object Constraint Language (OCL) that is used to specify constraints on ontology meta-model elements against which ontology models' consistency can be checked.

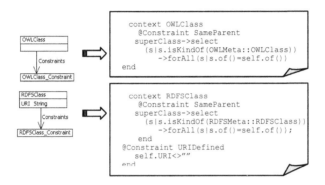

Fig. 2. Example of Constraints in Meta-models

Fig. 2 depicts two examples of constraints in ontology meta-models. OWLClass, an entity of the OWL meta-model, is augmented with constraint SameParent. This constraint coerces any OWLClass instance A to only subclass a class B if and only if B is also an instance of OWLClass and does not instantiate any other meta-model entity. In the OCL scripts, s.of() is used to get the superclass of an entity. Fig. 2 also shows constraint URIDefined imposed on class RDFSClass, which specifies every RDFSClass must have a non-empty URI (Uniform Resource Identifier) defined.

3.2 Context Ontology Model (COM)

An ontology of context represents knowledge about the context domain and comprises definitions of a set of *context entities*, the entity *attributes*, the *functions* the entities provide, the *relationships* between context entities, the *instances* of context entities and the *axioms* used for context reasoning.

We have defined COM that describes context for pervasive services. COM consists of two parts, namely, the Upper-Level Context Ontology Model (ULCOM) and the Extended Specific Context Ontology Model (ESCOM). ULCOM captures an ontology of concepts that are essential for generically characterizing context in the pervasive services domain. The ULCOM specification uses the RDFS/OWL meta-models. ESCOM defines specific concepts for context as extensions of ULCOM entities. Fig. 3 depicts a part of COM.

ULCOM includes three core concepts, namely, *Entity*, *EntityProperty*, and *EntitySpecification*:

- **Entity,** stereotyped as OWLClass, represents five types of context concepts that are usually involved in a typical pervasive service – *person, device*, communication-channel (*ComChannel*), *function*, and *event*.
- **EntityProperty:** Apart from the proprietary attributes an entity may have, EntityProperty is also used to characterize general attributes, such as, *time, identity, activity*, and *location*. These attributes are necessary to determine the when, who, what, and where type of knowledge relating to an entity. EntityProperty is a type of OWLProperty.
- **EntitySpecification** models the configuration of each entity and entity property in terms of constraints. It is an instance of OWLRestrictions and contains OCL scripts for constraints definition and model checking.

For simplicity, there are only a few of relationships depicted in Fig. 3. For instance, a person *owns* devices and a person is *nearby* another person.

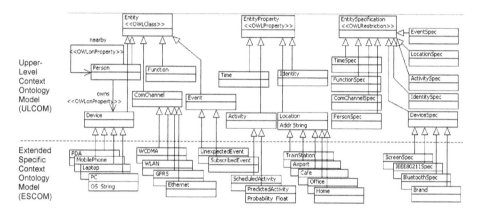

Fig. 3. A Part of the Context Ontology Model (COM)

ESCOM and ULCOM are M1 layer models. ESCOM is used to define more specific context entities and their corresponding properties and specifications. Some examples of ESCOM entities are *PDA, laptop, PC, mobile-phone* and *TV* which are devices normally used in a pervasive computing environment. These devices have specifications that define certain constraints on device features, e.g. *ScreenSpec*, or configurations of the device to support different types of network access e.g. *BluetoothSpec* and *IEEE80211Spec*. Further concepts in the ESCOM include different types of activities, such as *ScheduledActivity* or *PredictedActivity*, different types of locations, such as *home, office* or *café*, types of events that may emerge, e.g. *SubscribedEvent* and *UnexpectedEvent*, and types of communication channels supported by the devices or the user locations, e.g. *WLAN* and *GPRS*.

4   MDA-Based Context-Aware Application Development

This section presents our MDA-based approach for Context-Aware Application (CAA) development. Context ontology alone is useful but not sufficient to entirely support CAA development as it only captures knowledge about the CAA context. For CAA it is necessary to further specify models describing the application logic, the graphical user interfaces (GUI), the application data and the way the CAA integrates with other systems and services. Therefore, alongside COM, more meta-models have been developed to facilitate the automatic generation of CAAs.

Fig. 4 gives an overview of our Model Driven Integration Architecture (MDIA) for CAA development. At the meta-model layer there are three categories of artifacts: *CAA integration related meta-models, implementation languages meta-models*, and *mappings* between the meta-models.

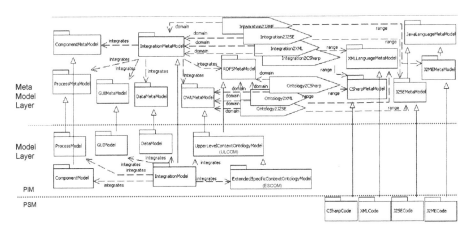

Fig. 4. Model Driven Integration Architecture (MDIA) for Context-Aware Application Development

The CAA integration related meta-models category includes the following six packages:

- **ComponentMetaModel** defines a language to model functional interfaces of existing functional components (such as ontology reasoning components in our application domain, or inventory components in OSS systems [5]). Using this language we can model at the M1 level ontology handling functionality of Commercial-Off-The-Shelf (COTS) components (or libraries) which we can then integrate into the models of CAAs.
- **ProcessMetaModel** represents a language that can be used on M1 to specify system logic in the form of a process. The meta-model defines elements of a UML activity diagram.
- **RDFSMetaModel and OWLMetaModel** are used to define context-aware ontology data in our architecture.
- **GUIMetaModel** defines basic elements of a language to describe a graphical user interface, such as window, label and textbox and an event-based model describing the dynamic way GUI elements can trigger logic associated with them.
- **DataMetaModel** describes a language for the specification of application-related data on M1. This meta-model is based on the UML class diagram.

- **IntegrationMetaModel** is fundamental as it defines the way all previous meta-models associate and integrate. It serves as the glue that brings all necessary elements together in order to compose a CAA. More specifically, this meta-model defines how (1) a flow of process activities integrates different components by invoking certain operations on each component to deliver an activity; (2) GUIs integrate with processes by events GUI elements generate and trigger process activities or entire processes representing the logic behind these elements; (3) data integrates with both components and processes that consume and produce information of different types.

All above CAA integration related meta-models are tools/languages that facilitate the technology-neutral specification of CAAs. In order to enable the generation of technology-specific CAA implementations, it is important to introduce another category of meta-models, namely, implementation languages meta-models. In this category, we defined *JavaLanguageMetaModel, XMLLanguageMetamodel*, and *CSharp-MetaModel,* which constitute specifications of the respective languages' syntax, including grammars, expressions, statements and programming structures (classes, operations, variables etc). It is worth to note that *J2SEMetaModel* and *J2MEMeta-Model* are defined which are extensions of *JavaLanguageMetaModel*. They are specifying to two sub-sets of Java language meta-data for generating the Java implementations for Standard and Micro Edition platforms, respectively.

What is still missing before MDIA is completely enabled to automatically generate CAA implementations is specifying precise transformations of technology-neutral into technology specific meta-models. More specifically, we define two types of mappings in the architecture:

- Mappings between integration and implementation language meta-models, namely, *Integration2Java, Integration2XML,* and *Integration2CSharp*. These are used to generate CAA implementations.
- Mappings between ontology language (*RDFSMetaModel* and *OWLMetaModel*) and implementation language meta-models, namely, *Ontology2Java, Ontology-2XML,* and *Ontology2CSharp*. These are used to generate technology-specific representations of ontological artifacts in the specified implementation languages.

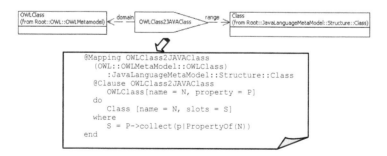

Fig. 5. A Mapping Example

Fig. 5 shows an example of a mapping specification that transforms OWLClass, of the OWLMetaModel, into Class, of the JavaLanguageMetaModel. The mapping script is written in XMap, the proprietary language of the XMF tool to define transformations. XMap uses pattern matching and the particular script of the example maps an `OWLClass` with a name and properties onto a Java class that has the same name and variables (slots) as the `OWLClass`.

Utilising the meta-models presented above, a designer can now specify the model of a CAA at the M1 layer. Fig. 4 illustrates the model layer being populated by generic forms of integration related model packages, corresponding to the CAA integration related category of meta-models that specify all aspects of a platform independent model for the CAA. These aspects are application logic (*ProcessModel* that can reuse and integrate COTS capabilities described in *OntologyComponentModel*), data (*DataModel*), context (*ULCOM* and *ESCOM*), GUIs (*GUIModel*) and the ways all aspects integrate (*IntegrationModel*). Rigorous specification of the CAA PIM allows for the automatic generation of complete PSMs represented in various implementation languages. Fig. 4 illustrates packages *JavaSourceCode*, *CSharpCode*, and *XMLCode* in the PSM of the model layer, that respectively include the code in Java, C# and XML representation of the CAA PIM as they are automatically generated by the correspondent transformations defined in the meta-model layer. For instance, *JavaSourceCode* results from the execution of the *Integration2Java* mapping that transform instances of the integration related meta-models into Java code. Similarly, the *Ontology2Java* mapping generates a Java code representation of an ontology.

5 Conclusion and Future Work

Our primary goal in this paper is to explore the feasibility of amalgamating UML, MDA and ontology languages (such as RDFS and OWL) towards context ontology modelling and an MDA-based integration architecture for automatic development of context-aware applications aiming at improving the accuracy and reducing time and costs.

We presented our Context Ontology Model (COM) which can be validated against precise meta-models. The Model Driven Integration Architecture (MDIA) is designed to integrate different types of DSLs and technologies. For instance, under the umbrella of the MDIA, GUI models, process models and ontology models can be integrated to build a platform independent CAA model representing user interfaces, business logic and ontology-based context data involved in the CAA.

This paper only presents the first step of our work towards a model driven ontology-based pervasive service engineering platform. As part of our future work, a comprehensive case study on ontology-based pervasive service provisioning is to be carried out to evaluate the new challenges introduced by ontology and MDA amalgamation. Our next big step will be the application of our MDA-based ontology approach to the design and integration of enterprise information systems in the telecom OSS domain.

References

1. A.K. Dey, D. Salber and G.D. Abowd, "A Conceptual Framework and a Toolkit for Supporting the Rapid Prototyping of Context-Aware Applications", Anchor article of a special issue on context-aware computing in the Human-Computer Interaction (HCI) Journal, Volume 16 (2-4), pp. 97-166, (2001)

2. P.J. Brown, J.D. Bovey and X. Chen, "Context-Aware Applications: From the Laboratory to the Marketplace", IEEE Personal Communications, 4(5), 58-64 (1997)
3. K. Yang, S. Ou, A. Liotta and I. Henning, "Composition of Context-aware Services Using Policies and Models", Proc. of IEEE GlobeCom 2005, IEEE Press, Dec. 2005, St. Louis, USA (2005)
4. K. Yang, S. Ou, M. Azmoodeh and N. Georgalas, "Policy-based Model-driven Engineering of Pervasive Services and the Associated OSS", BT Technical Journal (BTTJ), Vol 23, No 3, pp. 162-174 (2005)
5. N. Georgalas, M. Azmoodeh and S. Ou, "Model Driven Integration of Standard Based OSS Components", Proc. of the Eurescom Summit 2005 on Ubiquitous Services and Applications, Heidelberg, Germany (2005)
6. F. Fuchs,I. Hochstatter,M. Krause and M. Berger, "A Meta-model Approach to Context Information", Proc. of the 3rd Int'l Conf. on IEEE Pervasive Computing and Communications Workshops, pp. 8-14 (2005)
7. D. Duric, D. Gasevic and V. Devedzic, "A MDA-based Approach to the Ontology Definition Meta-model", Proc. of a 4th Workshop On Computational Intelligence And Information Technologies,Serbia (2003)
8. IBM and Sandpiper Software, Inc., "Ontology Definition Meta-model", http:// www. omg.org/docs/ad/05-08-01.pdf (2005)
9. X.H. Wang, T. Gu, D.Q. Zhang and H.K. Pung, "Ontology-Based Context Modelling and Reasoning using OWL", Context Modelling and Reasoning Workshop at PerCom (2004)
10. H. Chen, T. Finin and A. Joshi, "Using OWL in a Pervasive Computing Broker", In Proc. of Workshop on Ontologies in Open Agent Systems (AAMAS 2003) (2003)
11. K. Henricksen, S. Livingstone, and J. Indulska, "Towards a hybrid approach to context modelling, reasoning, and interoperation", Proc. of the 1st Int'l Workshop on Advanced Context Modelling, Reasoning And Management, UbiComp'2004 (2004)
12. Object Management Group (OMG), Model Driven Architecture, http://www.omg.org/mda
13. D.L. McGuinness and F. Harmelen, "OWL Web Ontology Language Overview", W3C Recommendation, http://www.w3.org/TR/owl-features/ (2004)
14. D. Brickley and R.V. Guha, "RDF Vocabulary Description Language 1.0: RDF Schema", W3C Recommendation, http://www.w3.org/TR/rdf-schema/ (2004)
15. H. Chen, F. Perich, T. Finin and A. Joshi, "SOUPA: Standard Ontology for Ubiquitous Pervasive Applications", Proc. Of the 1st Int'l Conf. on Mobile and Ubiquitous System, IEEE (2004)
16. G. Biegel, V. Cahill, "A Framework for Developing Mobile, Context-aware Applications", Proc. of 2nd IEEE Conf. on Pervasive computing and Communications (2004)
17. T. McFadden, K. Henricksen, J. Indulska, "Automating context-aware application development", First Int'l workshop on Advanced Context Modelling, Reasoning and Management, UbiComp 2004, England (2004)
18. QVT Partners. Initial Submission for MOF 2.0 Query/View/Transformations RFP, QVT-Partners, http://qvtp.org/downloads/1.1/qvtpartners1.1.pdf (2003)

Ontology-Based Composition and Transformation for Model-Driven Service Architecture

Claus Pahl

Dublin City University
School of Computing
Dublin 9, Ireland
`cpahl@computing.dcu.ie`

Abstract. Building service-based architectures has become a major area
of interest since the advent of Web services. Modelling these architectures
is a central activity. Model-driven architecture is a recent approach to
developing software systems based on the idea of making models the central artifacts for design representation, analysis, and code generation. We
propose an ontology-based composition and transformation approach for
model-driven service architecting. Ontology technology as a logic-based
knowledge representation and reasoning framework can provide answers
to the needs of sharable and reusable models and descriptions needed
for service engineering. Based on UML-style visual modelling of service
architectures and their mapping into an ontology representation, our
approach enables ontology-based semantic modelling based on representation, analysis, and code-generation techniques for Web services.

Keywords: Service-oriented Architecture, Service Process Composition,
Model-Driven Architecture, Service Ontology, Web Services.

1 Introduction

Model-driven architecture (MDA) is an approach to the development of software systems that has gained wide support over the past years [1]. MDA is
supported by major standardisation bodies such as the Object Management
Group (OMG). MDA emphasises the importance of modelling in the software
development process. Detailed models in MDA serve as design specifications
that support the maintainability of systems and can also provide the basis for
automated code generation. Service-oriented architecture (SOA) [2] is a specific
development and platform approach for service engineering that would benefit
from a tailored MDA solution in order to realise the MDA objectives.

Our focus is here on central development activities in service-oriented architecture [3,4]. Composition is central in a paradigm that addresses architectures of orchestrated services [2]. Service orchestration refers to the assembly or
composition of services to service processes [5]. Within the Web Services platform [3]– which is the concrete platform for service-oriented architecture that we

A. Rensink and J. Warmer (Eds.): ECMDA-FA 2006, LNCS 4066, pp. 198–212, 2006.

target here – the business process execution language WS-BPEL [6] is the most widely used implementation language for service processes.

Services description and composition has been combined with ontology technology [7,8]. Model-driven architecture has been enhanced to ontology-driven architecture [9]. However, the integrated application of both ontology technology and MDA to service architecture has so far not been adequately addressed. We propose an approach for architecting service-based software systems that embraces the MDA-philosophy. UML-based dynamic modelling is the starting point. A tailored UML profile based on activity diagrams provides the modelling notation for service process orchestration. The orchestration of services occurs in two forms. Firstly, the composition of services to processes at the abstract level using process operators. Secondly, the association of concrete provided services that match the requirements of abstract service process elements.

Supporting service engineering using MDA and ontologies is beneficial for the composition activity. For the SOA context, in particular Web services where compositions across organisations and network boundaries are the norm, explicit semantic descriptions of services are a prerequisite for the reliable composition of services [10]. We introduce an ontology framework, i.e. a logic-based knowledge representation framework, to enable sharable representations of semantic service and process descriptions. Various attempts in this direction include service ontologies such as OWL-S [11] and WSMO [12]. The OMG has also recognised the importance of logic-supported semantic modelling using ontologies, which is reflected in the OMG's Ontology Definition Metamodel (ODM) initiative [13]. The need for service providers to publish their services in an accepted, standardised format is another argument in favour of ontologies.

Our solution is UML-based service process modelling supported through a UML profile and a mapping from this profile into a semantic service ontology. The ontology acts as a service architecting engine for both forms of composition and also supports code generation for the process execution and service publication aspects. The aim is to apply the MDA philosophy to a specific software technology. Service-oriented architecture focusses on architectural problems such as process composition through service orchestration and the Web Services platform is characterised by specific languages such as WS-BPEL [6] for service process execution. Therefore, our solution will be dominated by semantic modelling techniques for these specific aspects.

We start with an overview of the service engineering process in our context in Section 2. In Section 3, we introduce UML-based modelling of service processes. Ontology-based composition is the topic of Section 4. We discuss the deployment of service processes in Section 5. We end with related work and some conclusions.

2   Engineering of Service-Based Software Architectures

In [4], a Web service is defined as a software system, whose public interfaces are defined and described using XML. Other systems can interact with the Web

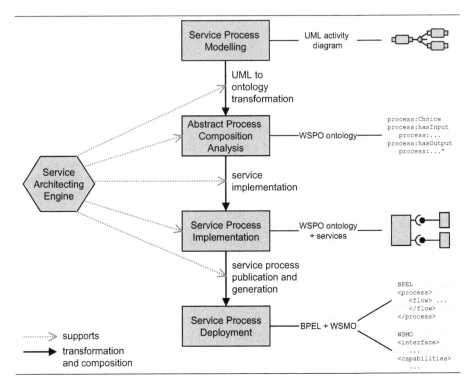

Fig. 1. Overview of the Ontology-based Service Architecture Technique

service in a manner prescribed by its definition, using XML based messages conveyed by Internet protocols. The composition of services to orchestrated processes is a major concern in current Web service research [14,15,2]. These recent developments have strengthened the importance of architectural questions such as service composition. Behaviour and interaction processes are central modelling concerns for service-based software architectures. Explicit semantic descriptions and exchangable models enable developers and clients of services to create reliable service architectures using tool support.

We embed our proposed service composition technique into an ontology-supported, MDA-based development approach for the platform-independent layer (PIM). Our service-specific software process model for ontology-driven semantic service architecture is based on the following steps, see Fig. 1:

- Service Process Modelling. This activity is about visual UML modelling of process activities. Activity diagrams with service-oriented semantic extensions form the notation. Individual actions represent services.
- Abstract Process Composition Analysis. The analysis activity part of the process modelling addresses the integrity of a process composition based on semantical model enhancements in an ontological representation; here we use

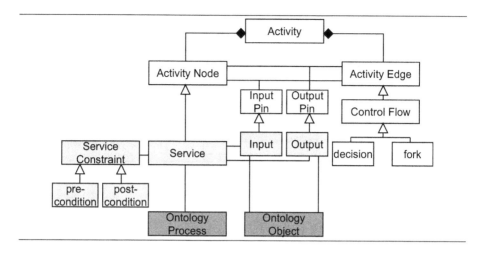

Fig. 2. UML Profile (Metamodel) for Semantic Service Process Modelling

the Web Service Process Ontology WSPO [16,17] – which we will motivate later on – to analyse for instance the integrity of service process definitions.
– Service Process Implementation. The focus of this activity is the discovery of individual services in repositories and directories that match the requirements of the actions specified in the process model. These concrete services can then be associated to the abstract services from the process model.
– Service Process Deployment. The deployment activity enables the implementation of the process as an executable WS-BPEL process [6] based on the associated services. Deployment also includes the publication of the overall process as a service in a service ontology; here we use the Web Service Modelling Ontology WSMO [12].

An ontology-based service architecting engine supports the composition activities within the platform-independent (PIM) layer and also guides the necessary transformations to the Service Deployment, i.e. platform-specific (PSM) layer.

3   Modelling of Service Processes

Service processes are assemblies of individual services or other service processes. This form of service composition is part of what is often called service orchestration [5] – the other aspect of orchestration is the association of concrete services to abstract service placeholders in the composed process description. It describes the control and data flow between services using basic flow operators.

UML activity diagrams capture activities that are to be performed as executable activity nodes in a graph-like structure. The overall system flow based on the activities is modelled. The basic diagram elements are executable activity nodes, called actions, and edges between these activity nodes that represent

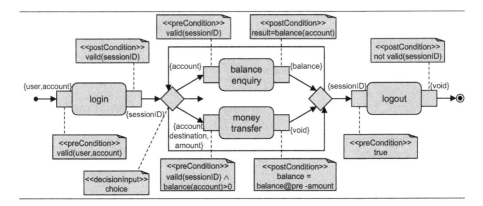

Fig. 3. Semantic Service Process Model based on UML Activity Diagrams

flow. Control flow nodes allow the description of choice (decision) or concurrency (fork) with their joining counterparts. The control flow can be enhanced by explicit objects and input and output pins that represent input and output elements at activities.

We require some extensions to activity diagrams, which we will capture in form of a UML profile, to address the needs of semantic service process description. This metamodel is defined in Fig. 2. White rectangles denote the standard UML activity diagram elements; medium grey ones denote our service-specific extensions; dark grey ones associated elements of a possible domain ontology[1]. A service is an activity. A service's input and output objects are linked to the input and output pins of activities. In addition to input and output elements, we need to add semantic service descriptions, here in the form of pre- and postconditions.

The application of the profile is presented in Fig. 3. It represents an online bank account application. The process of using such an account is described. This application is based on four individual services, each described in terms of input, output, precondition, and postcondition.

The following textual representation summarises the syntactical aspects in an IDL-style service interface format.

application AccountProcess
    service   login (user:string, account:int) : ID
                balance enquiry (account:int) : real
                money transfer (account:int, destination:int, amount:real) : void
                logout (sessionID:ID) : void
    process login; !(balance enquiry + money transfer); logout

---

[1] Often, a domain ontology or model captures central concepts, i.e. key objects and processes, of an application context [16]. The architecture model here is linked to the domain model. Although we do not discuss this aspect further, the integration with a domain model is central for a coherent ontology-based modelling approach.

The services are composed to a process, here using the combinators sequence (;), iteration (!), and choice (+) in the textual representation above, which is also captured in UML notation in Fig. 3[2].

4   Composition of Service Processes

Composition occurs, as already mentioned, in two forms in service architectures:

- Process composition. The assembly of services to processes is the first form of composition. The visual modelling of this composition form is supported by the UML profile. The semantic consistency of the process composition needs to be addressed at a different level.
- Refinement. The composition of the abstract service process as the client and individual concrete services as providers of functionality is the second form where the provider properties refine the required properties. The problem is the discovery of services in service repositories or directories that match the semantic requirements.

Both forms together are usually refered to as orchestration.

We introduce in this section an ontology-based engine to support the architecting of service-based systems based on these two composition forms. The notion of a service architecting engine – emphasising the focus on architecture development – captures semantic properties of services and processes, and supports process- and refinement-style composition. An operator calculus for process composition and inference rules to support matching are integral elements of this engine. As we will see later on, a service composition ontology can also provide the foundations for the generation of deployment code. We start with the composition ontology itself (Section 4.1), before looking at mappings between UML and this ontology (4.2) and process composition (4.3) and implementation (4.4).

4.1   A Service Composition Ontology

A number of service ontologies have been proposed, with OWL-S [11] and WSMO [12] as two prominent examples. The central aim of service ontologies is the semantic annotation of services. While OWL-S also supports service composition to a degree through its process model, we use the Web Service Process Ontology WSPO – whose foundations are presented in [17,18] and which we developed specifically to support service composition and architecture ontologically. WSPO is an OWL-DL (the Web Ontology Language – Description Logic variant) ontology. It uses description logic [19], which also provides the foundation of OWL, to capture composition techniques. WSPO is actually an encoding of a dynamic logic (a modal logic of programs) in a description logic format, which enables reasoning about dynamic service process properties such

[2] We have used iteration as an explicit control flow abstraction here, even though it is not part of the UML notation, since its simplifies expressions on the textual level.

as safety and liveness, making WSPO the most suitable candidate for ontology that supports the MDA PIM layer. The ontology can be used to check the integrity of service process definitions (a safety condition), e.g. determine if the output of a service satisfies the semantic requirements of the next service in the process.

Ontologies are knowledge representation frameworks formalised in an ontology language (such as OWL) [20,21], which is usually based on a terminological logic (such as description logic). Knowledge is represented in form of concepts and (quantified) relationships between these concepts to characterise them semantically. Services (and processes) in WSPO are not represented as concepts, as one might intuitively assume, but as relationships denoting accessibility relations between states of the system. The states are represented as concepts.

- The central concepts in this approach are states (pre- and poststates) for each service. Other concepts are parameters (input- and output-parameters) and constraints (pre- and postconditions).
- Two forms of relationships are provided. The services themselves or their composition to processes are called *transitional relationships*. These processes are based on operators such as sequence, choice (decision), and concurrency (fork) – other operators not present in activity diagrams, such as the iterator, could also be added as control flow abstractions. Essentially, the transitional relationships define a (labelled) transition system. Syntactical and semantical descriptions – here input and output parameter objects (syntax) and constraints (semantics) – are associated to individual services through *descriptional relationships*.

The benefit of this non-standard approach are improved reasoning capabilities for dynamic properties such as lifeness and safety. WSPO can be distinguished from other service ontologies by two specific properties.

- Firstly, although based on description logics, it adds a relationship-based process sublanguage enabling process expressions based on iteration, choice, and sequential and parallel composition operators.
- Secondly, it adds data to processes in form of in- and output parameters – introduced as constant process elements into the process sublanguage.

We will present WSPO here in a pseudo-OWL notation to avoid the full verbosity of XML-based descriptions, see e.g. Fig. 4. The @-construct used in some constraints refers to the attribute in the prestate, cf. [22].

A service process template with a central process element (the transitional relationship) and associated services (descriptional relationship) defines the basic structure of states and service processes. Syntactical parameter information in relation to the individual activities and also semantical information such as preconditions are attached to each activity as defined in the template. The pre- and poststates will remain implicit in the notation.

The three services on the right-hand side of Fig. 4 are part of a composed process, shown on the left-hand side. The process is based on a choice construction (based on the decision control flow operator of the UML activity diagrams).

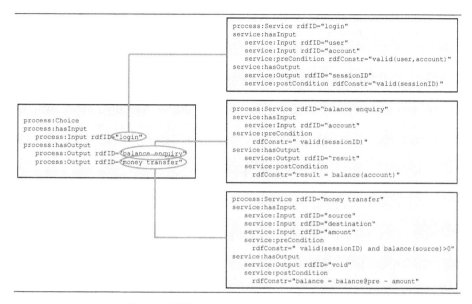

Fig. 4. WSPO Process and Service Model

The left-hand side is a transitional relationship expressing the composed process itself. The three services **login** (as input) and **balance enquiry** and **money transfer** (both as output of the control flow operator) are combined. Input and precondition are (implicitly) associated to the prestate and output and post-condition are (implicitly) associated to the poststate. Although the pre- and poststates are not explicit in the WSPO notation, their presence is necessary as the overall process specification is interpreted by labelled transition systems. The transitional relationships, i.e. the process specification itself, defines the accessibility relationship between pre- and poststates.

Pre- and postconditions for the composed process can be derived from the individual service specifications – once the overall consistency of the abstract composed process definition is established – in order to represent the process as a single service to potential users.

4.2 Mapping Activity Diagrams to Service Ontology

In our framework, UML activity diagrams and our extension to model service processes based on the UML profile serve mainly as a tool for visual modelling. The ontology framework provides the service architecting engine for the platform-independent and platform-specific model layers. It performs composition checks and creates executable process implementations.

The mapping from the activity diagrams based on the profile into the WSPO is straightforward. The ontology representation in Fig. 4 is the result of the transformation of the UML model in Fig. 3. WSPO is based on a standard template. A process specification forms the core, to which individual service specifications of services that participate in the process are associated. The standard activity nodes and edges from UML activity diagrams are mapped onto the process template:

– The activity nodes of services connected by the activity edges to processes (see Fig. 3) with their input and output elements are mapped onto the process part of the template. The UML control flow operators, such as decision and fork, are represented by the WSPO process combinators, such as choice and concurrency.
– For each service (activity node), a separate service part with input and output, precondition and postcondition information is generated, where each of the individual information elements is considered as attached through a descriptional relationship. The UML input and output pins are mapped to WSPO service input and output concepts. Pre- and postconditions of the UML extension are equally mapped to WSPO concepts.

We currently work with a subset of activity diagram features as shown in Fig. 3, which is sufficient to express abstract functional service and process properties. The transformation between this subset and WSPO is straightforward. Other diagram elements, such as activity partitioning mechanisms (swimlanes), could be used in extensions of this approach to consider non-functional aspects such as service distribution. We have investigated modelling of service distribution in [23].

The ontology acts as a formally defined internal representation that enables transformation, composition, and reasoning activities. UML provides an interface for visual modelling, but also interoperability, which allows existing UML models to be reused and integrated into our proposed framework.

4.3 Process Composition

Services that are visually composed do not necessarily match semantically. A semantical analysis of the composition between these abstract specifications is required. The excerpt of the bank account model.

The login service produces an output object `sessionID` that satisfies the postcondition `valid(sessionID)`. Although the `sessionID` is not required as an input element for the subsequent `balance enquiry` service, the validity of the `sessionID` is still required and guards this service. This case, even though a simple one, illustrates the need to check the consistency of the composition – both in terms of input elements in and output elements out and also the semantic matching of postcondition of the predecessor $post_P$ and precondition pre_S of the successor service. A required input element in of an output service of a composition must be provided as an output element of the preceding service in the process composition (cf. pipes) or must be supplied by the overall process instance (cf. calls). An implication $post_P \rightarrow pre_S$ is the semantic consistency constraint for the composition. This applies to all composition operators (sequence, choice, concurrency).

This type of composition can be characterised as horizontal, whereas in the following section, we will address the vertical dimension of composition by associating concrete provided services to abstract process models.

4.4   Composing Service Providers and Clients

The service process defined by modelling the control and data flow characteristics visually and by checking its consistency using the ontology engine is still an abstract description. Concrete services need to be found that match the requirements expressed in the abstract models, called service orchestration. Matching is often based on the so-called IOPE (Input Output Precondition Effect) characteristics. A refinement relation (e.g. weakening the precondition and strengthening the postcondition or effect, which we use here) defines the matching notion.

Ontologies enable reasoning about models and their properties. In [17], a refinement notion is integrated into an ontological framework, based on the ontological subsumption (subclass) relationship. There, we have presented an ontological matching notion that can be applied to determine whether a service provider can be connected to a service user based on their individual service and process requirements.

Assume that in order to implement an account process, an implementation for the `money transfer` service with input parameter `amount` needs to be integrated. For any given state, the process developer might require (using the `balance` enquiry)

```
service:preCondition  rdfConstr="balance() > amount"
service:postCondition rdfConstr="balance()= balance()@pre-amount"
```

which would be satisfied by a provided service

```
service:preCondition  rdfConstr="balance() > 0"
service:postCondition rdfConstr="balance()= balance()@pre- amount
    and lastActivity = 'transfer'"
```

The provided service would weaken the required precondition assuming that the transfer `amount` is always positive and strengthen the required postcondition as an additional result is delivered by the provided service. Note, that we have used a pseudo-RDF notation here to simplify the example.

5   Deployment of Service Processes

The deployment of services at the platform-specific layer involves two perspectives – clients invoking and executing service processes (5.1) and providers publishing abstract descriptions and making the process services available (5.2).

Rule	Aspect	Description
P1	WS-BPEL	The complex WSPO process relationships can be mapped to BPEL processes.
P1.1	WS-BPEL process partners	For each process create a BPEL partner process.
P1.2	WS-BPEL orchestration	Convert each process expression into BPEL-invoke activities and the client side BPEL-receive and -reply activities at the server side.
P1.3	WS-BPEL process activities	Convert the process combinators ';', '+', '!', and '∥' to the BPEL combinators sequence, pick, while, and flow, resp.

Fig. 5. Transformation Rules – Executable Processes

5.1 Code Generation for Service Process Invocation and Execution

Automated code generation is one of the central objectives of MDA. In the context of SOA, code generation essentially means the generation of exectuable service processes. WS-BPEL [6], which has been looked at from a semantic perspective [24], has emerged as the most widely accepted process execution language for Web services.

A summary of the transformation rules from WSPO to WS-BPEL is presented in Fig. 5. WSPO defines a simple language that can be fully translated into WS-BPEL. BPEL process partners are the client and the different service providers. The WSPO specification is already partitioned accordingly. Flow combinators can also be mapped directly.

5.2 Description and Publication of Services and Service Processes

The Web Services architecture proposes a specific platform based on services provided at certain locations, which can be located using directory information provided in service registries. The description of services – or service processes made available as a single service – is therefore of central importance. Information represented in the process model and formalised in the service process ontology can be mapped to a service ontology. Both OWL-S and WSMO would be suitable here. This transformation would only be a mapping into a subset, since these ontologies capture a wide range of functional and non-functional properties, whereas we have focussed on architecture-specific properties in WSPO.

We have chosen WSMO here to illustrate this type of code generation. A summary of the transformation rules from WSPO to WSMO is presented in Fig. 6. Some correspondences guide this transformation. WSPO input and output elements correspond to WSMO `messageExchange` patterns, which are used in WSMO to express stimuli-response patterns of direct service invocations, and WSPO pre- and postconditions correspond to their WSMO counterparts.

Rule	Aspect	Description
D1	WSMO	Based on the WSPO model, map process relationships to WSMO service concept and fill `messageExchange` and `pre/postCond` properties accordingly.
D1.1	WSMO messageExchange	Map the WSPO in and out objects onto WSMO `messageExchange` descriptions.
D1.2	WSMO pre-/postconditions	Map the WSPO pre- and postconditions onto WSMO `pre-` and `postconditions`.

Fig. 6. Transformation Rules – Semantic Service Descriptions

6 Related Work

Some developments have started exploiting the connection between ontologies – in particular OWL – and MDA. In [25], an MDA-based ontology architecture is defined. This architecture includes aspects of an ontology metamodel and a UML profile for ontologies. A transformation of the UML ontology to OWL is implemented. The work by [9,25] and the OMG [1,13], however, needs to be carried further to address the ontology-based modelling and reasoning of service-based architectures. In particular, the Web Services architecture needs to be addressed in the context of Web-based ontology technology. Some of the reasoning tasks we used ontologies for, could have also been addressed using OCL [22]. However, ontologies provide a full-scale logic and additionally allow XML-based sharing and exchange in a Semantic Web framework.

Grønmo et.al. [26] introduce – based on ideas from [25] – an approach similar to ours. Starting with a UML profile based on activity diagrams, services are modelled. These models are then translated into OWL-S. Although the paper discusses process composition, this aspect is not detailed. We have built on [26] in this respect by considering process compositions in the UML profile and by mapping into a service ontology that focusses on providing explicit support for service processes. Other authors [27,28] have directly connected UML modelling with WS-BPEL code generation, without the explicit ontology framework. Integrating ontologies, however, enhances the semantic modelling and reasoning capabilities in the context of service architectures.

WSMO [12] and OWL-S [11] are the two predominant examples of service ontologies. Service ontologies are ontologies to describe Web services, aiming to support their semantics-based discovery in Web service registries. WSMO is not an ontology, as OWL-S is, but rather a framework in which ontologies can be created. The Web Service Process Ontology WSPO [17,18] is also a service ontology, but its focus is the support of description and reasoning about service composition and service-based architectural configuration. An important current development is the Semantic Web Services Framework (SWSF), consisting of a language and an underlying ontology [29], which takes OWL-S work further and is also linked to convergence efforts in relation to WSMO. The FLOWS ontology in SWSF comprise process modelling and it equally suited to support semantic modelling within the MDA context.

Our framework has to be seen in the context of MDA initiatives. The OMG supports selected modelling notations and platforms through an adoption process. While Web technologies have not been adopted so far, the need for a specific MDA solution for the Web context is a concern. The ubiquity of the Web and the existence of standardised and accepted platform and modelling technology justify this requirement. The current OMG initiative to define and standardise an ontology metamodel (ODM) will allow the integration of our framework with OMG standards [13]. ODM will provide mappings to OWL-DL and also a UML2 profile for ontologies. ODM, however, is a standard addressing ontology description, but not reasoning. The reasoning component, which is important in our framework, would need to be addressed in addition to the standard.

7   Conclusions

Service-oriented architecture is developing into a service engineering paradigm with its own specific techniques. The development of a service engineering methodology should – similar to other approaches – adopt accepted technologies:

- MDA provides, based on UML, a modelling approach that can satisfy the modelling requirements necessary to develop service architectures and that emphasises tool support and automation.
- Ontology and Semantic Web technologies provide semantic strength for the modelling framework necessary for a distributed and inter-organisational environment.

Our main contribution is an ontology-based engine that supports the process of service architecting. The central element is a service ontology tailored to support service composition and transformation. An ontology-based technique is here beneficial for the following reasons. Firstly, ontologies define a rigourous, logic-based semantics modelling and reasoning framework thats support architectural design activities for services. Secondly, ontologies provides a knowledge integration and interoperability platform for multi-source semantic service-based software systems. Thirdly, service ontologies can also be integrated with domain ontologies to integrate different software development activities – for instance at the computation-independent layer of MDA. Our aim here was to demonstrate the suitability of ontologies for this environment – for both WSPO to support architectural issues but also for WSMO here to support service discovery. We have embedded this service composition ontology into an architecture modelling technique integrating visual UML-based modelling, transformation, ontology-based reasoning, and code generation.

In this approach ontologies replace the classical UML models, except that we keep the visual UML notation, but give semantics to a UML profile for service architecture by mapping UML models to ontologies. This approach has in addition to the visualisation of models also the benefit of allowing the reuse of existing models. Ontologies add rigorous semantic modelling and reasoning.

While we have outlined the core of an ontology-driven service architecture framework, a number of aspects have remained unaddressed. The integration of a wider range of UML models could be discussed in order to improve the reusability of UML models. For instance, interaction and sequence diagrams express aspects of relevance to service composition and interaction. Composition aspects such as time or error handling could be considered. A reversed mapping from ontologies into UML models could also be considered. A standardised ontology definition model (ODM) can be expected in the near future. The integration of our approach with this standard is necessary for interoperability reasons and will facilitate model reuse, but should turn out to be feasible due to OWL-DL as the common underlying ontology language.

References

1. Object Management Group. *MDA Model-Driven Architecture Guide V1.0.1.* OMG, 2003.
2. L. Bass, P. Clements, and R. Kazman. *Software Architecture in Practice (2nd Edition).* SEI Series in Software Engineering. Addison-Wesley, 2003.
3. G. Alonso, F. Casati, H. Kuno, and V. Machiraju. *Web Services – Concepts, Architectures and Applications.* Springer-Verlag, 2004.
4. World Wide Web Consortium. *Web Services Architecture.* http://www.w3.org/ TR/ws-arch, 2006. (visited 28/02/2006).
5. C. Peltz. Web Service orchestration and choreography: a look at WSCI and BPEL4WS. *Web Services Journal*, 3(7), 2003.
6. The WS-BPEL Coalition. *WS-BPEL Business Process Execution Language for Web Services – Specification Version 1.1.* http://www-106.ibm.com/ developer-works/webservices/library/ws-bpel, 2004. (visited 08/04/2005).
7. S. McIlraith and D. Martin. Bringing Semantics to Web Services. *IEEE Intelligent Systems*, 18(1):90–93, 2003.
8. T. Payne and O. Lassila. Semantic Web Services. *IEEE Intelligent Systems*, 19(4), 2004.
9. D. Gašević, V. Devedžić, and D. Djurić. MDA Standards for Ontology Development – Tutorial. In *International Conference on Web Engineering ICWE2004*, 2004.
10. J. Rao, P. Küngas, and M. Matskin. Logic-Based Web Services Composition: From Service Description to Process Model. In *International Conference on Web Services ICWS 2004*, pages 446–453. IEEE Press, 2004.
11. DAML-S Coalition. DAML-S: Web Services Description for the Semantic Web. In I. Horrocks and J. Hendler, editors, *Proc. First International Semantic Web Conference ISWC 2002*, LNCS 2342, pages 279–291. Springer-Verlag, 2002.
12. R. Lara, M. Stollberg, A. Polleres, C. Feier, C. Bussler, and D. Fensel. Web Service Modeling Ontology. *Applied Ontology*, 1(1):77–106, 2005.
13. Object Management Group. *Ontology Definition Metamodel - Request For Proposal (OMG Document: as/2003-03-40).* OMG, 2003.
14. R. Allen and D. Garlan. A Formal Basis for Architectural Connection. *ACM Transactions on Software Engineering and Methodology*, 6(3):213–249, 1997.

15. F. Plasil and S. Visnovsky. Behavior Protocols for Software Components. *ACM Transactions on Software Engineering*, 28(11):1056–1075, 2002.
16. C. Pahl. Layered Ontological Modelling for Web Service-oriented Model-Driven Architecture. In *European Conference on Model-Driven Architecture ECMDA2005*. Springer LNCS Series, 2005.
17. C. Pahl. An Ontology for Software Component Matching. *International Journal on Software Tools for Technology Transfer (STTT), Special Edition on Component-based Systems Engineering*, 7, 2006. (in press).
18. C. Pahl and M. Casey. Ontology Support for Web Service Processes. In *Proc. European Software Engineering Conference and Foundations of Software Engineering ESEC/FSE'03*. ACM Press, 2003.
19. F. Baader, D. McGuiness, D. Nardi, and P.P. Schneider, editors. *The Description Logic Handbook*. Cambridge University Press, 2003.
20. M.C. Daconta, L.J. Obrst, and K.T. Klein. *The Semantic Web*. Wiley, 2003.
21. W3C Semantic Web Activity. Semantic Web Activity Statement, 2004. http://www.w3.org/2001/sw. (visited 06/11/2005).
22. J.B. Warmer and A.G. Kleppe. *The Object Constraint Language – Precise Modeling With UML*. Addison-Wesley, 2003. (2nd Edition).
23. R. Barrett, L. M. Patcas, J. Murphy, and C. Pahl. Model Driven Distribution Pattern Design for Dynamic Web Service Compositions. In *International Conference on Web Engineering ICWE06. Palo Alto, US*. ACM Press, 2006.
24. D.J. Mandell and S.A. McIllraith. Adapting BPEL4WS for the Semantic Web: The Bottom-Up Approach to Web Service Interoperation. In D. Fensel, K.P. Sycara, and J. Mylopoulos, editors, *Proc. International Semantic Web Conference ISWC'2003*, pages 227–226. Springer-Verlag, LNCS 2870, 2003.
25. D. Djurić. MDA-based Ontology Infrastructure. *Computer Science and Information Systems (ComSIS)*, 1(1):91–116, 2004.
26. R. Grønmo, M.C. Jaeger, and H. Hoff. Transformations between UML and OWL-S. In A. Hartman and D. Kreische, editors, *Proc. Model-Driven Architecture – Foundations and Applications*, pages 269–283. Springer-Verlag, LNCS 3748, 2005.
27. K. Mantell. *From UML to BPEL –Model Driven Architecture in a Web services world*. IBM, http://www-128.ibm.com/developerworks/webservices/library/ws-uml2bpel/, 2005.
28. T. Ambühler. *UML 2.0 Profile for WS-BPEL with Mapping to WS-BPEL*. University of Stuttgart, 2005. Diploma Thesis.
29. Semantic Web Services Language (SWSL) Committee. *Semantic Web Services Framework (SWSF)*. http://www.daml.org/services/swsf/1.0/, 2006.

Harvesting Software Systems
for MDA-Based Reengineering

Thijs Reus[1], Hans Geers[2], and Arie van Deursen[3]

[1] Interactive Objects, Freiburg
Thijs.Reus@interactive-objects.com
[2] Delft University of Technology, The Netherlands
H.J.A.M.Geers@ewi.tudelft.nl
[3] Delft University of Technology and CWI, The Netherlands
A.vanDeursen@ewi.tudelft.nl

Abstract. In this paper we report on a feasibility study in reengineering legacy systems towards a model-driven architecture (MDA). Steps in our approach consist of (1) parsing the source code of the legacy system according to a grammar; (2) mapping the abstract syntax trees thus obtained to a grammar model that is defined in the Meta-Object Facility (MOF); (3) using model to model (M2M) transformations to turn the grammar model into a generic meta-model, called Generic-AST, in which information about software systems can be stored in a language-independent way; (4) mapping the GenericAST models, again using M2M transformations, to UML models that can be either used for code generation or for documentation purposes. The steps have been implemented in a prototype model harvesting tool that is based on Arc-Styler, the MDA environment provided by Interactive Objects. Our paper presents this approach, and reports on our experiences in applying the method to a 178 KLOC production system from the insurance domain written in PL/SQL.

1 Introduction

Model Driven Architecture (MDA) provides a promising basis for keeping software maintainable by using a series of models in the development process: models are the main software assets, as opposed to source code. In this paper we explore how MDA concepts can be applied to existing software systems. The key problem here is that usually no adequate models of actual systems are available. In order to overcome this gap, we investigate to what extent reverse engineering techniques can be used to extract adequate models from source code.

It is very unlikely that a fully automatic approach will ever be able to reconstruct models that are (1) at an appropriate level of abstraction; and (2) can be used to (re)generate the full functionality of the original application. Therefore, we will aim at the interactive reconstruction of models that serve the following purposes:

– The models can be used for system understanding and software exploration in order to support a transition to a model-driven reimplementation;

A. Rensink and J. Warmer (Eds.): ECMDA-FA 2006, LNCS 4066, pp. 213–225, 2006.

– The models can be used to generate code templates, that can subsequently be refined to include deeper application knowledge.

A distinctive characteristic of reengineering to an MDA context is that MDA provides a flexible environment for manipulating models, using open standards such as the Meta-Object Facility (MOF) [20], transformations using the Query/View/Transformation approach (QVT) [19] and the Unified Modeling Language UML. For that reason, we will investigate a reengineering approach which switches to the MDA "technological space" [15] as quickly as possible, after which model to model transformations are used to refine the initial raw results.

The work presented in this paper was carried out within a pilot study conducted at a major Dutch insurance company. The objective of this pilot study is to investigate the feasibility of adopting MDA techniques for their legacy systems, in order to safeguard the future maintainability of these systems. Within the study, tools were built to reverse engineer models from code —a process called "harvesting" — and these tools have been applied to the source code of a production system written in PL/SQL. Steps in our approach consist of

1. Parsing the source code of the legacy system according to a grammar;
2. Mapping the abstract syntax trees thus obtained to a grammar model that is defined in the Meta-Object Facility (MOF);
3. Using model to model (M2M) transformations to turn the grammar model into a generic meta-model, called GenericAST, in which information about software systems can be stored in a language-independent way;
4. Mapping the GenericAST models, again using M2M transformations, to UML models that can be either used for code generation or for documentation purposes.

The paper is structured as follows. We start out with a survey of related work in the area of reengineering to model-driven architectures. We then describe our approach (Section 3) as well as the prototype workbench we developed to support our approach (Section 4). The application of our approach to the PL/SQL production system is described next (Section 5) followed by a discussion of lessons learned (Section 6). We conclude by summarizing our main contributions as well as suggestions for future work.

2   Related Work

The Object Management Group is actively involved in the "reverse engineering to MDA" area, with the Architecture Driven Modernization (ADM) task force [11, 22]. A total of seven Requests for Proposal aim at standardizing an extensive reverse engineering framework towards an MDA target environment. Part of ADM are two generic intermediate models, for supporting analysis and refactoring. The generic models we use are inspired by but significantly simpler than the wide spectrum ADM models.

Mansurov and Campara [16] argue that a first step in the migration towards the MDA is the introduction of modeling in the software development process. They propose an approach to raise the maturity of software architectures to a level where software maintenance and evolution are driven by the architecture instead of by the code. For this they introduce so-called Container Models. They focus on the extraction of these Container Models from existing code.

A framework for language neutral representation of source code is presented by Al-Ekram and Kontogiannis [1]. A generic abstract syntax tree (AST) is part of the program representation framework. XML is used as the main language. It has the advantage of being a light weight solution, but comes with meta-model discovery problems. The meta-model must be hardwired into the programs that use it.

A view on language support for MDA also requiring a generic representation is discussed by Cepa and Mezini [4]. They propose a *generic annotated abstract syntax tree* that can be used to support domain-specific but platform-independent models. An explicit meta-representation is advocated for programs in an AST-like structure, together with the possibility for users to add their own annotations to this AST using a dedicated language.

Boronat *et al.* present a framework for automatic legacy system migration in MDA [3], using rewriting logic as their transformation engine. The results are UML models of the legacy system.

An approach aiming at incremental adoption of model-driven technologies is provided by Gannod and Carey [13], who rely on Java annotations that support the creation of models that fit in the Eclipse Modeling Framework EMF.

Harvesting MDA models from existing proprietary *models* is discussed by Doyle [9]. His starting point are models as used in a 4GL application generator also in use at Fortis. His approach involves reconstructing and normalizing models from database representations, which are subsequently transformed into MOF representations using EMF.

Reengineering from code towards the MDA involves a combination of parsing and model transformation. Kurtev et al. [15] refer to this as building bridges between *technological spaces*, in this case between the grammar-ware and MDA spaces. A very generic framework for bridging between technological spaces is discussed by Wimmer and Kramler [24]. In this framework a compiler-compiler is used that, based on an attributed grammar mapping EBNF to MOF, generates a so-called grammar parser. This grammar-parser not only transforms EBNF grammars into MOF-based metamodels, but also generates a tool to transform programs associated with that EBNF grammar into models associated with the generated metamodel.

A general introduction to reengineering and system renovation is provided in [5,7]. Reengineering generally consists of a series of *reverse engineering* steps that reconstruct system representations at a higher level of abstraction. These representations can subsequently be used for code generation. Since fully automated reengineering often is not feasible, much reverse engineering research focuses on supporting *system exploration*, i.e., helping software engineers in

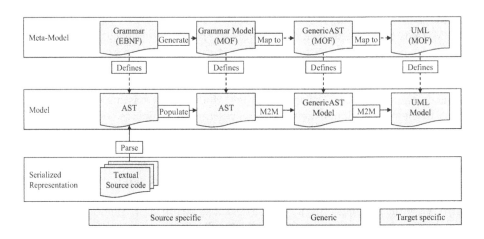

Fig. 1. Reengineering Framework

understanding the legacy system at hand [17]. A reverse engineering process tailored towards reconstructing software architectures from source code is provided in [6].

3   Harvesting Approach

The approach we used for harvesting models from the source code of an existing application is depicted in Figure 1. It consists of the following steps.

The starting point is a grammar of the legacy language, expressed in an EBNF-like formalism. We first of all use this grammar to generate a parser capable of processing the system's source code and representing it by means of abstract syntax trees (ASTs).

Existing parser generators generally produce proprietary AST representations. In order to benefit from standards and available tool support from MDA technologies, we therefore need to transfer these abstract syntax trees to a MOF-based representation. To that end, we use the EBNF grammar to generate:

1. A MOF-based *Grammar Model*, i.e., a metamodel of the Grammar defined with MOF, that offers a one-to-one mapping between EBNF-based ASTs and MOF-based ASTs; and
2. A series of transformations coded in Java mapping EBNF-based AST nodes to their Grammar Model counterparts.

Following the terminology of Kurtev *et al.*, we thus switch from the grammar-ware technological space to the MDA technological space [10, 15].

Our next step consists of mapping the source language abstract syntax trees to a generic, domain-independent model, which we have dubbed *GenericAST*. From this generic model, we subsequently generate models that can be used either for documentation or for code generation purposes. In some cases these models will be based on UML, whereas in other situations these models will be domain specific. The main reason for introducing such a generic layer is that it increases opportunities for reuse when, for example, extending the framework with additional source languages.

The GenericAST meta-model is based on UML, especially for representing structural information such as containers, entities, features, constraints, or types. Regarding behavioral constructs, various meta-classes have been defined for representing common programming language constructs, such as a conditional-statement (similar to an if-statement or switch-statement) and a loop-statement (similar to a for-loop or while-loop). Note that these statements can be represented independent of a specific concrete syntax, which is abstracted in the transformations to a GenericAST model. UML support for representing behavioral constructs is limited (we used version 1.4), which is another reason for using a GenericAST as intermediate model in the transformation process, instead of transforming directly to UML. The GenericAST meta-model furthermore includes facilities for storing custom information in model elements by using tagged values, and for including references to the original source code.

4   Harvesting Workbench Developed and Used

We created a prototype tool set implementing the approach described that allowed us to harvest models from PL/SQL applications. This tool set makes use of the following components.

- The basis for our tool set is Interactive Objects' MDA environment Arc-Styler.[1] ArcStyler is an extensible platform for MDA-based software architecting and engineering. It integrates a UML modeling environment with a collection of model transformations with can generate models or textual output base on UML models. It provides an open, flexible environment for tasks relating models, such as visualization, transformation (both model to model, and model to text), and manipulation. We mostly used the model to model transformation and visualization facilities, and to a lesser extend the model to text transformation facilities offered.
- We used the Grammatica[2] parser generator to obtain a PL/SQL parser. We have been able to reuse an existing PL/SQL grammar, which we tuned for our purposes.
- The mapping from grammars to MOF was set up according to the method proposed by [2], with some extensions in order to turn Grammatica parse trees into true abstract syntax trees.
- The MOF repositories were generated and manipulated using Interactive Objects' MDA-environment ArcStyler. In particular, ArcStyler's Carat.MOF functionality was used to generate a Java repository implementation, conforming to the Java Metadata Interface JMI [14], from a repository model represented in the UML profile for MOF.

---

[1] http://www.arcstyler.com

[2] http://grammatica.percederberg.net

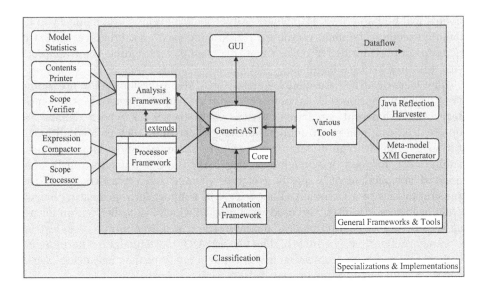

Fig. 2. GenericAST Framework and Tools

- The language independent analysis and transformation facilities offered at the GenericAST level are illustrated in Figure 2. They include tree traversals, transformations, a user interface for manipulating models, and an annotation framework.
- Model to model transformations (M2M) (e.g. from GenericAST to UML) were implemented in ArcStyler's prototype M2M-transformation engine called AIM – Atomistic Information Mapping. AIM provides a graphical user interface for defining transformations, which can be expressed in the Jython[3] scripting language.

5   Case Study

We have applied the harvester tools to HiBob, a 178 KLOC production system at De Amersfoortse Verzekeringen, a major insurance company based in The Netherlands. The system has been developed in Oracle's PL/SQL[4] and consisted of a data model with business logic that calculates insurance offers. The size of the application is shown in Table 1, both in KLOC PL/SQL and in the number of items.

For each main construct a grammar has been developed that describes part of the PL/SQL language, to generate parsers and meta-models that can process the input. The GenericAST has been used as an intermediate model, to reuse previously developed analyses and M2M-transformations to UML. ArcStyler has been

---

[3] http://www.jython.org
[4] http://www.oracle.com/technology/tech/pl_sql

Table 1. System size per main construct

Main Construct	Size (KLOC)	Item count
Tables with fields	70	163 with 4052
Triggers	28	468
Stored procedures (global)	7	46
Packages with procedures	73	23 with 538

used as MDA-environment for executing M2M-transformations and presenting the generated UML models.

Before commencing harvesting, the anticipated architecture of HIBOB was determined. This first of all gives suggestions for the specific harvesting approach. Secondly, it will help to determine where there are mismatches between the current and the target architecture.

Only a small part of the harvesters is specific for HIBOB, which is implemented in the model to model transformations from a grammar model to a GenericAST model. Using HIBOB specific information, we were able to automatically modularize the application, based on known naming conventions. The modularization was implemented in one transformation rule, whereas all other transformation rules (more than 100) can be reused for harvesting other PL/SQL applications. The grammars can be completely reused for harvesting other PL/SQL applications. A grammar only regards syntax, which is not application specific.

Although there is no conceptual restriction on what target models are generated, in the case study only UML models were generated, including class diagrams, state-chart diagrams and collaboration diagrams. Class diagrams (such as in Figure 3) were used to gain insight in the data structure of the application (tables, fields, relations, triggers and constraints) and the structure of the behavior (stored procedures, packages with stored procedures, direct call dependencies). The generated model can be used for both documentation and code generation purposes.

Collaboration diagrams (such as in Figure 4) were derived to obtain insight in all required methods for executing a certain initial method, which is derived from direct call dependencies. The example diagrams shown here are relatively simple, there are for example collaboration diagrams with over 10 objects and more than 1000 method invocations required for more complex calculations.

Table 2 shows several performance measurements from the case study, performed on a Pentium4 3.0 GHz computer with 1 GB RAM. The measurements give an indication on the performance of parsing and populating a generated MOF repository. The table also shows that the cost of compressing and saving models by means of XMI are substantial. No explicit measurements have been done for the M2M-transformations, because we used a prototype M2M-transformation engine with known scalability issues. M2M-transformations ran for hours before completing which is due to the current implementation of the engine. A custom (Java) transformation may run much faster, but it is harder to keep a good overview of the transformation implementation.

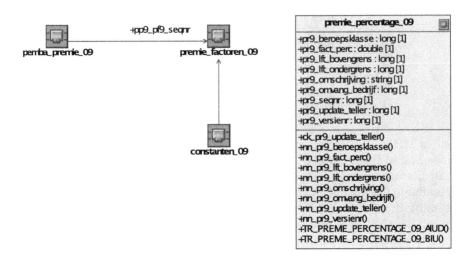

Fig. 3. Harvested Data Structures

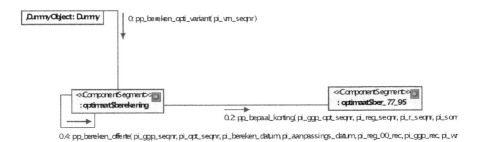

Fig. 4. Harvested Collaboration Diagram showing Required methods for executing method `pp_bereken_opti_variant`

Table 2. Performance measurements from Text to MOF-based model

Property	Unit	Tables	Triggers	Stored Procedures	Packages
Grammar size	LOC	190	240	250	250
Input size	KLOC	70	28	7	73
Parse time	Sec	6	13	3	33
Population time	Sec	9	42	7	144
Compressed XMI file size	KB	2580	15600	1800	41000
XMI save time	Sec	117	827	103	2660

The case study has shown the feasibility of harvesting existing source code (in this case 178 KLOC PL/SQL) to UML models, although the current prototype implementation suffers from scalability issues regarding M2M-transformations. Using the GenericAST has successfully enabled transformation reuse as intended, although being an extra step in the extraction process. The extracted models have successfully been used for documentation and forward engineering purposes. Although currently no full migration has been done, experiments have been conducted in generating J2EE code from the harvested UML models, using standard model to text transformations shipped with ArcStyler. For data structures (tables with fields) complete J2EE code has been generated, whereas for the business logic (e.g. trigger implementations, stored procedures, and PL/SQL packages) only structural code has been generated (e.g. classes with methods, with an empty body).

Further details of the case study conducted can be found in [21].

6   Lessons Learned

Have a clear picture of what to harvest. It is important to have a specific question to answer or problem to solve before harvesting, and to know how to find the answer or solution: if you don't know where you're going, any road will take you there. In other words, constructs of interest that appear in the input must be specified, such that a harvester can recognize them. For example, if for a database system a question is 'what is the data structure?' then constructs of interest are table definitions, field definitions and relations between the tables.

Know the anticipated target models in detail. Having good knowledge on the target models that need to be harvested increases usability of the harvested models. For example, if the harvested models will be used for code generation and the code generator requires that associations have names then association should be given names during harvesting, which might not be necessary when generating models solely for documentation. This results in models that can be used directly for their purpose.

Make use of coding guidelines and naming conventions. The more system-specific information is used during harvesting, the better quality the initial models have. For example, if a table name contains a number that indicates the module it is part of, it can be used to automatically relocate the table to the right module. It improves the usability of the initial models.

Keep grammars small and focused. Smaller grammars are easier to maintain than bigger grammars. When a complete grammar is not available for a harvesting project, a minimal grammar should be developed. A minimal grammar has exactly the right information to describe the anticipated input, but not a complete language. This approach, which is based on the notion of *island grammar* [8,18] has been taken while harvesting HiBob.

Modularize grammars. Modular grammars improve reusability of commonly used grammar parts, such as statement and expression definitions. In the case study, four different grammars were composed from several grammar parts. Not only does this save work while developing grammars, it also allows reuse of several M2M-transformation parts, which correspond with the grammar parts. This has successfully done in the case study.

Design grammar towards a target meta-model. Grammars should be developed with a certain target meta-model in mind, including how to map the grammar to the target meta-model. This improves reusability of M2M-transformation parts. For example, if in a target meta-model statements are all contained by a certain container, this should be reflected in the grammar. This could be done by having a production `statement_container` which contains other statements and acts the entry-point for statements in the grammar. This creates an extra node in the AST that can be mapped to the statement container model element in the target meta-model.

Avoid usage of XMI to store model contents. Persistence of harvesting results using XMI should be avoided, because it is a slow mechanism. Instead of saving and loading every time to and from XMI, as much as possible should be done without XMI. In the case study, parsing and populating a repository took in the order of seconds, while streaming to XMI took in the order of minutes. Therefore, it is more efficient to parse the input every time the models are needed for M2M-transformations. Because generation of a GenericAST model takes more time than saving and loading XMI, it should be used to save a generated GenericAST model.

Optimize M2M-transformations. M2M-transformations should be optimized everywhere possible. In the case study, M2M-transformations were the longest operations, which took in the order of days to complete. Simple optimizations could improve the performance, for example by doing calculations once, pass on the results to child rules where filtering takes place. In the case study, calculations where done at the same time as filtering, requiring each calculation to be executed multiple times instead of once.

Genericity Mismatch. The genericity (or expressiveness) of the GenericAST could be inadequate for a given harvesting project. It means that the GenericAST cannot represent constructs that appear in the project's source code. This risk is hard to identify and predict; it will show up during individual harvesting projects.

Possible ways of minimizing or dealing with the consequences are:

- Provide extension points in meta-model: Currently each element can be extended by tagged-values, which is a light-weight, pragmatic extension mechanism. This will not be sufficient for all situations, but it is a start.
- Extend GenericAST meta-model: Evolving the meta-model requires extensive testing in both the meta-model and tools, because it is a heavy-weight extension mechanism. It has impact on compatibility with existing models and transformations.

The genericity (or expressiveness) of the GenericAST could be too large. It happens when a semantic construct can be represented in more than one way. If this is true it is harder to create generic transformations and analyses on GenericAST models, because there could be two semantically equal models that do not result in the same target model and/or analysis result. This risk is hard to identify and predict.

Possible ways of minimizing the consequences are:

- Thorough meta-model review: For each meta-model element make sure why it exists and what can be represented with it. It should not be able to represent the same construct with any other element.
- Definition of well-formed model guidelines: Identified ambiguities must be resolved by making one option 'preferred' and the other options 'illegal', which can be done with a guideline. Any model that violates a guideline is not a valid GenericAST model. It may be enforced by providing a model-checker which detects and reports violations.

7   Concluding Remarks

Reverse engineering to an MDA target context requires a flexible, automated process that uses open standards as propagated by the OMG. Our reverse engineering framework provides an abstract process with minimal transformations to generate UML models from textual source code. The process consists of several transformations: textual source code is parsed into an AST, which is populated into a MOF-based repository with a meta-model conforming to the grammar that describes the structure of the textual source code. The contents of the MOF-based repository are transformed to an initial target model, which can be a UML model. The benefits of MDA can now be used to their full potential: generated models can be used for documentation, or even for MDA-based forward engineering.

To automate the process our prototype implementation uses generators. The source code structure is described in a grammar and from the grammar a specialized harvester and repository are generated. An improved mapping from an EBNF grammar to a MOF meta-model results in concise and usable repositories.

The generic intermediate model allows us to reuse M2M-transformations and analyses. For specific harvesters a transformation can be developed to generate a generic model. Available transformations and analyses can then be applied to the generic model to get the desired target models.

The case study has shown that the prototype implementation of the reverse engineering framework is able to extract models from a production system of 178 KLOC: UML models have been generated that give insight in structure and behavior. These models can be used for documentation purposes as well as for (partial) forward engineering: in our case Java classes have been generated from the harvested models that represent the application's structure.

Future work firstly regards solving scalability issues for our prototype implementation with the current M2M-transformation engine. An improved version of such an engine is required to support larger M2M-transformations without running into performance problems. A functional extension of the prototype implementation is replacing the parser generator with a more powerful one, such as a Generalized LR parser generator [23] or an expression grammar parser generator [12]. A more powerful parser generator enables usage of island grammars [18], which is a powerful technique to quickly develop grammars for complex structured source code. In an island grammar constructs of interest can be specified in detail while the parser is told to ignore any other construct encountered in the input.

Secondly, it should be investigated whether information in GenericAST models is sufficient to generate target source code, such that method implementations can be generated as much as possible (at least for several constructs this expected to be feasible). A particular challenge is how to represent business logic. It is an open issue to what extend UML Action Semantics can help for the case at hand. To fully evaluate the current GenericAST prototype implementation should be tested on more source languages and evolved accordingly.

Last but not least, a full system migration should be attempted to assess feasibility of using reverse engineered models in an MDA-based forward engineering track. This might require transformation to specific UML profiles, domain specific languages and/or abstraction of platform dependent constructs to platform independent constructs.

References

1. R. Al-Ekram and K. Kontogiannis. An XML-based framework for language neutral program representation and generic analysis. In *CSMR '05: Proceedings of the Ninth European Conference on Software Maintenance and Reengineering (CSMR'05)*, pages 42–51, Washington, DC, USA, 2005. IEEE Computer Society.
2. M. Alanen and I. Porres. A relation between context-free grammars and meta object facility meta-models. Technical Report 606, TUCS Turku Center for Computer Science, 2003.
3. A. Boronat, J. A. Carsi, and I. Ramos. Automatic reengineering in MDA using rewriting logic as transformation engine. In *CSMR '05: Proceedings of the Ninth European Conference on Software Maintenance and Reengineering (CSMR'05)*, pages 228–231, Washington, DC, USA, 2005. IEEE Computer Society.
4. V. Cepa and M. Mezini. Language support for model-driven software development. *Science of Computer Programming*, 2006. Special issue on model-driven architectures; to appear.
5. E.J. Chikofsky and J.H. Cross. Reverse engineering and design recovery: a taxonomy. *IEEE Software*, pages 13–17, January 1990.
6. A. van Deursen, C. Hofmeister, R. Koschke, L. Moonen, and C. Riva. Symphony: View-driven software architecture reconstruction. In *Proceedings Working IEEE/IFIP Conference on Software Architecture (WICSA'04)*, pages 122–134. IEEE Computer Society Press, 2004.
7. A. van Deursen, P. Klint, and C. Verhoef. Research issues in software renovation. In J.-P. Finance, editor, *Fundamental Approaches to Software Engineering (FASE '99)*, Lecture Notes in Computer Science, pages 1–21. Springer-Verlag, 1999.

8. A. van Deursen and T. Kuipers. Building documentation generators. In *Proceedings International Conference on Software Maintenance*, pages 40–49. IEEE Computer Society, 1999.

9. D. Doyle. Transforming proprietary domain-specific modeling languages to model-driven architectures. Master's thesis, Delft University of Technology, 2005. URL: `swerl.tudelft.nl`.

10. J.-M. Favre and T. Nguyen. Towards a megamodel to model software evolution through transformations. *Electr. Notes Theor. Comput. Sci.*, 127(3):59–74, 2005.

11. ADM Task Force. Architecture-driven modernization roadmap. Technical report, OMG, 2006. Draft #1 dated 1/12/2006, `adm.omg.org`.

12. B. Ford. Parsing expression grammars: a recognition-based syntactic foundation. In *Proceedings of the 31st ACM SIGPLAN-SIGACT Symposium on Principles of Programming Languages*, pages 111–122. ACM, 2004.

13. G. Gannod and M. Carey. Evolution of java programs to a model-driven environment using EMF. In *Proceedings EDOC Workshop on Model-Driven Evolution of Legacy Systems (MELS)*. IEEE Computer Society Digital Library, 2004.

14. Java Specification Requests. *JSR 040: Java Metadata Interface (JMI) Specification Version 1.0*, 2002.

15. I. Kurtev, J. Bézevin, and M. Aksit. Technological spaces: An initial appraisal. In *CoopIS, DOA 2002 Federated Conferences*. Springer-Verlag, 2002. Industrial Track.

16. N. Mansurov and D. Campara. Managed architecture of existing code as a practical transition towards MDA. In *UML Modeling Languages and Applications: ≪UML≫ 2004 Satellite Activities*, volume 3297 of *Lecture Notes in Computer Science*, pages 219–233. Springer-Verlag, 2005.

17. L. Moonen. *Exploring Software Systems*. PhD thesis, Faculty of Natural Sciences, Mathematics, and Computer Science, University of Amsterdam, December 2002.

18. L. Moonen. Lightweight impact analysis using island grammars. In *Proceedings of the 10th International Workshop on Program Comprehension (IWPC 2002)*. IEEE Computer Society Press, June 2002.

19. OMG. *Meta Object Facility (MOF) 2.0 Query/View/Transformation Specification*, 2002. Final Adopted Specification, ptc/05-11-01.

20. OMG. *Meta Object Facility (MOF) Specification Version 1.4*, 2002.

21. T. Reus. Harvesting existing software systems for MDA-based reengineering. Master's thesis, Delft University of Technology, 2006. URL: `swerl.tudelft.nl`.

22. W. Ulrich. A status on OMG architecture-driven modernization task force. In *Proceedings EDOC Workshop on Model-Driven Evolution of Legacy Systems (MELS)*. IEEE Computer Society Digital Library, 2004.

23. E. Visser. *Syntax Definition for Language Prototyping*. PhD thesis, University of Amsterdam, September 1997.

24. M. Wimmer and G. Kramler. Bridging grammarware and modelware. In *Satellite Events at the MoDELS 2005 Conference: MoDELS 2005 International Workshops*, volume 3844 of *Lecture Notes in Computer Science*, pages 159–168. Springer-Verlag, 2006.

A Methodology for Database Reengineering
to Web Services

Ignacio García-Rodríguez de Guzmán, Macario Polo, and Mario Piattini

ALARCOS Research Group
Information Systems and Technologies Department
UCLM-Soluziona Research and Development Institute
University of Castilla-La Mancha
Paseo de la Universidad, 4 – 13071 Ciudad Real, Spain
{Ignacio.GRodriguez, Macario.Polo, Mario.Piattini}@uclm.es

Abstract. Databases are one of the most important components of information systems, since they keep all the information of organizations. Although new standards in databases have appeared in the last years, most databases are still based on SQL-92, and are thus true legacy systems. Most of the services offered by information systems are based on the information stored in their databases. In order to allow interoperability, current trends advise exposing some of these services to the Web, making them available for other users and also for the information system itself. Since dealing with old databases and their associated software is difficult, a methodology to discover services from SQL-92 databases and to offer them via Web Services is proposed. This methodology is based on the MDA approach and implements a reengineering process, which starts from an SQL-92 database and obtains a set of services that can be exposed as Web Services.

Keywords: reengineering, reverse engineering, metamodel, Web Service, QVT, patterns, MDA.

1 Introduction

Information systems are composed of many elements, for example documentation, programs, hardware, databases, etc. Of these, the database can be considered as the cornerstone. This importance is due to the role played by databases: they store all the information required for system operation.

Despite the fact that new versions of the SQL standard are being developed (i.e. SQL-99, SQL-2003), many systems are still working with relational databases [1], mainly based on the SQL-92 paradigm [2] .

Programs that use legacy databases are sometimes also legacy programs with low maintainability. Because of that, the effort spent on improving these systems (adding new features, integration into the web, etc.) can be taxing [3] .

Any attempt to deal with this kind of legacy system is difficult for many reasons, such as the size of both the applications and the databases [4] , lack of experience in the source code language, lack of documentation, etc.

A. Rensink and J. Warmer (Eds.): ECMDA-FA 2006, LNCS 4066, pp. 226 – 240, 2006.

Reengineering is a very useful tool for dealing with this kind of problem. According to [5] , reengineering is a process composed of two sub-stages: reverse and forward engineering.

Recently, reverse engineering (the most important stage of reengineering) has become closely related to MDA [6] . In just a few words, MDA makes is possible to separate business logic from the implementation platform [6] . MDA proposes to work at both model and metamodel levels: thus, the implementation stage is not as critical as in the earlier times, because this step can be performed by means of automatic transformations. The relation of reverse engineering and MDA has been strengthened by ADM (*Architecture-Driven Modernization*), which aims to integrate reverse engineering and MDA. Many metamodels have been standardized to support legacy systems, such as CWM [7] . It is essential to represent this kind of systems by means of these metamodels by a reverse engineering stage.

According to [6, 8] , the basic elements of the MDA approach are PIMs (Platform Independent Models), PSMs (Platforms Specific Models), and PDMs (Platform Description Models). When MDA is applied, the software engineer works at a business level with one or more PIMs. Later, and by means of some transformations, one or more PSMs are generated depending on the target platform. If the starting point is not a PIM but a PSM (the legacy system), the process involves two transformations, one to obtain a PIM (representation of the legacy platform) and a second transformation to obtain the target PSM from the PIM [8] . The latter situation is what leads to the aforementioned term "Architecture-Driven Modernization". In this situation, reverse engineering is required to pass from the starting PSM to the PIM: therefore, reverse engineering is a core element in the application of the MDA approach.

In this respect, a methodology based on the idea of reengineering and focusing on databases, using the concepts of MDA and ADM has been developed. The starting PSM is the SQL-92 database; the different PIMs are the set of metamodels used during the process; while the target PSM is the final set of Web Services to be generated.

The methodology also takes into account the fact that, as happens in many applications, the domain layer used is a reflection of the structure of the database which supports the information managed by the application. In other words, having a multi-tier application [9] , the domain (or business) tier is chiefly responsible for implementing the operations required to achieve the objective for which the system was developed. Because of this, the database can be used not only to extract the static structure in a reengineering process, but also to infer many of the original system functionalities.

The development of a general and partially-automated reengineering process for relational databases requires specifying which kind of relational databases are involved. As far as we know, despite the fact that SQL-2003 is the current standard, most databases are still defined in SQL-92 (or the corresponding subset of SQL-2003). For this reason, we are now mainly focused on obtaining all the characteristics of SQL-92 based databases. By means of a set of inference patterns, it is possible to find potential services in the schema of the database, using a model-driven pattern matching process as a sub-step of our general reengineering process.

This paper is organized as follows: Section 2 provides a brief description of the related work; Section 3 overviews our proposal; Section 4 summarizes the reengineering task to be performed until the services are discovered; Sections 5 and 6 depicts the service discovery; Section 7 deals with service implementation, Section 8 puts forth some conclusions and possibilities for future work.

2 Background

Until recently, data reengineering (and more specifically data reverse engineering) had not been one of the most important topics in reengineering for two straight-forward reasons: (1) the traditional partition of software engineering and database systems, and (2) source code reverse engineering seemed more interesting in many aspects in the academic environment [10] . Database reverse engineering can be performed for the following purposes [11-13] : redocumentation, model migration, restructuring, maintainance or improvement, tentative requirements, software assessment, integration, conversion of legacy data, and assessment of the state-of-the-art.

Recovering metadata from databases is a very important issue, because our process starts with a database from which no documentation is available. Here, much research has been done on algorithms and techniques to recover metadata stored in database catalogs. In [14, 15] the authors studied algorithms to extract information about the structure of relational databases. In [16] J.L. Hainaut also made a deep study of the database reverse engineering field.

[17, 18] present a reengineering database project named DB-MAIN. DB-MAIN is a generic methodology supported by a tool of the same name, with the following steps: (1) database structure extraction, and (2) data structure conceptualization.

The MIDAS framework [11] tackles the migration of databases, specifically from net databases to relational databases. This framework also allows for the replacement of database access subroutines by SQL code.

In the field of migration, not all the research tries to tailor the original database to the new model in order to adapt it to a new technology. *Wrapping* can be seen as another kind of migration, in which a logical layer is displayed between the databases and the system. This technique used to be implemented by means of *wrappers* which can be seen as a kind of component, such as an adapter. Wrappers make it possible to transform queries for a particular data model into another one, for example from a particular DMS (*Data Management System*) into a different model [19] . Wrappers are used not only to adapt one data model to another, but also for other purposes, for example adapting a relational database to a distributed environment [20] . In this case, the wrappers work as a *façade* between the database and any external system which attempts to access the information.

However, databases are not always subjects of transformations or migration in reengineering, that is, of operations that (sometimes) modify their structure and require complex data transformations. In [21] , the authors implement a whole reengineering process in a tool, *RelationalWeb*. This tool takes a relational database as input (nowadays it accepts four sorts of DBMS, namely Microsoft Access, SQL Server, Caché Intersystems and Oracle) and generates a full operational application to manage it.

Traditionally, research in database reengineering has focused on the tasks discussed above (migration, restructuring, etc.), but not much research has been done (to our best knowledge) on generating services from relational databases. As with [21], our intention is not to generate applications but rather Web Services, offering operations based on the structure of the database.

Our methodology starts with a particular sort of relational database (as noted above), SQL-92. This is due to the fact that industrial studies show that many information systems are still running over relational databases [1, 22] .

3   An Overview of the Methodology

Fig. 1 illustrates the different steps of the methodology. The first step reverse engineers the SQL-92 database in order to obtain its structure. It obtains an instance of a relational database metamodel representing its complete logical schema.

In the next step, the instance (a model) of the database metamodel is transformed into an instance (also a model) of a metamodel describing an object-oriented representation. This model is instrumented with basic operations and state machines to define its behavior.

Then, the engineer guides the process of service discovery, applying different techniques. As a result, a set of services are shaped in an abstract manner.

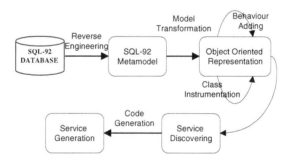

Fig. 1. Process overview

The last stage is the service generation. By means of transformations, a code implementation of the abstract service description is generated. All the stages are explained in the following sections.

4   Preparing the Environment: A Reverse Engineering Task

This section explains the different steps of the methodology in detail.

4.1   Database Metadata Extraction for Schema Representation

An effective strategy for recovering the database schema is used in [23, 24], where database metadata is extracted via specific queries thrown against the database data dictionary.

All these metadata are stored and represented via the SQL-92 metamodel in Fig. 2, proposed by [25] , which considers all the elements of the SQL-92 standard [2]. By means of this metamodel, all the metadata stored in the original database can be represented. From now on we call this sub-metamodel SQL92Schema.

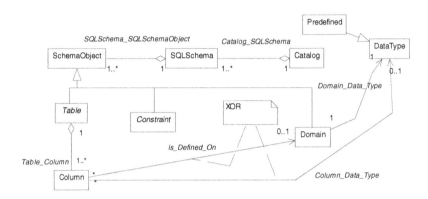

Fig. 2. General View of the SQL-92 metamodel

4.2   An Object-Oriented Representation of the Database

Once the structure of the database has been recovered, the next step in the process translates the instance of the database metamodel (SQL92Schema) into an instance of an object-oriented metamodel, representing the conceptual schema corresponding to the database. This object-oriented representation is the starting point for inferring and building services, establishing a layer between the exposed services and the database itself.

The object-oriented metamodel is extracted from the UML 2 specification [26]. This metamodel has been made up by a subset of the *Classes* package of UML2, but has not been included here due to the lack of space.

4.3   Transforming the SQL92Schema into the OOSv2 Metamodel

This section explains how to obtain an object-oriented representation from a database schema by means of a QVT composed transformation.

All the elements managed are models: thus, the reengineering process is platform-independent and the database service discovery is performed in a conceptual level. In this way, the generation of source code is deferred to the final stage, when the artifacts implementing the services must be generated.

The QVT language [27] was chosen to perform the transformations. QVT is a powerful language to specify transformations among models (and in the same fashion metamodels). QVT includes both a syntactical and graphical notation to define transformations.

Due to the extension of the complete transformation, Table 1 shows only a small part of the QVT algorithm to transform an instance of the SQL92Schema metamodel into an instance of the OOSv2 metamodel.

Table 1. QVT transformation to obtain an object-oriented system from an SQL-92 Schema

transformation SQLSchemaToOOSv2
 (sql92db: SQL92Schema, oos2: OOSv2){
 	
 key Class{name, owner};
 key Association{name, owner};
 key Property{name, owner};
 	
 top relation SQL92SchemaToOOSv2{...}
 top relation TableToUMLElement{...}
 top relation ConstraintToUMLElement{...}
 relation
    ReferentialConstraintToAssociation{...}
 relation UniqueConstraintToProperty{...}
 relation BaseTableToClass{...}
 relation ColumnToProperty{...}
	relation DomainToUMLConstraint{...}
	 relation ViewToClass{...}
	 relation AssertToConstraint{...}
	 relation TableCheckConstraintToUMLConstraint{...}
	 //Funciones
	 function SQL92_ValueToOOSv2V_Value
	   (domain sql92 col:Column{ }):
	   domain oos2 val:ValueSpecification{ }
	 function SQL92_TypeToOOSv2_Type
	   (domain sql92 type: DataType{ }):
	   domain oos2 type:DataType{ }
	 function DomConstraintToUMLClassInvariant
	   (domain sqp92 cons:Constraint{ }):
	   domain oos2 cons:Constraint{ }

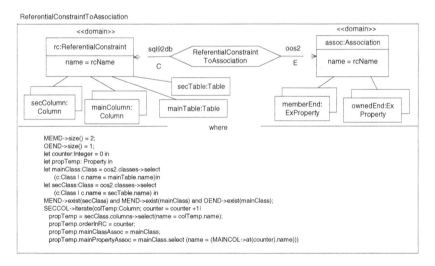

Fig. 3. QVT transformation to obtain a UML association from an SQL-92 foreign key

The algorithm here is a composed function that triggers the functions shown in Figs. 3 and 4 (graphical representation): for example, *View2Class, ReferentialConst-raint2Association, BaseTable2Class, Assertion2UMLConstraint*, etc. In the same way, other transformations are triggered later, as a consequence of the execution of the main transformation (Table 1).

Transformation in Fig. 4 is in charge of transforming a column from a table to a property of a class. In the same way, we have developed another transformation which is also invoked by the *SQL92S_2_OOSv2*, the *ReferentialConstraint2-Association* transformation in Fig. 3. This takes a foreign key (which is composed of one set of referencing columns and one of referenced columns) and generates a UML Association (between one class representing the referencing table and other class representing the referenced table).

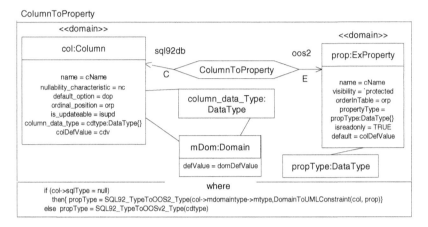

Fig. 4. QVT transformation to obtain a UML property from an SQL Column

5   Class Instrumentation

At this stage of the process, all the work is focused on the instance of the OOSv2 metamodel (that is, the representation of the relational database schema). That means that all classes involved in a service are in fact an object-oriented representation of the relational database tables and the parameters of a service are required to perform an operation over the database.

Before performing any task for service discovery, the set of obtained classes must be instrumented with methods. Up to now classes have been created from tables, and each class owns properties but no methods. Thus, before composing any service, methods must be assigned to all classes.

The basic CRUD operations (*C*reate, *R*ead, *U*pdate and *D*elete, shown in Fig. 5) are added to all classes.

In addition, other operations may be required to add extra behavior to our classes. Imagine the class *Account* representing a banking account (previously recovered from a table). It is very likely that this class would require operations such as *deposit*, *withdraw* or *getBalance*. In other words, many classes would require operations to shape their behavior.

In addition to these operations, a state machine for some classes is also provided in order to give the class a more similar behavior than it has in reality. See [21] for further explanations.

The set of states corresponding to each class can be assigned by hand or be inferred from the data saved in the database. Transitions, however, must always be designed by the engineer, since there is no information about them.

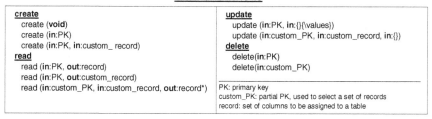

create	update
create (**void**)	update (**in**:PK, **in**:{}{\values})
create (**in**:PK)	update (**in**:custom_PK, **in**:custom_record, **in**:{})
create (**in**:PK, **in**:custom_ record)	delete
read	delete(**in**:PK)
read (**in**:PK, **out**:record)	delete(**in**:custom_PK)
read (**in**:PK, **out**:custom_record)	
read (**in**:custom_PK, **in**:custom_record, **out**:record*)	PK: primary key
	custom_PK: partial PK, used to select a set of records
	record: set of columns to be assigned to a table

Fig. 5. CRUD operations to be added

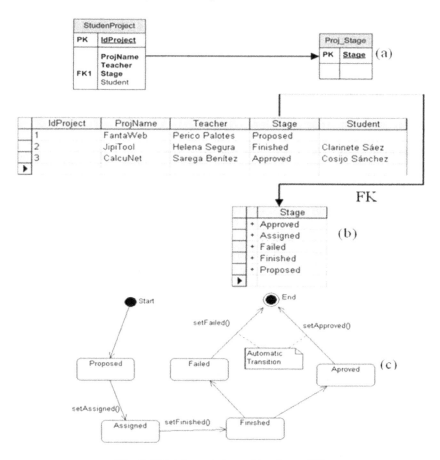

Fig. 6. Obtaining a state machine from a FK

The automation of state discovery inside classes relies on some heuristics. Some of these rules are the following:

- *Use of limit values*: in numeric columns (later transformed to properties), limit values are suggested in order to identify intervals that, at the end, can be seen as states. For example, remember our *Account* table. The *Balance* column (repre-senting the money in the banking account) must be of a numeric data type. Three limit values can be obtained, namely negative values, zero and positive values. According to this, any account would be in any of these intervals: *Balance-Negative* ($-\infty$ < Balance <0), *BalanceZero* (Balance = 0) and *BalancePositive* (0 < Balance < ∞).

- Now suppose a table, and one of its columns referencing via a foreign key another table with just one column (with a short set of values, such as an enumeration). It is possible that these values are defining the state of the corresponding table record and class instance. For example, in Fig. 6 (a) two tables are observed, the first one representing projects developed by students and the second representing the possible stages a project may have: thus, the *stage* column in the first table is constrained by the second table via referential constraint (Fig. 6 (b)). Taking the values of the *Proj_Stage* table as possible states, a suitable state machine results from this supposition (Fig. 6 (c)).

In order to integrate the class instrumentation inside the full process, the State Machine metamodel of the UML2 specification has been taken into account.

6 Extracting Services for SQL-92 Databases

6.1 Service Extraction

A service is a function that is well-defined, self-contained, and does not depend on the context or state of other services [28] . Also, a service can be seen as an operation which may need a set of parameters and that may return a result.

One of the first issues before generating services automatically is how to build these services in a generic manner. Since a metamodel is an abstract language for some kind of metadata [29] , a service metamodel has been developed to represent any database-based service.

A service can be divided into two basic parts: the static and the dynamic compo-nent. The static component of the metamodel represents all the artifacts involved in the service such as classes, parameters, etc. The dynamic component of the service is related to the behavior of the service, that is, the execution flow of the service. This dynamic component lets the engineer model the set of steps that must be taken to achieve the goal of the service.

In the methodology, a service will be translated into an (more or less) complex SQL sentence. That is, both the result of the Model-Driven Pattern Matching (see section 6.2) and the CRUD operations (see section 5).

Due to the SQL representation of services, a dynamic description is not required, but a complete one of the structural elements of the service is essential. With this aim in mind, a service metamodel has been developed. This metamodel does not cover the full syntax of the SQL-92 standard but the required the methodology. Instead of the BNF description of SQL-92 standard this metamodel has been build because (1) it is easier to manage and integrate in the MDA process, (2) also to have a service representation compatible with the other metamodels involved in the process, (3) because this metamodel contains all the required elements to generate the requited source code to implement services in the code generation stage, and is more suitable than the SQL-92 BNF notation to represent services.

Together with this metamodel, a complete OCL set of invariants has been added to many of the classes in order to specify with are the correct models (of services) that could be generated having the kind of service and the operations involved in the service. Due to the lack of space, these OCL invariants will be studied in further publications.

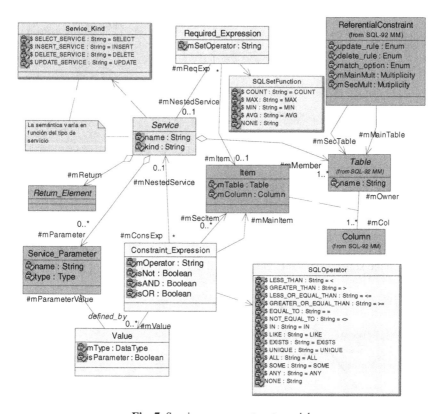

Fig. 7. Service component metamodel

6.2 Model-Driven Pattern Matching

As noted above, the database schema is considered as the reflection of the domain layer, so it is very possible that many of the functionalities of the application are reflected in the schema of the relational databases.

Being M_A the set of elements that could take part in a service, it is possible to match this model against a bigger model, namely M_B, in order to find occurrences of M_A. That is, M_A may be used as a pattern to search inside M_B.

In our context, M_B could be either the SQL92Schema or the OOSv2. The goal of this process would be to obtain a set with all the occurrences of the elements of the model that matches the given specification, and choose among them those that fit our intention.

The idea explained above corresponds to the *model-driven pattern matching* (from now on, MDPEM) concept. This idea is briefly outlined in the MDA specification [6], but emphasized more in the QVT specification [27]: *"The essential idea behind pattern matching is to allow the succinct expression of complex constraints on an input data type; data which matches the pattern is then picked out and returned to the invoker"*.

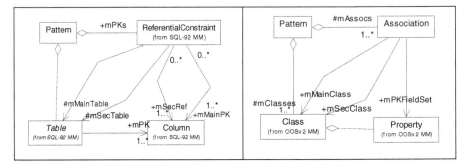

Fig. 8. Pattern metamodels

In this context, the pattern (or the mechanism to shape something that could be offered as a service) is a generic description of a pattern to do the matching against a model. In this respect, the metamodels in Fig. 8 are proposed. These metamodels does not work in the same way as the one proposed in [30], which is more general.

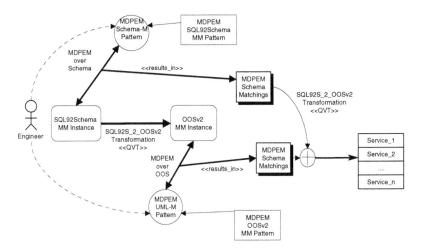

Fig. 9. MDPEM: inputs and results

Because MDPEM can be performed at two different levels of abstraction (namely the SQL92Schema and the OOSv2 level), a pattern metamodel has been designed for each one. While Fig. 8 (a) depicts the metamodel for building a pattern at a OOSv2 level, Fig. 8 (b) depicts a metamodel for builing patterns at the SQL92Schema level.

Looking at the metamodels, it can be seen that both of them represent the same concepts, but at the two different levels of abstraction. This fact means that the MDPEM can be performed over the two models without distinction. Since there is a QVT transformation to obtain an OOSv2 instance from a SQL92Schema instance (see Section 0), this mechanism can be also applied to transform results from MDPEM at the SQL92Schema level to OOSv2 results. This means that the engineer can choose to apply MDPEM to any of the abovementioned levels.

Fig. 9 helps explain the MDPEM process. As Fig. 9 shows, MDPEM is guided by the engineer in charge of the reengineering process. Having both the instance of the SQL-92 metamodel and the object oriented system metamodel, the engineer can choose where to apply the MDPEM technique, depending on the skill of the engineer and his/her preferences, because at the end, all matchings found in the SQL92Schema instance could be transformed to OOSv2 ones by means of our QVT transformations. An example of this process is presented below.

6.2.1 An Example of the Application of MDPEM

Given the relational database in Fig. 10 (b), a pair of patterns (Fig. 10 (a)), which will be applied later, are going to be proposed, both over the SQL92Schema and OOSv2 metamodel instances.

The pattern of Fig. 10 expresses four tables (namely C_p, D_p, E_p and M_p) and three foreign keys (namely FK_{p1}, FK_{p2} and FK_{p3}), where FK_{p1} is a foreign key from M_p to C_p, FK_{p2} is a foreign key from M_p to D_p, and Fkp_3 is a foreign key from M_p to E_p. These elements belong to a conceptual set, namely S, which represents all the elements of the recovered schema. The MDPEM process could be also be expressed by means of a pseudo-SQL query:

$$SELECT \ C_S, D_S, E_S, M_S, FK_{S1}, FK_{S2}, FK_{S3} \in S . FK_{S1}(C_S, M_S)$$
$$\land FK_{S2}(D_S, M_S) \land FK_{S3}(E_S, M_S)$$

In this pseudo-SQL query, A_S, B_S, C_S and M_S represents tables and FK_{S1}, FK_{S2} and FK_{S3} represents foreign keys, both from the recovered schema. The result of the MDPEM over the schema represented by Fig. 10 will be composed of two occurrences. One of these results (which is only a view of the whole model) will be composed of *Classroom*, *Academic_Year*, *Teacher* and *Give* tables (which match the C_p, D_p E_p and M_p tables of the pattern respectively) and their corresponding foreign keys (which have no names in the schema but probably numerical identifiers). It is important to note that the result of the MDPEM can be represented by the service metamodel proposed in Fig. 7.

Implementing the patterns with an abstract description of an operation, in which all the elements of the pattern are involved, could be very useful for the semi-automatic generating of source code in further steps. In this way, after matching is done, the result is the abstract specification of an operation where the elements involved are real elements of the schema and not abstract entities of the pattern. Obviously, many parts of the abstract operation must be customized before the services are generated. This point is currently being researched and we think that would be useful to provide a special language to express these abstract operations together with our proposal.

At the end of the MDPEM process, each instance of the patterns is susceptible to being transformed to a Web Service (see the following section). Because the entire process revolves around models and views of these models, the target implementation platform does not matter, because it is automatically generated. It only depends on the available factories to generate code in different platforms (such as J2EE, .NET, etc.).

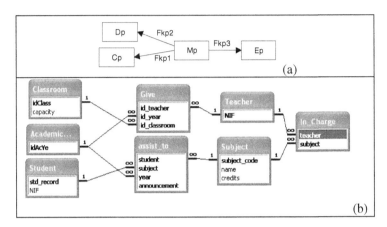

Fig. 10. Two patterns for searching in an SQL-92 Schema

7   Service Implementation: The Last Step

In the previous sections, a methodology to reengineer SQL-92 databases to discover services was explained. The main goal of this work is to develop a method to help the software engineer expose services from a legacy system, in our case an SQL-92 database.

Our choice for publishing these services is Web Services technology. The reason for using Web Services instead of other types of component or software artifacts is that Web Services were created for system integration and to wrap legacy systems [31]. Specifically, the use of Web Services for legacy system integration is a fact [32]. So, on one hand, Web Services were chosen because the target of the methodology is true legacy systems such as an SQL-92 database which is still widely in use and on the other hand, Web Services work over any technology due to the fact that this technology lean on standard protocols such as SOAP, WSDL and UDDI.

Currently, QVT transformations to generate Web Services from abstract service specifications are being defined. In this case, the core of the transformation is the obtained services and the WSDL specification of a Web Service. The WSDL documents work as a contract between the provider and the customer, because this specification is where the customer can learn which operations the Web Service provides, along with the signature of each operation. Different strategies to perform this transformation are being studied.

The source models for the last transformation in our process are the services, while the target model is the WSDL document metamodel and the implementation of the services as well. Different versions of transformations would be created in order to generate Web Services in different platforms.

8 Conclusions and Future Work

Up to now, a complex but fully functional environment for database reengineering (Relational Web) has been developed, and its efficiency has been proven in many projects [21] .

Despite the fact that SQL-92 technology is obsolete, most legacy systems and most companies are still working over this kind of database. For this reason, an effective process for reengineering this kind of database towards the web, exposing functionalities and operations, is being designed.

In section 4.1, the SQL-92 part of the metamodel presented in [25] was chosen to work with, but current results will be extended to subsequent versions of SQL (namely 1999 and 2003 versions).

Our research is mainly focused on discovering hidden functionalities by means of pattern matching and state machines. These functionalities are exposed by means of Web Services, which are also automatically generated inside the reengineering process.

Transformations are described using QVT as transformation language. Due to the novelty of this language, not too much tools support the full syntax of QVT. However, until a suitable QVT engine could be used, transformations will be represented by means of an implemented algorithm.

Acknowledgements. This work is partially supported by the MÁS project (Mantenimiento Ágil del Software), Ministerio de Ciencia y Tecnología/FEDER, TIC2003-02737-C02-02, and the ENIGMAS project, Plan Regional de Investigación Científica, Desarrollo Tecnológico e Innovación, Junta de Comunidades de Castilla La Mancha, PBI-05-058.

References

1. Blaha, M. A Retrospective on Industrial Database Reverse Engineering Projects-Part 1. in Proceedings of the 8th Working Conference on Reverse Engineering (WCRE´01). 2001. Suttgart, Germany: IEEE Computer Society.
2. ISO/IEC, ISO/IEC 9075:1992, Database Language SQL. 1992.
3. Zimmermann, O., M. Tomlinson, and S. Peuser, Perspectives on Web Services. Applying SOAP, WSDL and UDDI to Real-World Projects. Primera Edición ed. Springer Professional Computing. 2003, Germany: Springer. pp. 645.
4. Wang, X., et al. Business Rules Extraction from Large Legacy Systems. in Proceedings of the Eighth Euromicro Working Conference on Software Maintenance and Reengineering. 2004. Tampere, Finland.
5. Chikofsky, E.J. and J.H. Cross, Reverse Engineering and Desing Recovery: A Taxonomy. IEEE Software, 1990(January): p. 13-17.
6. OMG, MDA Guide Version 1.0.1. 2003, Object Management Group. p. 62.
7. Favre, J.-M., M. Godfrey, and A. Winter. Integrating Reverse Engineering and Model Driven Engineering. in Proceedings of the Second International Workshop on Meta-Models and Schemas for Reverse Engineering (ateM 2004). 2004. Delft, The Netherlands.
8. Bézivin, J. Model Engineering for Software Modernization. in Guest Talk in the 11th IEEE Working Conference of Reverse Engineering. 2004.
9. Larman, C., Applying UML and Patterns. 1998, New York: Prentice Hall, Upper Saddle River.

10. Müller, H.A., et al. Reverse Engineering: A Roadmap. in International Conference on Software Engineering - Proceedings of the Conference on The Future of Software Engineering. 2000. Limerick, Ireland.
11. Cohen, Y. and Y.A. Feldman, Automatic High-Quality Reengineering of Database Programs by Abstraction, Transformation and Reimplementation. ACM Transactions on Software Engineering and Methodology, 2003. **12**(3): p. 285-316.
12. Blaha, M. Dimensions of Database Reverse Engineering. in Fourth Working Conference on Reverse Engineering (WCRE '97). 1997. Amsterdam, The NETHERLANDS.
13. Henrard, J. and J.-L. Hainaut. Data dependency elicitation in database reverse engineering. in Fifth European Conference on Software Maintenance and Reengineering (CSMR´01). 2001. Lisbon, Portugal: IEEE Computer Society.
14. Soutou, C., Relational database reverse engineering: algorithms to extract cardinality constraints. Data & Knowledge Engineering, Elsevier Science Publishers B. V., 1998. **28**(2): p. 161-207.
15. Sousa, P.M.A., et al. Clustering Relations into Abstract ER Schemas for Database Reverse Engineering. in Proceedings of the Third European Conference on Software Maintenance and Reengineering. 1999. Amsterdam, Netherlands: IEEE Computer Society.
16. Hainaut, J.-L., et al. Database Design Recovery. in Eighth Conferences on Advance Information Systems Engineering. 1996. Berlin.
17. Henrard, J., et al. Program understanding in database reverse engineering. 2002.
18. Hick, J.-M. and J.-L. Hainaut, Strategy for Database Application Evolution: The DB-MAIN Approach. LNCS 2813, 2003: p. 291-306.
19. Thiran and J.-L. Hainaut. Wrapper Development for Legacy Data Reuse. in Eighth Working Conference on Reverse Engineering (WCRE'01). 2001. Suttgart, Alamania: IEEE Computer Society.
20. Bychkov, Y. and J.H. Jahnke. Interactive Migration of Legacy Databases to Net-Centric Technologies. in Proceedings of the Eighth Working Conference On Reverse Engineering (WCRE´01). 2001: IEEE Computer Society.
21. García-Rodríguez de Guzmán, I., M. Polo, and M. Piattini. An Integrated Environment for Reengineering. in Proceedings of the 21st International Conference on Software Maintenance (ICSM 2005). 2005. Hungary, Budapest: IEEE Computer Society.
22. Blaha, M. A Retrospective on Industrial Database Reverse Engineering Projects-Part 2. in Proceedings of the 8th Working Conference on Reverse Engineering (WCRE´01). 2001. Suttgart, Germany: IEEE Computer Society.
23. Polo, M., et al., Generating three-tier applications from relational databases: a formal and practical approach. Information & Software Technology, 2002. **44**(15): p. pp. 923-941.
24. García-Rodríguez de Guzmán, I., M. Polo, and M. Piattini. An integrated environment for reengineering. in 21st IEEE International Conference on Software Maintenance. 2005. Budapest, Hungría: IEEE Computer Society.
25. Calero, C., et al., An Ontological Approach To Describe the SQL:2003 Object-Relational Features. Accepted in "Computer Standards and Interfaces", 2005: p. 28.
26. OMG, Unified Modeling Language: Superstructure. Versión 2.0. 2005.
27. QVTP, Revised submission for MOF 2.0 Query / Views /Transformations RFP (Version 1.1). 2003, QVT-Partners (http://qvtp.org/).
28. WSSOA, Web Services and Service-Oriented Architectures. 2005.
29. OMG, Meta Object Facility (MOF) Specification. 2002.
30. Pagel, B.-U. and M. Winter. Towards Pattern-Based Tools. in Proceedings of EuropLop. 1996.
31. Alonso, G., et al., Web Services. Concepts, Architectures and Applications, ed. M.J. Carey and S. Ceri. 2004, Berlin: Springer. pp. 354.
32. Lavery, J., et al. Laying the Foundations for Web Services over Legacy Systems. in Proceedings of the Fourth International Workshop on Web Site Evolution (WSE'02). 2002. Montreal, Canada.

Business Process Modeling: Defining Domain Specific Modeling Languages by Use of UML Profiles

Steen Brahe and Kasper Østerbye

IT University of Copenhagen, Copenhagen, Denmark
stbr@itu.dk, kasper@itu.dk

Abstract. General-purpose modeling languages are inadequate to model and visualize business processes precisely. An enterprise has its own vocabulary for modeling processes and its specific tasks may have attached data that define the tasks precisely. We propose using Domain Specific Modeling (DSM) languages to model business processes, such that an enterprise can define its own DSM language(s) capturing its vocabulary and data requirement. We suggest using UML profiles and UML activity diagrams as the semantic base for these DSM languages and present tools that are able to create a DSM language and tool support for a given domain. One tool, called ADSpecializer, can generate a UML profile and its tool support of a given application domain. The other tool, ADModeler, is used to create UML activity diagrams within such a domain-specific UML profile. The two tools enable an enterprise to efficiently define and utilize their own DSM language.

1 Introduction

Model Driven Engineering (MDE), as an approach for describing and implementing business processes, is believed to speed up the development time and be less error prone compared to traditional software development. Several standards have been proposed for modeling and implementing business processes [2]. Based on experiences at using MDE for describing and implementing business processes in a large Scandinavian bank, we recognize a need to have domain specific modeling languages to be able to succeed using the MDE approach. Each enterprise has its own terms for modeling business processes and has enterprise specific implementation patterns for these terms. The development of a common vocabulary in a large enterprise is crucial for efficiency. To tailor modeling tools efficiently to this common vocabulary is therefore a prerequisite for us to apply MDE.

A general language is too abstract to be used by people working in a specific domain. As Bézivin and Heckel state [1 p. 1], "model-driven approaches to software development require precise definitions and tool support for modeling languages, their syntax and semantics".

We see at least three obstacles to use a general purpose modeling language compared to a domain specific modeling (DSM) language for business process modeling:

- *Semantics*. Specific semantics for custom tasks like RegisterInvoice cannot be defined. A modeler has to remember to define necessary data when using the task

A. Rensink and J. Warmer (Eds.): ECMDA-FA 2006, LNCS 4066, pp. 241–255, 2006.
© Springer-Verlag Berlin Heidelberg 2006

in models and there is no tool support for providing and validating the data. A transformation engine does not recognize a task like RegisterInvoice because it is modeled as a general task.

- *Visualization*. There is no customized visual presentation of the model. Visualization is important because different people such as users, business analysts, architects and developers all have to understand the model.
- *Abstraction*. A business process may be modeled at a high abstraction level. A task such as RegisterInvoice may not have a simple implementation as e.g. a web service invocation. Instead, it could have an implementation pattern, for instance a sequence of three web service calls, and mechanisms for handling exceptions. These details are not relevant for the model, but have to be modeled when using a general language to make transformation to an implementation possible.

The primary argument against using DSM languages and customized tasks for each enterprise or even each business unit inside the enterprise is that the set of necessary languages and tasks to define will continue to evolve. We address this argument by providing tool support for definition and generation of custom tasks and new languages.

This is in line with Bézivin and Heckel [1, p. 1] who state "In order to support model-driven development in a variety of contexts, we must find efficient ways of designing languages, accepting that definitions are evolving and that tools need to be delivered in a timely fashion". Software systems are evolving all the time and enterprises will also have to extend and enrich their DSM languages. To do this efficiently they need ways to get customized modeling tools for the extended DSM languages.

We have developed two Eclipse-based UML2 tools, *ADModeler* and *ADSpecializer*. ADModeler is a plug-in that implements a UML activity diagram editor. ADSpecializer can define and generate UML profiles and data entry wizards encapsulated as Eclipse plug-ins for ADModeler. The modeler who uses a DSM language generated by ADSpecializer is not aware that she is modeling in UML. Both the language and tool support appear domain specific.

1.1 Background

The Model Driven Architecture (MDA) initiative by the Object Management Group (OMG) is an implementation of the general MDE approach for developing software around a set of standards like MOF, UML, CWM etc. [5]. UML is a visual language for specifying, constructing and documenting software systems [4]. It is a broad-spectrum language and consists of several diagram types. One of these, the activity diagram, has modeling of organizational processes as one of its purposes. UML is defined by the Meta Object Facility (MOF) [3]. MOF is a meta-meta model because it is used for defining other meta-models like UMF. MOF is defined by itself.

When using MDA standards, there are two possible approaches for creating DSM languages. The first approach is the definition of a new language based directly on MOF. Such a language becomes an alternative to UML. The Common Warehouse Meta model (CWM) is an example of such a language. The syntax and semantics of the elements of the new language can be defined to match the specific domain.

The second approach is based on specialization of the existing UML entities using UML profiles. The intention of profiles is to give a straightforward mechanism for adapting UML with constructs that are specific to a particular domain, platform, or method. A profile is constructed by using the extensibility elements: stereotypes, tagged values, and constraints. Stereotypes are specific meta-classes, tagged values are standard meta-attributes, and constraints are restrictions on how an element can be used in models. Using profiles is considered a lightweight method of defining a DSM language, while basing the language on MOF is considered a heavyweight method.

UML Profiles have been made for many specific purposes. For example several profiles have been defined for business process modeling [13, 18] or for implementation technologies such as J2EE, where refined UML Class diagram differentiate between home and remote interfaces. Each of these profiles defines UML for a particular context.

Meta-modeling tools like MetaEdit+ [12] and GME [7] show that it is possible to provide generic tool support for domain specific modeling languages. At present such tools do not exist for MOF although work is going on in projects like GMF (Graphical Modeling Framework)[22]. In contrast, the use of UML profiles for customizing the modeling language is supported by several UML modeling tools.

Business process models are sufficiently similar to the fundamental abstractions of activity diagrams so that we believe using profiles for defining DSM languages is feasible. UML Activity diagrams can model most of the workflow patterns described in [9] and have more expressive power than most of the industrial workflow management standards [10, 11] for implementing business processes. It is therefore a natural choice to use activity diagrams for modeling business processes.

1.2 Our Work

We use UML activity diagrams and UML profiles to create domain specific modeling languages for business processes. Activity diagrams have the formal expressive power to formulate the business processes we want to model. UML is a specification and is supported by general tools such as Rational and Poseidon, which support creation and use of profiles.

However, using profiles for domain specific modeling in general modeling tools requires good knowledge of both UML and profiles as the general tools do not support modeling directly in domain specific terms. The usability of the tools remains low, in particular:

1. The abstract notion of actions lies far from concrete tasks like "change reservation". This makes the tools less useful to domain experts.
2. There is no way to customize how attributes for a particular stereotype such as "RegisterInvoice" should be entered.
3. There is no design-time validation of attribute values or model element relationships.

The general tools do not support these requirements, and the commercial tools are not sufficiently open to tailor them. We will therefore work with the open source tool Eclipse [19]. The UML2 eclipse project [20] provides an implementation of the

UML2 specification and is based on the Eclipse Modeling Framework (EMF) [21] which implements a subset of MOF.

We address the vision of providing enterprise specific process modeling tools in a two-step fashion. First, our ADModeler is a general-purpose extensible and open source UML activity-diagram editor, and is to our knowledge the first such for the Eclipse framework. Special emphasis has been placed on rendering UML profiles containing specification of icons for each stereotype, and the definition and management of mandatory auxiliary data.

Secondly, our ADSpecializer enables efficient development of enterprise specific profiles. It can generate a profile for use by ADModeler. It creates icons, images and text to present the specific profile in ADModeler, and wizards to enter data for the specific tasks. The Eclipse framework provides a rapid and seamless profile-development cycle for testing plug-ins, which we leverage by making ADSpecializer generate the profile as an Eclipse plug-in. ADSpecializer is a no-coding-required tool and requires only limited knowledge of UML activity diagrams.

We define two different roles, a tool developer and a modeler. The tool developer is a person responsible for developing tools in an enterprise. He uses ADSpecializer to create DSM languages. The modeler is a domain expert. She uses ADModeler with extensions created by the tool developer to model business processes precisely in domain specific terms.

The usability of ADModeler is enabled for a particular domain as the specific tasks are available directly from the editor's tool palette, addressing point one above. When adding a task, the modeler is presented a wizard to define data for the attributes of the task. This addresses point two above. Point three is addressed by allowing a tool developer to define validation rules in the generated wizards for the different tasks, so consistency in the model is ensured.

A tool developer can use ADSpecializer to create a DSM language and customized tool support for it with only limited insight into UML. Further, using the ADModeler it is possible for a modeler to work with domain specific terms without any knowledge of UML.

The rest of the paper is structured as follows: In section 2, we give an example of using our tools to model processes in a human family. We first identify domain specific tasks for modeling processes in the family, then we create a new language for modeling processes using the ADSpecializer, and last we create a model of the process of getting home from work using the newly generated DSM language. In section 3, we describe the architecture of the tools, and in section 4 and 5 we describe related work, give a summary, and outline future work.

2   Example: DSM Language for Processes in a Family

We illustrate the power of defining a DSM language and a customized tool for a particular domain by looking at the processes in a human family. The family domain has been chosen since it is well known to all and easy to illustrate. Example of processes in a family are *Getting home from work*, *Go to the cinema* and *Drive on vacation*.

First, we define the language. We ask: what specialized tasks do we require to model processes in the family, what are the attributes for these tasks, and what new data types do we need. Secondly, we use the ADSpecializer to define the language and to generate a plug-in to the ADModeler. Thirdly, we use the generated plug-in together with the ADModeler to model the process of getting home from work.

2.1 Language Definition

We limit the language for modeling processes in the family to deal with six different task types. These are Transport, Clean, Cook, Shop, Relax and Nurse Kid, and are described below in table 1 including the images used for their graphical representation.

Table 1. Custom tasks for the Family DSML

Task	Icon	Description
Transport		Transport family members to a destination using some kind of transportation, e.g. a car, a bus or a train
Clean		Clean a room. The cleaning can be of different types, e.g. vacuum cleaning, wash the floor etc.
Cook		Cook a meal. It must be specified which kind of meal should be created; breakfast, lunch or dinner
Shop		Do some specific shopping, such as groceries or clothes.
Relax		Take some time for watching TV, exercise or sleep. For the task it must also be specified for how long time relaxation can be done.
Nurse kid		Take care of the children, play with them, put them to bed, etc.

To be able to define these tasks and their attributes we must also define some data types. For example we must have a data type defining that we can choose between the kitchen, the toilet and the living room when we use the Clean task and have to decide which room to clean. Table 2 lists the different data types for our new language. Here we define only Enumeration data types, although we could also have defined composite data types containing attributes of other data types. When we have specified the required data types, we can define the custom tasks and their attributes. These can be found in table 3.

Table 2. Data types for family DSML

Data type	Possible values
TransportationType	Car, Bicycle, Train, Bus
CleanType	Vacuum clean, Wash floor
RoomType	Kitchen, Toilet, Living room
MealType	Breakfast, Lunch, Dinner
ShoppingType	Grocery, Clothes, Lumberyard
ActivityType	Sleep, Play soccer, Watch TV
NurseType	Play, Bath, Change nappies, Put to bed

Now, after having described the custom tasks, their attributes, and the required data types, we can generate the language using the ADSpecializer.

Table 3. The custom tasks and their attributes

Task	Attributes	Type	Description
Transport	meansOfTransport	TransportationType	Which transport?
	destination	String	Where to go?
Clean	room	RoomType	What room to clean?
	cleanWhat	CleanType	What to clean?
Cook	Meal	MealType	Which meal to cook?
	Persons	Integer	Number of persons.
Shop	shopKind	ShopType	What to shop?
Relax	activity	ActivityType	What to do?
	duration	integer	How many minutes?
Nurse kid	activity	NurseType	What to do?
	duration	integer	How many minutes?

2.2 Language Creation

The ADSpecializer creates an extension to the ADModeler after a tool developer has used a wizard to define the previously described language. The wizard contains three steps. First, the language or the profile is named and described. Then the tasks are defined, and at last, the custom data types and attributes for the tasks are defined.

Completing the wizard, a new Eclipse plug-in project is created containing an UML profile with stereotypes, attributes and data types as defined in the wizard. Further, the plug-in extends the ADModeler so the defined tasks can be used within ADModeler. The generated plug-in project also contains generated wizards for each task to be used to collect data for the defined attributes when a modeler inserts a task of a given type into a model.

2.3 The Process of Getting Home from Work

While it would have been useful to demonstrate a process from an industrial application, we have chosen to show a process from the domain of a human family because it is well known to all. Here we describe a simplified process of getting home from work and try to model it by using our domain specific language.

After getting off from work, you drive to the daycare to pick up your child. Then you go to the grocery shop to buy food for dinner and, then you drive home. At home a lot of things now happen in parallel; you start cooking dinner, you have to check the nappies on your kid and optionally change it, also you have to play with the kid, and you have to clean the floor. When dinner is ready, you stop cleaning, and the family eats. After dinner, you put your kid to bed, and exhausted, go to relax in front of the television for an hour before going to sleep.

This process has been modeled in ADModeler using the Family language and can be found in figure 1, which also illustrates the ADModeler working with the generated plug-in containing the Family language. In the tool palette to the right, all the customized tasks as defined in table 1 can be found. A task instance can be dragged from the palette onto the model. As the figure illustrates, we have also customized the general UML decision and merge nodes to use a question mark as image. Doing this makes the tool more intuitive to use by a domain expert.

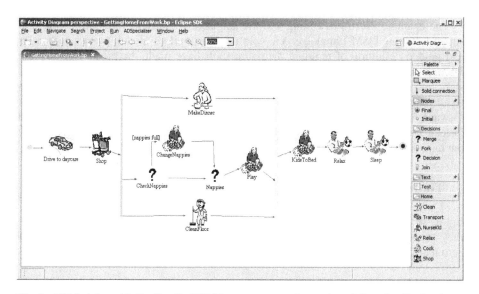

Fig. 1. ADModeler with the Family DSM language extension and modeling the *Getting home from work* process

Still the modeler could be customized further, e.g. unnecessary menus and toolbars could be removed from the tool, and a special view for accessing attribute data could be created.

Whereas the customized diagram is syntactic sugar over plain UML, the semantics of the task instances is the real force of our approach. When a task instance is added to the model, the modeler is presented with a customized wizard for collecting data

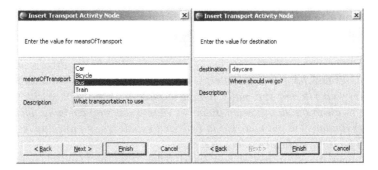

Fig. 2. Generated wizard pages for defining data for the Transport Task attributes

for the attributes defined for the task. Figure 2 shows the two generated wizard pages for entering attribute data for a Transport task, which are the transportation type and the destination. A tool developer can customize these pages if the generated ones are insufficient for a particular task, e.g. if some specific validation is required or data has to be retrieved from a database.

The example illustrates having a DSM language when modeling and having tool support for this DSM Language. We gain a more intuitive model, precise semantics and guided definition of required data. Our tools have made the process of creating DSM languages and tool support for them automatic with no need for technical insight into UML and eclipse plug-in development. The example shows that using activity diagrams and profiles for creating DSM languages using our tools is straight forward. Using the generated tools hides the complexity and generality of UML and instead provides domain specific terms, symbols and wizards to be used directly by the modeler.

3   Tool Details

In this section, we give an overview of the ADModeler and ADSpecializer tools, how they use meta-models, how ADModeler can be extended, and how ADSpecializer automates the task of creating such extensions.

3.1   ADModeler

The ADModeler is a general-purpose UML activity diagram editor but provides an Eclipse extension point that enables tool developers to extend the editor for specific purposes, i.e. they can define their own domain specific languages and customize the editor and tool palette. ADModeler will appear as if it was created for the specific domain. A model can be defined by adding instances of the domain specific tasks directly from the palette. A domain specific task represents a specific UML ActivityNode, for instance an Action or a DecisionNode with an applied stereotype such as Transport which indicates an action of transporting oneself from one destination to another. The stereotype is defined in a profile that is contained in the plug-in that extends ADModeler.

Furthermore, the tool developer is able to define how a modeler is supported in providing attribute data for the specific tasks. This is done by creating a wizard containing a number of wizard pages for each custom task. The wizard is able to validate input from a modeler before an element is inserted into the model. The validation check can be everything ranging from simple validation of text strings to validation against values in databases or from web services. Wizards are not always considered a good strategy for providing tool support [23, p. 126] so this approach may be revised in the future.

ADModeler provides a graphical editor for creating and editing UML2 activity diagrams. We have built the editor using a number of open source eclipse plug-ins providing a framework for making graphical editors and implementations of MOF and UML 2.0 specifications. These plug-ins are

- Graphical Editor Framework (GEF). The project provides an easy way to create a rich graphical environment based on a model.
- Eclipse Modeling Framework (EMF). The EMF project provides an implementation of a subset of the MOF specification. Using this project enables a tool developer to define his own modeling languages based on MOF.
- UML2. The project provides an implementation of the UML2 specification and builds on EMF. The project makes it possible to create models which conform to the UML2 specification although it does not provide any graphical annotations or possibilities of making visual diagrams of models.

3.1.1   Meta-models in ADModeler

Because the Eclipse UML2 project contains no implementation of the UML2 Diagram Interchange Specification or other visual data, we have to decide how to define visual information for an activity diagram. We could define a profile containing the visual information and apply it to all model elements. But a lot of irrelevant information would pollute the model. Another approach could be to create a new meta-model which contains both visual and semantic information and from which UML could be exported. We have chosen neither of these. Instead we have created a new MOF based meta-model called ADModel representing all visual information about the activity diagram. This meta-model does not contain any semantics. Instead it wraps or links to the UML2 meta-model, which represents the semantic model of activity diagrams. The ADModel meta-model could be thought of as a decorator of the UML2 meta-model.

When creating a model in ADModeler two models are produced. One model based on the ADModel meta-model contains all visual information and one model based on the UML2 meta-model contains all semantic information. The strengths of this approach are:

- Separation of visual and semantic information in two models.
- Semantic model is directly available from file system for other UML tools like modeling tools or transformation engines, which do not require visual information.
- Simple visual model extensible for plug-ins.

Because the UML model is not encapsulated in another model, no extraction or export has to be done from the visual model. The UML model can be edited directly, except actions like adding or deleting elements, in another tool and the corrections will be reflected in the editor when shown in ADModeler.

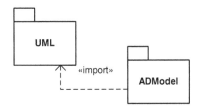

Fig. 3. Meta-model dependency from the UML meta-model

The meta-model used by ADModeler is illustrated in figure 3 and figure 4. Each element in the meta-model has a reference to an element in the UML meta-model. The most interesting part of the meta-model is the Node element which represents the ActivityNodes, or the building blocks, in the activity diagram.

It contains attributes for various visual presentations like coordinates and size. It further contains a typeId attribute and has a link to the abstract UML class ActivityNode. Concrete implementations of the ActivityNode class include classes like Action, Decision-, Join-, Fork-, and Merge nodes. An instance of a Node in a concrete model will have a reference to an instance of one of these concrete ActivityNode types.

The typeId attribute at the node indicates which kind of ActivityNode and optional stereotype the Node represents. Using a typeId and a reference to the abstract ActivityNode enables us to make the model extensible for others. For example, the Transport task contained in the Family language has a typeId equal Family.Transport and extends an Action node. It also represents the stereotype Transport. When a Transport task is inserted into a model, a Node and an Action instance is created. The Transport

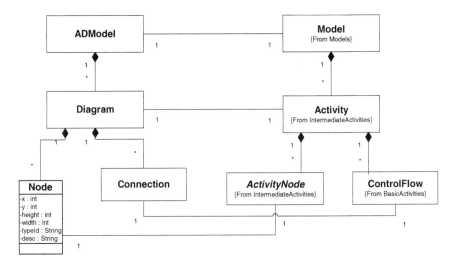

Fig. 4. The ADModel meta-model and references to elements in the UML meta-model

stereotype is applied to the action. The Node instance has a link to the Action instance and a typeId equal Family.Transport.

The tool provides standard typeId's for the most common ActivityNodes; Initial-Node, ActivityFinalNode, Action, DecisionNode, MergeNode, ForkNode and Join-Node. Next section provides more information about how to define an extension to the ADModeler.

3.1.2 Extension Point

ADModeler provides an extension point for extending the editor and its underlying meta-model. By default, the modeler supports modeling with seven different node types as described above. These are registered in a NodeRegistry which maps a typeId to a specific kind of UML ActivityNode, an optional stereotype, an icon, image, label, description and group, and a wizard for collecting data for stereotype attributes. When opening the editor, its tool palette is built by reading the NodeRegistry and creating a tool for each entry.

Each element in the palette contains a typeId. When an element is dragged onto the editor, ADModeler from the NodeRegistry retrieves the kind of ActivityNode to instantiate, the stereotype to apply at the ActivityNode, a wizard, etc. based on the typeId. After looking up the typeId it presents the wizard to the modeler to collect data. Then it instantiates the concrete ActivityNode type, optionally applies the stereotype, sets stereotype attributes and at last presents the Node in the diagram using the image registered in the NodeRegistry.

To extend ADModeller, one has to provide the data described in table 4.

Table 4. ADModeler extension point attributes

Attribute	Description
PaletteLabel	The label to be used in the tool palette, e.g. *Transport.*
PaletteTip	The tool tip text for the palette, e.g. *Transportation to somewhere.*
Group (Optional)	The tool group in which the extension should be present.
PaletteIcon path	A relative path to the icon for the palette.
EditorImage path	A relative path to the image for the editor.
ActivityNode type	The type of UML activity node, e.g. Action.
Profile path	A relative path to the profile containing the required stereotype.
Stereotype name	The name of the stereotype to be applied to the ActivityNode
Wizard class name	A wizard class for collecting data for the stereotype attributes.
typeId	A unique Id for this type to be used in the NodeRegistry, e.g. org.mda4bpm.homeprofile.Transport.

One limitation of the tool is that only the control flow part of activity diagrams can be modeled. Modeling of the object flow is not implemented. Furthermore, it does not support defining restrictions in e.g. OCL or Java for how new tasks may be used in

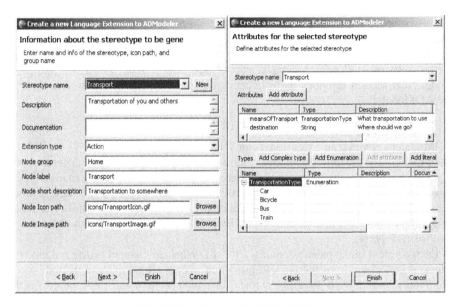

Fig. 5. Wizard pages for ADSpecializer

the model or how to validate stereotype attributes. Attribute validation can be done in the wizard class, but one has to do this in plain Java code.

3.2   ADSpecializer

To extend ADModeler, a tool developer has to create a new plug-in project and define the extension. As part of defining the extension, he has to create a wizard and an UML profile. This requires good technical insight into both the Eclipse platform and into UML. Further, it requires a UML tool supporting profiles to be able to define the profile. To aid in this task we have developed the ADSpecializer tool.

To define a new DSM language, a tool developer is guided though a wizard. Figure 5 shows the pages used to define a new stereotype. The first page defines the graphical appearance, and which UML-type that is extended. The second page is used to define the custom attributes to be associated with this new stereotype. Currently attributes of type integer, Boolean, and string, and user defined enumerations are supported. In addition, it is possible to define aggregations of such values, which we call complex types.

Complex types as well as enumerations are defined in the right hand window shown in figure 5. An additional page (not shown) is used to define the name of the profile. The data model behind the wizards conforms to a MOF based meta-model that we call ADProfile, which is shown in figure 6. In particular, complex types and enumerations are represented in the underlying model. Based on this model, ADSpecialiser generates an eclipse plug-in that contains one extension to ADModeler for each custom task defined. Further, it generates all resources required for the extension point defined by ADModeler.

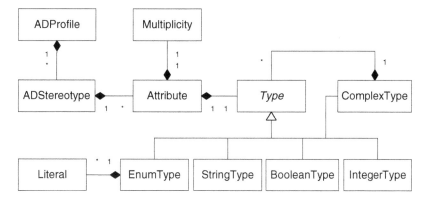

Fig. 6. Meta-model used by ADSpecializer

In the next section, we describe related work in the area of business process modeling notations and particular the use of activity diagrams.

4 Related Work

Many standards have been proposed for modeling business processes and their implementations. Two notations are dominating the modeling field. The Business Process Modeling Notation (BPMN) [15] is a graphical notation intended for business analysts. The UML activity diagrams, on the other hand, are part of the UML suite of technical diagramming notations. Both notations are able to model most of the workflow patterns described in [9] which means they are feasible for modeling business processes [10, 14]. On the implementation side, the most important standard is the Business Process Execution Language for Web services (BPEL4WS or just BPEL) [6].

Transformation rules have been proposed for both the BPMN notation [15] and UML activity diagrams [8, 13] to BPEL, so an implementation can be generated directly from a business process model.

Several others before us have used UML activity diagrams for business process modeling. Heckel and Voigt [8] suggest using a profile for UML activity diagrams for modeling business processes with the purpose of generating BPEL code. Combined with graph transformation as a meta-language for defining model transformations such models are transformed into BPEL. Heckel also presents techniques to analyze the models. Staikopoulos and Bordbar [16] have studied how the UML meta-model and the Web-services meta-models can be integrated so transformations can be facilitated. They present a method to support meta-model integration and interoperability and exemplify this with the BPEL meta-model. In [17] the same authors have used activity diagrams to capture the behavioral aspects of composing web-services and to transform these diagrams into BPEL. Eriksson and Penker have written a complete book about using UML for business modeling and have among other thing defined a profile to be used for business process modeling [18].

Common to the above-mentioned work on using UML activity diagrams and profiles for business process modeling is that they suggest using *one* profile for process modeling regardless of application domain. Our contribution is to enable enterprise specific tailoring of the modeling tools, and to give tool support for the tailoring process. We believe this tailoring is necessary to ensure the semantics, visualization, and abstraction of business process modeling as mentioned in the introduction.

5 Summary and Future Work

We have suggested UML activity diagrams as a general-purpose business process modeling language and using UML profiles for creating DSM languages for a specific enterprise.

We presented the general-purpose UML activity-diagram modeling tool ADModeler, and the ADSpecializer that automates the process of defining DSM languages and create customized tool support for them. The effectiveness and efficiency of these tools to model a solution in domain specific terms were demonstrated in the human family domain.

Several open issues remain. Currently, presence of mandatory attribute data is validated. However, we lack mechanisms to define restrictions on their values. In addition, it should be possible to constrain the manner in which concrete task types are combined (e.g. invalidate concurrent cleaning and transport by the same person). The modeling tool should be able to interpret these constraints and guide the modeler. Further, it should be possible to model object flows and to extend already defined languages with new even more specialized languages, i.e. specialize profiles.

A motivation for this work has been a wish to combine domain specific modeling with model transformations toward an implementation. For each custom task type defined in a profile, we need to define custom transformation rules and model templates representing patterns at lower abstraction levels.

In the future, we expect to evaluate the strength and weaknesses of the proposed tools for modeling business processes. We will evaluate it using real business processes together with our industrial partner. Further, we will start to work on customized model transformations and the use of model templates to automate the development of implementation specific code like BPEL.

We believe that having the combination of domain specific modeling languages, customized model transformations, model templates, and tool support for these for a single enterprise will be a crucial step towards the MDE vision: To heighten the abstraction level in software development.

References

1. Bézivin, J., Heckel, R.: Language Engineering for Model-driven Software Development. Dagstuhl Seminar Proceedings 04101(2005) 1-8
2. Havey, M: Essential Business Process Modeling. O'Reilly Media, Inc. (2005)
3. OMG: Meta Object Facility 2.0 Specification. Document id: ptc/04-10-15 (2003)
4. OMG: UML 2.0 Superstructure Specification. Document id : formal/05-07-04 (2005)

5. Kleppe, A., Warmer, J., Bast, W.: MDA Explained: The Model Driven Architecture- Practice and Promise. Addison-Wesley (2003)
6. BPEL: BEA, Microsoft, IBM, SAP, Siebel, Business Process Execution Language for Web Services, Version 1.1. (2003)
7. GME, Generic Modeling Environment, http://www.isis.vanderbilt.edu/Projects/gme, last accessed 29 Jan 2006
8. Heckel, R., Voigt, H.: Model-Based Development of Executable Business Processes for Web Services. Lecture Notes in Computer Science, Vol. 3098. Springer-Verlag (2003) 559-584.
9. van der Aalst, W.M.P., Hofstede, A.H.M., Kiepuszewski, B., Barros, A.P.: Workflow Patterns. Distributed and Parallel Databases, 14(1) (2003) 5-51
10. Wohed, P, van der Aalst, W.M.P., Dumas, M., Hofstede, A.H.M., Russell, N.: Pattern-based Analysis of UML Activity Diagrams. Technical report #129, Beta Research School, Eindhoven University of Technology, December 2004
11. Dumas, M., Hofstede, A.H.M: UML Activity Diagrams as a Workflow Specification Language. Lecture Notes in Computer Science, Vol. 2185, Springer-Verlag (2001) 76-90
12. MetaEdit+, MetaCase modeling tool, http://www.metacase.com. last accessed 29 Jan 2006
13. Gardner, T.: UML Modelling of Automated Business Processes with a Mapping to BPEL4WS. Presented at 17th European Conference on Object-Oriented Programming (ECOOP), Darmstadt, Germany (2003)
14. White, S.: Process Modeling Notations and Workflow Patterns. In L. Fischer, editor, WorkflowHandbook 2004. Future Strategies Inc., Lighthouse Point, FL, USA (2004) 265–294
15. White, S.: Business Process Modeling Notation, Version 1.0 http://www.bpmn.org/Documents/BPMN%20V1-0%20May%203%202004.pdf May 2004. Last accessed 29 Jan. 2006.
16. Staikopoulos, A., Bordbar, B.: A Comparative Study of Meta-model Integration and Interoperability in UML and Web Services. Lecture Notes in Computer Science, Vol. 3748, Springer-Verlag (2005) 145-159.
17. Bordbar, B. Staikopoulus, A.: On behavioural Model Transformation in Web Services. Proc. Conceptual Modelling for Advanced Application Domain (eCOMO), Shanghai, China (2004) 667-678
18. Eriksson, H.E., Penker, M.: Business Modeling with UML. Business Patterns at Work. John Wiley & Sons, Inc. (2000)
19. Eclipse Project, http://www.eclipse.org/
20. Eclipse UML2 project, http://www.eclipse.org/uml2/
21. Eclipse EMF project, http://www.eclipse.org/emf/
22. Eclipse GMF project, http://www.eclipse.org/gmf/
23. Lauesen, S.: User Interface Design: A Software Engineering Perspective. Addison Wesley (2005)

Constraint Support in MDA Tools: A Survey

Jordi Cabot[1] and Ernest Teniente[2]

[1] Estudis d'Informàtica i Multimèdia, Universitat Oberta de Catalunya
jcabot@uoc.edu
[2] Dept. Llenguatges i Sistemes Informàtics, Universitat Politècnica de Catalunya
teniente@lsi.upc.edu

Abstract. The growing interest in the MDA (Model-Driven Architecture) and MDD (Model-Driven Development) approaches has largely increased the number of tools and methods including code-generation capabilities. Given a platform-independent model (PIM) of an application, these tools generate (part of) the application code either by defining first a platform-specific model or by executing a direct PIM to code transformation. However, current tools present several limitations regarding code generation of the integrity constraints defined in the PIMs. This paper compares these tools and shows that they lack expressiveness in the kind of constraints they can handle or efficiency in the code generated to verify them. Based on this evaluation, the features of an ideal code-generation method for integrity constraints are established. We believe such a method is required to extend MDA adoption in the development of industrial projects, where constraints play a key role.

1 Introduction

The goal of automating information systems building was already stated in the late sixties [32]. However, thanks to the definition and standardization of the MDA [28] this goal has revived and seems now more feasible than ever. As a matter of fact, we have recently witnessed an explosion of tools and methods promising a full and automatic generation of the application code from its specification. Even more, nowadays, code-generation capabilities of current CASE tools and their adhesion to the MDA vision is a key issue in their development and marketing strategy.

Nowadays, almost all methods and tools are able to generate the skeleton of Java classes or relational schemas from a platform-independent model (PIM). A few also generate the code of the application operations when its behavior is specified with state diagrams or action semantics [27]. Nevertheless, most methods and tools tend to skip the integrity constraints (ICs) specified in the PIM when generating the application code. We believe this is a major drawback since ICs are a fundamental part in the specification of an application [18], and thus, they must be taken into account when generating its implementation. In fact, the problem of generating an efficient integrity checking code from the ICs defined in a PIM has been classified as one of the open problems to solve before MDA, and in general MDD approaches, can be widely used in the industrial development of information systems [25].

A. Rensink and J. Warmer (Eds.): ECMDA-FA 2006, LNCS 4066, pp. 256–267, 2006.

This paper surveys the capabilities of current tools regarding the explicit definition of ICs in a PIM and the code generation to enforce them. As we will see, all of them present important limitations regarding the expressivity of the ICs they can handle and/or the efficiency of the generated code. From such analysis, we will be able to draw the desirable features that should be satisfied by any tool generating code to enforce the ICs.

In our study, we have considered MDA tools in a broad sense since we have chosen the most representative examples from the different kinds of tools (from CASE tools extended with code-generation capabilities to full MDD methods). Moreover, we have included in the study all tools supporting a textual language to define ICs, commonly OCL (Object Constraint Language [26]) or similar. Support for such a language is required in order to specify all kinds of ICs in the PIM.

As far as we know, ours is the first paper addressing this topic. Several tool lists and comparisons exist, like the one we find in [31] which is the closest to our work. We extend the work reported there by evaluating a larger number of tools and by analyzing the support they provide regarding expressivity of the ICs and efficiency of the code generated to enforce them (while [31] only points out whether the tools support OCL or not).

The paper is organized as follows. Next section defines the different evaluation criteria. Section 3 presents the evaluation of the selected tools and methods. Given their limitations, section 4 defines the features that all code-generation method for ICs should have. Finally, section 5 presents some conclusions.

2 Evaluation Criteria

This section presents the criteria used to select and/or to evaluate the tools. We have considered expressivity of the constraint definition language they allow, efficiency of the generated code and target technologies they address since they are the most relevant ones regarding the automatic treatment of ICs defined at the PIM level.

a) *Expressivity of the constraint definition language*
Although some ICs can be expressed by means of the graphical constructs provided by the modeling language (as the cardinality constraints), most ICs require the use of a general-purpose constraint definition language, commonly OCL in our case.

The expressivity of tools supporting such a language differs depending on the complexity of the operators permitted in the constraint definitions. We distinguish three basic complexity levels (adapted from [33]):

- Intra-object ICs: constraints restricting the value of the attributes of a single object.
- Inter-object ICs: constraints restricting the relationships between an object and other objects, instances of different classes. Within this category, it is worth to distinguish the subcategory of ICs containing aggregator operators (like *sum*, *count*, *size*...).
- Class-level ICs: constraints restricting a set of objects of the same class (in OCL, these ICs require the *allInstances* operator).

b) *Efficiency of the code generated to enforce the ICs*

An IC states a condition that each state of the Information Base (IB), i.e. the set of objects and links of the class diagram at a certain time point, must satisfy. Hence, after each change of the contents of the IB the generated code must check efficiently that the new state of the IB satisfies also the ICs. We define two different levels of efficiency:

1. An IC must only be enforced after changes that may induce its violation [5]. For instance, if one of the ICs states that the value of an attribute *at* of a class *cl* must be lower than *X*, we do not need to verify the IC after changes over other attributes of *cl* or when deleting *cl* instances.
2. The enforcement of an IC must be done incrementally by considering the lowest possible number of objects [6]. In the previous example, once a new instance of *cl* is created we should only evaluate the constraint over that new instance instead of taking all instances of *cl* into account.

c) *Target technologies of the code generation process*

The IB must be implemented in a particular technology. Typically the IB is implemented by means of a (relational) database or by means of a set of classes in some object-oriented language.

When using a database, the ICs are checked over the tuples of the tables created to represent the classes of the class diagram. When using a set of classes (for instance Java classes) representing the class diagram, the ICs are verified over the set of objects instance of these classes. Usually, after the objects have been verified they are also permanently stored in a database or a file system.

Therefore, to study the constraint code-generation capabilities we focus on these two technologies: 1 – Relational databases and 2 – Object-oriented languages, in particular Java. Even though some tools also deal with other technologies (like .NET or C++), this decision does not restrict the set of tools to study since these two are the most widely covered.

3   Tool Evaluation

To facilitate the evaluation, we have classified the different tools in the following categories: CASE tools, MDA specific tools, MDD methods and OCL tools. For each group we have selected the tools we believe are the most representative or the ones that offer a better IC support. Some of the tools could be classified in more than category since most of them are usually considered as MDA-tools although in our classification we reserve this category to the tools closest to the MDA standard.

Following the criteria stated in the previous section, for each tool we have evaluated its constraint generation capabilities for Java and for relational databases. For each technology we have studied the allowed expressivity and the efficiency of the generated implementation. See the appendix for a summary table.

As a running example we will use the simple PIM of Figure 1. Apart from the cardinality constraints (each employee works in a department and each department has from three to ten employees) the PIM includes three textual ICs defined with

OCL. The ICs state that all employees are over 16 years old (*ValidAge*), that all departments contain at least three employees over 45 (*SeniorEmployees*) and that no two employees have the same name (*UniqueName*).

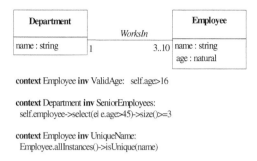

Fig. 1. PIM used as a running example

As we will see in the next subsections, even such a simple example cannot be fully generated using the current tools since none of them is able to provide an efficient implementation of the schema and its ICs.

3.1 CASE Tools

Even though the initial aim of CASE tools was to facilitate the modeling of software systems, almost all of them have extended their functionality to offer, to some extent, code-generation capabilities. From all CASE tools (see [23] for an exhaustive list) we have selected the following ones: *Poseidon*, *Rational Rose*, *MagicDraw*, *Objecteering/UML* and *Together*. In what follows we comment them in detail:

a) *Poseidon* [15] is a commercial extension of *ArgoUML*. The Java generation capabilities are quite simple. It does not allow the definition of OCL ICs and it does not take the cardinality constraints into account either. It only distinguishes two different multiplicity values: '1' and 'greater than one'. In fact, when the multiplicity is greater than one the values of the multivalued attributed created in the corresponding Java class are not restricted to be of the correct type (see the *employee* attribute of the *Department* class in Figure 2, the attribute may hold any kind of object and not only employee instances).

The generation of the relational schema is not much powerful either. The only constraints appearing in the relational schema are the *primary keys*. The designer must explicitly indicate which attributes act as primary keys by means of modifying the corresponding property in the attribute definition.

```
public class Department {
    private string name;
    public java.util.Collection employee = new java.util.TreeSet();
}
```

Fig. 2. *Department* class as generated by Poseidon

b) *Rational Rose* [30]. The Java generation process is similar to that of *Poseidon*. The database generation is better because the class diagram can be complemented with the definition of additional properties. For instance, the *ValidAge* constraint can be specified as a property of the *age* attribute (Figure 3). Given this property, the tool adds to the *Employee* table the constraint *check(age>16)* to control the employees' age.

Recently, a Rational Rose plug-in [13] is available to permit the definition of OCL ICs on rose models. However, these ICs are not considered when generating the application code.

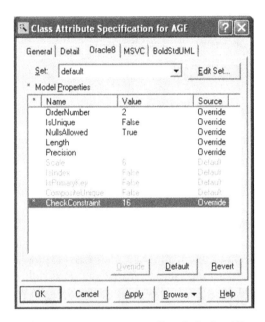

Fig. 3. Properties of the *Age* attribute in Rational Rose

c) *MagicDraw* [22] offers a specific UML profile to define relational schemas which allows to improve the code generation for that kind of databases. In this way, the user may annotate the class diagram with all the necessary information (*primary* and *foreign keys*, *unique* constraints and checks over attributes).

Figure 4 shows the relational schema definition of the PIM in Figure 1 once annotated with the profile. This diagram could be considered as the PSM (Platform-Specific Model) of the initial PIM. The tool partially generates this PSM from the PIM. The schema includes the primary keys of each table, the foreign key from employee to department and the *ValidAge* IC. The other ICs cannot be specified since the database does not provide any predefined mechanism to verify them (and MagicDraw does not generate for itself any code excerpt to verify them either).

Though *MagicDraw* allows the definition of OCL ICs, they are completely omitted during the PSM or code generation. For instance, when transforming the initial PIM (Figure 1) to the PSM (Figure 4), *MagicDraw* is unable to transform *ValidAge* in the corresponding *check* in the PSM, we are force to manually redefine the constraint again in the PSM.

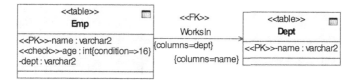

Fig. 4. PSM for the relational schema in *MagicDraw*

d) *Objecteering/UML* [29] presents as a special feature with respect to the previous tools that supports (and generates) any multiplicity value in the associations. When generating the Java code it uses a predefined class library to enforce the cardinality constraints. Moreover, it creates a set of triggers during the generation of the relational schema. For instance, the trigger in Figure 5 checks that a department contains less than ten employees before allowing the assignment of a new employee. Otherwise, it raises an exception. The starting point for the database generation is, as in the previous tool, a PSM that can be obtained from the initial PIM. It does not allow the definition of ICs in OCL.

```
CREATE TRIGGER TI_dept_emp_INSERT
 ON employee
 FOR INSERT
 AS
 IF NOT((SELECT COUNT(*)
     FROM employee, inserted
     WHERE employee.department = inserted.department) <= 10)
 BEGIN
   ROLLBACK TRANSACTION
   RAISERROR 20501, "dept_emp : May not insert element,
       dept_emp_FK maximum cardinality constraint violation"
 END
```

Fig. 5. Trigger to control the maximum number of employees per department

e) *Together* [4] offers similar capabilities to *Rational Rose* regarding the database generation. Moreover, it includes full OCL support to define constraints and pre/ postconditions in the PIMs. However, when generating the Java code, only intra-object constraints are correctly generated. Moreover the generation is not efficient since constraints are verified after every single method and not only after methods possibly violating the constraints.

3.2 MDA Tools

We classify in this category tools having as main goal to support the definition and execution of model transformations from PIMs to PSMs and from the PSMs to the final code. We evaluate in this section some of the well-known MDA tools: *ArcStyler*, *OptimalJ* and *AndroMDA*.

ArcStyler [17] concentrates in the generation of Java, J2EE and .NET applications (with its *cartridge* architecture the designer can define additional transformations). When generating Java programs, the constraint support is like the one in Poseidon, with the only difference that automatically creates a set of methods to modify the attributes representing the associations of the original class diagram. *ArcStyler* includes the *Dresden OCL* tool (see section 3.4) to define and generate ICs.

OptimalJ [9] is devoted to generate J2EE applications where all the business logic concentrates in the Java classes (Enterprise Java Beans in this case). It only supports constraints over the attribute values using constant values or regular expressions. For more complex ICs, the designer must write the corresponding Java code directly.

AndroMDA is an open source code generation framework that follows the MDA paradigm. According to the tool information, it takes model(s) from CASE-tool(s) and generates fully deployable applications. *AndroMDA* supports the definition of OCL query expressions and transforms them to the Hibernate-QL or EJB-QL query languages. However, no explicit support for OCL ICs is provided.

3.3 MDD Methods

In this section we grouped several MDD methods although some of them may not follow exactly the MDA approach nor use OMG standard languages.

OO-Method [14] is based on the formal language OASIS, though admits the definition of UML class diagrams with constraints defined in an OCL-like language. ICs may include aggregator operators but class-level constraints are not allowed. ICs are verified over the objects instance of the Java classes implementing the class diagram. Every time a method of a Java class is executed, all ICs defined on that class are verified (and not only the ICs that may be affected by that method execution). To verify the ICs, they add a special method in the Java classes (Figure 6). The method contains a set of conditions (one for each constraint defined on the class). When a condition is not satisfied, the method throws an exception.

```
Protected void checkIntegrityConstraints() throws Error
{
  if (! (age>16))
  throw new error ("Constraint Violation. Invalid age");
}
```

Fig. 6. Java method verifying the *ValidAge* constraint

WebML [8] is specialized in the generation of web applications. It presents little support for defining ICs. It only admits the definition of *validity predicates* on the web page forms. A validity predicate is a boolean expression that checks the correctness of the value entered by the user in a form included in a web page. The boolean expression may consist of boolean operators, arithmetic operators, comparisons (=,>,<,...) and constant values.

Executable UML [21] proposes to specify the behavior of an application in sufficient detail so that it can be directly executed. Specifications in executable UML consist merely of class diagrams, state diagrams and action semantics to describe the operation behavior. Using a model compiler, then, the specification is internally transformed into Java or C++. It supports a predefined set of constraints like cardinality constraints, unique constraints or checks over the attribute' values. These ICs are afterwards expressed using the *Action Language* they provide. For more general ones, the designer must define them using this Action Language directly. That is, the designer is forced to define them in an imperative way and not declaratively (although action languages may contain query expressions they are basically an imperative language). Figure 7 shows the *UniqueName* expressed in the action language. Tools following this approach (like *BridgePoint* or *iUML*) are mainly used in the real time and embedded domains.

```
select many employees from instances of Employee
Where selected.name==self.name
Return (cardinality employees)==0)
```

Fig. 7. *UniqueName* defined with an Action Language

3.4 OCL Tools

This section evaluates all tools generating code from OCL constraints. Tools supporting OCL with other purposes (as model validation [16] or verification [1]) are not considered.

Dresden OCL [11] generates the Java classes corresponding to the classes in a class diagram, including all ICs except for the class-level ICs, which are not supported. ICs are verified only after modifications over the attributes and associations (represented also as attributes in the Java classes) referenced in the constraint definition. This represents an efficiency improvement regarding previous methods, but, as shown in [5], it is still inefficient since not all kinds of changes over the attributes may violate the IC. For instance, the *SeniorEmployees* IC can be violated when removing an employee from a department but not when assigning a new one. This is exactly the same limitation of [34].

OCLtoSQL is another tool comprised in the previous toolkit, based on the method proposed in [10]. It generates the relational schema from the class diagram. Additionally, for each IC, it creates an SQL view. The view selects those tuples of the database not satisfying the constraint, and thus, a non-empty view indicates that the IC has been violated. As an example, Figure 8 shows the view corresponding to the *ValidAge* IC. Note that the view selects those employees *not* verifying the age condition. The views are not efficient since they examine the whole table population instead of considering only those tuples modified during the transaction (in the example, the view accesses all employees and not just the inserted or updated ones).

```
CREATE OR REPLACE VIEW ValidAge as
(select * from EMPLOYEE SELF where not (SELF.AGE > 16));
```

Fig. 8. View for the *ValidAge* constraint

The code-generation capabilities of Octopus [20] are more restricted. For each IC, it creates a new method in the Java class corresponding to the context type of the IC. To know whether the IC holds we call this method. If it does not hold the method throws an exception. However, the decision about *when* the IC needs to be verified (i.e. when we should call this method) is left to the designer. *OCLE* [2] and *KMF* {KentModellingFramework, #154} provide a similar functionality.

OCL2J [12] (and similarly *OCL4Java* [24]) generate a Java implementation of a PIM including all intra-object and inter-object ICs. The constraint verification is inefficient since ICs are verified before and after any method of the class executes.

Finally, *BoldSoft* [3] permits to execute an OCL expression over a set of objects stored in main memory or in the database (in this latter case, the expressivity is restricted, for instance, operators as count, collect, difference, asSet, asBag and so forth are not allowed). However, the tool is focused in the definition of derived elements and not in the verification of ICs.

4   Desirable Features of an IC Generation Method

From the previous evaluation it is clear that tools must incorporate and/or develop new methods to cope with IC enforcement. The aim of this section is to propose a set of features that should be considered when developing such methods.

Apart from the two basic features (expressivity and efficiency) we define also the *technology-aware generation*, *technological independence* and *checking time* characteristics. The description of each characteristic is the following:

1. *Expressivity*: The whole expressivity of the OCL language should be allowed.
2. *Efficiency*: The generated code should verify the ICs only when it is strictly necessary and using an efficient approach.
3. *Technology-aware generation*: To improve the efficiency of the generated code, the method should take into account the special characteristics of each target technology platform. For instance, when Java is the target technology *disjoint* ICs (stating that the intersection between objects of two given classes must be empty) can be discarded since they are enforced by the Java language itself (Java does not admit multiple classification, and thus, all classes are necessarily disjoint).
   The same idea applies when the target technology is a relational database. Relational databases offer some predefined constraint constructs as primary keys, checks over attribute values or unique constraints. OCL ICs should be mapped into one of this predefined constructs when possible, instead of creating our own checking code. It is reasonable to assume that the database management system will be always more efficient in managing them.
4. *Technological independence*: Following the MDA vision, at least the first stages of the code generation process (as the processing of the ICs to determine the kind of changes that can violate them) should be independent of the target technology platform. In this way we could reuse the same method to generate the checking code in several technologies. Just the last step (the code generation itself) should be technologically dependent and take into account the previous *technology-aware generation* characteristic.
5. *Checking time*: In general there are two different possibilities regarding the moment when ICs are verified. They can be verified immediately after each single modification or their verification can be deferred until the end of the operation/s or the transaction. The method should be flexible enough to allow the designer define the preferred checking time for each IC.

5 Conclusions

In this paper we have surveyed the support of current tools regarding the automatic generation of the code required to enforce the ICs specified in a PIM. These tools have been evaluated regarding the expressivity of the IC definition language they provide, the efficiency of the generated code and the target technology they allow.

From our study, we may conclude that current tools have not yet seriously addressed such an issue since the support they provide is still rather limited. The main shortcomings encountered are the lack of expressivity of the ICs that may be defined; the need to use proprietary profiles and/or properties of each tool since in many tools ICs may not be expressed directly in OCL; and the lack of efficiency of the code generated to enforce the ICs.

We believe that the main reasons why the tools are making so little progress in this matter are the difficulty of performing IC checking with OCL (because of the high expressivity of this language) and the focus of the tools on the automatic code generation for more basic capabilities (such as translation of the class diagram, automatic interface generation, etc.). Additionally, we think that the increasing number of OCL auxiliary tools (parsers, compilers, APIs...) provides the tool vendors with a feasible opportunity to enhance tools' functionality with full OCL support.

So, there is still a huge amount of research to be pursued to achieve the goal of generating automatically the code required to enforce the OCL ICs defined in the PIM. Methods dealing with this problem are likely to be an extension of previous work on incremental integrity checking in relational and deductive databases. A first proposal has been recently presented in [7].

Acknowledgments

This work has been partly supported by the Ministerio de Educacion y Ciencia under project TIN 2005-06053.

References

1. Ahrendt, W., Baar, T., Beckert, B., Bubel, R., Giese, M., Hähnle, R., Menzel, W., Mostowski, W., Roth, A., Schlager, S., Schmitt, P. H.: The KeY tool, Integrating object oriented design and formal verification. Software and Systems Modeling 4 (2005) 32-54
2. Babes-Bolyai. Object Constraint Language Environment 2.0. http://lci.cs.ubbcluj.ro/ocle/
3. Borland. Bold for Delphi. http://info.borland.com/techpubs/delphi/boldfordelphi/
4. Borland. Together Architect 2006. http://www.borland.com/us/products/together/
5. Cabot, J., Teniente, E.: Determining the Structural Events that May Violate an Integrity Constraint. In: Proc. 7th Int. Conf. on the Unified Modeling Language, LNCS, 3273 (2004) 173-187
6. Cabot, J., Teniente, E.: Computing the Relevant Instances that May Violate an OCL constraint. In: Proc. 17th Int. Conf. on Advanced Information Systems Engineering, LNCS, 3520 (2005) 48-62

7. Cabot, J., Teniente, E.: Incremental Evaluation of OCL Constraints. In: Proc. 18th Int. Conf. on Advanced Information Systems Engineering, LNCS, 4001 (2006) 81-95
8. Ceri, S., Fraternali, P., Bongio, A., Brambilla, M., Comai, S., Matera, M.: Designing Data-Intensive Web Applications. Morgan Kaufmann (2002)
9. Compuware. OptimalJ. http://www.compuware.com/products/optimalj/
10. Demuth, B., Hussmann, H., Loecher, S.: OCL as a Specification Language for Business Rules in Database Applications. In: Proc. 4th Int. Conf. on the Unified Modeling Language, LNCS, 2185 (2001) 104-117
11. Dresden. Dresden OCL Toolkit. http://dresden-ocl.sourceforge.net/index.html
12. Dzidek, W. J., Briand, L. C., Labiche, Y.: Lessons Learned from Developing a Dynamic OCL Constraint Enforcement Tool for Java. In: Proc. MODELS 2005 Workshops, LNCS, 3844 (2005) 10-19
13. EmPowerTec. OCL-AddIn for Rational Rose.   http://www.empowertec.de/ products/ rational-rose-ocl.htm
14. Fons, J., Pelechano, V., Albert, M., Pastor, Ó. Development of Web Applications from Web Enhanced Conceptual Schemas. In: Proc. 22nd Int. Conf. on Conceptual Modeling, LNCS, 2813 (2003) 232-245
15. Gentleware. Poseidon for UML v. 4. http://www.gentleware.com
16. Gogolla, M., Bohling, J., Richters, M.: Validation of UML and OCL Models by Automatic Snapshot Generation. In: Proc. 6th Int. Conf. Unified Modeling Language. LNCS 2863 (2003)
17. Interactive Objects. ArcStyler v.5. http://www.interactive-objects.com/
18. ISO/TC97/SC5/WG3: Concepts and Terminology for the Conceptual Schema and Information Base. ISO, (1982)
19. Kent Modelling Framework. Kent OCL Library. http://www.cs.kent.ac.uk/projects/kmf/
20. Klasse Objecten. Octopus: OCL Tool for Precise Uml Specifications. http:// www. klasse. nl/octopus/index.html
21. Mellor, S. J., Balcer, M. J.: Executable UML. Object Technology Series. Addison-Wesley (2002)
22. No Magic Inc. MagicDraw UML v. 10.5. http://www.magicdraw.com/
23. Objects by Design. List of UML tools. Available: http://www.objectsbydesign.com/
24. OCL4Java. http://www.ocl4java.org
25. Olivé, A.: Conceptual Schema-Centric Development: A Grand Challenge for Information Systems Research. In: Proc. 17th Int. Conf. on Advanced Information Systems Engin-eering, LNCs, 3520 (2005) 1-15
26. OMG: UML 2.0 OCL Specification. Adopted Specification (ptc/03-10-14) (2003)
27. OMG: UML 2.0 Superstructure Specification. Adopted Specification (ptc/03-08-02) (2003)
28. OMG: MDA Guide Version 1.0.1. (2003)
29. Softeam. Objecteering/UML v. 5.3. http://www.objecteering.com/products.php
30. Software, R. Rational Rose. http://www-306.ibm.com/software/rational/
31. Tariq, N. A., Akhter, N.: Comparison of Model Driven Architecture (MDA) based tools. In: Proc. 13th Nordic Baltic Conference (NBC), IFMBE Proceedings, 9 (2005)
32. Teichroew, D.: Methodology for the Design of Information Processing Systems. In: Proc. 4th Australian Computer Conference, (1969) 629-634
33. Türker, C., Gertz, M.: Semantic integrity support in SQL:1999 and commercial (object-)relational database management systems. The VLDB Journal 10 (2001) 241-269
34. Verheecke, B., Straeten, R. V. D.: Specifying and implementing the operational use of constraints in object-oriented applications. In: Proc. Tools Pacific 2002, (2002) 23-32

Appendix A

The following table summarizes the comparison of the different tools. For each tool we indicate its expressivity and efficiency regarding the Java and relational database generation of the ICs. In the *expressivity* columns, the symbol *X* means that the tool does not support any kind of constraint definition while the symbol √ means a full constraint support and *n/a* indicates that the tool does not generate code for that technology. Otherwise, we explicitly indicate the type of ICs admitted, according to the classification of section 2. Likewise for *efficiency* columns. In the *DB efficiency* column, cells are defined as *DBMS* when the tool relies on the constraint constructs offered by the database-management system (*primary keys*, *checks*...) to verify the ICs.

Table A.1. Tool comparison

Tools	Java		DB	
	Expressivity	Efficiency	Expressivity	Efficiency
Poseidon	X	n/a	PK	DBMS
Rational Rose	X	n/a	PK, intra	DBMS
Magic Draw	X	n/a	PK, intra	DBMS
Objecteering	cardinality	√	PK,cardinality	√
Together	√	ICs are verified after every method	PK, intra	DBMS
ArcStyler	Uses DresdenOCL	n/a	PK, intra	DBMS
OptimalJ	intra	√	PK, intra	DBMS
AndroMDA	X	n/a	PK, intra	DBMS
OO-Method	intra, inter	ICs are verified after every method	PK	DBMS
WebML	intra	√	PK	DBMS
ExecutableUML	intra, predefined types	√	n/a	n/a
DresdenOCL	intra, inter	ICs are verified after methods modifying the constrained elements	n/a	n/a
OCLtoSQL	n/a	n/a	√	Views evaluate all table population
Octopus	intra, inter	n/a	n/a	n/a
OCLE	intra, inter	n/a	n/a	n/a
KMF	intra, inter	n/a	n/a	n/a
OCL2J	intra, inter	ICs are verified before and after every method	n/a	n/a
OCL4Java	intra, inter	ICs are verified before and after every method	n/a	n/a

Automatic Generation of Modelling Tools

Jan P. Nytun, Andreas Prinz, and Merete S. Tveit

Faculty of Engineering, Agder University College
Grooseveien 36, N-4876 Grimstad, Norway
{andreas.prinz, jan.p.nytun, merete.s.tveit}@hia.no

Abstract. Higher-level modelling is considered to be the answer to many of the problems computer science is faced with. In order to do modelling, it is necessary to use proper tools. This article is about modelling tools and how they can be generated automatically out of (modelling) language descriptions. Language descriptions in turn are given in meta-models. In this article, we define a terminology for aspects of meta-models and check how they are supported by existing meta-modelling tools. In particular we look at semantic aspects of the meta-models.

1   Introduction

Information technology is spreading more and more into all areas of daily life, leading to an ever increasing amount of information and applications of a very high complexity. Traditional methods of software production and data handling cannot cope with this ever increasing complexity. New ways of complexity handling take higher levels of abstraction and describe systems using models. In particular, OMG puts forward their idea of a model-driven architecture (MDA) [21] which focuses on software development by means of high-level models. We will use the term MDD (model driven development) in the sequel to denote an approach taking high-level descriptions for the generation of low-level results, e.g. executable code. For an effective application of MDD it is necessary to use models that fit their application domain, which means to use domain specific languages (DSLs) or domain specific adaptations of languages.

This leads to the problem of the development of DSL tool support. The currently existing tools support common multi-purpose languages, but are not particularly adapted to a specific domain. On the other hand, developers insist on integrated development environments to be effective in their daily work. In this context, the choice is either to take a not fitting language with a good tool support or to use a well fitting language with no tool support. Of course, none of these alternatives is satisfactory.

So the problem is to provide tool support for modelling languages. There are basically two ways to achieve this, either by manually building such tools or by having higher-level tools that generate modelling tools. In any case it is necessary to have a description of the language first. We will call such a description of the language a meta-model. There are varying levels of accuracy when it comes to

A. Rensink and J. Warmer (Eds.): ECMDA-FA 2006, LNCS 4066, pp. 268–283, 2006.

describing meta-models and also a whole range of tools that support parts of this tool production by automation. Of course, also meta-models are just a special kind of models and for their handling we again need (meta-)modelling tools. This closes the circle and we can apply the same reasoning on the next level. So in all the levels we have the need of powerful tools that are able to handle models of different kind.

In this paper we will focus on this need for generating modelling tools. We will first in section 2 look at the different requirements coming for these tools. Then we will look at a new class of integrated tools claiming to support the complete description of languages in Section 3. Section 4 concludes the paper.

2   Meta-modelling and Tool Production

A modelling tool is a tool that is able to handle models of a certain kind. The description of the model kind is given by a meta-model, or in simpler cases by an abstract grammar or even by a concrete grammar.

[12] defines meta-modelling as: ... *the construction of an object-oriented model of the abstract syntax of a language.* However, in our article we use the term meta-model in a wider sense: *A meta-model is a model that defines a language completely including the concrete syntax, abstract syntax and semantics.*

The current situation of meta-model use is characterized by the following observations.

- Meta-models are usually *not given explicitly*, but are built-in into the tools that provide them; this can be seen as a sort of hard coded implementation of a meta-model. In particular there is no direct relation between an external meta-model and the representation in the tool.
- Meta-models *change over time*. Tool builders adapt their meta-models along with their tools and do only provide means to align with their own old versions.
- Meta-models *are not standardized*. Although several organisations, in particular OMG, try to publish standards for meta-models, the standards are far from being formal and implementations deviate more or less severely from the standards.

This leads to the fact that users are bound to one tool at a time. They are allowed to import models from other tools, but then they are again encapsulated. On the other hand, most meta-modelling tools provide a set of basic facilities that are the same and some advanced facilities that are specific. A user is usually not able to combine the positive parts of different tools.

In this section we will be looking at tools, aspects of meta-models and how tools and meta-models are related.

2.1   Aspects of Meta-models

The meta-model can have several aspects that are to be covered by the modelling tool. In figure 1 we have shown the essential parts of a meta-model. There is no

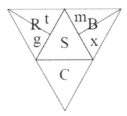

Fig. 1. Structure of a Meta-model

complete agreement about these parts, but in most contexts the same or similar parts are identified. In the picture, we have shown the following parts.

Structural information for the meta-model including all the information about which concepts exist in the domain and how they are related. An example of this would be a MOF class diagram. In our understanding this part does just include very simple structural properties and not more advanced concepts that rely on the use of constraints.

Constraints giving additional information about the structure in that they identify the allowed structure according to additional logical constraints. This will include first-order logic constraints (e.g. written in OCL) as well as multiplicity constraints. In classical compiler theory these are collected under the name of static semantics and in a meta-model context they are called well-formedness rules.

Representation description includes model serialization syntax and information about how the models are to be (re)presented to the user. The textual grammars (concrete textual syntax) are well understood in terms of compiler theory. When it comes to graphical grammar (concrete visual syntax), there is less agreement and also some open research topics.

Behaviour description describes how the model is used. This item includes execution of the model as well as mappings. By mapping we will understand a relation between the model itself and another representation, e.g. in another language. A typical example would be a compiler from UML to Java, or mapping from PIM to PSM. An execution is the real run of the model, which is of course only possible if the model is executable. A typical example here would be a run of a UML state diagram.

In the picture given, the structure is the central aspect and all the other parts relate to the structure. This is quite clear for the constraints, which need the structure to be meaningful, but also for the representation and the semantics. Most language descriptions do currently follow this approach, i.e. defining a structure first and attaching all the static and dynamic semantic information to this basic structure.

When we take a step back, we will notice that the representation as well as the semantics are not that closely bound to the structure. In fact, several modelling languages use the same representation in order to represent similar things and also the semantics is largely comparable although the internal structure might be different.

For this situation, the MVC (model-view-controller) pattern is better suited. This means in our case that the connection between the representation and the structure and between the semantics and the structure is not direct, but mediated via a controller. This will allow to associate both with each other as shown in figure 2.

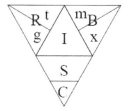

Fig. 2. Decoupling the Structure of a Meta-model

In the new structure, the middle is just connecting the parts as described below.

Integration gives the connections between the different model parts. Each part forms a unit of its own, e.g. the syntax is described separately without reference to the basic structure of the language. Afterwards, the integration allows to connect these separate parts.

Please note that the explicit connections are already implicitly present in figure 1. We have just extracted them explicitly in order to allow a better handling of model descriptions. In the following we will ignore the explicit connections and use the figure 1 as a reference.

2.2   Tools as Meta-model Implementations

We have discussed in the previous section how meta-models describe the possible models to be handled. When we now look at tools, we can see that tools have the same property as meta-models. They also define what kind of models are allowed, how they look and what you can do with them. This way, a tool can be considered a special meta-model as shown in figure 3.

The meta-model gives a description of the tool, which in turn can be transformed into tool code. This code has then to be executed in order to be a running tool, which then can handle a model.

Figure 3 does also match nicely with the OMG 4-level architecture. The model would here stay on the level 1 (models), the tool code and the meta-model would be on level 2 (meta-models) and then we do also have languages described on level 3 (meta-meta-model).

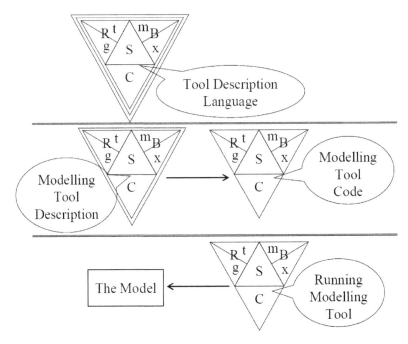

Fig. 3. Tools and Meta-models

This meta-meta-aspect goes into the next level of description. In order to have (formal) description of the meta-model, we need a (formal) meta-meta-model which can be used to provide this description. Alternatively, we can use known ad-hoc solutions, e.g. using a low-level programming language for doing the description. Of course, all the aspects identified in figure 1 for a meta-model have to be supported on all levels. For the tool, there should be code for each of them; in the meta-model we need a description for each of them and in the language level we need a language for each of them.

2.3   Tool Production Requirements

When it comes to tools that produce modelling tools, we will look at the following requirements:

Generativeness: As we speak about tools that produce modelling tools, the most important requirement is that they are able to automatically produce the tool. In figure 3 this amounts to the mapping from the meta-model to the tool code.

High-Level Description: The descriptions are more easily handled when they are given in a high-level notation. This means that a tool should provide high-level notations for the different modelling language aspects. This is reflected in the figure 3 by the top-level layer.

Completeness amounts to the coverage of the different aspects introduced in the previous section. A good meta-tool will allow the expression of all important aspects of a modelling language. This requirement is reflected in figure 3 by the amount of the meta-model aspects that are covered. Please note that completeness is applicable for the tool, for the tool description and for the tool description language.

Conformance to Standards is given in this respect very easily when the tools are produced automatically from the corresponding standards documents. For this to be possible the standards documents have to be given in a formal way.

User Friendliness: Of course, for generated tools there is also the aspect of user friendliness. As we focus on the very generation of the tools, this end-user aspect is out of our focus.

When we look at the requirements, we see that they are all completely covered in the two upper levels of figure 3. Therefore we will use these two levels as the reference for comparing several meta-modelling tools in the next section. There, we just identify which aspects are supported and if they are described formally or built-in. If they are described formally, we check if they have a high-level notation or if they are given using a low-level language. The template for the comparison is therefore the two upper levels of figure 3.

3 Some Meta-modelling Frameworks and Tool Production

In this section, we will compare different meta-modelling frameworks according to the structure presented in the previous section.

3.1 MDA Meta-modelling

Karl Frank [5] states the following:

> At the core of MDA are the concepts of models, of meta-models defining the abstract languages in which the models are captured, and of transformations that take one or more models and produce one or more other models from them.

Since OMG introduced MDA in 2001, much work has been done in defining this approach with proposed specifications and implementations. Please find below some specifications that together cover all langues aspects of figure 3:

- For serialization: XMI [24] based on XML and UML 2.0 Diagram Interchange Specification [27].
- For concrete textual syntax: Human-Usable Textual Notation [22].
- For concrete graphical syntax: Human-Usable Graphical Notation [22].
- For transformations: Query/View/Transformation Specification [23] which also has a reference implementation.

 – For execution: Action Semantics [26] (no concrete syntax defined).
 – For constraints: OCL [25].
 – For abstract syntax: MOF [28].

When it comes to tool production the specifications are important with respect to "input" and "output", e.g. code conforming to the Action Semantics specification [26] might be produced as output and run on some UML virtual machine.

The QVT [23] might turn out to be important since the jobs a tool does in many respects can be seen as transformations.

Today there is no single tool or coherent set of tools producing a family of tools that conforms to the listed specifications.

For MDA to work in practice models have to be unambiguous and their semantics have to be precisely defined - UML does not fully comply with this demand [12].

In many respects UML has been defined as a general modelling (programming) language (but without fully described semantics) - a DSL, on the other hand, is specific (by definition), such that a UML tool might not be the right tool for expressing statements in a DSL (considering a DSL a subset of UML).

If the UML tool allowed advanced configuration (e.g. excluding parts of the UML language), supported the extension mechanism of UML (profiling), then the UML could be set up as a DSL tool; but even this might not work well in all cases since UML after all is a predefined language based on some language design decisions - this is the opposite argument of the "missing semantic" argument, UML might be to specific in "the wrong way"! It seems harder to reject MOF in the context of defining DSLs (which is done in [12]); if some semantic is missing then add it!

3.2 XMF-Mosaic

XMF-Mosaic from Xactium is a platform for building tailored tools that should provide high level automation, modelling and programming support for specific development processes, languages and application domains. The tool is implementing a layered executable meta-modelling framework called XMF that provides semantically rich meta-modelling facilities for the design of languages. This way the Mosaic platform is realizing the Language Driven Development (LDD) process presented by Xactium in [31]. LDD is a model-driven development technology based on MDA [21] standards, and it involves adopting a unified and semantically rich approach to describe languages. A key feature of the approach is the possibility to describe all aspects of a language in a platform-independent way, including their concrete representation and behaviour. The thought is that these language definitions should be rich enough to generate tools that can provide all the necessary support for use of the languages, such as syntax-aware editors, GUI's, compilers and interpreters.

XMF provides a collection of classes that form the basis of all XMF-Mosaic defined tools. These classes form the kernel of XMF and are called XCORE. XCORE is a MOF-like meta-meta-modelling language, and it is reflexive, i.e. all XCORE classes are instances of XCORE classes. XMF provides an extensive language for describing language properties called XOCL (eXtensible Object Command Language). XOCL is built from XCORE and it provides a language for manipulating XCORE objects. In addition to XCORE, XMF provides a collection of languages and tools defined in XOCL.

The general architecture of a tool or a language built using XMF-Mosaic is as follows:

Structure. At the heart of most XMF-Mosaic tools is a meta-model, in XMF called the domain model. This meta-model describes the structure of the concepts in a language or in a domain. The language for building the structure is XCORE.

Constraints. For adding constraints to the domain model, XMF-Mosaic supports a constraint language based on OCL. It is also possible to create instances of the domain model and test them against their constraints.

Representation. This is also called the user-interface model in XMF, and describes the concrete representation of the concepts in the domain model. For this purpose XMF-Mosaic provides XBNF, which is a grammar definition language for defining the textual syntax, and XTools which is used to specify the concrete graphical representation of a language and to model user interfaces.

Behaviour. The langugage XOCL is used to build executable tools with executable semantics. XMF-Mosaic also supports the representation of model-to-model transformation and model-to-code mappings, including generation of Java from XCore models and XML serialization of models. The language XMap is a pattern-based language that is used to write model-to-model transformations.

According to this, XMF-Mosaic is fully covering all the aspects of the template in figure 3.

3.3 Coral

Coral [15] is a meta-model independent framework, which means that it positions itself at the top of the OMG's meta-model architecture and then creates a meta-meta-model interface. In figure 4 it is shown which parts of the template (see fig. 3) Coral supports by indicating them in grey. It was a bit problematic to describe Coral according to the template, because the tool is not fully documented.

Coral is divided into two main components: the kernel and the graphical user-interface. The kernel is implementing a model repository. This repository could be seen as a program library or an application framework that is used to manage models described in the user-defined modelling language. This model repository is based on a specific modelling language, Simple Metamodel Description Language, which defines the structure of all modelling languages in Coral. SMD can

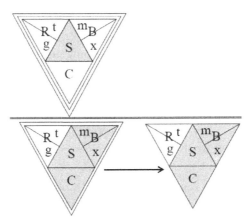

Fig. 4. Aspects supported by Coral

be seen as analogue to MOF, but SMD contains some extensions to deal with models described in multiple modelling languages. When Coral needs the definition of a modelling language, the SMD model for this language is loaded and converted to a meta-model internally. This way Coral provides full support for all structural aspects of meta-models.

The graphical user-interface in Coral can be used to view and edit models manually. The kernel and the graphical user-interface are independent. This means that the kernel can manage and transform models even if the user-interface cannot render them graphically.

Currently Coral is coming with some predefined modelling languages, such as UML 1.1, UML 1.3, UML 1.4 and UML 1.5, and also the XMI-DI 2.0 [27]. Coral can load and save models and meta-models using XMI 1.0 and XMI 2.0 format. It is also possible to load and save models containing diagram interchange information using XMI-DI, and this format is also used to represent diagrams. When it comes to interactive graphical support, this is missing, and support for every diagram must be written explicitly.

One feature in Coral is the possibility to query and modify models at runtime. This is done by creating Phyton wrappers around the Coral kernel, which is written in C++. Model transformation can be written as Phyton programs with separate phases for precondition, query and modification and postconditions. The Phyton interface in Coral makes it possible to query models in a very similar way to OCL [25], thus allowing constraints and transformations and executions to be expressed. Because there is no specific language to express these things, but just Python modules, we have not indicated these parts in the top-most language layer.

3.4 Software Factories

Software Factories are described in [12] in the following way:

A software factory is a product line that configures extensible development tools like Microsoft Visual Studio Team System (VSTS) [17] with packaged content and guidance, carefully designed for building specific kinds of applications ... the software factory schema specifies which DSLs should be used and describes how models based on these DSLs can be transformed into code and other artefacts, or into other models ... the software factory template ... provides the patterns, guidance, templates, frameworks, samples, custom tools such as DSL visual editing tools, scripts, XSDs, style sheets, and other ingredients used to build the product ... When configured with the software factory template, VSTS becomes a software factory for the product family.

Software Factories are promoted by Microsoft and can be based on tools like VSTS - which is a tool that lets you develop Microsoft .Net Framework applications. In .Net many different languages can be used; compilation is done to a common binary language (IL) which can be executed by the same runtime engine. The .Net approach gives integration of different general purpose languages (e.g. C# and C++) and this seems to be a good starting point for the development of a DSL framework.

The Software Factories method describes a MDD approach that is not based on UML or MOF; it opposes the MDA which is based on UML and claims it to give insufficient support to development of DSLs.

A comprehensive example is given in [12]; the following list describes the elements that constitute a DSL:

1. Abstract syntax graphs instantiated from meta-models and also abstract syntax trees instantiated from context-free grammars.
2. Layout information instantiated from concrete syntax. Concrete syntax is described with annotations on meta-model elements, e.g. class Identifier has annotation: [$shape: TextBox].
3. Serialized abstract syntax graphs and layout information which conforms to defined serialization syntax. Serialization is not based on XMI, which is seen as too strongly coupled to the target language meta-model and also hard to read; they advocate the following: "..., the XML syntax should be designed on a language-by-language basis, so that the language designer has the flexibility to change the mapping to accommodate different rates of change on either side."
4. Well-formedness rules defined with some "OCL-like" language.
5. Trace-based semantics describing what happens during execution; this semantics is described with a meta-model attached to the meta-model of the DSL; well-formedness rules can be attached in the "normal way"; a concrete syntax for the trace-based semantics is described (as above).

Software factories do also demonstrate how a meta-models can be broken down to parameterized language elements, called language design patterns, that can be glued together in different configurations - this gluing is considered a special case of model mapping.

Item 2 above describes how graphical layout can be attached; OMG has a different approach [27] which seems to be more flexible since it defines a separate graph for the graphics - a graph that will be connected to the abstract syntax graph, e.g. one element of the abstract syntax graph might be represented with several nodes in the concrete syntax graph.

The arguments concerning the rejection of XMI (item 3) seems hard to follow, e.g. change from one XMI version to another can be performed by some (simple) transformation. It seems likely that this approach will lead to yet another standard!

It is hard to get an overview of tool support (tools that makes tools) when it comes to software factories since a product line is put together in a somewhat ad hoc way and since there is no specialized complete framework (as we know of) for supporting the software factory method - only more general frameworks with some pre-made components. On the other hand, [12] and articles like [11] present a vision that includes full language support (a fulfillment of all the aspects of figure 3).

3.5   More Examples

Of course, the idea to generate language processing tools out of language descriptions is not new. The first attempts were grouped around the idea to generate grammar handling tools out of grammars. They have been successful in the area of lexical handling (e.g. [14]) and in the area of parsers (e.g. [29], [13]). It was quickly clear that these properties did not fully describe a language and several other approaches have been defined to capture the complete range of language aspects. However, none of these has had real success.

Currently, there are several initiatives towards the idea of a more complete language handling coming from different starting points. We have a closer look at four of them.

Intentional Software [9,1] is an attempt to use the informal descriptions of a software in order to generate code from them. This way, the *intent* of the code is still visible later and the connection to the real code stays alive. It is very difficult to get deeper understanding of their technology from the publicly available information. What we have seen is that they allow the definition of languages that capture the intent at the level that the developer has meant it. Then they apply tools that make these descriptions valuable, i.e. they are transformed to code. It is not visible which kind of description languages are used in order to describe languages.

Meta-programming System [18] is coming from JetBrains. The name does already say that this is a tool for meta-programming. They state "MPS is an implementation of Language Oriented Programming [3], whose goal is to make defining languages as natural and easy as defining classes and methods is today. The purpose is to "raise the level of abstraction", which has been a major goal of programming since the first assembly language was born." This way they also allow the definition of languages and the generation of tools out of the descriptions. It is not easy to see what languages they use for language description and which aspects they cover. On their website it is possible to get a pre-release of their tools for experiments.

GMF The Eclipse Graphical Modeling Framework (GMF) [7] is a promising open-source technology based on the Eclipse Modeling Framework (EMF) and the Graphical Editing Framework (GEF). One purpose of GMF is to support definition and implementation of Domain-Specific Languages. EMF provides its own meta-model, called Ecore which is very similar to EMOF (a subset of MOF 2.0). EMF includes support for XMI 2.0 serialization and reflection APIs; support for OCL has also been added. GEF is an MVC-based framework to create graphical editors. GMF brides EMF and GEF; it supplies a set of tools that allows you to define and then automatically generate a graphical Eclipse-based modelling tool. GMF seems quit complete already and it will probably play an important role as a tool making tool. This new approach has not had the time to mature and it is left to see if it is flexible enough to meet the demands of tomorrow.

MetaEdit+ [16] is a commercial metaCASE tool developed by the company MetaCase Consulting, Finland. The tool consists of two parts: the Method Workbench and the CASE tool. The Method Workbench is a dialog based interface, which allows the user to define the language concepts, their properties, associated rules, symbols etc. To describe the language concepts, a meta-modelling language called GOPPRR is used. GOPPRR stands for Graph, Object, Property, Port, Relationship and Role, which are the meta-types used to describe modelling languages. The CASE tool MetaEdit+ follows the language definition given in the Workbench, and provides a modelling tool according to this specification. MetaEdit+ support automatic code generation for predefined and user-defined programming language. The predefined includes: Smalltalk, C++, Java, Delphi, SQL and CORBA IDL.

3.6   The SMILE Framework

The SMILE project [19,6,20] started as an attempt to implement a technology that allows high-level language descriptions to be interpreted or compiled into real tools.

The basic idea of SMILE is the application of MDD to the language handling itself. This is done by using high-level descriptions of the languages for creating complete development environments. The descriptions are given in high-level languages, thus allowing the application of the SMILE principle to itself, which is usually called bootstrapping or self-reference. This idea came out of the success of this technology in the implementation of the SDL formal semantics [10,4,30].

For language modelling, the SMILE methodology takes three steps:

1. the description of structure and semantics,
2. the automated generation of specific repositories and tools, and
3. the use of the generated repositories and tools for concrete models.

This methodology is based on a combination of meta-modelling for information structure description with technologies to describe the semantics of that information accordingly. These description techniques, covering different language aspects, have to be adopted and aligned to create a common language modelling framework. With this new technology that integrates structure and semantics, the SMILE toolset will be able to generate data repositories and language tools that reflect the given semantics.

The SMILE methodology will be supported by a domain-independent framework that provides language support for information structure and semantic descriptions, making SMILE applicable to the described domains. To describe the information structure SMILE will use existing standards to describe a repository, e.g. MOF or RDFS. In the area of semantics SMILE distinguishes between five kinds of semantics: Static semantics that is described with a condition language based on OCL, execution semantics that will be handled through the ASM method, transformations formally described by rules and two ways to describe concrete representations, textual and graphical. SMILE will provide a) languages to handle these semantics and b) implementations that allow the generation of tools (model checkers, transformation engines, model editors and parsers) from descriptions in these languages.

The SMILE approach is best understood by looking at the meaning of the project abbreviation, which is Semantic Model-based Integrated Language Environment. These parts stand for the following concepts.

Semantic: SMILE acknowledges the importance of explicit semantic descriptions in all places of the technology. The current approach to have informal descriptions of parts of modelling languages (most prominently the dynamic aspects) is not fitting the state of the art. There is enough knowledge about how language semantics can be formalised and there are even tools that can transform such explicit semantics descriptions into real tools (interpreters or compilers).

Model-Based: The whole approach of SMILE is focused on the idea to handle models. Not only the descriptions of the software are models, but also the descriptions of the languages and the languages to describe them and even the generated code. In order to handle these models in a unified way, a basic model representation is used allowing to capture models internally. This is detailed below.

Integrated: The integration within SMILE starts with the unified model representation. Every bit of information in SMILE is handled similarily. This is achieved by using a basic instance representation with an explicit interface between meta-modelling levels. This means, SMILE follow a strict meta-modelling approach without connecting the levels to each other by default. In SMILE, a model can be connected to different meta-models if the interface between them allows this coupling.

Language: The most prominent examples of using SMILE are languages. In fact, in SMILE a model is just a kind of a language and vice versa. Therefore, the concentration on languages is not that special, because everything is a language in the end.

Environment: The final aim of SMILE is providing a complete modelling environment, which would also be a meta-modelling environment. Moreover, the SMILE technology does also an easy integration of external modelling or meta-modelling tools. The SMILE implementation is started in the scope of the Eclipse [2] platform using EMF [8].

The SMILE project is still in its early phases and is not yet completely implemented. A basic representation called MATER (see [6]) was defined that allows the representation of any model (and meta-model) independently of the corresponding meta-model. This is possible since SMILE has the complete information about the model and the meta-model encoded into structural properties. This allows models to be connected to different meta-models in SMILE.

4   Concluding Remarks

In this article, we have defined a terminology for the comparison of environments that generate modelling tools. This framework is very heavily related to meta-modelling. There are several current initiatives to create such an environment, and although very few results exist so far, we can conclude that almost all approaches focus on the same aspects of languages, namely structure, constraints, representation (textual and graphical), and behaviour (mapping and execution).

Despite these striking commonalities, there are also several differences, that mostly relate to the semantics of the parts. In all MDA-related approaches a fixed exchange format (XMI) is taken as part of the structure semantics. Software factories argue that this is not needed and will use a specific format defined for each language instead. This kind of reasoning is understandable when one thinks of the many versions of XMI and that they do not really achieve the goal of exchangability. However, we still think that in an ideal setting a basic exchange format should be defined independently of the concrete language. This is taken into account in the SMILE framework in that we consider also the semantics of structural information to be given by the description language of structural information, and a general way of exchange can be described there in terms of textual representation. This way, it is just a special case and would also be possible the same way in software factories.

Another difference are the concrete languages put forward for expressing the different aspects of meta-models. Surprisingly, very concrete languages are used, although they are defined based on meta-models. There is not much work in integrating these different formalisms. Only the SMILE project tries to tackle this problem, but they are at the very beginning of their work.

Finally, it remains to be said that almost all approaches take the language structure for granted and do not allow handling of changes to the meta-model. As these approaches are that similar, it would be a very good idea to allow them to integrate, i.e. that there are ways to use the models of one approach also in another approach.

The plans described in the different environments sound very promising and could lead to a completely different way of software development, once they are fully implemented.

References

1. K. Czarnecki and U. W. Eisenecker. *Generative Programming. Methods, Tools, and Applications*, chapter 11: Intentional Programming. Addison Wesley, 2000.
2. Jim d'Anjou, Scott Fairbrother, Dan Kehn, John Kellermann, and Pat McCarthy. *The Java Developer's Guide to Eclipse*. Addison-Wesley, 2004.
3. Sergey Dmitriev. Language oriented programming: The next programming paradigm. *onBoard*, 2004. See
   `http://www.onboard.jetbrains.com/is1/articles/04/10/lop/`.
4. Robert Eschbach, Uwe Glässer, Reinhard Gotzhein, Martin von Löwis, and Andreas Prinz. Formal definition of SDL-2000: Compiling and running SDL specifications as ASM models. In *Abstract State Machines 2001: New Developments and Applications*. J.UCS Special issue vol. 7, no. 11, 2001.
5. Karl Frank. A proposal for an MDA foundation model. An ORMSC White Paper V00-02 ormsc/05-04-01, Object Management Group (OMG), accessed August, 2005. Available at
   `http://www.omg.org/docs/ormsc/05-04-01.pdf`.
6. Terje Gjøsæter, Jan P. Nytun, Andreas Prinz, and Merete S. Tveit. Accessibility testing XHTML documents using UML. In Kai Koskimies, Ludwik Kuzniarz, Jyrki Nummenmaa, and Zheying Zhang, editors, *Proc. of the Nordic UML Workshop*. University of Tampere, Finland, 2005.
7. *Eclipse Graphical Modeling Framework*. See `http://www.eclipse.org/gmf`.
8. Catherine Griffin. Using EMF. Technical report, IBM: Eclipse Corner Article, 2003. See also
   `http://www.eclipse.org/articles/Article-Using EMF/using-emf.html`.
9. *Intentional Software*. See `http://intentsoft.com/`.
10. ITU-T. SDL - ITU-T Specification and Description Language, Formal Semantics. ITU-T Recommendation Z.100, Annex F, 1999.
11. Jack Greenfield and Keith Short. *Moving to Software Factories*, July 2004. Available at `http://blogs.msdn.com/askburton/articles/232021.aspx`.
12. Jack Greenfield and Keith Short, with contributions by Steve Cook and Stuart Kent. *Software Factories: Assembling Applications with Patterns, Frameworks, Models & Tools*. John Wiley & Sons, September 2004.
13. Stephen C. Johnson. *yacc – Yet Another Compiler-Compiler*. See also `http://dinosaur.compilertools.net/yacc/index.html`.
14. M. E. Lesk and E. Schmidt. *Lex – A Lexical Analyzer Generator*. See also `http://dinosaur.compilertools.net/lex/index.html`.
15. Ivan Porres Marcus Alanen. The coral modelling framework. In Kai Koskimies, Ludwik Kuzniarz, Johan Lilius, and Ivan Porres, editors, *Proc. of the 2nd Nordic Workshop on the Unified Modeling Language NWUML'2004*. Turku Centre for Computer Science, Finland, 2004.
16. MetaCase. MetaEdit+. Version 4.0. Evaluation Tutorial. Technical report, Meta-Case, 2005. Available at
   `http://www.metacase.com/support/40/manuals/eval40sr2a4.pdf`.

17. Microsoft. Information on Visual Studio Team System. Technical report, Microsoft, 2006. Available at
    `http://lab.msdn.microsoft.com/vs2005/teamsystem`.
18. *Meta Programming System.* See `http://www.jetbrains.com/mps/`.
19. J. P. Nytun, A. Prinz, and A. Kunert. Representation of levels and instantiation in a metamodelling environment. In Kai Koskimies, Ludwik Kuzniarz, Johan Lilius, and Ivan Porres, editors, *Proc. of the Nordic UML Workshop.* Turku Centre for Computer Science, Finland, 2004.
20. Jan Pettersen Nytun and Andreas Prinz. Metalevel representation and philosophical ontology. In *Proc. of ECOOP workshop on Philosophy, Ontology, and Information Systems.* University of Oslo, Norway, 2004.
21. OMG. *Model Driven Architecture Guide, Version 1.0.1.* Object Management Group, June 2003. omg/03-06-01.
22. OMG. Human-Usable Textual Notation (HUTN) Specification Version 1.0 formal/04-08-01. OMG document, Object Management Group, 2004. Available at
    `http://www.omg.org/docs/formal/04-08-01.pdf`.
23. OMG. Meta Object Facility (MOF) 2.0 Query/View/Transformation Specification Final Adopted Specification ptc/05-11-01. OMG document, Object Management Group, 2005. Available at `http://www.omg.org/docs/ptc/05-11-01.pdf`.
24. OMG. MOF 2.0/XMI Mapping Specification, v2.1 formal/05-09-01. OMG document, Object Management Group, 2005. Available at
    `http://www.omg.org/docs/formal/05-09-01.pdf`.
25. OMG. *OCL 2.0 Specification.* Object Management Group, June 2005. ptc/2005-06-06.
26. OMG. UML 1.4 with Action Semantics. OMG document, Object Management Group, 2005. Available at `http://www.omg.org/cgi-bin/doc?ptc/02-01-09`.
27. OMG. Unified Modeling Language: Diagram Interchange version 2.0, ptc/05-06-04. OMG document, Object Management Group, 2005. Available at
    `http://www.omg.org/docs/ptc/05-06-04.pdf`.
28. OMG Editor. Revised Submission to OMG RFP ad/2003-04-07: Meta Object Facility (MOF) 2.0 Core Proposal. Technical report, Object Management Group, April 2003. Available at
    `http://www.omg.org/docs/formal/06-01-01.pdf`.
29. T. J. Parr and R. W. Quong. ANTLR: A predicated-LL(k) parser generator. In *Software – Practice and Experience, Vol. 25(7).* ACM Press New York, 1995.
30. Andreas Prinz. *Formal Semantics for RSDL: Definition and Implementation.* PhD thesis, Humboldt-Universität zu Berlin, June 2000.
31. Tony Clark, Andy Evans, Paul Sammut, James Williams. *Applied Metamodelling. A Foundation for Language Driven Development.* Xactium, 2004. Available at `http://www.xactium.com`.

Model Driven Development of Multi-Agent Systems

Juan Pavón, Jorge Gómez-Sanz, and Rubén Fuentes

Facultad de Informática, Universidad Complutense Madrid
Ciudad Universitaria s/n, 28040 Madrid, Spain
{jpavon, jjgomez, ruben}@sip.ucm.es

Abstract. From a software engineering point of view, the agent paradigm has shown its potential for modelling in different domains. However, moving from agent models to implementation is not fully addressed by most agent-oriented methodologies in a systematic way. In most cases, they focus on the agent concept at the analysis level or look for visual or formal representations of elements present in an already implemented agent framework. Here we show that model driven development with agent-based models can facilitate the implementation of methods and tools for the development of multi-agent systems. This is illustrated with the INGENIAS methodology and its tools, the INGENIAS Development Kit (IDK), which are founded on the definition of the INGENIAS meta-models for multi-agent systems, and implement most of the facilities that a model driven development approach requires.

1 Introduction

Agent Oriented Software Engineering addresses the development of complex and dynamic distributed systems using the agent paradigm [3]. An agent is a software entity that has its own thread of control and is modelled in terms of behavioural and social concepts such as goals, intentions, evidences, tasks, organizations, roles, etc. Many agent-oriented methodologies have focused on modelling concerns, leaving open the mapping to concrete implementations. In fact, multi-agent systems (MAS) are usually implemented with object oriented programming languages, with the support of some middleware for agent communications and lifecycle management. However, the fact of using agent modelling concepts makes the design and analysis simpler to understand since these concepts are, in principle, closer to human thinking. They are specially appropriate to deal with social issues (organization, interaction, coordination, negotiation, cooperation, distribution) and complex behaviours (autonomy, mental state, goals, tasks, emergence) [13]. The issue then is twofold: how to map these concepts, and how to associate them with concrete implementations.

Most of the agent oriented methodologies propose a data model and provide predetermined mappings to very specific implementation frameworks or do not deal with implementation at all [4]. This leaves a significant gap between design and implementation, which is put in evidence when trying to apply some methodologies to specific application domains, i.e., losing generality. Given this context, we have been surprised by the fact that almost no agent-oriented methodological proposal bases on MDD,

A. Rensink and J. Warmer (Eds.): ECMDA-FA 2006, LNCS 4066, pp. 284–298, 2006.

which would help to address this important issue. This idea has driven us to reformulate an agent-oriented methodology, INGENIAS [15], in terms of the MDD paradigm. INGENIAS defines a development process, a specification of the results to produce, i.e. models, and support tools for modelling and transformation of models. The experience of using the methodology in several projects has been synthesized into a set of meta-model specifications for MAS and transformations (code generation) for several target platforms. These are supported by the INGENIAS Development Kit (IDK) [15], which provides capabilities for model edition, model verification and automatic code generation. These are ingredients that make INGENIAS suitable for applying MDD.

However, we have also identified two main open issues with INGENIAS. First, meta-models may change (evolve) due to new requirements in new application domains. Second, producing the transformations of the models into code for different target platforms requires a development process by itself. These issues were not addressed by the INGENIAS development process when it was first formulated. They point out the need of reviewing the problems inherent to a model drivel development in the context of agent systems. So, the contribution in this paper is a reformulation of INGENIAS methodology that increases the relevance of the model creation, definition, and transformation in the context of multi-agent systems.

The next section discusses MAS meta-models and introduces the scope the INGENIAS meta-models. Section 3 presents IDK facilities, more concretely, model edition, model verification, and automatic code generation. Section 4 describes the steps required in the IDK to produce a transformation module. Section 5 takes into account the support of IDK to define an Agent MDD process for INGENIAS. Section 6 gives information on the evaluation of the approach as it has been applied in the development of several projects and compares it with similar works. Section 7 discusses conclusions derived from such experiences.

2 Multi-Agent Systems Meta-models

Meta-models in agent-oriented software engineering have been generally used for presenting concepts and only recently they are being considering as a foundation for MAS development tools. Probably, AALAADIN [7] has been the first meta-model for MAS. It intends to represent the MAS structure, not behaviour, in terms of three main concepts: agent, group and role. AALAADIN meta-model concepts have been implemented on the MadKit platform. A more formal proposal for the definition of agent organizations is given in [12], by extending the UML superstructure using MOF, although we have not found any tool that implements it. These meta-models were quite simple, but represent seminal work in the agent research area.

Recently, the use of meta-models has grown. It has being used in the agent community as a tool that can help to compare different methodologies, such as in [2] for Adelfe, Gaia and Passi. More pragmatic purpose has [5], which tries to identify a generic meta-model for MAS that could serve as the basis to apply a method engineering approach to integrate various agent-oriented methods. This approach has been also followed by recent work in AgentLink III, as reported in [3]. All these works are convincing agent researchers of the advantages of defining meta-models. Whether these meta-models will be detailed enough to serve as foundation for the appropriate

tools is something that we should see in the coming future. In this line, we are wit-
nessing an emergence of many meta-models for already existing agent-oriented methodologies, like in Tropos, where a modelling tool is built on Eclipse using EMF and
GEF [17].

Our contribution in the application of meta-models to agent-oriented software engineering started with MESSAGE/UML [6], an extension to UML with the definition
of a meta-model for MAS specification. In principle, an editor based on this metamodel was implemented with MetaEdit+ [10]. With the application in several projects, we have refined the MESSAGE/UML meta-model (see for instance [9]), which
has evolved into INGENIAS [15]. As we show below, INGENIAS has succeeded to
specify a complete metamodel for MAS on which it is possible to build a full set of
tools for Agent MDD.

Since its conception, INGENIAS uses meta-modelling as the foundation for its
methods and tools. This has facilitated the extension of the methodology when new
concepts have been considered for their integration in INGENIAS. The specification
is structured in five packages (Fig. 1) that represent the viewpoints from which a
MAS can be regarded: organization, agent, goals/tasks, interactions, and environment.

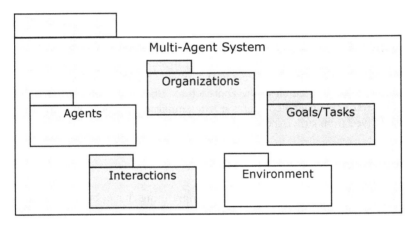

Fig. 1. INGENIAS viewpoints

For instance, the agent viewpoint considers the elements to specify agent behaviour. Agents are considered as intentional entities that pursue the satisfaction of goals
as they play roles in a MAS organization. Taking into account their mental state (a set
of facts, goals, believes) the agent decides which actions (tasks) will try to perform.
The mechanisms to make such decision are encapsulated in a Mental State Processor
(P) and the management of mental state entities (creation, modification, deletion) is
encapsulated in a Mental State Manager (G). These concepts and their dependencies
are represented in meta-classes of the meta-model (see Fig 2). They may be assigned
with a graphical representation for the modelling language, which can be particular to
the INGENIAS tools or UML like (see Fig 3).

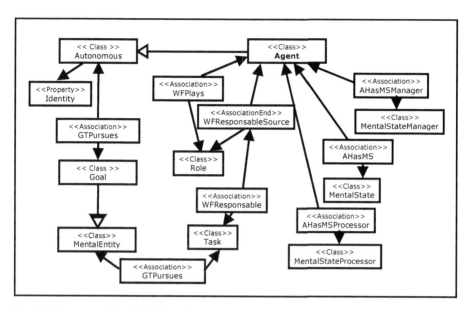

Fig. 2. Fragment of the INGENIAS Agent viewpoint meta-model. Stereotypes indicate the intended use of each entity at M1 level, i.e., the model level. A *class* stereotype means that instances of the entity (in the model) will be classes. *Association* means that the entities will be instantiated into edges among *class* instances. *AssociationEnd* details which kind of entities will be connected by an *Association*. The stereotype notation is based on GOPRR [10] and helps making the diagram more compact and readable. The UML superstructure, also, defines special entities to represent relationships, namely *Relationship*, *Association*, or *Directed Relationship*, all of them elements of the *Kernel* package.

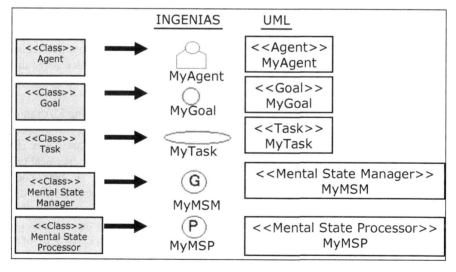

Fig. 3. Correspondence of meta-model entities with graphical representation in the model with INGENIAS notation and UML-like

The current INGENIAS MAS meta-model is rather complex (at least in size). The interested reader can navigate through the specification, which is available on-line at http://grasia.fdi.ucm.es/ingenias/metamodel. Some statistics of the number of entities are given in Table 1.

Table 1. Statistics of basic MOF primitives applied in the INGENIAS meta-model

Class	87
Association	85
AssociationEnd	137

This complexity is due to the required level of detail for producing complete models which could be transformed into executable code. However, it is a decision of the developer to use the meta-model with an adequate degree of abstraction. In the initial specification of the INGENIAS methodology there are guidelines, based on the Unified Process, that indicate which elements and diagrams should be produced in each stage of the development. Indeed, the more precise has to be the description of the functionality, the more information the models should incorporate.

3 Agent MDD Tools: The INGENIAS Development Kit (IDK)

A MDD process requires support tools for modelling, verification and for transformation of the models. These functionalities are available in the IDK. The IDK is an open source set of tools for the development of MAS. The foundation of the IDK is the INGENIAS MAS meta-model, presented in the previous section. The IDK is meta-model independent in the sense that it can be regenerated automatically from the meta-model, though this feature is not available in the open source version. Therefore, changes in the meta-model can be quickly applied in the tools. This is necessary to support the evolution of the meta-model as we gain experience in the entities needed to build MAS applications. Besides, as INGENIAS is a research project, it requires the ability to extend and refine the meta-model specification in order to integrate new features from experimental and theoretical results.

For instance, the IDK MAS Model Editor (a graphical tool for defining MAS models), is generated, as shown in Fig. 4, from the meta-model specification, graphical representations for concepts (icon files), and a description of editor attributes (for instance, the associations between entities in the meta-model and their graphical representation, as icon files). The generation is driven by an interpreter of meta-model descriptors and an editor template (which determines the general aspect and distribution of editor elements) following a similar mechanism as the *modules* which will be presented below. An advantage of this approach is that changes in the definition of meta-models can be easily applied to generate personalized editors. As a proof of concept, an editor for holonic manufacturing systems has been built by another research group using the IDK framework [8].

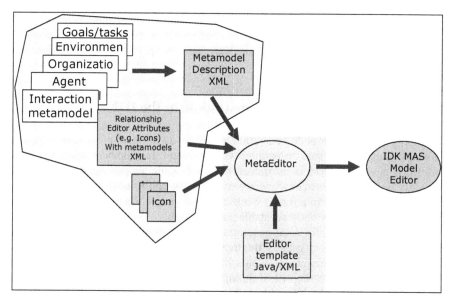

Fig. 4. Generation of the IDK MAS Model Editor from meta-model specifications

The editor is the primary tool for the MAS developer, but a MDD approach requires also verification and validation tools, and transformation engines to derive source code in the target platform, documentation, or some other model. This is supported in the IDK by *modules*. Modules (or *plugins*) in INGENIAS are programs that process specifications and produce some output:

- *Source code.* There is an infrastructure that facilitates the transformation of the specification into source code. This is based on the definition of code templates for each target platform and information extraction procedures from the current models.
- *Reports.* Specifications can also be analysed to check, for instance, whether they have certain properties or whether special semantics (defined by the developer) are being respected, or to collect statistics of usage of different elements.
- *Modifications on current specification diagrams.* Though this feature is in beta stage, a module could insert and/or modify entities in the diagrams, or insert/delete diagrams. This feature is useful to define personal assistants that interact with the tool.
- *Other models.* As we produce source code, there is no difference in producing as well other models following different meta-models.

Modules are built in the top of a framework that provides facilities to traverse specifications, extract information from specifications, and put the extracted information into templates. A module is typically written in Java according to some strict instructions (implementing concrete interfaces, model information extraction procedures, templates, packaging it all into jar files, and deploying the result in a concrete folder) if the developer intends to integrate it with the IDK, though another alternatives may be used. Models are stored in XML, so other transformation techniques could be used, like XSLT, and custom model to text conversions could be applied, like a raw DOM parsing of the XML tree and producing as output directly some code.

4   Developing a Transformation Module in the IDK

Developing a module for code generation is usually an iterative process through several steps. This process runs in parallel with the main development when the target platform is new (i.e., there is no transformation module supporting it in IDK). The main development process consequently relies in the ability of the module construction process to elaborate in a timely manner a code generation process that enacts the transformation of models into executable code.

In our case, the basis for code generation is the availability of code templates for the target platform. This is usually the most difficult to obtain as it requires a good knowledge of how to implement agents in the target platform. Our experience has shown that this can be accomplished through an iterative process, in which the developer defines progressively the architecture of the code for the target platform and the transformations from specification to code templates. This process could be sketched in several steps:

1. *Small initial prototype.* The developer produces a simple prototype of the application. Initially, the developer would centre into one or more features of the specification, easy to implement if possible. For instance, how to use the specific facilities of the target platform to make two agents interact. As a result, the developer gains knowledge on the target platform and has a prototype of an application on the target platform that realizes a small part of the specification with a selected set of features.

2. *Marking up the prototype code.* Looking at both the prototype and the specification, it is possible to identify parts of the prototype that match parts of the specification. As a result, the developer identifies possible mappings from the specification to the prototype code. This is reflected in a prototype code marked up with tags. The marked-up pieces of source code are called *templates*.

3. *Generating/modifying a module.* A module has to traverse the specification in order to obtain the information required to instantiate and fill in the prototype templates. The IDK provides an API for traversing specifications and Java packages for building modules. In concrete, the module engineer has to extend the class *BasicToolImp* for verification and validation modules or the class *BasicCodeGeneratorImp* for code generation modules. Other classes may be created as well.

4. *Deploying the module.* The resulting Java classes and templates of the module are put together into a jar file. This jar file is deployed in a specific folder where the IDK MAS Model Editor can load it dynamically.

5. *Testing the module.* Testing is performed from the IDK MAS Model Editor. By executing the module over the specification, the developer can check if the diagram is traversed properly and if all templates have been filled in as they

should. Also, as templates demand concrete information, it may be possible that this is not present or that it is not expressed as it should. Therefore, it may turn out that the specification was not correct or incomplete. In this sense, any module can be useful to validate the specification against some completeness criteria. As a result, several kinds of problems may appear: with the code generated by the module, with the traversal of the specification, or with the specification itself.

6. *Debugging.* If something goes wrong, debug the prototype and go to:
    a.   Step 2. If there is new code that was not marked up before.
    b.   Step 3. If the failure was in the module and the data traversal.
    c.   Step 4. If there was a failure in the prototype and could be solved without marking up the code again.
7. *Refinement and extension.* When the module is finished, it can translate diagram specifications into code or perform verification of some properties. However, the module performs these tasks with a reduced set of the diagram specification. The next step would be to take the code generated by the module and extend it so that it can satisfy other parts of the specification. Therefore, we would go back to step 1.

In this way, modules produce code using a template based approach. As an example, Fig. 5 shows how to generate code for a rule based system, in this case *JESS* (Java Expert System Shell, http://herzberg.ca.sandia.gov/jess). A developer defines a template of a JESS rule (steps 1 and 2) and extracts data from the MAS specification (step 3) to generate the rest of rules. Rules need a condition, an action, and a name. These data are expressed using a concrete structure that will be presented later. As a result, we get two different rules, which are instantiated from the same template.

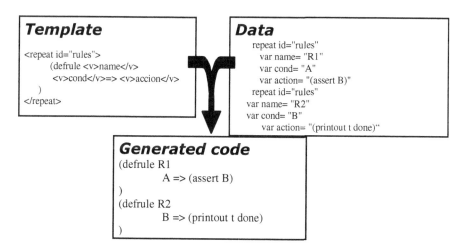

Fig. 5. An example of code generation for a set of JESS rules

These elements are configured within a module and deployed in the IDK (step 4), and tested over the specification of a MAS (step 5). As a result of the testing, we would obtain the generated code presented in Fig. 5. Whether this satisfies the requirements or not would trigger step 6. This procedure has been used in several developments, which are commented in section 6.

As readers may deduce, other transformation techniques based on XML transformations to get source code may be similar: they all need to determine what source code is to be produced, what information from the model is relevant, and go through a strong testing process to ensure that the transformation chain works as expected. In any case, producing source code from a model requires time and expertise of both the expected semantics of the models and the target platform where the source code will be deployed. Besides, a module intending to process a whole specification rarely can be built in one iteration. It requires a step-wise analysis of the requirements detailed in the models

Assuming this hypothesis, there are several common conflicts between this flow of activities and the main development flow that one may expect:

- Models can be modified without knowledge of the workers involved in the development of a module. The specification of the problem may grow in different directions, and some of them may be incompatible with the assumptions made to develop the transformation.
- The transformation procedure, whatever it is, determines the models and vice-versa. On one hand, obtaining source code implies assuming unambiguous semantics of the models. At the end, only models which are valid according to these semantics will be considered, but is all the relevant information being considered? On the other hand, a step-wise construction of a transformation implies that each step is compatible with the previous one, and, sometimes, this happens to be false. A transformation may consider new elements of the specification that could require to identify new dependencies that did not exist before.

These problems are not easily solvable. We have alleviated them by synchronizing the activities in the MDD version of INGENIAS. So, instead of building independently models and the model transformation, both flows should evolve in parallel with frequent cross-checks to ensure that current transformation can indeed grow to incorporate new elements of the specification and to avoid adding information which would not be realized in the final delivers.

5 An Agent MDD Process

To solve previous dependencies between the elaboration of the models and the construction of the transformations, we have refined the initial INGENIAS process taking into account MDD principles.

This starts by considering two main roles in the development process:

- The MAS developer, as shown in Fig. 6, uses the IDK MAS Model Editor to specify MAS models. These models can be verified and validated with analysis and simulation modules. Once they have been validated, code generation modules facilitate the implementation to deploy in a target platform. When the system has been produced, the testing activities start. In case of

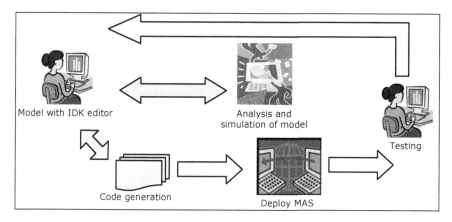

Fig. 6. MAS developer activities

- detecting failures, the developer would come back to the modelling. Also, the developer may come back to modelling to add new features.
- The INGENIAS engineer, as shown in Fig. 7, knows the INGENIAS meta-model and can customize the editor for a specific purpose (this may require modifications on the meta-model) and produce new modules for verification and validation, or for code generation in some target platform.

Most development process identify more roles, but here we are interested in solving the dependencies between the model transformation construction and the model

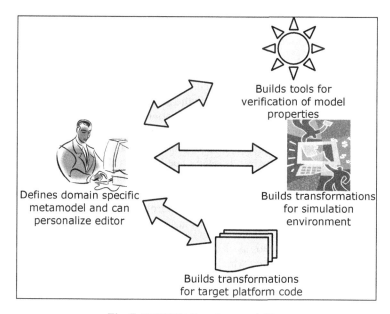

Fig. 7. INGENIAS engineer activities

elaboration activities. Sometimes these roles can be played by the same person, which normally occurs when the application under development has to be deployed in a novel target platform, so a new code generation module is required. But, in principle, at least one person of the development team needs to have the skills of a INGENIAS engineer to create new modules, the rest can just edit models and execute modules to work on the specifications. In the later case, the INGENIAS developer and the MAS developer have to synchronize their activities.

Defects in the meta-model will appear when the MAS developer is modelling. Hence, the INGENIAS engineer should ensure that a new editor is available before the new modelling – system generation round happens.

The transformation has to be built during the modelling or testing stage. Initially, there are available transformations for the initial stages that can be used in the mean time (they are included in the IDK). However, these, probably, have to be adapted to the new domain. By scheduling the module adaptation effort during the modelling and testing stages, the MAS developer should not be affected by the delays. Therefore, new versions of the module should be ready right before the code generation. This deadline can be too strict sometimes, and, indeed, it can be a bottleneck in the development, since it prevents the generation of new bug-free systems. Our experience with this respect is that having already tested initial generic transformations saves most of the effort and makes this process more feasible.

6   Evaluation and Related Works

The INGENIAS approach to code generation is in line with Wasserman [18], who proposes a rapid application development environment where graphical specifications are translated to executable code by using code skeletons. This technique has evolved into more sophisticated scripting languages that acted as mappers of specification to code. Examples of such environments are METAEDIT+ [10] and WithCLASS [11]. The first is a meta-case tool that supports mapping of specifications to any kind of code. The second, a UML compliant tool, also provides facilities to translate diagrams to code, which is based on script language. There is, however, one significant difference between IDK and those tools, apart of the scope of INGENIAS, which is clearly oriented to agent-oriented systems. The IDK offers programmatic infrastructure to generate new modules with a clear interface to manipulate meta-models.

The experience of this approach in several projects has shown increase in productivity as transformations allow to reuse the experience on the use of platforms in further projects using similar infrastructure. Also, the smooth approach to the platform with the incremental-iterative method towards the development of modules, in parallel with the modelling of the MAS, facilitates learning through a risk-driven process. However, the application of transformations has revealed some problems, such as:

- Debugging transformations. For instance, it is not trivial, given a chain of transformations, to detect which one is not working as it should. Also, a transformation may meet the requirements set initially and, at the same time, be insufficient according to the code generation needs. This may happen, for instance, if there are different developers for different transformations to be chained later on.

- The maintenance of the transformations. Once created, a transformation should be reused in different developments. This implies documenting appropriately the transformation or elaborating extension points to incorporate new functionality with low impact.

So far, there are some relevant experiments where these ideas have been validated and have contributed to the evolution of the IDK tools. These tools provide some code generation facilities and have allowed us to study the ability of other people to create IDK modules:

- Robocode. Based on a work from Elsa Yañez, an undergraduate student. Robocode is a platform for learning JAVA by describing the behaviour of fighting tanks in a simulated environment (see http://robocode.sourceforge.net/). This is interesting from an agent perspective as tanks can be driven autonomously and collaborate in teams. The goal of the student was to provide a graphical front-end with the IDK for the design of the control of individual tanks and of the team. Once defined, the module developed by the student produces source code that can be compiled and executed by Robocode.
- Tank Soar. Based on a work from Juan Antonio Recio, a PhD student. It defines transformations for a model describing an example of the SOAR architecture for the control of tanks within a labyrinth. Control of the tanks are expressed by means of several rules according to what SOAR expects. These rules are expressed in terms of the elements identified by the INGENIAS Development Kit.
- *Juul BokHandle* case study. It describes a bookshop that sells books to university students. The company has an agreement with professors and students to obtain a list of books used in their courses and sell them at special prices. The bookseller is considered an organization in which there are departments in charge of sales and departments in charge of logistics. This organization has to negotiate with other organizations, editorials, for acquiring books at the best prices and with specific timing constraints. It can also negotiate for special arrangements for certain books that are demanded in concrete courses. Sales can be conventional or through internet.

- Cinema Ticket Selling. Based on a work from Carlos Celorrio, a PhD student. It describes a scenario where an interface agent interacts with a buyer agent to buy a ticket to go to the cinema. The buyer agent has to locate a seller agent that will sell the cinema ticket, and move towards the node the seller agent is allocated into. After migrating, it buys the ticket, and then moves back to its original location to give back the ticket to the interface agent.

Some models used for these developments are included within the IDK and serve as examples of the use of transformation modules included in the IDK distribution:

- Communication facilities. There are two variants of this module, one based on JADE (http://jade.tilab.com) and another based on JADE Leap. In both, it produces session oriented communication facilities for different process entities. Concretely, the code generator produces state machines each one representing the partial knowledge a participant has of a conversation modelled with the IDK. The JADE Leap code generator adds to these the capability of code mobility and task execution. Mobility and task execution is specified again in the IDK. JADE and JADE Leap provide a FIPA compliant middleware for agent communications. They differ in how communication is envisioned and that JADE provides also management services for agents and agent platform domains.

- Servlet Based Workflow Simulation. It transforms a specification of task execution into a servlet. This servlet simulates different existing workflows where different tasks and actors take part. By traversing the specification, it detects which tasks are the initial ones and what happens, i.e. what tasks are enabled, when a concrete one is executed.
- Document generation. To facilitate development, it is important to be able to document the specification. This module, instead of producing code, uses templates of reports to produce different HTML documents that can be reviewed by developers.

All these transformation modules were built according to the process presented in section 4.

7   Conclusions

Our experience in the application of MDD techniques to the development of multi-agent systems (MAS) with INGENIAS has shown the convenience of the parallel evolution of both application modelling and transformations definition, especially when the target environment and application domain are new for the developer. The proposed process promotes the evolution of the MAS model and transformations for the chosen target platform, in a sequence of small incremental steps. Each step goes trough strict testing before proceeding to the next step. In this way, the MDD process becomes agile, in the sense that iterations take into consideration small parts of the MAS model, which determine the elements of the meta-model that are taken into account by the implementation of the transformation. Note that in this process, while building the transformation, there may be elements of the model that are required and where not considered. So there is a feedback between model and transformation developments.

Once that the transformation modules for a target platform are available, this experience can be reused in further developments. It is also interesting to note that, given the IDK infrastructure, it is possible to specify different implementation strategies for the same target platform. Each strategy may depend on particular application concerns, for instance.

An advantage of using agent-based modelling in a MDD context is that agent concepts promote a more abstract language for problem domain modelling than standard UML. This makes it easier to consider the definition of domain modelling languages as extensions of the agent-oriented language. In INGENIAS, this has been done to adapt the language to a more specific one for holonic manufacturing systems [8] and for social simulation environments [16].

Our experience in the development of IDK is that, as a general framework, MDD favours the use of meta-models and these ideas can be used when considering building tools for agent oriented development in the same way as for other software paradigms (such as the object one). However, it is quite difficult to provide complete meta-models suitable for specific platforms (such as JADE) in a similar way as MDA proposes. For this reason we propose a process for partial and incremental transformations that can be driven by application needs. This can provide support to developers, but getting the whole solution still requires further research.

Acknowledgments

This work has been funded by the Spanish Council for Science and Technology with grant TIN2005-08501-C03-01.

References

1. Amor M., Fuentes L., and Vallecillo A.: Bridging the Gap Between Agent-Oriented Design and Implementation Using MDA. In: *Agent-Oriented Software Engineering V: 5th International Workshop, AOSE 2004*. Lecture Notes in Computer Science 3382, Springer Verlag, (2005) 93-108
2. Bernon, C. et al.: A Study of Some Multi-agent Meta-models. In: *Agent-Oriented Software Engineering V: 5th International Workshop, AOSE 2004*. Lecture Notes in Computer Science, Vol. 3382. Springer-Verlag, Berlin Heidelberg (2005) 78–77
3. Bernon, C., Cossentino, M. and Pavón, J..: Agent Oriented Software Engineering. *The Knowledge Engineering Review 20, 2* (2005), 99-116.
4. Bernon, C., Cossentino, M. and Pavón, J..: An Overview of Current Trends in European AOSE Research. *Informatica, An International Journal of Computing and Informatics 29, 4* (2005), 379-390
5. Beydoun, G., González-Pérez, C., Low, G. and Henderson-Sellers, B.: Synthesis of a Generic MAS Meta-model. In: *Proc. Software Engineering for Large-Scale Multi-Agent Systems, SELMAS'05*
6. Caire G., et al.: Agent Oriented Analysis using MESSAGE/UML. In: *The Second International Workshop on Agent-Oriented Software Engineering (AOSE 2001)*, Lecture Notes in Computer Science, Vol. 2222. Springer-Verlag (2002) 119-135.
7. Ferber, J., and Gutknecht, O.: A Meta-Model for the Analysis and Design of Organizations in Multi-Agent Systems. In: *Proc. 3rd International Conference on Multi-Agent Systems*, IEEE Computer Society (1998), 128-135
8. Giret, A., Botti, V., and Valero, S. MAS Methodology for HMS. In: *Holonic and Multi-Agent Systems for Manufacturing: Second International Conference on Industrial Applications of Holonic and Multi-Agent Systems, HoloMAS 2005*. Lecture Notes in Artificial Intelligence, Vol. 3593. Springer-Verlag (2005) 39-49
9. Gómez-Sanz J. J., and Pavón, J.: Meta-modelling in Agent-Oriented Software Engineering. In: *Advances in Artificial Intelligence - IBERAMIA 2002*. Lecture Notes in Artificial Intelligence, Vol. 2527. Springer-Verlag (2002) 606-615

10. Kelly, S., Lyytinen, K. S., and Rossi M.: MetaEdit+: A Fully Configurable Multi-User and Multi-Tool CASE and CAME Environment. In: *Advances Information System Engineering, 8th International Conference, CAiSE'96.* Lecture Notes in Computer Science, Vol. 1080. Springer-Verlag (1996) 1-21

11. Microgold. WithCLASS. http://www.microgold.com/, 2003.

12. Odell, J., Nodine, M., and Levy, R.: A Metamodel for Agents, Roles, and Groups. In: *Agent-Oriented Software Engineering V: 5th International Workshop, AOSE 2004.* Lecture Notes in Computer Science, Vol. 3382. Springer-Verlag, Berlin Heidelberg (2005) 78–92

13. Odell, J.: Objects and Agents Compared. *Journal of Object Technology 1, 1* (2002), 41-53

14. OMG: *Meta Object Facility (MOF) Specification. Version 1.4* (2002) formal/02-04-03

15. Pavón, J., Gómez-Sanz, J.J. & Fuentes, R.: *The INGENIAS Methodology and Tools.* In: Henderson-Sellers, B. and Giorgini, P., editors: *Agent-Oriented Methodologies.* Idea Group Publishing (2005), 236—276

16. Sansores, C., Pavón, J. and Gómez-Sanz, J.J.: Visual Modeling for Complex Agent-Based Simulation Systems. In: J.S. Sichman and L. Antunes (Eds.): *Int. Workshop on Multi-Agent-Based Simulation 2005*, Lecture Notes in Artificial Intelligence, Vol. 3891, Springer-Verlag (2006) 174–189

17. Susi, A. et al. The Tropos Metamodel and its Use. *Informatica, An International Journal of Computing and Informatics 29* (2005), 401-408

18. Wasserman, A. and Pircher, P. A graphical, extensible integrated environment for software development. In: *Proceedings of the Second ACM SIGSOFT/SIGPLAN Software Engineering Symposium on Practical Software Development Environments*, 131–142. ACM Press, 1987.

19. Weis, T., Ulbrich, A., and Geihs, K: Model Metamorphosis. *IEEE Software 20, 5* (2003), 46-51

Limes: An Aspect-Oriented Constraint Checking Language

Benjamin Mesing[1], Constantinos Constantinides[2], and Wolfgang Lohmann[1]

[1] University of Rostock, Germany
{benjamin.mesing, wolfgang.lohmann}@informatik.uni-rostock.de
[2] Concordia University, Montréal, Québec, Canada
cc@cs.concordia.ca

Abstract. In object-oriented software development, UML artefacts are used to illustrate and define the structure and the behaviour of the software system, while the semantics is usually described in a formal or informal specification language. The specification often consists of sets of constraints defined over the software components. When implementing the model, the specification is taken into consideration by the implementor. Since a significant proportion of the implementation consists of human-generated code, errors may be introduced in the implementation model. To detect these errors, the specified constraints need to be checked in the implementation. In this paper, we present *Limes*, an imperative constraint implementation language, which adopts aspect-oriented programming to describe constraint checking in a non-invasive way. *Limes* can be used at the design level, and can add constraint checking to the implementation.

1 Introduction

The Unified Modeling Language (UML) is a language for specifying and constructing the artefacts of software systems, and thereby allows to create models of systems. While UML models specify the structure and behaviour of systems, the semantics of the individual artefacts are usually captured in specifications expressed in a number of languages, most of them being declarative. Often specifications consist of sets of constraints specified over the artefacts. One specification language is the Object Constraint Language (OCL). Originally developed by IBM, the OCL is now part of the UML specification. In model driven engineering (MDE), UML models are often transformed directly into an implementation language. Since the transformation from the model to the implementation is not fully automated, some level of manual implementation is required. However, human-generated code might deviate from the specification, due to possible programming errors, or a misinterpretation or disregard of it. It is, therefore, desirable to be able to automatically check the implementation against the specification. However, an automatic translation of the specified constraints into executable code, and an instrumentation of this code into the target program is not a straightforward task. This is due to the large gap between the abstraction level of the specification language and that of the implementation

A. Rensink and J. Warmer (Eds.): ECMDA-FA 2006, LNCS 4066, pp. 299–315, 2006.

language. While the former is normally a declarative language specificly designed for writing specifications, the latter is normally an imperative general-purpose language. Even though tools exist to instrument OCL constraints to the target program, these tools are language specific and they often make assumptions about implementation details.

In this paper we introduce *Limes*[1], a language which allows to imperatively specify how and when to check the constraints of a model in a platform independent way. It provides information to add constraint checking to the implementation of the model, and by adopting aspectual behaviour it is able to perform the checking in a non-invasive way, i.e. without the need to manipulate the implementation. *Limes* code does not rely on any implementation specific information, and can therefore be written while still being a the design level. The specification of *Limes* is confined within the domain of constraint checking. Alltogether, *Limes* allows to narrow the gap between specification and implementation and integrates well with MDE. *Limes* code provides all the information necessary to put the constraints into operation, and thus can be considered an implementation of the constraint checking.

The remainder of this paper is organised as follows: Section 2 provides a discussion on the fundamental concepts behind aspect-oriented programming. Section 3 forms the main part of the paper and provides an overview of the language, demonstrating its main features with examples. Section 4 outlines the architecture of our current prototypical *Limes* compiler. Section 5 discusses related work, followed by Sect. 6 discussing some general aspects of *Limes*. Section 7 concludes the paper and sketches some areas of future work.

2   Background: Aspect-Oriented Programming (AOP)

Despite the success of object-orientation in the effort to achieve separation of concerns, certain properties cannot be directly mapped in a one-to-one fashion from the problem domain to the solution space, and thus cannot be localised in single modular units, but their implementation cuts across other units. This crosscutting phenomenon manifests over the inheritance hierarchy. As a result, developers are faced with a number of problems including a low level of cohesion of modular units, strong coupling between modular units and difficult comprehensibility, resulting in programs that are more error prone. Crosscutting concerns include persistence, authentication, synchronisation and logging.

Aspect-Oriented Programming (AOP) [1,2] addresses those concerns by introducing the notion of an aspect definition, which is a modular unit that explicitly captures and encapsulates a crosscutting concern, and therefore "can not be cleanly encapsulated in a generalized procedure (i.e. object, method, procedure, API)" [1]. Even though AOP is neither limited to object-oriented programming nor to the imperative programming paradigm, we will restrict this discussion to the adoption of AOP in that context. There is currently a growing number of

---

[1] ['liːməs], named after the ancient Roman wall built to keep out "barbarians". *Limes* was designed to keep out bugs.

approaches and technologies to support AOP. Our work is based on the linguistic model introduced by the general-purpose aspect-oriented language AspectJ [3] which is perhaps the most notable technology today, with a collection of supporting tools and an active developer community.

AspectJ has influenced the design dimensions of several other general-purpose aspect-oriented languages, and provided the community with a common vocabulary based on its own linguistic constructs. In the AspectJ model, an aspect definition provides behaviour to be inserted over functional components. This behaviour is defined in method-like blocks called *advice* blocks. However, unlike a method, an advice block is never explicitly called. Instead, it is activated by an associated construct called a *pointcut* expression. A pointcut expression is a predicate over well-defined points in the execution of the program which are referred to as *join points*. When the program execution reaches a join point captured by a pointcut expression, the associated advice block is executed. Even though the specification and level of granularity of the join point model differ from one language to another, common join points in current language specifications include calls to methods and execution of methods. Most aspect-oriented languages provide a level of granularity which specifies exactly when an advice block should be executed, such as executing before, after, or instead of the code defined at the associated join point. As a result, with an aspect-oriented language we are able to make quantified statements such as "whenever there is a call to a particular method (or a group of methods), before running the code that should run, execute the code in a given advice block."

A program in any general-purpose aspect-oriented language is essentially two-dimensional: One dimension describes the functional components written as definitions of classes, while another dimension describes aspect definitions written in an *aspect language* [1]. Like a class definition, an aspect definition can also contain state and behaviour (variables and methods). Additionally it can contain pointcut expressions and advice blocks. Furthermore, much like functional components must be composed to perform a computation, functional components and aspects must also be composed. This composition is referred to as "weaving" and it is performed by a special tool called a *weaver*. The weaver evaluates the pointcut expressions and determines the join points where the code of the advice block is inserted. The weaving process (Fig. 1) may take place either statically or dynamically.

As an example, consider a system where all calls to any method of some target classes should be logged. The implementation of logging would be scattered over a number of modules. In this example, the method calls constitute the join points where logging behaviour must be executed. An aspect definition encapsulating the logging behaviour would contain an advice block to perform the logging—perhaps creating an entry in a log file—and bind the advice block to a pointcut expression defined as a disjunction over relevant method calls. Once any of the methods captured by the pointcut expression is called, the associated advice block executes. The join point model and the related pointcut expression mechanism of AspectJ is highly expressive, including support

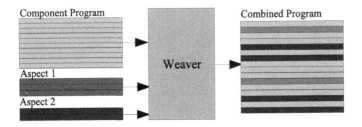

Fig. 1. The weaving process

for pattern expressions. In the example, pattern expressions would allow the definition of a logging aspect with such a complex behaviour as: "log all calls of set* methods in subclasses of a certain base class."

3   *Limes*: A Constraint Checking Language

Limes is a language to specify how and when to check constraints. It allows the description of constraint checking for a model, relying exclusively on structural information. Therefore *Limes* code can be written independently of the particular implementation of the model, and provides a platform independent model (PIM) for the constraint checking. In order to transform it to a platform specific model (PSM), we can follow either one of the following two approaches: First, constraints written in *Limes* can be transformed into the implementation language of the program to be checked, and second, these constraints can be transformed directly into executable code.

In the subsequent subsections we will first discuss the requirements for *Limes* and then provide an overview of the language, demonstrating its main features with examples. We will also discuss the problem of invariant checking and list conditions which an implementation of a system must fulfil in order to allow for the instrumentation of the model generated from its corresponding *Limes* definitions. The core specification of the *Limes* grammar is listed in the appendix of this paper.

3.1   Requirements for *Limes*

Our objective in building the requirements of *Limes* was to create a language which allows the specification of constraint checking for an implementation of a model without knowledge about implementation details. We aimed at the constraints defined by the types of assertions in the Design by Contract (DbC) principle [4]: preconditions, postconditions and invariants. Additionally, we placed the following requirements:

Describe constraints separately. Constraint checking should be described separately, without the need to modify the model or its implementation.

Free of side effect. The instrumentation of constraints should not affect the normal execution of the program, except for some unavoidable overhead in the execution speed of the program.

Platform independence. *Limes* code should not rely on any platform specific features.

Customisability. To allow the refinement of the constraint checking with implementation specific code, constraint checking specified in *Limes* should be modifiable in a non-invasive way.

Detailed context information. When detecting a violation of a constraint, as much information about the location of the error as possible should be made available.

Transformable. *Limes* should be easily transformable into different aspect-oriented languages. This allows to rapidly develop a transformation into various target languages, and thereby support a transformation to PSMs.

3.2   Features of *Limes*

Limes offers the following features:

Encapsulation of constraint checking. Constraint checking information is encapsulated in aspect definitions.

Minimisation of side effects. Though imperative by nature, *Limes* prevents the introduction of any side effects other then changing terminating to non-terminating behaviour, and changes in exectution speed and ressource usage.

Semantic checking at Design Level. The semantic analysis of *Limes* code is based exclusively on structural model information and hence it can be performed with only a PIM available. It is not necessary to defer the semantic checking until the source code is generated.

Non-invasive customisability. It is possible to customise how and when to perform the constraint checking in the implementation of the main program using aspect inheritance.

Transformable. The specification of *Limes* was held as simple as possible. Additionally, we added only language features which can be mapped to existing aspect-oriented languages such as AspectC++ [5], AspectJ and Eos [6] (an aspect-oriented extension for C#). Therefore, transformation of *Limes* to common aspect-oriented languages should be straightforward.

3.3   An Overview of *Limes*

Limes is an imperative aspect-oriented language to implement constraint checking. It uses the notion of aspect definitions, pointcut expressions and advice blocks to encapsulate the checking of constraints. The constraint checking code relies on type information from the model which can be available in various forms, e.g. as a UML model, as the source of the implementation or as the byte code of the checked program.

In this subsection, we will provide an overview of *Limes*, illustrating its main features with examples. The examples will implement constraints for the class shown in Fig. 2.

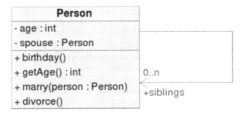

Fig. 2. Example class diagram

Aspects to Encapsulate Constraint Checking. *Limes* uses aspect definitions to encapsulate the checking of constraints. One aspect specifies the constraints for a single class. The name of the class to be checked is given in square
brackets after the aspect name. Listing 1 shows the basic syntax of an aspect.

```
1 aspect PersonConstraints [Person] {
2   // constraint checking code here
3 }
```

Listing 1. Aspect stub

Pointcuts and Advices to Attach the Constraint Checking Code. A
pointcut expression specifies the points in the execution where a constraint must
be checked, and an advice block specifies the checking policy. The deployment
of the pointcut and advice mechanism allows a non-invasive addition of the
constraint checking to the corresponding class. Listing 2 shows the grammar
rule specifying the syntax for the definition of an advice block. The syntax is
specified in EBNF according to the rules provided in the appendix.

```
1 advice_def = advice_type ( typed_parameter_list ) [[
2                    pointcut_expr ]] advice_body.
3 advice_type = before | after | before after | around.
```

Listing 2. Grammar rule for an advice definition

The `typed_parameter_list` specifies the *pointcut signature*, a list of parameters
available in the advice body. The parameters must be bound by (i.e. provided by)
the pointcut expression. A pointcut expression is a predicate of atomic pointcut
expressions. Among others, the following atomic pointcut expressions are available:

1. `execution`(*methodPattern*): matches the execution of any method matching
   the specified method pattern.
2. `this`(*identifier*): binds the current object (`this`) to the parameter of the
   pointcut signature named *identifier*.

3. args(*identifier1, identifier2,...*): binds the parameters of the matched methods to the parameters named *identifier1, identifier2, ...* of the pointcut signature.

The body of the advice block contains the code performing the checking of constraints. An advice block can be executed **before**, **after**, **before** and **after**, or instead of (**around**) the code corresponding to the join point(s) specified in the pointcut expression. During the execution of an **around**-advice, the original behaviour defined by the join point can be invoked through a call to the special function **proceed()**. Listing 3 shows an advice definition implementing the checking of a precondition of the **divorce()** method. The pointcut expression given in line 2 together with the type of the advice (before) specify that the advice is executed before the execution of the **divorce()** method in class **Person**. Additionally, the current **Person** instance is bound to the parameter **self**. The meaning of the keyword **const** in line 1 is explained subsequently. To check the precondition, the advice calls the special function **precondition()** which tests the condition given as the first argument.

```
1   before(const Person self)
2     [[ this(self) && execution(void Person.divorce()) ]] :
3   { precondition(self.spouse != null , "divorce()"); }
```

Listing 3. Demonstrating precondition checking

Concepts to Prevent Side Effects. The specification of *Limes* provides various concepts to avoid the introduction of side effects through code written in *Limes* into the checked program.

To reduce the possibility of introducing an infinite loop, no conditional loop construct was added. The only type of loop in *Limes* is a **foreach** loop which allows the iteration over a collection with a fixed set of elements. However, it is still possible to create infinite loops by using recursive function calls.

Another provision is that every **around** advice must contain exactly one **proceed()** call which must not be conditional[2]. This ensures that the original behaviour defined by the join point is executed.

Finally we added a *const* concept similar to the one supported by the C++ programming language [7]. This concept allows to define an object as being constant, i.e. denoting that its fields cannot be modified and none of its mutator methods (methods that modify its object) can be called. This relies on the model to provide the information which methods are mutators. In our implementation which utilises the UML model, every non-query method is assumed to be a mutator. Similarly, a constant object can only be given as an argument to a method, if the method declares that parameter not to be modified, which again relies on the model providing this information. Furthermore, whenever a call to

---

[2] A less restrictive condition would be that in every execution path **proceed()** must be called exactly once, but this is harder to check at compile time.

a method of a constant object returns an object, the returned object is assumed to be constant to prevent exposing internal objects. The const keyword can be added as a modifier to a variable definition, marking its referenced object to be constant. Advice parameters bound by pointcut expressions must be defined as const, since they expose objects of the main program. Consequently a constant variable can only be assigned to another constant variable.

Special Functions to Perform the Condition Checking. *Limes* offers a number of special functions to support the implementation of constraint checking. First, there are precondition(), postcondition(), and invariant(), each of them checking the corresponding constraint. As the first argument they require a boolean expression specifying the condition to be checked. Additional arguments can be given to specify context information about the constraint. To allow transformations to a target implementation language to implement different strategies in order to handle constraint violations, the semantics of those functions is only partially defined Only that the constraint is violated if the first argument evaluates to false, that those functions do not return a value, and the meaning of the additional arguments is defined by *Limes*. For example, while one transformation might raise an exception, another might choose to merely log the constraint violation. A possible Java implementation corresponding to the precondition() call given in Listing 3 line 3 is shown in Listing 4.

```
1 if (!(self.spouse != null))
2   System.err.println("Precondition " + expression.toString()+
3     " for "+class+"."+method+" violated");
```

Listing 4. Transformed precondition call

Other special functions available in *Limes* include copy() and equals(). Function copy() is defined to return a non-constant, deep copy of a given object. Function equals() performs a value comparison of its two arguments. Additionally there is an == operator, which checks whether its operands refer to the same object. Listing 5 shows an advice definition using copy() to save the old state of an object.

```
1 around(const Person self)
2   [[ this(self) && execution(void Person.birthday()) ]] :
3 {
4   Person old = copy(self);
5   proceed();
6   postcondition(old.getAge()+1==self.getAge(), "birthday()");
7 }
```

Listing 5. Advice definition utilising the copy() function

foreach to Deal with Collections. Associations with a multiplicity greater than one are common in software models and therefore a constraint language must support this concept. For *Limes* a small hierarchy of `Collection` classes including `Collection`, `Bag`, `Set` and `Sequence` is defined. Those classes provide a small interface allowing the convenient implementation of the most common constraints. Additionally, we introduced a `foreach` loop which iterates over a `Collection` and allows to check more complex conditions. An advice definition implementing the invariant that each sibling's siblings must contain the self-object is shown in Listing 6. The information on whether a variable refers to a collection, must be provided by the model providing the type information. The UML model utilised by the current *Limes* implementation provides this information by explicitly illustrating collections through associations with a multiplicity greater than one.

```
1 before after(const Person self) [[ publicFunction(self) ]] : {
2   foreach(const Person current : self.siblings) {
3     invariant(current.contains(self));
4   }
5 }
```

Listing 6. Advice definition utilising `foreach`

Function and Pointcut Overriding to Support Customisability. *Limes* was designed to support the implementation of complex constraints. However, unanticipated needs occur in practice, which would usually lead to unconventional, error prone and unreadable workarounds (i.e. hacks). To reduce the need for those hacks, *Limes* supports aspect inheritance which enables the non-invasive customisation of constraint checking specified in *Limes*. If *Limes* proves not to be powerful enough to specify *how* to perform the constraint checking, virtual methods can be used to allow the target implementation language to refine the constraint checking code. If *Limes* proves not to be powerful enough to specify *when* to perform the constraint checking, pointcut definitions can be overridden in the target implementation. An example to illustrate this is given in Listing 7.

```
1  aspect PersonConstraints [Person] {
2    abstract void checkComplexPrecondition(const Person self);
3    before(const Person self) [[ this(self) &&
4      execution(void Person.marry(Person)) ]] :
5    {
6      checkComplexPrecondition(self);
7    }
8    abstract pointcut underageCheck(const Person self);
9    before(const Person self) [[ underageCheck(self) ]] : {
10     invariant(self.age>=18 || self.spouse==null, "notUnderage");
11   }
12 }
```

Listing 7. Customisable aspect

Here, the advice definition to check the precondition of the `marry()` method (lines 3–7) calls the abstract method `checkComplexPrecondition()`. This requires that the method is implemented in a derived aspect. In line 8 we define an abstract pointcut named `underageCheck`, which is used in the second advice definition (lines 9–11) to specify when to check the invariant `notUnderage`. Because the pointcut is abstract, it must be implemented in a derived aspect. The derived aspect can be defined in the implementation language used for the main program, and thereby use its full feature set for both the pointcut definition and the implementation of the abstract method. Listing 8 shows an AspectJ definition of an aspect that extends and customises the aspect `PersonConstraints` shown above. It is also possible to override method and pointcut definitions. The concept of overriding pointcut definitions is similar to the overriding of methods. Note that when overriding or implementing pointcut definitions, the pointcut signatures must match.

```
1 aspect PersonConstraintsRefine extends PersonConstraints {
2   void checkComplexPrecondition(Person self)
3   { /* an AspectJ precondition check */ }
4   pointcut underageCheck(Person self) : <an AspectJ pointcut expression>;
5 }
```

Listing 8. Customising an aspect in AspectJ

3.4   Invariant Checking with *Limes*

While specifying when to check pre- and postconditions is rather straightforward, specifying when to check invariants requires careful consideration. According to Bertrand Meyer, "[an] invariant must be satisfied after the creation of every instance of the class, (and) be preserved by every exported routine of the class (that is to say, every routine available to clients)" [4]. Most often this is interpreted as *an invariant must be satisfied after the constructor execution, and before and after the execution of every public method.* However, we believe that it is valuable to also be able to specify invariants which must hold true before and after the execution of protected methods. The example in Listing 9 shows the code for checking the constraint that a married person should not be underage.

```
1 aspect PersonConstraints [Person] {
2   pointcut protectedPublic(const Person self) [[
3     (execution(* Person.ctor(..)) || execution(protected+ * Person.*(..)))
4     && this(self) && !cflow(within(PersonConstraints)) ]];
5   before after(const Person self) [[ protectedPublic(self) ]] : {
6     invariant(self.getAge()>=18 || self.spouse==null, "notUnderage");
7   }
8 }
```

Listing 9. Demonstrating invariant checking

In lines 2–4 the pointcut `protectedPublic` is defined. It captures the execution of the constructor (`ctor`) and the execution of every method specified protected or less restrictive (i.e. protected and public). The `!cflow(within(PersonConstraints))` pointcut expression excludes every join point where the control flow is within the execution of any code in the `PersonConstraints`. It avoids invoking the advice when calling `getAge()` from the advice itself which would trigger an infinite loop. The `before after` advice in lines 5–7 executes before *and* after the join points captured by `protectedPublic`. This is equivalent to defining the same advice twice, once as a `before`, and once as an `after` advice. Note that even though this seems to execute the advice before a constructor call, *Limes* defines that `before after` does not execute advice blocks before constructor calls.

While it is easy to provide a pointcut expression to check invariants after the constructor execution and before and after the execution of every (public) method, this has two major drawbacks. First, it results in checking invariants unnecessarily frequently, and second it does not necessarily detect invariant violations at the points in the execution of the program where these violations take place. Consider, for example, an object **A** containing a reference to an object **B**. Now, if an invariant is specified for **A** which involves **B**, and **B** is changed outside of **A**, this constraint might be violated. The violation will go undetected until a (public) method of **A** is called. Using the pointcut language, it is possible to give a more sophisticated definition of when to check an invariant. Through abstract pointcuts it is also possible to delegate the definition of when to perform the checking to the implementation of the model. There the implementation language might provide a sophisticated join point model. Since a fine-grained specification of the condition under which invariants must be evaluated normally requires intimate knowledge of the implementation, we believe it would be justified to delegate this task to the implementor of the model in this case.

3.5   Target Language Requirements

When *Limes* should be transformed into the general-purpose implementation language used for the rest of the system, the target implementation must meet some requirements to allow for an easy transformation, the most notable of which are listed below:

1. The implementation must be written in an aspect-oriented language (or an aspect-oriented extension for the language must exist) which supports the notion of aspect definitions, pointcut expressions and advice blocks.
2. The implementation language must be able to express the pointcut expressions available in *Limes*.
3. The implementation must allow to perform a value comparison of objects.
4. The implementation must provide a consistent way to iterate over collections.
5. The implementation must provide a consistent way to create deep-copies of objects.

4   Implementation

We have implemented a parser and analyser for *Limes* in AspectJ. Together they create an abstract syntax tree (AST) decorated with type information. The AST can be used as the basis for further transformations, and is accessible through a Java API using the Visitor design pattern, but could also be serialised and read using another programming language. The parser is generated using the Java Compiler Compiler (JavaCC) [8] and creates the initial AST. The analyser decorates the AST with type information, accessing the type information of the model through a type information provider. Information providers based on different types of models can be implemented. We have only implemented one provider, based on the UML model. Other possible models include various internal models of CASE tools, but also the source code of a program or some kind of byte code. The support of different model types allows for an easy integration of *Limes* support into existing CASE tools, which often have their own internal model format. It also allows to add constraint checking to existing applications without any high-level models available.

We have also implemented a *Limes* to AspectJ converter, which transforms the decorated AST into AspectJ. The implementation was mostly straightforward. The only major difficulty was the transformation of the atomic `return` pointcut expression available in *Limes* which exposes the return value of a method, since there is no such pointcut expression in AspectJ.

5   Related Work

Besides DbC, Unit testing [9] is another approach that aims at detecting implementation errors. It is used to test software artefacts by calling operations of them with a fixed set of input data, and checking assertions about the state after the operation. However, unit testing can only test with input data provided by the test case designer, who might not forsee all the input data possible during the execution of the program. On the other hand, constraint checking can check the constraints during the whole test cycle of the software. Nevertheless, unit testing provides a valuable addition to constraint checking, as it allows the specification of a fixed set of input data which is consequently tested. In fact, the combination of unit testing and automated constraint checking provides a powerful method for error detection [10].

Even though for many major programming languages without native DbC support frameworks and tools exist to add this missing feature, limited support exists for an automatic instrumentation of constraints specified for a model. Java is a notable exception here, where OCL is the main target for research dealing with constraint instrumentation. For example, the Dresden OCL Toolkit (DOT) [11,12] provides support for parsing and semantic checking of OCL expressions. Through a generator, the DOT is capable of generating Java code. In his work, Wiebicke [13] extends the DOT with the capability to instrument constraints to Java programs. To achieve this, the original source code is modified and the constraint checking code is added. Wiebicke also lists a number of other tools dealing with the instrumentation of constraints. Since the DOT can also be utilised by other code generators, we feel it could also provide the basis for transforming OCL expressions to *Limes* code.

Another approach towards monitoring OCL constraints is proposed by Richters and Gogolla [14]. It is based on the USE tool [15] which allows to validate OCL constraints for an instance of a UML model. In order to test and validate an implementation, the authors use aspect orientation to detect changes in the implementation objects, and map those back to the modelling level, keeping an instance of the UML model synchronised with the implementation objects. They then validate the OCL constraints for the model instance. This approach requires a duplication of the application data and is implemented for the Java language.

Briand et al. [16] propose the adoption of grammar rules to transform OCL constraints into aspects, which instrument the constraint checking to the target program. Even though the approach is based on AspectJ and on some assumption about the implementation of the UML model, it could be adapted to transform OCL constraints to *Limes* code. In [17] the authors generalise their ideas and explain how AspectJ can be used to instrument constraints in general. Since the join point model used in *Limes* is similar to the one of AspectJ, this work could provide valuable guidelines for implementing constraint checking in *Limes*.

The issue when to check invariants and how to achieve this using AspectJ is discussed in [18]. The authors analyse OCL invariants and classify them according to the navigation paths. For each type, they provide a pattern to create aspects to check the invariants, focussing on specifying when to perform the check. The work provides guidelines for defining more sophisticated pointcut expressions for the check of invariants, then simply checking before and after every (public) method call. However, some of those patterns rely on per-instance aspects which are not available in *Limes*.

In [19] the authors facilitate AspectJ to implement internal and external operation contracts. Since the contracts are defined on the design level, *Limes* seems to be well suited to implement the operation contracts, and thereby enforcing operation semantics independently of the implementation language.

6   Discussion

There are two elements in *Limes* which will probably have a significant impact on the performance of the program where the constraints are checked. The first is the special function `copy()`, used to create a deep copy of an object. This can become very expensive for deep object hierarchies. Note that the problem of circular references must be addressed by *Limes* compilers implementing a deep copy mechanism. The second is the iteration over a collection, as this can lead to a large number of iterations. Particularly in combination with a frequent invariant checking (e.g. after every public method), this might significantly slow down the program. Even though this is not a problem for the program deployed to the end user since the constraint checking can be disabled, it will become a problem if the program becomes so slow that it cannot be tested anymore.

The avoidance of introduction of side effects is a major concern for a constraint checking language. When using a fully compliant *Limes* compiler and having a model that truthfully provides information about its components, the only side effect that can be introduced through *Limes* code is changing terminating into non-terminating behaviour. However, in reality this might not always be given. We therefore discuss possible limitations that might lead to an introduction of side effects. First, there is the information about a method not modifying the object. For UML models this is defined by the modeller through the isQuery-attribute, but its enforcement is not supported in most implementation languages. Therefore, the implementation of a supposedly non-modifying method might not hold up to its promise and modify some properties of the object, allowing to introduce side effects through *Limes* code calling such a method. In the same way, the const-information about method parameters might not be honoured in the implementation. Another source for a potential introduction of side effects is the case where the implementation of the special function copy() does not create a full deep copy, but copies some parts flat.

One might argue about the use of a high-level, imperative constraint checking language. After all, there exist formal specification languages like OCL or Z and general-purpose aspect-oriented languages capable of implementing constraints. Especially so, since techniques exist for the automatic conversion from OCL to AspectJ. However, we believe that it would be valuable to have a platform independent language specifically designed for the specification of constraint checking. First, there are persons more comfortable with using imperative languages which might find writing *Limes* code easier than writing a declarative specification. Second, the conversion from a declarative to an imperative language requires a complex transformation which must be written once for each specification language to each implementation language. Here, *Limes* could serve as an intermediate language, first converting the specification language into *Limes*, and then converting *Limes* into the implementation language. For each specification language, this requires the complex transformation from the declarative to an imperative language to be implemented only once, leaving only the easier transformations from *Limes* to the target implementation language to be done multiple times. Compared to implementing the constraints manually in the target implementation language, *Limes* provides the advantage of being platform independent and being specifically designed for this task.

7   Conclusion and Future Work

In this paper we provided an overview of *Limes*. By demonstrating its main features with examples, we discussed how *Limes* can be utilised to implement DbC constraints. Conceptually, *Limes* is located between an expression based specification language like OCL, and a general-purpose implementation language. It can help bridging the semantic gap between the high level expression and the low level implementation language.

Even though we have tested *Limes* in a small scale, a test in a real system including measurements of the runtime performance needs to be done in order to see how well *Limes* can scale up. Furthermore, until now we have only implemented a translator of *Limes* to AspectJ. To prove that our approach is not limited to that particular language, we plan to implement translations to AspectC++ and Eos. The current specification of *Limes* provides the basic features necessary to implement constraint checking. However, there are a number of improvements to be done. For example, an atomic pointcut expression to match query methods could be used to avoid invariant checking for methods which cannot modify the state of the object. In case of well known error conditions, e.g. signalled by exceptions, it might be reasonable to allow a violation of certain constraints. Hence, allowing to restrict constraint checking to take place only if methods exit normally is another desirable feature. Also, we plan to provide access for the advice definitions to context information about the current join point. This can provide valuable information, like the called method, in case of a constraint violation, and thereby support the *detailed context information* requirement listed in Sect. 3.1. Currently this information must be explicitly handed in the form of an argument to the checking functions.

References

1. Kiczales, G., Lamping, J., Menhdhekar, A., Maeda, C., Lopes, C., Loingtier, J.M., Irwin, J.: Aspect-oriented programming. In Akşit, M., Matsuoka, S., eds.: Proceedings of the 11th European Conference on Object-Oriented Programming (ECOOP). Volume 1241., Springer-Verlag (1997) 220–242
2. Elrad, T., Filman, R.E., Bader, A.: Aspect-oriented programming: Introduction. Communications of the ACM **44**(10) (2001) 29–32
3. Kiczales, G., Hilsdale, E., Hugunin, J., Kersten, M., Palm, J., Griswold, W.G.: An overview of AspectJ. Lecture Notes in Computer Science **2072** (2001) 327–355
4. Meyer, B.: Applying "Design by Contract". Computer **25**(10) (1992) 40–51
5. Spinczyk, O., Gal, A., Schröder-Preikschat, W.: AspectC++: An aspect-oriented extension to the C++ programming language. In: CRPITS '02: Proceedings of the Fortieth International Conference on Tools Pacific, Australian Computer Society, Inc. (2002) 53–60
6. Rajan, H., Sullivan, K.: Eos: instance-level aspects for integrated system design. SIGSOFT Softw. Eng. Notes **28**(5) (2003) 297–306
7. Stroustrup, B.: The C++ Programming Language, Third Edition. Addison-Wesley Longman Publishing Co., Inc. (1997)
8. JavaCC: JavaCC home page. https://javacc.dev.java.net/ (2006)
9. Beck, K., Gamma, E.: Test infected: Programmers love writing tests. Java Report **3**(7) (1998)
10. Cheon, Y., Leavens, G.T.: A simple and practical approach to unit testing: The JML and JUnit way. In: ECOOP '02: Proceedings of the 16th European Conference on Object-Oriented Programming, Springer-Verlag (2002) 231–255

11. Finger, F.: Design and implementation of a modular OCL compiler. Diploma thesis, TU-Dresden (2000)
12. TU-Dresden: Dresden OCL toolkit. `http://dresden-ocl.sourceforge.net/` (2006)
13. Wiebicke, R.: Utility support for checking OCL business rules in Java programs. Diploma thesis, TU-Dresden (2000)
14. Richters, M., Gogolla, M.: Aspect-oriented monitoring of UML and OCL constraints. In: Proceedings of the 4th AOSD Modeling With UML Workshop. (2003)
15. Richters, M.: The USE tool: A UML-based specification environment. `http://www.db.informatik.uni-bremen.de/projects/USE/` (2006)
16. Briand, L.C., Dzidek, W.J., Labiche, Y.: Using aspect-oriented programming to instrument OCL contracts in Java. Technical Report SCE-04-03, Software Quality Laboratory, Carleton University (2004)
17. Briand, L.C., Dzidek, W.J., Labiche, Y.: Instrumenting contracts with aspect-oriented programming to increase observability and support debugging. In: Proceedings of the 21st IEEE International Conference on Software Maintenance (ICSM'05), IEEE Computer Society (2005) 687–690
18. van der Straeten, R., Casanova, M.: Stirred but not shaken: Applying constraints in object-oriented systems. In: Proceedings of the NetObjectDays2001. (2001)
19. Constantinides, C., Skotiniotis, T.: The provision of contracts to enforce system semantics throughout software development. In: Proceedings of the Eighth IASTED International Conference on Software Engineering and Applications. (2004)
20. International Organization for Standardization: ISO/IEC 14977:1996: Information technology — Syntactic metalanguage — Extended BNF. International Organization for Standardization (1996)

A   Grammar

In this appendix we provide the grammar for *Limes*. The grammar is described in EBNF, as defined by the ISO 14977 standard [20], with the following two deviations from the standard: First a sequence of terminals and non-terminals is not separated by commas, and second we use a "+" to denote that the proceeding group must be repeated one or more times. Besides, we mark terminals by setting them in **bold** font or by underlining them.

```
unit = [package] {aspect}.
package = package identifier {. identifier}.
aspect = aspect identifier [ type ] { aspect_body }.
aspect_body = {variable_def | method_def | pointcut_def | advice_def}.

full_qualified_name = identifier {. identifier}.
type = full_qualified_name.
simple_method_call = identifier ( argument_list ).
argument_list = [expr {, expr}].
nested_identifier = {(identifier | simple_method_call) .} identifier.
identifier = letter alphanum*.
alphanum = letter | digit.
letter = a | b | .. | z | A | B | .. | Z | _.
digit = 0 | 1 | .. | 9.

method_def = abstract_method_def | concrete_method_def.
abstract_method_def = abstract  method_signature ;.
concrete_method_def = method_signature block.
method_signature = ([const] type | void) identifier ( typed_parameter_list ) [const].
```

```
variable_def = variable_decl [ = expr() ] ;.
variable_decl = [const] type identifier.
typed_parameter_list = [variable_decl {, variable_decl}].
untyped_parameter_list = [identifier {, identifier}].

advice_def = advice_type ( typed_parameter_list ) [[ pointcut_expr ]] advice_body.
advice_type = before | after | before after | around.
advice_body = block.

pointcut_def = abstract_pointcut_def | concrete_pointcut_def.
abstract_pointcut_def = abstract pointcut pointcut_signature ;.
concrete_pointcut_def = pointcut pointcut_signature [[ pointcut_expr ]] [;].
pointcut_signature = identifier ( typed_parameter_list );

expr = unary_expr {binop unary_expr}.
unary_expr = simple_expr | ( expr ) | unop unary_expr.
simple_expr = method_call | nested_identifier | real_literal | integer_literal |
              string_literal | bool_literal | null.
method_call = {(identifier | simple_method_call) .} simple_method_call.
binop = logical_binop | arithmetical_binop.
unop = logical_unop | arithmetical_unop.
arithmetical_unop = ++ | -- | -.
arithmetical_binop = + | - | * | / | < | > | <= | >= | == | !=.
logical_binop = && | ||.
logical_unop = !.
bool_literal = true | false.
real_literal = digit+ . digit+.
integer_literal = digit+.
string_literal = " any_char_not_quote* ".

pointcut_expr = unary_pc_expr {logical_binop unary_pc_expr}.
unary_pc_expr = simple_pointcut_expr | ( pointcut_expr ) | logical_unop unary_pc_expr.
simple_pc_expr = call_pc | execution_pc | within_pc | cflow_pc | target_pc |
                 this_pc | args_pc | return_pc | pointcut_reference.
call_pc      = call      ( method_pattern ).
execution_pc = execution ( method_pattern ).
within_pc    = within    ( type_pattern ).
cflow_pc     = cflow     ( pointcut_expr ).
target_pc    = target    ( full_qualified_name ).
this_pc      = this      ( full_qualified_name ).
result_pc    = result    ( full_qualified_name ).
args_pc      = args      ( full_qualified_name {, full_qualified_name} ).
pointcut_reference = identifier ( untyped_parameter_list ).
method_pattern = [access_pattern] (type_pattern | void) [type_pattern .]
                 id_pattern (signature_pattern) [const].
id_pattern = wildcard_literal.
type_pattern = wildcard_literal {. wildcard_literal} [+].
signature_pattern = [type_pattern {, type_pattern} [, ..] | ..].
access_pattern = [!] access_modifier [+].
access_modifier = public | protected | package | private.
wildcard_identifier = * {alphanum+ [*]} | letter {alphanum} {* alphanum+} [*].

block = { command_sequence }.
command_sequence = (block | try_block | statement)+.
try_block = try block (catch ( variable_decl ) block)+.
statement = foreach_stmt | if_stmt | expr_stmt | assign_stmt | return_stmt |
            loop_control_stmt | skip_stmt.
foreach_statement = foreach ( variable_decl : expr ) block.
if_else_statement = if ( expr ) block [else block].
expr_stmt = expr ;.
assign_stmt = (variable_decl | nested_identifier) = expr ;.
return_stmt = return [expr] ;.
loop_control_stmt = (break | continue) ;.
skip_stmt = skip ;.
```

An Algebraic Specification of Generic OCL Queries Within the Eclipse Modeling Framework*

Artur Boronat, Joaquín Oriente, Abel Gómez, Isidro Ramos, and José Á. Carsí

Department of Information Systems and Computation
Technical University of Valencia
C/Camí de Vera s/n
46022 Valencia-Spain
{aboronat, joriente, agomez, iramos, pcarsi}@dsic.upv.es

Abstract. In the Model-Driven Architecture initiative, software artefacts are represented by means of models that can be manipulated. Such manipulations can be performed by means of transformations and queries. The standard Query/Views/Transformations and the standard language OCL are becoming suitable languages for these purposes. This paper presents an algebraic specification of the operational semantics of part of the OCL 2.0 standard, focusing on queries. This algebraic specification of OCL can be used within the Eclipse Modeling Framework to represent models in an algebraic setting and to perform queries or transformations over software artefacts that can be represented as models: model instances, models, metamodels, etc. In addition, a prototype for executing such OCL queries and invariants over EMF models is presented. This prototype provides a compiler of the OCL standard language that targets an algebraic specification of OCL, which runs on the term rewriting system Maude.

Keywords: MDA, OCL queries and invariants, metamodeling, algebraic specification.

1 Introduction

Model-Driven Development is a field in Software Engineering that, for several years, has represented software artefacts as models in order to improve productivity, quality, and economic income. Models provide a more abstract description of a software artefact than the final code of the application. A model can be built by defining concepts and relationships. The set of primitives that permit the definition of these elements constitutes what is called the metamodel of the model.

Interest in this field has grown in software development companies due to several factors. Previous experiences with Model Integrated Computing [1] (where embedded systems are designed and tested by means of models before generating them automatically) have shown that costs decrease in the development process. The consolidation of UML as a design language for software engineers has contributed to

---

* This work was supported by the Spanish Government under the National Program for Research, Development and Innovation, DYNAMICA Project TIC 2003-07804-C05-01.

A. Rensink and J. Warmer (Eds.): ECMDA-FA 2006, LNCS 4066, pp. 316–330, 2006.
© Springer-Verlag Berlin Heidelberg 2006

software Model-Driven Development by means of several CASE tools that permit the definition of UML models and automated code generation. The emergence of important model-driven initiatives such as the Model-Driven Architecture [2], which is supported by OMG, and the Software Factories [3], which is supported by Microsoft, ensures a model-driven technology stock for the near future.

Model-Driven Development has evolved into the Model-Driven Engineering field, where not only design and code generation tasks are involved, but also traceability, model management, metamodeling issues, model interchange and persistence, etc. To fulfil these tasks, model transformations and model queries are relevant tasks that must be solved. In the MDA context several open-standards are proposed to handle this. The standard Meta-Object Facility (MOF) [4] provides a way to define metamodels. The standard proposal Query/Views/Transformations (QVT) [5] will provide support for both transformations and queries. While model transformation technology is being developed [6-8], the Object Constraint Language (OCL) remains as the best choice for queries.

OCL [9] is a textual language that is defined as a standard "add-on" to the UML standard. It is used to define constraints and queries on UML models, allowing the definition of more precise and more useful models. It can also be used to provide support for metamodeling (MOF-based and Domain Specific Metamodeling), model transformation, Aspect-Oriented Modeling, support for model testing and simulation, ontology development and validation for the Semantic Web, among others. Despite its many advantages, while there is wide acceptance for UML design in CASE tools, OCL lacks a well-suited technological support.

In this paper, we present an algebraic specification of generic OCL queries, by using Maude [10], that can be used in a MOF-like industrial tool. Maude is a high-level language and a high-performance system supporting executable specification and declarative programming in rewriting logic. From a technological point of view, Maude provides a flexible parser, reflection, parameterization and an efficient implementation of associative-commutative-pattern matching that permits obtaining efficient executable specifications, among many other features. From a theoretical point of view, rewriting logic is an expressive logical framework, in which many other logics can be naturally expressed due to its reflective character. In addition, several formal analysis tools have been build for Maude taking advantage of its reflective features: the Maude Church-Rosser Checker, the Maude Inductive Theorem Prover, the Maude Sufficient Completeness Checker, the Maude termination tool, among others (see [11] for a roadmap).

The algebraic specification of OCL has been developed in the MOMENT framework (MOdel manageMENT) [12], which provides a set of generic operators to deal with models. The MOMENT operators use OCL queries to perform model queries and transformations, so that the part of OCL that provides support for methods and messages has not been taken into account.

The structure of the paper is as follows: Section 2 provides an example; Section 3 describes the algebraic specification of OCL, indicating the support for basic data types and collection types, and the support for collection operations; Section 4 presents the integration of the algebraic specification of OCL within an industrial modelling framework; Section 5 provides the architecture of the prototype; Section 6 presents some related works; Section 7 provides some conclusions and ongoing work.

2   The Coach Company Example

The Meta-Object Facility standard (MOF) [4] provides a metadata management framework and a set of metadata services to enable the development and interoperability of model and metadata-driven systems. The main achievement of this standard is the definition of a common terminology in the Model-Driven Architecture initiative, which can be used conceptually in other model-driven approaches.

As an example we have modelled a simple coach company in UML. In this design, a coach has a specific number of seats and can be used for regular trips or for private trips. In regular trips, the tickets are bought individually. In private trips, the whole coach is rented for a trip. The model is shown in UML notation in Fig. 1. The example provides a specific UML model, and the queries are applied to its instances. The OCL-like specification that is presented can also be used for queries over any software artefact that might be defined following the MOF conceptual framework: metamodels, regular models, and instances of models.

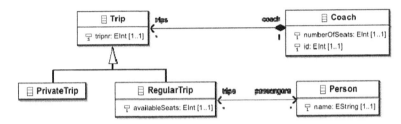

Fig. 1. Coach company model

OCL queries[1] permit a more precise definition of the model above by adding constraints. For instance, we can indicate that overbooking is not allowed in a regular trip by means of the following invariant:

> **context** *Coach:*
> **inv:** *self.trips -> select(t:Trip | t.oclIsType(RegularTrip))*
>   *-> forAll(r:Trip | r.oclAsType(RegularTrip).passengers -> size()*
>   *<= r.coach.numberOfSeats -> sum())*

3   Algebraic Specification of Generic[2] OCL Queries

In this section, we describe the parameterized algebraic specification of OCL that permits the query of either metamodels or UML models. The Maude term rewriting system [10] has been used for this purpose. Maude provides an algebraic specification language that belongs to the OBJ family[3]. Its equational rewriting mechanism

---

[1] We consider that an invariant is built on an OCL query that returns a Boolean value. Thus, although we talk about invariants, we are also using OCL queries.

[2] In this work, OCL genericity refers to the possibility of reusing the OCL specification for any software artefact that can be represented as a model, including metamodels.

[3] In this paper, we assume some basic knowledge about algebraic specifications and OBJ-like notation. We refer to [12] for more details.

animates the OCL algebraic specification over a specific model instance, providing the operational semantics for OCL expressions. We have developed a plug-in that embeds the Maude environment into the Eclipse framework so that we can use it for our purposes.

3.1 Overview of the Parameterized OCL Algebraic Specification

In Maude, functional modules describe data types and operations on them by means of membership equational theories. Mathematically, such a theory can be described as a pair $(\Sigma, E \cup A)$, where: Σ is the signature that specifies the type structure (sorts, subsorts, kinds, and overloaded operators); E is the collection of equations and memberships declared in the functional module; and A is the collection of equational attributes (associativity, commutativity, and so on) that are declared for the different operators. Computation is the form of equational deduction in which equations are used from left to right as simplification rules, with the rules being Church-Rosser and terminating.

OCL collection types and their operations have been defined in a parameterized algebraic specification, called *OCL-SUPPORT{X :: TRIV}*. Fig. 2 shows the elements involved in the parameter passing mechanism diagram. *TRIV* is the algebraic specification of the formal parameter, which is called theory in Maude.

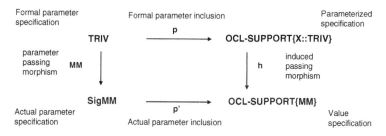

Fig. 2. Parameter passing diagram for the *OCL-SUPPORT{X :: TRIV}* parameterized module

SigMM is an algebraic specification that is obtained from a specific metamodel automatically. The *SigMM* specification constitutes the actual parameter for the *OCL-SUPPORT{X :: TRIV}* module and provides a constructor for each type that is defined in the metamodel and an inheritance hierarchy among the types that appear in the metamodel. The *MM* view is the morphism that relates the elements of the *TRIV* formal parameter to the elements of the *SigMM* actual parameter.

OCL collection types and related operations have been generically specified in the parameterized module *OCL-SUPPORT{X :: TRIV}*, where the formal parameter *X* has the trivial theory as type. The trivial theory only contains a sort *Elt* (referred to as *X$Elt* in the OCL specification) that represents the sort of elements that can be contained in an OCL collection. This sort represents the *OCLAny* type of the standard OCL specification. The *OCL-SUPPORT{X::TRIV}* module imports the basic data types and provides the constructors that are needed to define collections of elements. It provides collection operations as well.

In Fig. 2, p and p' are inclusion morphisms that indicate that the formal parameter specification is included in the parameterized specification, and that the actual parameter specification is included in the value specification, respectively. The h morphism is the induced passing morphism that relates the elements of the parameterized module to the elements of the *OCL-SUPPORT{MM}* value specification by using the *MM* parameter passing morphism.

3.2 Algebraic Specification of OCL Types

Types in OCL are divided into basic data types, collection types, and user-defined types. In this section, the algebraic support for the first two kinds of types is presented.

3.2.1 Basic Data Types

In OCL, there are four basic data types that have a direct correspondence to Maude basic data types. In Table 1, we show the correspondences between OCL 2.0 and the Maude data-type system and their corresponding primitives. In the table, when the operations have different symbols in OCL and Maude, we indicate the Maude symbol in brackets.

Table 1. OCL and Maude data-type correspondences

OCL 2.0	Maude	Common operators
Boolean	Bool	or, and, xor, not, = (==), <> (=/=), implies, if-then-else-endif (if-then-else-fi)
Integer	Int	= (==), <> (=/=), <, <=, >, >=, +, -, *, / (quo), mod (rem), abs, max, min
Real	Float	/, round (ceiling), floor
String	String	concat (+), size (length), substring(substr), = (==), <> (=/=)

3.2.2 Collection Types

OCL provides four specific collection types that are defined as follows:

– A Set is a collection that contains instances of a valid OCL type, where order is not relevant and duplicate elements are not allowed.
– An OrderedSet is a set whose elements are ordered.
– A Bag is a collection that may contain duplicate elements. Elements in a bag are not ordered.
– A Sequence is a bag whose elements are ordered.

To take into account the uniqueness and order features of an OCL collection, we introduce two intermediate sorts and their constructors (shown in Table 2): *Magma{X}* and *OrderedMagma{X}*. Basically, we define the sort *Magma{X}* as the sort of the term that represents a group of elements that are not ordered by means of the association and the commutativity attributes. The constructor for this sort has the symbol ",", and is associative and commutative. Thus, working with integers, "*1, 2, 3*" is a term that represents a valid *Magma{Int}*. In addition, we can state that "*1,2,3*" and "*3,2,1*" represent the same group of elements modulo the commutative and asso-iative attributes.

Instead, the constructor of the sort *OrderedMagma{X}* does not have the commutativity property, producing terms that represent ordered concatenations of elements.

The constructor for this sort has "::" as symbol and permits building ordered groups of elements by using the common syntax for lists in functional programming. Thus, the term "*1 :: 2 :: 3*" represents a valid ordered magma of integers, and "*1 :: 2 :: 3*" is different from "*3 :: 2 :: 1*" because the constructor "::" is not commutative.

Table 2. Specification of groups of elements

```
1.  sort Magma{X} OrderedMagma{X} .
2.  subsort X$Elt < Magma{X} OrderedMagma{X} .
3.  sorts Collection{X} Set{X} OrderedSet{X} .
4.  subsort Collection{X} < X$Elt .
5.  subsorts Set{X} OrderedSet{X} < Collection{X} .
6.  op _,_ : Magma{X} Magma{X} -> Magma{X} [assoc comm ctor] .
7.  op _::_ : Magma{X} Magma{X} -> Magma{X} [assoc ctor] .
8.  op Set{_} : Magma{X} -> Set{X} [ctor] .
9.  op empty-set : -> Set{X} [ctor] .
10. op OrderedSet{_} : OrderedMagma{X} -> OrderedSet{X} [ctor] .
11. op empty-orderedset : -> OrderedSet{X} [ctor] .
```

Terms of the sort *Magma{X}* are used to define sets (line 8), while terms of the sort *OrderedMagma{X}* are used in ordered sets (line 10). In Table 2, we show the Maude code that specifies the *Set* and *OrderedSet* types. In our specification, collections of collections are allowed by indicating that one collection can be an element of another collection (line 4). The sort *Collection{X}* can be considered as an abstract concept on the grounds that there is no specific constructor for it. Each collection has a constant constructor that defines an empty collection (lines 9, 11). The types *Bag* and *Sequence* have also been specified, similarly to the *Set* and *OrderedSet* types, respectively. In this specification, the uniqueness property of both the collection *Set* and the collection *OrderedSet* is checked in the operations that join two collections: *union*, *intersection* and *including* for *Set*, and *union*, *append*, *prepend*, *insertAt* and *including* for *OrderedSet*.

A view has been defined for each Maude simple data type in order to deal with collections of simple data types. For instance, to deal with collections of integers, the following view is defined: *view Int from TRIV to INT is sort Elt to Int . endv*

This view is used to instantiate the OCL-SUPPORT{X} module as OCL-SUPPORT{Int}. This way, the following example is a valid collection of integers:

OrderedSet{ Set{1, 2, 3} :: Bag{1, 2, 3, 3} :: Sequence{3 :: 3 :: 2 :: 1}}

3.3 Loop Operations or Iterators

Two kinds of operations on collection types can be distinguished in OCL 2.0: regular operations and loop operations or iterators. Regular operations provide common functionality over collections. Loop operations or iterators permit looping over the elements in a collection while performing a specific action. In this paper, we focus on the second type of operations.

Every loop operation has an OCL expression as parameter. This is called the body, or body parameter, of the operation. As a guiding example, we use a standard OCL expression that permits obtaining the odd numbers from a set of integers:

Set{1,2,3,4,5,6} -> select(i | i.mod(2) <> 0)

In this expression, *select* is the iterator operation and the expression *(i | i.mod(2)) <> 0)* is the body. Both iterator operations and body expressions are considered in the algebraic specification separately. This separation is needed to simulate higher-order functions in Maude by considering body functions as terms that can be passed as arguments to iterator operations.

Using the example of the selection of odd numbers from an integer set, we study first how to specify the body of the select expression *i | i.mod(2) <> 0*. Expression bodies can be evaluated to several types depending on the kind of operator in which they are used. For instance, the body expression of a *select* evaluates to a boolean value. Depending on the return type of the body expression, a symbol is associated to it indicating the name of the body expression. For the example, we obtain:

> *op isOdd : -> BoolBody{Int} [ctor] .*

The body expression is built by using the following operation:

> *op _::_`(_;_`) : Magma{X} BoolBody{X} ParameterList Collection{X} -> Bool .*

where the first argument is a term that represents a magma of elements, the second argument is the corresponding body symbol, the third argument is a variant list of parameters that can be empty, and the fourth argument is the whole initial collection to which the first argument belongs. To define a body function, the axioms must be provided by the user in Maude notation. For the example, we define the following equation:

> *var intN : Int . var intCol : Collection{Int} . var PL : ParameterList .*
> *eq intN :: isOdd (PL ; intCol) = ((intN rem 2) =/= 0) .*

Once the body expression has been defined, we provide an algebraic specification of the operational semantics of the select operation for sets. The different collection operations have been defined as function symbols (terms of the sorts that are shown in Table 3), depending on the return type of each operation. For instance, the select operation, which returns a collection of elements, is defined as follows:

> *op select : -> Fun{X} [ctor] .*

The operational semantics of iterator operations is defined independently of body operations. This fact permits the reuse of the algebraic specification of iterator operations simulating them as higher-order functions. Three axioms constitute the algebraic specification of the *select* operator for sets (as shown in Maude notation in Table 4). These are the arguments of select: BB is a variable that contains the boolean body expression, PL is a parameter list for the body operator, and Col is the original set. The first axiom considers the recursion case where there is more than one element in the set. If the body function validates to a true value, the element is added to the resulting set. Finally, the recursion over the rest of the elements continues. The second axiom considers the recursion case when only one element remains in the set so that the recursive trail ends. The third axiom considers the case where the set is empty.

To invoke an iterator in an OCL-like way, the following operation is used:

> op _->_`(_;_;_`) : Collection{X} Fun{X} BoolBody{X} ParameterList Collection{X} ->
> Collection{X} .

where the first argument is the collection to be looped, the second argument is an iterator symbol, the third argument is the body operation, the fourth argument is a list of arguments for the body operation, and the fifth argument is the proper collection that is looped. The fifth argument is useful when the collection must be navigated in the body operation. When the iterator is processed, if this argument is not added, the recursion mechanism consumes the elements of the collection, and queries over the whole collection would not be complete. To invoke the select iterator over a set of integers with the body isOdd we use: *Set{1, 2, 3, 4, 5, 6} -> select(isOdd ; empty-params ; empty-set)* .

Table 3. OCL collection operations that have been specified

	Return type	Collection operator symbols					Iterator symbols
		Collection	Set	Ordered-Set	Bag	Sequence	Collection
Fun{X}	Collection	union, flatten, including, excluding, iterate	--, inter-secti-on	--, insertAt, append, prepend	intersection	insertAt, append, prepend	select, reject, any, sortedBy, collect, collectNested, iterate
EltFun{X}	Element			first, last, at		first, last, at	
BoolFun{X}	Boolean value	includes, includesAll, excludes, excludesAll, isEmtpy, notEmpty					one, forAll, forAll2[4], exists, isUnique
IntFun{X}	Integer value	count, size, sum, product		indexOf		indexOf	

Table 4. Axiomatic specification of the select operation for sets

```
eq Set{ N , M } -> select ( BB ; PL ; Col ) =
   if (N :: BB ( PL ; Col )) then
         Set{ N } -> including ( ( Set{ M } -> select ( BB ; PL ; Col )) ) -> flatten
   else Set{ M } -> select ( BB ; PL ; Col ) fi .
eq Set{ N } -> select ( BB ; PL ; Col ) = if (N :: BB ( PL ; Col )) then Set{ N } else empty-set fi .
eq empty-set -> select ( BB ; PL ; Col ) = empty-set .
```

4 Algebraic Specification of Metamodels and Models

The advantage of OCL is that user-defined types can be used in expressions to perform queries on software artefacts (namely models). User-defined types are the types that can be used in a model: classes, associations, enumerations, and so on. One of the keys to success in the use of the OCL algebraic specification is the integration with an industrial modelling environment. In this way, OCL expressions can be

---

[4] The forAll2 operation has been included to provide support when two iterators are being used in the forAll operation.

evaluated in a graphical model without having to prepare the information in a specific format manually.

In our case, we have chosen the Eclipse Modeling Framework (EMF) [13]. EMF is a modeling environment that is plugged into the Eclipse platform and provides a sort of implementation of the MOF. It brings code generation capabilities and enables the automatic importation of software artefacts from heterogeneous data sources.

Within the EMF, Ecore is the set of primitives that is used as metametamodel. Ecore can be viewed as an implementation of a subset of the class diagram of the MOF metamodel (or of the UML metamodel). An Ecore model is mainly constituted by EClass instances (informally called classes) that are related to each other by means of inheritance relationships and EReference instances (informally called references in Ecore and associations in UML)[5]. Using the MOF terminology, an Ecore model may represent either a metamodel at the M2-layer (for instance, the UML metamodel) or a model at the M1-layer (for instance, a UML model). Similarly, an Ecore model instance may represent either a model that conforms to a metamodel at the M1-layer (for instance, a UML model) or a model instance at the M0-layer (for instance, the instances of a UML model). From now on, the OCL support is explained by using the example of the UML model, although it would be exactly the same as defining OCL queries over Ecore metamodels.

To perform OCL queries over EMF software artefacts, three types of projection mechanisms have been specified. The first obtains an algebraic specification from a metamodel. The second represents a model as a term in Maude. Finally, the third is the OCL expression compiler that targets Maude code.

4.1 A Model as an Algebraic Specification

The first projection mechanism obtains the algebraic specification[6] that corresponds to a specific Ecore model automatically by assigning a code template to each concept of the Ecore metamodel. The algebraic specification that is generated by means of these templates is used as an actual parameter for the *OCL-SUPPORT{X::TRIV}* module (see Fig. 2).

As example, we explain the code that is generated for an Ecore class. An Ecore class is constituted by attributes and references. This information is used to generate an algebraic sort that represents the collection of instances of this class and a constructor, whose arguments are: an internal identifier (represented by the type Qid[7] in Maude), a group of arguments that represent the attributes (basic data types in Maude) and a group of identifier collections (representing references). For instance,

---

[5] For further information on the Ecore metamodel and the representation of Ecore models we refer to [13].

[6] The algebraic specification that is generated for a given metamodel (defined in EMF as an Ecore model) permits the representation of models as algebraic terms. Thus, models can be manipulated by our model management operators. Algebraic specifications of this kind do not specify operational semantics for the concepts of the metamodel; they only permit the representation of information for model management issues.

[7] A Qid value is defined by a quote followed by an string (see [12] for further details). For instance, *'trip1* is a valid Qid value. Qid values are used to define implicit instance identifiers in our framework.

when this code template is applied to the *RegularTrip* class in Fig. 1, we obtain the following Maude code:

```
sort RegularTrip .
op `(RegularTrip_ _ _ _ _`) : Qid Int Int OrderedSet {QID} OrderedSet {QID} -> RegularTrip [ctor] .
```

where the first argument is the internal identifier of the instance, the second argument is the inherited *tripnr* attribute, the third argument is the *availableSeats* argument, the fourth argument is the inherited *coach* reference (UML role), and the fifth argument is the *passengers* reference (UML role). This template is only applied to specific classes. When a class is defined as abstract, the code only contains the declaration of the sort and no constructor is generated, indicating that this class cannot be instantiated.

4.2 An Instance of a Model as an Algebraic Term

The second projection mechanism permits us to serialize an Ecore model instance as a term of the algebraic specification that corresponds to the Ecore model. The instance of a model is represented as a set of instances of the classes that constitute the model *MM*. This second projection mechanism is constituted by several code templates that serialize each class instance to a term of the sort that has been generated from the corresponding class by means of the first projection mechanism.

For example, the instance of the model *Trip* (shown in Fig. 3) is serialized as a set, where all the elements are instances of the classes of the model, by using the constructors of the serialized algebraic specification *sigMM*, as follows:

```
Set { (Coach 'coach1 1 10 OrderedSet { 'person1 } ),
(RegularTrip 'trip1 1 9 OrderedSet {'coach1 } OrderedSet { 'person1} ),
(Person 'person1 "Peter" OrderedSet { 'trip1 } ) }
```

The internal structure of a term is transparent to the user of the algebraic specification due to some navigation operations, which permit the user to navigate in an OCL-like way throughout the roles and attributes of the objects of the model instance.

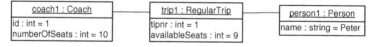

Fig. 3. Object diagram defined as an instance of the model defined in Fig. 1

Finally, the *OCL-SUPPORT{MM}* module provides all the operations that are needed to define an instance of a model (constructors to define collections, to define basic data type values and user-defined types) and to apply OCL queries to instances of any model (collection operations, iterators, and user-defined navigation operations).

4.3 Translation of OCL Expressions into Maude Code

The third projection mechanism compiles standard OCL code to Maude code that uses operations of the *OCL-SUPPORT{MM}* module, which have been introduced in

Section 3. As example of this compilation process, we show that the query that is used in the invariant in Section 2 can be written by defining the body expression of the *forAll* iterator as a body operation. This body operation checks that all regular trips have a lower number of passengers than the number established by the *numberOfSeats* attribute of the corresponding *Coach* instance. The Maude code that is automatically obtained for the body expression of the *forAll* operator (by using the operator that is explained in Section 3.3) in the example is as follows:

```
var self : trip-Trip . var tripModel : Set{trip} .
op notOverbooked : -> BoolBody{trip} [ctor].
ceq self :: notOverbooked ( PL ; tripModel ) =
    (((((self :: oclAsType ( ? "RegularTrip" ; tripModel )) :: passengers ( tripModel))
    -> size) <= ((self :: coach ( tripModel ) :: numberOfSeats) -> sum))
if self :: trip-Trip .
eq self :: notOverbooked ( PL ; tripModel ) = false [owise].
```

where: *self* is a variable of type *Trip* and *tripModel* is a set that represents the model instance to be queried; expressions with the form *c :: att* permit the navigation of an attribute *att* of the class instance *c*; and expressions with the form *c :: ref (ModelInstance)* are used to navigate the instances associated to the class instance *c* through the reference *ref* in the model instance *ModelInstance*. The invariant is coded as follows:

```
red tripModel -> select ( oclIsTypeOf ; ? "Coach" ; tripModel ) -> forAll(notOverbooked; empty-params ;
tripModel) .
```

where *tripModel* is a variable that contains the model instance to be checked, and the *select* and the *forAll* operation provide the body expression of the invariant in Maude code by using the *oclIsTypeOf* operator and the above body expression *notOverbooked*. Thus, we check if all the instances of the class Coach hold the *notOverbooked* invariant.

5 MOMENT-OCL: A Prototype for Executing Algebraic OCL Expressions Within the Eclipse Modeling Framework

The OCL algebraic specification that has been presented in the paper permits both the representation of models as sets and the use of queries and invariants over them. This permits the use of OCL expressions in algebraic model transformations, such as those presented in [6]. In addition, we have developed a simple OCL editor that permits the evaluation of OCL queries and invariants over EMF models or model instances. In this section, we provide a brief description of the architecture of this prototype, which is called MOMENT-OCL.

Fig. 4 shows the components of the MOMENT-OCL prototype that permit the execution of algebraic OCL expressions over EMF models:

– The *OCL Projector* component is the module that projects the OCL expression to Maude code. It makes use of the *Kent OCL* library [14] to validate the syntax and the semantics of the expression. The process of compilation from OCL to Maude follows the typical structure of a language processor. The process is divided in two phases: an initial analysis phase and a second synthesis phase.

In the first phase, we have reused the OCL support of the Kent Modelling Framework (KMF) [14], which provides lexical, syntactical and semantical analysis of OCL expressions over an EMF model. KMF analyzes an OCL expression, taking into account the semantics of the model, and produces an Abstract Syntax Tree (AST) to represent the data that is needed in the synthesis phase.

Fig. 4. MOMENT-OCL Architecture

In the second phase, once an OCL expression has been analyzed by KMF correctly, the AST is parsed and Maude code for body expressions, queries and invariants are produced in order to evaluate OCL expressions over EMF models in Maude.

- The *Module Loader* component obtains the algebraic specification from a meta-model, by instantiating the *OCL-SUPPORT{X::TRIV}* module with the signature obtained for a specific metamodel. This algebraic specification is extended with the Maude code obtained from the compilation of OCL expressions by means of the OCL Projector component. The *Module Loader* uses three other components: the M2 Projector, which projects a metamodel *MM* (the Coach model in the example) as the signature *SigMM*; the M1 Bridge, which projects a model (model instance in the example) as a term of the corresponding algebraic specification *OCL-SUPPORT{MM}*; and the Kernel Loader, which instantiates the parameterized algebraic specification of OCL with the signature *SigMM*, providing the formal environment where OCL expressions for the model *MM* can be evaluated.
- The OCL Editor permits the definition of OCL queries and invariants over EMF models and provides syntactical and semantical analyses of the expressions by reusing this functionality from the KMF. It permits the evaluation of queries and invariants. If we consider an invariant or query, we can analyze the expression syntactically and semantically, evaluate it by showing the result, or parse it to Maude code, as indicated in Fig. 4.

6   Related Works

Although OCL is not as well supported as UML in some CASE tools, there is a growing interest in providing support for OCL in order to achieve different goals. In [15], several tools that support OCL are studied. Taking them and others into account, some technological examples, which are classified by their main goal, are provided:

- Model transformation: MOMENT, ATL, YATL.
- Model verification: the KeY System.
- Requirements validation: ITP/OCL, the USE tool, the Dresden OCL Toolkit, Borland Together, OSLO, Rational Software Modeller.
- Code generation (also for requirements validation): Octopus, OCLE, Kent OCL tool.
- OCL Testing: HOL/OCL.

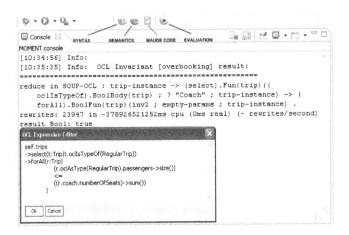

Fig. 5. MOMENT-OCL screenshot

Nevertheless, only a few of them rely on formal methods to provide support for the operational semantics of OCL, and even fewer tools are integrated in (commercial) CASE tools. We focus on some tools that rely on formal methods in this section.

The KeY system [16] provides functionality for formal specification and deductive verification within a commercial CASE tool (Together Control Center). In this approach, the user defines a software artefact in UML that can be annotated with OCL constraints. The OCL constraints are translated into formulas of JavaDL (a dynamic logic for Java) that can be reduced by means of an interactive theorem prover.

The USE tool [17] provides interactive validation of OCL constraints over a model. This tool reads the input model and the OCL constraints from textual resources, supporting class diagrams, object diagrams and sequence diagrams. Afterwards, objects and links can be graphically created to define a snapshot of a running system. This tool has been extended for the automatic generation of test cases and validation cases.

The ITP/OCL tool [18] provides automatic validation of UML static class diagrams with respect to OCL constraints. It provides an algebraic OCL specification using Maude, where UML class diagrams and object diagrams are formalized by means of algebraic specifications in membership equational logic and where OCL constraints are defined as formulas in membership equational logic theories. A graphical front-end is being developed for the ITP/OCL tool, which permits the definition of class diagrams and the definition of correct object diagrams.

In these last approaches, only UML diagrams are considered for validating OCL expressions. In the MOMENT-OCL specification, OCL queries can be automatically applied either to metamodels or to models that may be defined in EMF by making use of the Maude parameterization mechanism, following a more automated model-driven oriented approach. In our approach, while Maude is used to execute OCL expressions, the OCL expressions can be applied to graphical model-based software artefacts through the EMF. Whenever EMF, and related support, is used to develop a (domain specific or UML) modelling environment, we can use MOMENT-OCL to provide invariant checking and query evaluation. Thus, our philosophy does not consist in developing a new modelling environment to provide OCL support, we provide it for other existing modelling approaches. Other java-based approaches that integrate OCL within the EMF are [14, 19, 20], from which we took the Kent library to reuse the analysis phase for the ocl compilation.

By using Maude, we avoided the development of a new plugin for providing support for OCL from scratch. We specified many first-order properties in membership equational logic by means of operators that are applied modulo associativity and commutativity. In addition, the underlying membership equational logic enjoys a precise mathematical semantics [21] and an efficient implementation in Maude [22].

7 Conclusions and Further Work

OCL is becoming a de-facto standard for defining constraints and queries in the Model-Driven Engineering field. The number of tools that provide support for this language is growing, and although the operational semantics of OCL is said to be formal, only a few tools rely on formal methods to define its operational semantics.

In this paper, we have introduced an algebraic specification of part of the operational semantics of OCL 2.0 from an implementation point of view. This specification takes advantage of several features of Maude for the sake of reuse: parameterization, associative-commutative-pattern matching, a flexible parser, among others.

In the specification we have taken into account the Ecore metamodel[8] and part of the OCL standard that permits the definition of queries and invariants. This specification is used to perform model queries in the EMF and to represent EMF software artefacts as algebraic specifications or as terms. Such terms can be manipulated by means of model management operators in the MOMENT framework (MOdel manageMENT) [12], which provides a set of generic operators to deal with models. The MOMENT operators use OCL queries to perform model queries and transformations, so that the part of OCL that provides support for methods and messages has not been taken into account.

The OCL specification has been developed generically so that it can be used for any kind of metamodel, model or model instance. Thus, not only can OCL be studied in an algebraic setting, it can also be used in the well-known modelling environment EMF. Further work consists in exploiting the formal features of the OCL specification from a more-theoretical point of view and its application to real case studies.

---

[8] Interface and simple data type definition has not been addressed yet in the specification.

References

1. Sztipanovits, J., Karsai, G.: Model-Integrated Computing. IEEE Computer Society Press **30** (1997) 110-111
2. Kleppe, A., Warmer, J., Bast, W.: MDA Explained: The Model Driven Architecture--Practice and Promise. (2003)
3. Greenfield, J., Short, K., Cook, S., Kent, S.: Software Factories: Assembling Applications with Patterns, Models, Frameworks, and Tools. John Wiley & Sons (2004)
4. OMG: Meta Object Facility (MOF) 2.0 Core Specification, ptc/04-10-15. (2004)
5. OMG: MOF 2.0 QVT final adopted specification (ptc/05-11-01). (2005)
6. Boronat, A., Carsí, J.A., Ramos, I.: Algebraic Specification of a Model Transformation Engine. Fundamental Approaches to Software Engineering, FASE'06 Springer LNCS.Vienna, Austria (2006)
7. Bézivin, J., Dupe, G., Jouault, F., Pitette, G., Rougui, J.E.: First experiments with the ATL model transformation language: Transforming XSLT into XQuery. OOPSLA 2003 Workshop.Anaheim, California (2003)
8. The Model Transformation Framework. http://www.alphaworks.ibm.com/tech/mtf
9. Warmer, J., Kleppe, A.: The Object Constraint Language, Second Edition, Getting Your Models Ready for MDA. Addison-Wesley (2004)
10. Clavel, M., Durán, F., Eker, S., Lincoln, P., Martí-Oliet, N., Meseguer, J., Quesada, J.F.: Maude: specification and programming in rewriting logic. Theor. Comput. Sci. **285** (2002) 187-243
11. Martí-Oliet, N., Meseguer, J.: Rewriting Logic: Roadmap and Bibliography. Theoretical Computer Science **285** (2002) 121-154
12. Boronat, A., Carsí, J.A., Ramos, I.: Automatic Support for Traceability in a Generic Model Management Framework. Model Driven Architecture - Foundations and Applications, First European Conference, ECMDA-FA 2005 Springer LNCS.Nuremberg, Germany (2005)
13. Budinsky, F., Steinberg, D., Merks, E., Ellersick, R., Grose, T.J.: Eclipse Modeling Framework. Addison Wesley Professional (2003)
14. Kent, U.o.: Kent Object Constraint Language Library. http://www.cs.kent.ac.uk/ projects/ocl/index.html
15. Toval, A., Requena, V., Fernández, J.L.: Emerging OCL tools. Software and System Modeling **2** (2003) 248-261
16. Ahrendt, W., Baar, T., Beckert, B., Giese, M., Hähnle, R., Menzel, W., Mostowski, W., Schmitt, P.H.: The KeY System: Integrating Object-Oriented Design and Formal Methods. Fundamental Approaches to Software Engineering. 5th International Conference, FASE 2002 Springer.Grenoble, France (2002)
17. Richters, M.: The USE tool: A UML-based Specification Environment. (2001). http:// www. db.informatik.uni-bremen.de/projects/USE/
18. Egea, M., Clavel, M.: The ITP/OCL tool. (2006). http://maude.sip.ucm.es/itp/ocl/
19. Vanwormhoudt, G.: EMF OCL Plugin. (2006). http://www.enic.fr/people/ Vanwormhoudt/ siteEMFOCL/maven-reports.html
20. Eclipse Modeling Framework Technologies. (2006). http://www.eclipse.org/emft/projects/
21. Clavel, M., Durán, F., Eker, S., Lincoln, P., Martí-Oliet, N., Meseguer, J., Talcott, C.: Maude 2.2 manual and examples. (2005)
22. Eker, S.: Associative-Commutative Rewriting on Large Terms. Proceedings of the 14th International Conference on Rewriting Techniques and Applications (RTA 2003),Lecture Notes in Computer Science (2003)

A Comparison of Configuration Techniques for Model Transformations

Dennis Wagelaar* and Ragnhild Van Der Straeten

Vrije Universiteit Brussel, Pleinlaan 2, 1050 Brussels, Belgium
{dennis.wagelaar, rvdstrae}@vub.ac.be

Abstract. MDA generally involves applying multiple model transformations. These transformations need to be applied in a particular configuration, depending on the targeted platform. Several techniques exist to manage the configuration of various software elements or components. These techniques focus on the composition rules of the various elements. A well-known application area of such techniques are Software Product Lines, in which the various features that make up a software product need to be configured. In this paper, we will investigate how several of these techniques can be applied to manage the configuration of model transformations in an MDA context.

1 Introduction

Model transformations play a central role in Model-Driven Engineering, but currently they are often applied stand-alone, much like a compiler. In an MDA context, however, various model transformations need to be combined and integrated in a build process. The type of transformations that are generally used in combination are refinement and refactoring transformations. Since these model transformations cannot always be combined safely [1], configuration techniques can help manage the composition of model transformations in an MDA context. In a model-driven build process, however, other transformations than refactoring and refinement transformations can occur (e.g. translation to other languages), which means that the configuration techniques must support model transformations in general.

Several techniques exist to manage the configuration of various software elements or components. These techniques focus on the composition rules of the various elements. The problem domain of configuration existed already within the Artificial Intelligence research area, and several techniques were used to support configuration decisions [2]. In the domain of Software Product Lines (SPL) [3], configuration techniques are used heavily to express the composition rules of the various *features* that make up a software *product*.

---

* The author's work is part of the CoDAMoS project, which is funded by the Institute for the Promotion of Innovation by Science and Technology in Flanders (IWT-Flanders).

A. Rensink and J. Warmer (Eds.): ECMDA-FA 2006, LNCS 4066, pp. 331–345, 2006.

In this paper, we will investigate how several of these techniques can be applied to manage the configuration of refinement and refactoring transformations in an MDA context. First, an introduction of the configuration techniques is given. A running example is introduced to illustrate the model transformation configuration issues that can occur. Several criteria that are relevant for the configuration of model transformations are introduced for the purpose of comparison. After applying the selected configuration techniques to our running example, a comparison is made, based on the criteria given earlier. To conclude, we discuss the scope and impact of this comparison.

2   Configuration Techniques

This section gives an introduction of several techniques that can be used to configure model transformations.

2.1   Knowledge-Based Systems

Since the 1980's *configuration* and a *configuration task* are well-known problem domains in Artificial Intelligence (AI). A *configuration* is defined in AI as *an arrangement of parts* and a *configuration task* is defined as *a problem-solving activity that selects and arranges combinations of parts to satisfy given specifications* [2]. Knowledge-based systems are used to make configuration decisions. Other AI approaches are constraint reasoning, model-based reasoning, case-based reasoning and Description Logics.

In configuration tasks, much of the "design" work goes into defining and characterising the set of possible parts. The set of parts must be designed so they can be combined systematically and so they cover the desired range of possible functions. A specification language for a configuration task describes the requirements that configurations must satisfy. Configuration decisions are made incrementally. Depending on the alternatives chosen, different required parts will be needed, and different further requirements will be noted. This dynamic aspect of the problem suggests the use of dynamic and hierarchical constraint methods.

One of the first and best known knowledge-based configuration systems is the XCON system for configuring VAX computer systems [4]. This configuration system has a component database containing the parts and a container template database that describes how parts can physically contain other parts. The knowledge for driving the configuration task is represented mostly by production rules. The decision making process is organised in stages and subtasks.

2.2   Domain-Specific Languages

Domain-specific languages (DSLs) cover a broad spectrum of applications [5]. For the purpose of this paper, we focus on the use of DSLs for configuring refactoring and refinement transformations. The tools for developing a DSL can be classified into the following two categories:

- Grammar definition and/or meta-modelling languages and frameworks
- Transformation engines (including rule-based rewrite engines and code generators)

The main vehicle for expressing the constraints within which transformations may be combined, is the grammar definition formalism (e.g. SDF [6]) or meta-modelling language (e.g. MOF [7] or Ecore [8]). Since the expressiveness/efficiency of grammar definition and meta-modelling languages is limited, additional tools are used to express complex constraints. These tools include transformation languages (e.g. ASF+SDF [6] rewrite rules, Stratego/XT [9] and the ATLAS Transformation Language (ATL [10]) and specialised constraint languages (e.g. OCL [11]).

2.3   Feature Modelling

Feature Modelling has its origin in the Feature Oriented Domain Analysis method (FODA) [12]. Its initial goal was to document the results of analysing the commonalities and variabilities [13] of software product families/lines. Feature models allow to express variability at an abstract level without committing to any particular variability mechanism. The modelling of the semantic context of features requires some additional modelling formalisms. For example, constraints can specify the valid and invalid feature combinations. These constraints can be expressed in, for example, OCL. Several graphical tools for feature modelling exist, however, tool support for transformations and code generation is limited.

Recently some efforts have been made to formalise feature models. In [14] a translation of feature models into a context-free grammar is presented.

Feature models can also be used for configuration purposes, demonstrated by Czarnecki *et al.* [15]. In this context, a *configuration* consists of the features that were selected according to the variability constraints defined by the feature model. Configuration also refers to the process of deriving a configuration from a feature model. The configuration process is a *transformation process that takes a feature model and yields another feature model, such that the set of the configurations denoted by the latter diagram is a true subset of the configurations denoted by the former diagram* [15].

The relationship between feature modelling and domain specific languages (see subsection 2.2) is explored by van Deursen *et al.* in [16]. An important conclusion is that feature models can be translated into a DSL grammar (or meta-model). This is illustrated by their Feature Description Language (FDL), which follows the same structure as a BNF grammar.

3   Running Example: Instant Messaging Client

As a running example, we use the case study of an instant messaging client, which has been designed using the Unified Modeling Language (UML). Fig. 1 shows a UML class diagram of parts of the Platform-Independent Model (PIM) for a simple instant messaging client. The instant messaging client is able to send and to receive messages over different kinds of networks (e.g. Jabber/Internet or SMS)[1]. It also keeps a list of contacts for each supported network. The Instant-MessagingClient both uses and implements the ExceptionReporter interface: it reports raised exceptions either on the command line or on a Network that implements ExceptionReporter (e.g. a Loop-back network). The design is split up in a model, edit, view and networking part, each in their own package (the edit and view packages are not shown). Concrete view and network types are specified in separate models. These "satellite" models can be merged with the central PIM using a merging model transformation.

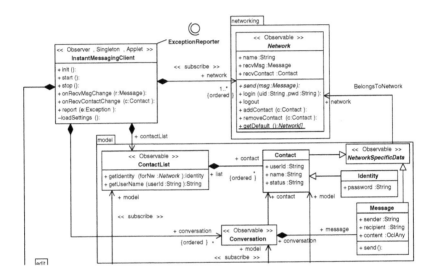

Fig. 1. Partial PIM class diagram for a simple instant messaging client

The example PIM contains several elements that are not available in the programming language used for the target platform. These elements are the "Applet", "Observer", "Observable", "subscribe" and "Singleton" stereotypes, the "String", "Integer", "Exception" and "OclAny" data types, association relationships and specifications of operations (e.g. in OCL, a dynamic diagram or an Action Language). Model transformations are used to translate each of these elements to one or more elements that are available in the target programming environment. The following transformations are applied:

– There are two alternative refinement transformations that generate implementing attributes for associations. Each of them uses a different API for representing collection types.

---

[1] The Network class in the model actually represents a network connection; this is why InstantMessagingClient "owns" Network.

- Depending on the result of these transformations, there are two alternative transformations that generate accessor methods for each attribute, again using different collection type APIs. Note that if one chooses a particular "associations-to-attributes" transformation, one has to choose the "attributes-to-accessors" transformation that uses the same collection type API.
- There are two alternative transformations that generate observer pattern infrastructure: one uses existing API and the other generates all infrastructure. Since the "observer" transformations need to adapt accessor methods, they depend on the "attributes-to-accessors" transformations.
- There are two alternative transformations that either generate Java applet infrastructure or J2ME MIDlet infrastructure.
- There is one transformation that generates singleton pattern infrastructure. This transformation needs to take into account the initialisation control flow of a class, which is non-standard for applets and MIDlets (the singleton pattern is not allowed to create an object). Hence, this transformation depends on the applet infrastructure transformations.
- There is one transformation that generates wrappers for asynchronous methods.
- There are two alternative transformations that translate any OCL types to native Java types. One uses the simple Java collections, which are provided by all Java implementations. The other uses the Java 2 collections framework. Note that these are the two collection type APIs that are also used in the "associations-to-attributes" and "attributes-to-accessors" transformations. Hence, one again has to choose the transformation with the same collection type API as has been chosen before. In addition, this transformation should be run after all other transformations that may introduce references to OCL types.

After these transformations are run, a final transformation is run that translates the model into code (i.e. a code generator).

4   Criteria for Comparison

Model transformations have specific properties that impose their requirements on the configuration technique. This section discusses the requirements for each of these properties and states the comparison criteria for evaluating the requirements.

4.1   Generality

Model transformations are more general than the software model they are applied to; they can also be applied to models of another software product line. The configuration rules for the transformations must therefore be separated from the configuration rules of the software product line itself. This way, the configuration rules of the transformations are reusable over multiple software product lines. The comparison criteria can be summarised as follows:

- modularity (of configuration rules);
- reusability (of configuration rule modules).

4.2 Mutual Conflicts and Dependencies

The result of applying two or more particular transformations may yield an inconsistent result or two transformations cannot even be executed in combination at all [1]. This issue is generally known as the *feature interaction problem* [17]. Such constraints are inherent to the specific transformations and the configuration rules must be sufficiently expressive to capture them. In addition, the configuration rules must express the interaction constraints in an efficient way, allowing for better maintainability of the configuration rules. To allow the configuration technique to scale up to a large number of transformations, it must be possible to check the transformation interaction constraints locally. The comparison criteria can be summarised as follows:

- expressiveness (of interaction constraints for transformations);
- maintainability (of configuration rules);
- locality (of configuration rule verification).

4.3 Platform Dependencies

The result of applying a particular refinement transformation may introduce requirements on the execution context (or target platform) of the software (e.g. require library `javax.swing` or `javax.microedition.lcdui`). It is possible that the selected transformations impose platform dependencies that cannot be satisfied by any concrete execution context (that is currently available). In [18], a method for specifying context constraints independently from concrete context is described. This method uses a query that searches for concrete context *instances* that satisfy a particular context constraint. Explicitly including this query into a configuration model results in a higher-order model. It is sufficient to enable the inclusion of the parameters for such a query, however, since the query never changes. This can be done by annotating the model transformation rules in the configuration. The comparison criteria can be summarised as follows:

- extensibility (of configuration rules with annotations).

5   Case Study

In this section, the configuration techniques introduced in section 2 are applied to the Instant Messaging running example. The particular advantages and limitations are discussed for each technique.

5.1 Knowledge-Based Systems

A knowledge-based formalism that promises useful properties for configuration is Description Logics [19]. An implementation of Description Logics that has proven its scalability and modularity is the OWL-DL ontology language [20]. Below is an ontology that describes the configuration rules for our running example[2]:

$$
\begin{aligned}
Refinement &\sqsubseteq owl : Thing \\
implies &: Refinement \times Refinement \ (transitive) \\
Java1Refinement &\sqsubseteq Refinement \\
Java2Refinement &\sqsubseteq Refinement \\
Accessors &\sqsubseteq Java1Refinement \\
Java2Accessors &\sqsubseteq Java2Refinement \\
Applet &\sqsubseteq Refinement \\
MIDlet &\sqsubseteq Refinement \\
AssociationAttributes &\sqsubseteq Java1Refinement \\
Java2AssociationAttributes &\sqsubseteq Java2Refinement \\
AsyncMethods &\sqsubseteq Refinement \\
UMLtoJava &\sqsubseteq Refinement \\
DataTypes &\sqsubseteq Java1Refinement \\
Java2DataTypes &\sqsubseteq Java2Refinement \\
Observer &\sqsubseteq Refinement \\
JavaObserver &\sqsubseteq Refinement \\
Singleton &\sqsubseteq Refinement \\
RefinementConfiguration &\sqsubseteq Refinement \\
CompleteRefinementConfiguration &\sqsubseteq RefinementConfiguration \\
CompleteRefinementConfiguration &\equiv \exists \ implies \ UMLtoJava \\
&\sqcap \exists \ implies \ (Accessors \ \sqcup \ Java2Accessors) \\
&\sqcap \exists \ implies \ (Applet \ \sqcup \ MIDlet) \\
&\sqcap \exists \ implies \ (AssociationAttributes \ \sqcup \\
&\quad Java2AssociationAttributes) \\
&\sqcap \exists \ implies \ AsyncMethods \\
&\sqcap \exists \ implies \ (DataTypes \ \sqcup \ Java2DataTypes) \\
&\sqcap \exists \ implies \ (JavaObserver \ \sqcup \ Observer) \\
&\sqcap \exists \ implies \ Singleton \\
InvalidRefinementConfiguration &\sqsubseteq RefinementConfiguration \\
ImpliesInvalidConfiguration &\sqsubseteq InvalidRefinementConfiguration \\
ImpliesInvalidConfiguration &\equiv \exists \ implies \ InvalidRefinementConfiguration \\
Java1AndJava2 &\sqsubseteq InvalidRefinementConfiguration \\
Java1AndJava2 &\equiv \exists \ implies \ Java1Refinement \\
&\sqcap \exists \ implies \ Java2Refinement \\
AppletAndMIDlet &\sqsubseteq InvalidRefinementConfiguration \\
AppletAndMIDlet &\equiv \exists \ implies \ Applet \\
&\sqcap \exists \ implies \ MIDlet \\
ObserverAndJavaObserver &\sqsubseteq InvalidRefinementConfiguration \\
ObserverAndJavaObserver &\equiv \exists \ implies \ JavaObserver \\
&\sqcap \exists \ implies \ Observer
\end{aligned}
$$

---

[2] The abbreviated syntax of the Protégé ontology editor (http://protege.stanford.edu) is used.

Note that only the refinement transformations are covered in this ontology. A separate ontology has been defined for the features that are specific to the Instant Messaging product line, which includes references to this ontology. This separate ontology is not shown here due to size constraints.

The ontology uses the "implies" property to determine which refinement transformations are included in the transformation. This property is transitive, which allows refinement transformations that are implied by other refinement transformations to be transitively included in the global refinement configuration.

The "CompleteRefinementConfiguration" concept is equivalent to a logic expression, which allows for automatically determining its instances. This logic expression states which refinement transformations should at least be implied to have a complete configuration. The sub-concepts of "InvalidRefinementConfiguration" again use logic expressions, this time to express the conditions for an invalid combination of refinement transformations. For each instance of "RefinementConfiguration" one can check whether it is complete and/or invalid. If neither can be inferred, it is an incomplete configuration. If both are inferred, it is an inconsistent configuration. In OWL-DL, it is also possible to define annotations for each element. Such annotations can be used to define external (context) constraints for each refinement transformation.

Note that the order in which transformations have to be executed cannot be efficiently defined within the chosen concept structure. An alternative structure can be defined that uses separate properties to chain the refinement transformations together. For example, the following property can be used to chain AssociationAttributes and Accessors together:

$$impliesAccessors : AssociationAttributes \times Accessors$$

Such a property cannot be made transitive, because the domain and range are different. Because of this, completeness and incorrectness concepts will have to be defined separately for each refinement transformation concept.

Since OWL is built on top of RDFS [21], OWL supports annotation through RDFS. Therefore, OWL-DL supports attaching external constraints such as platform dependencies.

5.2 Domain-Specific Languages

Using the DSL technique, one can define a grammar or meta-model that describes the legal configurations of model transformations. Below is an EBNF grammar for our running example:

```
InstantMessagingClient  = 'InstantMessagingClient' UserInterface+
                          Network+ RefinementConfiguration .
UserInterface           = 'AWT' | 'Swing' | 'LCDUI' .
Network                 = JabberNetwork | 'Local' | 'SMS' .
JabberNetwork           = 'Jabber' JabberTransport .
JabberTransport         = 'DefaultJabber' | 'MEJabber' .
```

```
RefinementConfiguration = AssocAttrRefinement
                          AccessorsRefinement
                          ObserverRefinement
                          AppletRefinement
                          SingletonRefinement
                          AsyncMethodsRefinement
                          DataTypesRefinement
                          CodeGenerator .
AssocAttrRefinement     = 'AssociationAttributes' |
                          'Java2AssociationAttributes' .
AccessorsRefinement     = 'Accessors' | 'Java2Accessors' .
ObserverRefinement      = 'Observer' | 'JavaObserver' .
AppletRefinement        = 'Applet' | 'MIDlet' .
SingletonRefinement     = 'Singleton' .
AsyncMethodsRefinement  = 'AsyncMethods' .
DataTypesRefinement     = 'DataTypes' | 'Java2DataTypes' .
CodeGenerator           = 'UMLtoJava' .
```

The part up to **RefinementConfiguration** is specific to the Instant Messaging product line. The part after describes the configuration rules for the refinement transformations in general. Note that EBNF does not provide a means to separate the specific part of the grammar from the general part. The grammar allows for configurations that have one or more user interfaces, one or more network protocols and exactly one refinement configuration. It is not possible to express that there may only be one user interface of each kind in an efficient way (without dropping the "at-least-one-user-interface" constraint). Similarly, the valid combinations of refinement transformations cannot be efficiently expressed (see sub-section 5.1). In such a case, transformations can be used to explicitly validate a configuration using additional configuration rules. The ASF+SDF grammar framework provides a rule-based rewriting system for this purpose.

An alternative for defining an EBNF grammar for our DSL is to define a meta-model. The Eclipse Modeling Framework (EMF) [8] provides the Ecore language that allows one to define and use meta-models. Fig. 2 shows a graphical representation of the meta-model that describes the configuration rules for the instant messaging client. This meta-model refers to another meta-model for the "RefinementConfiguration". The meta-model that describes the configuration rules for the refinement transformations is shown in Fig. 3. Only part of this meta-model is shown due to space constraints.

EMF allows for defining annotations for each element. For our example, we have used annotations to associate platform dependencies to the meta-classes. These platform dependencies are defined in a separate model [18]. In our example, the "InstantMessagingClient" meta-class (see Fig. 2) has an annotation "InstantMessengerConstraints.owl#InstantMessagingClientPlatform". This annotation points to the "InstantMessagingClientPlatform" element in the "InstantMessengerConstraints.owl" model. Similarly, the "AssociationAttributes" meta-class (Fig. 3) has an annotation to the "AssociationAttributesPlatform" element in separate platform constraints model for the refinement transformations. Note that there is also a "ContextConstraint" annotation in Fig. 3. All context constraint annotations point to this annotation to indicate they are of the context constraint "type".

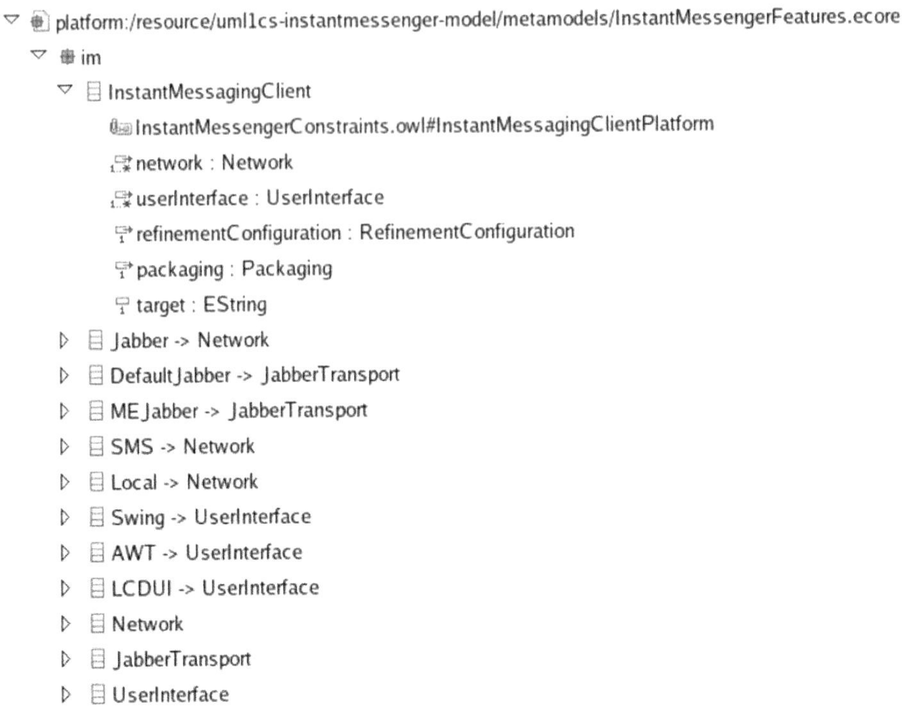

▽ ⊕ platform:/resource/uml1cs-instantmessenger-model/metamodels/InstantMessengerFeatures.ecore

   ▽ ⊞ im

      ▽ ⊟ InstantMessagingClient

          ⌸ InstantMessengerConstraints.owl#InstantMessagingClientPlatform

          ⌗ network : Network

          ⌗ userInterface : UserInterface

          ⊤ refinementConfiguration : RefinementConfiguration

          ⊤ packaging : Packaging

          ⊤ target : EString

      ▷ ⊟ Jabber -> Network

      ▷ ⊟ DefaultJabber -> JabberTransport

      ▷ ⊟ ME Jabber -> JabberTransport

      ▷ ⊟ SMS -> Network

      ▷ ⊟ Local -> Network

      ▷ ⊟ Swing -> UserInterface

      ▷ ⊟ AWT -> UserInterface

      ▷ ⊟ LCDUI -> UserInterface

      ▷ ⊟ Network

      ▷ ⊟ JabberTransport

      ▷ ⊟ UserInterface

Fig. 2. EMF meta-model of the instant messaging client features

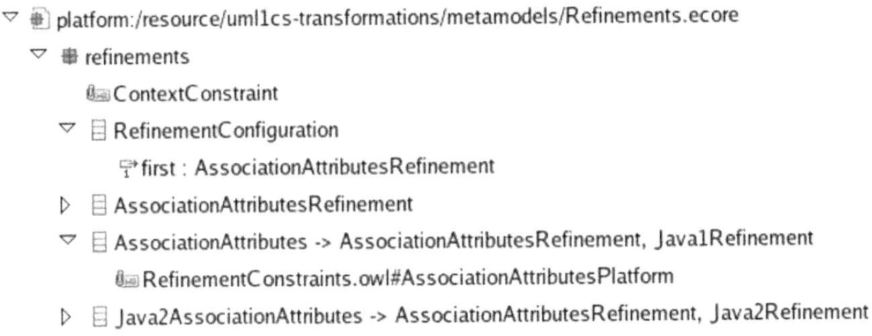

▽ ⊕ platform:/resource/uml1cs-transformations/metamodels/Refinements.ecore

   ▽ ⊞ refinements

      ⌸ ContextConstraint

      ▽ ⊟ RefinementConfiguration

         ⊤ first : AssociationAttributesRefinement

      ▷ ⊟ AssociationAttributesRefinement

      ▽ ⊟ AssociationAttributes -> AssociationAttributesRefinement, Java1Refinement

         ⌸ RefinementConstraints.owl#AssociationAttributesPlatform

      ▷ ⊟ Java2AssociationAttributes -> AssociationAttributesRefinement, Java2Refinement

Fig. 3. Part of the EMF meta-model of the refinement model transformations

Similarly to grammars, Ecore meta-models also cannot express certain constraints in an efficient way. One can use OCL expressions to define extra constraints or one can define a model transformation that explicitly checks the extra constraints. In the case of Ecore, ATL can be used to transform the model into a "true" or "false" statement, indicating either a valid or an invalid model. In addition, it is harder to enforce sequence for the refinement transformations, because meta-modelling is closer to a graph structure than a tree structure. The only way to enforce sequence in the meta-model is to use nesting of model elements, since the nesting follows a tree structure again. An alternative way of enforcing the sequence is to encode it in a model transformation. Such a model transformation could be used to place the chosen refinement transformations in the correct order.

5.3   Feature Modelling

Feature models are generally visualised with feature diagrams. Fig. 4 shows a partial feature diagram for our running example. Not all features are shown due to space constraints.

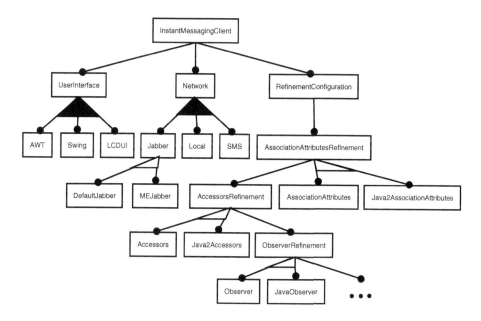

Fig. 4. Partial feature diagram of the instant messaging client features

Similar to meta-modelling, a tree structure is necessary to express sequence. Note that it is possible to express the constraints of having at least one user interface, yet any of them may occur only once. This is due to the nature of feature diagrams in which features can occur only once by default. Extensions to feature diagrams exist that allow for expressing feature multiplicities [14]. It is not possible to efficiently express the additional constraints on valid refinement transformation combinations. The Feature Modeling Plugin tool[3] solves this problem by allowing XPath constraints to be defined. Note that this solution works on the XML representation level, not on the feature diagram level.

---

[3] http://gp.uwaterloo.ca/fmp/

The Feature Modeling Plugin also allows for annotations, such that external constraints can be attached.

6   Comparison and Discussion

This section compares the different configuration techniques for each criterion listed in section 4. Table 1 gives an overview of how well each technique fulfils the requirements. The scale is divided into five steps, ranging from -- to ++.

Regarding modularity, meta-modelling provides the best mechanism, since it explicitly supports modules of language elements (i.e. packages and meta-models). The OWL-DL knowledge-based approach supports different ontology namespaces, but this is implemented on the level of RDFS. Grammars and feature models have no explicit support for modularity. This can be added by building on top of a language – and corresponding tool – that supports modularity. The Feature Modeling Plugin, for example, is built on top of EMF's Ecore language. This way, the Feature Modeling Plugin can use EMF to access elements of the feature model. This mechanism works the same for local and inter-model references.

OWL-DL is designed for reusability: OWL-DL allows for the definition of common vocabularies with particular semantics. Each ontology that builds on top of that vocabulary inherits those semantics. Meta-modelling does not provide real reuse by itself. EMF supports reuse of meta-models through its XMI [22] layer. Feature modelling more or less provides reusability through staged configuration: specialisations of feature models are derived from a general feature model to outline the scope for a product line subset. Grammars offer no native support for reuse, but this can again be added by building the grammar on top of a language that does support reuse.

If one includes the transformation engines for DSLs (both for grammars and meta-modelling), the expressiveness is beyond what is necessary for our purposes. The expressiveness of the OWL-DL knowledge-based system is sufficient, but is inefficient for expressing sequence. The expressiveness of feature models is also sufficient, but inefficient for expressing more complex constraints.

Table 1. Comparison of configuration techniques

Techniques / Criteria	modularity	reusability	expressiveness	maintainability	locality	extensibility
Knowledge-based systems	+	++	+	-	+/-	++
DSL - grammar	-	-	++	+	+/-	+/-
DSL - meta-modelling	++	+	++	+	+/-	++
Feature modelling	-	+/-	+	-	+	+

The inefficiency in expressing certain constraints can cause reduced maintainability for both the knowledge-based approach as well as feature modelling. A change in these constraints may require extensive refactoring of the configuration rules. This is not such an issue for the DSL-based techniques, which allow complex constraints to be expressed in a separate constraint checking transformation.

The locality principle requires that configuration constraints do not require global checking for a local modification of the configuration. This principle inherently holds for feature modelling, since constraints can only apply to the directly neighbouring elements. For all other techniques, the user of that technique is responsible for keeping the complexity of the constraints in check. If one constraint requires the checking of too many related constraints, the constraint checking will not scale sufficiently.

Extensibility, in this context, refers to the possibility to annotate the configuration rules with external constraints (e.g. platform dependencies), such that the configuration system can be "extended" with an extra constraint checking mechanism. Both OWL-DL and meta-modelling are built on top of languages that provide support for annotations. Feature models in general do not provide annotation support, but the Feature Modeling Plugin implementation does. The Feature Modeling Plugin annotations can be accessed through the underlying modelling framework. EBNF grammars in general also do not provide annotation support, but most grammar frameworks support comments. These comments are not as easily accessible through the grammar framework, however (one must usually know the navigation path to these comments).

7   Conclusion

In this paper, we have introduced and compared a number of configuration techniques for the purpose of configuring model transformations in an MDA context. Based on a number of specific model transformation properties, several comparison criteria have been derived. The comparison shows the feasibility of each configuration technique for each of these criteria. The paper then discusses which aspects of the configuration techniques contribute to the required criteria.

In the discussion of DSLs, the language definition formalism is used to describe a particular set of model transformations. DSL techniques can also be used to define a "Transformation Configuration DSL". This allows for representing concepts like "platform dependency" as first-class language elements instead of annotations. If "model transformation" and "platform dependency" are part of the language definition, the particular instances of model transformations and their platform dependencies become an expression in that language. Configurations of transformations again contain occurrences (i.e. instances) of the various model transformation instances. This is commonly addressed by adding an explicit "instanceOf" relationship to the language definition (examples are UML and OWL). Of course, when adding your own "instanceOf" relationship, you also have to provide the semantics for it. This usually boils down to providing your own tool support to check whether your particular configuration of model transformation occurrences complies with the configuration rules you defined for the model transformations. This comes close to a "DSL-within-a-DSL" and leads to the discussion of whether we need a special language definition formalism for "Transformation Configuration". Such a special language definition formalism is considered out of the scope of this comparison, since it does not yet exist.

In the comparison, we did not explicitly consider step-wise refinement [23]. This is a paradigm for developing a complex program from a simple program by adding features incrementally. In the AHEAD tool an arbitrary number of programs and features is expressed as nested sets of equations. This model uses algebraic specifications, which can be reduced to a DSL approach that provides a language definition formalism and an algebra that operates on this formalism.

Acknowledgement

The authors would like to thank the anonymous review committee for their comments, which included some very useful points for consideration and discussion.

References

1. Mens, T., Taentzer, G., Runge, O.: Detecting Structural Refactoring Conflicts Using Critical Pair Analysis. Electr. Notes Theor. Comput. Sci. **127** (2005) 113–128
2. Stefik, M.: Introduction to Knowledge Systems. Morgan Kaufmann Publishers Inc. (1995)
3. Clements, P., Northrop, L.: Software Product Lines: Practices and Patterns. The SEI Series in Software Engineering. Addison Wesley Professional (2001)
4. McDermott, J.: XSEL: a computer sales person's assistant. In J.E.Hayes, Michie, D., Y-H.Pao, eds.: Proceedings of the Tenth Machine Intelligence Workshop, held at Case Western Reserve University, Cleveland, USA, Ellis Horwood (1982) 325–338
5. Deursen, A.v., Klint, P., Visser, J.: Domain-Specific Languages: An Annotated Bibliography. ACM SIGPLAN Notices **35** (2000) 26–36
6. Brand, M.v.d., Deursen, A.v., Heering, J., Jong, H.A.d., Jonge, M.d., Kuipers, T., Klint, P., Moonen, L., Olivier, P.A., Scheerder, J., Vinju, J.J., Visser, E., Visser, J.: The ASF+SDF Meta-environment: A Component-Based Language Development Environment. In Wilhelm, R., ed.: Proceedings of the 10th International Conference on Compiler Construction (CC 2001). Held as Part of the Joint European Conferences on Theory and Practice of Software, ETAPS 2001 Genova, Italy, April 2-6, 2001, Proceedings. Volume 2027 of Lecture Notes in Computer Science., Springer-Verlag (2001) 365–370
7. Object Management Group, Inc.: Meta Object Facility (MOF) 2.0 Core Specification. (2003) Version 2.0, Available Specification, ptc/04-10-15.
8. Budinsky, F., Steinberg, D., Merks, E., Ellersick, R., Grose, T.J.: Eclipse Modeling Framework. The Eclipse Series. Addison Wesley Professional (2003)
9. Bravenboer, M., Dam, A.v., Olmos, K., Visser, E.: Program Transformation with Scoped Dynamic Rewrite Rules. Fundamenta Informaticae **69** (2005) 1–56

10. Jouault, F., Kurtev, I.: Transforming Models with ATL. In: Model Transformations in Practice Workshop at MoDELS 2005, Montego Bay, Jamaice. (2005)
11. Object Management Group, Inc.: OCL 2.0 Specification. (2005) Version 2.0, ptc/2005-06-06.
12. Kang, K., Cohen, S., Hess, J., Nowak, W., Peterson, S.: Feature-Oriented Domain Analysis (FODA) Feasibility Study. Technical report CMU/SEI-90-TR-021, Software Engineering Institute, Carnegie Mellon University, Pittsburgh, PA, USA (1990)
13. Coplien, J., Hoffman, D., Weiss, D.: Commonality and Variability in Software Engineering. IEEE Software **15** (1998) 37–45
14. Czarnecki, K., Helsen, S., Eisenecker, U.W.: Formalizing cardinality-based feature models and their specialization. Software Process: Improvement and Practice **10** (2005) 7–29 Special Issue on Software Variability: Process and Management.
15. Czarnecki, K., Helsen, S., Eisenecker, U.W.: Staged configuration through specialization and multilevel configuration of feature models. Software Process: Improvement and Practice **10** (2005) 143–169 Special Issue on Software Product Lines.
16. Deursen, A.v., Klint, P.: Domain-Specific Language Design Requires Feature Descriptions. Journal of Computing and Information Technology **10** (2002) 1–17
17. Reiff-Marganiec, S., Ryan, M., eds.: Proceedings of the 8th International Conference on Feature Interactions in Telecommunications and Software Systems (ICFI2005), Leicester, UK, IOS Press (2005)
18. Wagelaar, D., Jonckers, V.: Explicit Platform Models for MDA. In: Proceedings of the ACM/IEEE 8th International Conference on Model Driven Engineering Languages and Systems (MoDELS 2005), Montego Bay, Jamaica. Volume 3713 of Lecture Notes in Computer Science., Springer-Verlag (2005) 367–381
19. Baader, F., Calvanese, D., McGuinness, D., Nardi, D., Patel-Schneider, P., eds.: The Description Logic Handbook: Theory, Implementation and Applications. Cambridge University Press (2003)
20. Smith, M.K., Welty, C., McGuinness, D.L.: OWL Web Ontology Language Guide. World Wide Web Consortium. (2004) W3C Recommendation 10 February 2004, [Online] http://www.w3.org/TR/owl-guide/.
21. Dan Brickley, R.G.: RDF Vocabulary Description Language 1.0: RDF Schema. World Wide Web Consortium. (2004) W3C Recommendation 10 February 2004, [Online] http://www.w3.org/TR/rdf-schema/.
22. Object Management Group, Inc.: MOF 2.0/XMI Mapping Specification. (2005) Version 2.1, formal/05-09-01.
23. Batory, D., Sarvela, J.N., Rauschmayer, A.: Scaling Step-Wise Refinement. IEEE Transactions on Software Engineering **30** (2004) 355–371

A Canonical Scheme for Model Composition

Jean Bézivin[1], Salim Bouzitouna[2], Marcos Didonet Del Fabro[1],
Marie-Pierre Gervais[2], Fréderic Jouault[1], Dimitrios Kolovos[3],
Ivan Kurtev[1], and Richard F. Paige[3]

[1] ATLAS Group (INRIA & LINA), Université de Nantes, France
{Jean.Bezivin, Frederic.Jouault,
Marcos.Didonet-Del-Fabro, Ivan.Kurtev}@univ-nantes.fr
[2] Université de Paris-6, France
{Salim.Bouzitouna, Marie-Pierre, Gervais}@lip6.fr
[3] Department of Computer Science, University of York, UK
{paige, dkolovos}@cs.york.ac.uk

Abstract. There is little agreement on terminology in model composition, and even less on key characteristics of a model composition solution. We present three composition frameworks: the Atlas Model Weaver, the Epsilon Merging Language, and the Glue Generator Tool, and from them derive a core set of common definitions. We use this to outline the key requirements of a model composition solution, in terms of language and tool support.

1 Introduction

Model composition involves combining different models in a Model-Driven Development process. Model composition is an emerging research field, based on related work in aspect-oriented modelling [14], database schema integration [11,12], and model transformation [15]. There is not, as yet, an agreed vocabulary, glossary, and set of definitions on model composition. Nor is there an agreed set of basic requirements for model composition languages and tools.

This paper addresses these issues by deriving a common set of definitions for model composition, and from this deriving a set of fundamental requirements for model composition languages and tools. We base our presentation on an assessment of three functional frameworks: the Glue Generator Tool [7, 8], the Epsilon Merging Language [6], and the Atlas Model Weaver [10]. Based on these frameworks, we derive a set of common definitions, before presenting a set of solution requirements.

Let us consider the simplified situation where there are three models Ma, Mx and Mb conforming to metamodels MMa, MMx and MMb. A typical transformation problem may be stated as follows: given Ma and Mx compute Mb. Mx is the transformation model that, when applied to Ma, produces Mb. There are no specific constraints on metamodels MMa and MMb, but metamodel MMx defines the transformation language, for example ATL [15]. Alternatively, computing Mx from Ma and Mb is clearly a more difficult issue, different from a transformation. This situation corresponds to one kind of composition problem which is, in general more complex. In this case we have usually no constraint on metamodels MMa, MMx or MMb. We see here that model transformation is quite well understood while model composition still needs further investigation. Furthermore, a composition may

A. Rensink and J. Warmer (Eds.): ECMDA-FA 2006, LNCS 4066, pp. 346–360, 2006.
© Springer-Verlag Berlin Heidelberg 2006

sometimes also be perceived as a transformation with two input models and one output model.

Which kind of composition scheme are we going to use in the aforementioned composition examples? Can the composition of Ma and Mb to produce Mx be completely automated or do we need in some cases to resort to some external inter-vention? Can we define merging heuristics that could be applied to Ma and Mb in order to produce Mx? Should model composition be considered as a one shot operation or could it be decomposed in several phases of discovering correspondences first and then transforming these correspondences into operational mappings that could be solved by multi-input model transformation? There are many open questions in the field of model composition. There are also several partial solutions. What we need is to place these various solutions within one common conceptual framework in order to identify a canonical scheme that will allow us to compare them and to show their complementarities.

This paper is organized as follows. Section 2 describes three model composition solutions that have been independently developed in the context of the ModelWare European Integrated project. These solutions are addressing different goals and may be typical of which kind of problems could be solved by model composition techniques. Section 3 provides a glossary and some common definitions because we recognize that without solid foundations it will not be possible to produce any canonical scheme for model composition. These definitions are based on graph theory. Building on the two previous parts, Section 4 proposes an initial set of requirements for model composition frameworks. While this work does not claim completeness, it concludes that the problem of model composition should not be confused with plain model transformation. The issues are much broader and there is an urgent need for additional work in this field.

2 Model Composition Frameworks

We now describe three functional model composition frameworks, and from these descriptions identify a canonical scheme for model composition based on a glossary and a common set of definitions. A significant summary of the state-of-the-art in model composition would be a useful contribution but goes beyond the scope of this paper. In particular, related work may be found in XML, aspect-oriented program-mming, data engineering, the semantic web, and elsewhere.

2.1 Atlas Model Weaver (AMW)

The Atlas Model Weaver is a model composition framework that uses model weaving and model transformations to produce and execute composition operations. The model resulting from a composition may contain parts or all of the elements of the input models, and it may also have new elements. AMW has been used to handle several problems in data engineering [16]. The tool is available as open source from the Eclipse GMT project [10].

Let us illustrate the composition of two simple object models M_A and M_B into a model M_{AB}. M_A contains class *Teacher*. M_B contains classes *Professor* and *AssistantProfessor*. From this example, we illustrate three possibilities (there may be more) of output model. First, M_{AB} contains one class *Professor* that contains the information from all the other three classes. Second, M_{AB} contains classes *Professor* and *AssistantProfessor*; *Teacher* is combined with *Professor*. Third, M_{AB} has three classes: *Professor*, *AssistantProfessor* as in the previous scenario, and a new class *VisitingProfessor*. This class contains information about occasional visitors.

There are different options to implement a composition operation. One is to write a transformation by hand. However, model composition scenarios have a set of frequently used primitives with specific semantics, such as "merge", "override" or "extends". These primitives link concepts that represent similar information. We must raise the abstraction level of current transformation languages to create composition links. The links must be saved, as they are the specification of the operation.

In AMW, the production of a composition operation is divided in two phases. First, a weaving model captures the links between the input model elements, for example indicating that *Teacher* and *Professor* are combined into *Professor*, or that *Visiting-Professor* is a new class to be created. The weaving model conforms to a weaving metamodel. It is a domain specific metamodel dedicated to composition scenarios. It contains elements such as "rename", "override", "merge", and elements specifying how to solve conflicts between the input models.

Second, the weaving model is used to generate a transformation. This transformation is the final composition operation. The code complexity is not an issue here because the transformation is automatically produced. The transformation takes two input models and produces the composed model as output.

2.1.1 Weaving Model

In order to provide a description of a weaving model, let us suppose we have two metamodels *LeftMM* and *RightMM*. We need to establish links between their elements. The type of links specifies how the elements are composed. Some issues need be considered regarding the set of links between elements of both metamodels:

- The set of links cannot be automatically generated because it is often based on design decisions or various complex heuristics;
- It should be possible to save this set of links as a whole, in order to use them later to produce the composition operation.

The weaving model conforms to a weaving metamodel *WMM*. The weaving model is produced by a match operation. A match operation is a combination of automatic techniques with user interaction. The produced weaving model relates with the source and target metamodels *LeftMM* and *RightMM*. Figure 1 illustrates the conformance relations of *LeftMM*, *RightMM* and *WM*.

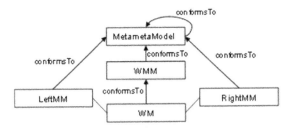

Fig. 1. Weaving conformance relations

Each composition link conforms to *WMM*, which specifies a composition operation. The link types are divided into *matching* and *composition* links. Matching links specify the equivalences between elements. Composition links specify how to solve conflicts and how to compose the related elements, e.g., equivalent elements are merged into one and the right element name is taken as default.

There is no standard weaving metamodel capable of capturing every semantics to compose models. However, various weaving metamodels have a set of common concepts: all provide means to establish links between model elements. We capture this in a *basic weaving metamodel*, and obtain different semantics by extending it. This *extension operation* takes two metamodels as input and returns a weaving metamodel. The output metamodel contains all elements from the input metamodels.

Figure 2 describes our basic weaving metamodel, which contains a *WElement*, the base element from which all the elements inherit. *WModel* is the root element. *WLink* can be extended to define different matching and composition links, and refers to multiple endpoints. *WLinkEnd* indicates the type of elements that are be composed. *WElementRef* has an identifier (ID) that points to the elements of the input models. Each extension of *WElementRef* implements a different identification mechanism, for example XMI-ID. *WModel* also contains *WModelRefs*, which is equivalent to the reference of *WLinkEnd* and *WElementRef*, but for models as a whole.

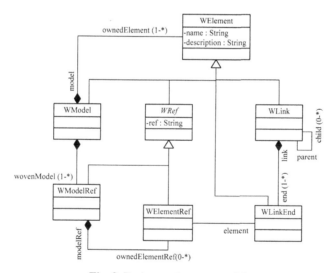

Fig. 2. Basic weaving metamodel

2.1.2 Weaving and Transformations as a Composition Operation

The weaving model is a high-level specification for the composition operation. It is not an executable entity, i.e., there is no specific composition engine to execute it. The composition operation is obtained by translating the weaving model into a transformation model. It is automatically produced by a higher-order transformation (HOT). A HOT is a transformation that either takes a transformation model as input, either produces a transformation model as output, or both. There is one different HOT for every weaving metamodel, which defines the semantics of the weaving meta-model by transforming its instances to executable transformations.

The elements of the weaving models are transformed into specific composition code patterns. For instance one may define an element called *Union* that combine *Professor* and *AssistantProfessor* into a single element. Every time the weaving model is modified, the composition operation is regenerated. The composition operations are produced for different transformation languages, such as ATL, SQL or XSLT. They are further serialized into the appropriated format (often text). The serialized form takes as input the models to be composed. It executes the composition between the data sources in the dedicated transformation engine.

2.2   Glue Generator Tool

The Glue Generator Tool (GGT) [7, 8] is a framework dedicated to the reuse of existing MDA [1] applications, without alteration, to build new ones. In the MDA approach, this reuse relates to both PIM and PSM reuse, and to composition as well as extension or modification of existing PIMs and PSMs.

The GGT framework comes with:

- a metamodel of composition rules, implemented with EMF. Three categories of rules are proposed [7]. The *correspondence rules* are used to put in correspondence related model elements. The *merge rules* are dedicated to the composition. They identify which model elements from the source models will merge. The *override rules* are dedicated to the modification. They identify which model elements in a source model will be replaced.
- a Glue Generator Tool for EJB 2.0, implemented using an EMF repository.

2.2.1   Scope of Work and Approach

GGT supports construction of a new application from existing ones in the case where the original applications were built using PIMs, PSMs, transformations and code. It also supports functionality extension of applications built using an MDA approach, and in both cases without modifying the original applications.

As a preliminary requirement, GGT considers that the reuse of PIMs must not modify the existing PIMs. Consequently it provides a designer with means to express PIM reuse in terms of model composition, extension, and modification. Currently, PIMs are expressed in UML 2.0 in terms of class and sequence diagrams. This expression of composition (*EC*) is in addition to the existing PIMs to be composed (or extended or modified). Once this expression *EC* is available, GGT provides a means for its automatic translation into its corresponding pieces of model at the PSM level. The result of this translation is called *glue*, since it binds the existing PSMs according to *EC*. As such, the Glue depends not only on the expression *EC* but also on the type of PSMs that it binds.

For the sake of concreteness, we focus on a specific type of PSM in the presentation that follows: Enterprise Java Beans (EJBs).

2.2.2   Glue for EJB PSMs

The authors in GGT defined the concept of Glue for EJB PSMs according to three statements we established from the analysis of the mapping rules of the UML class and sequence diagrams onto EJB platforms:

- R1) a business class maps onto an Entity bean. Its attributes, depending on whether they are persistent or not, map onto persistent or simple fields.
- R2) a process class maps onto a Session bean. Its attributes map onto fields.
- R3) An association or a dependency between classes, depending on the nature of the class (business or process), maps onto EJB Relationships or EJB references between the corresponding beans.

These three statements can be detailed as follows:

S1) Translating EC is mapping the composition and the override rules expressed between PIM elements onto effective merge and replacement of their corresponding EJB PSM elements.

The three rules Ri illustrate how to map PIM elements onto EJB PSM elements, and can be used for the translation of *EC* defined at PIM level by a designer.

S2) The unit of composition or override at PIM level is the class.

At the PIM level, the designer can express some composition rules aimed at merging some PIM elements, such as:

1)   The merge of features (attributes/ operations) of different classes into one feature (attribute/ operation);
2)   The merge of classes of different packages into one class;
3)   The merge of sub-packages of different other packages into one package.

However, since the encapsulation unit of PIM is the class, all these merges consist in merging classes. The merge of the packages consists of merging their corresponding classes. In addition, the merge of attributes or operations must initially deal with the merge of their container, which are classes. This also holds for the override rules, which consist of replacing elements of one PIM by those of another.

S3) The composition or the override of classes is the merge or the replacement of the corresponding beans

When considering the three rules Ri mentioned above, we note that the classes at PIM level map onto beans.

These three statements enable us to define the Glue as a PSM binding entity responsible for the merge or replacement of beans. These two operations and how the Glue achieves them are described in depth in [8].

2.2.3   Architecture of the Tool

The Glue Generator Tool is responsible for automatic generation of the Glue from the expression of composition defined at PIM level by a designer. To this end, it inputs a composition model defining a set of composition rules, and outputs the Glue that will bind the corresponding PSMs. It consists of the Analyzer, the Generator and the Controller (Figure 3).

The *Analyzer* parses the input composition rules to build a merge tree or a replacement tree according the categories of these rules while checking the semantic and syntactic well-formedness of rules. For semantic well-formedness, the authors of GGT defined a set of constraints on the rules and have developed automated constraint checking operations that run at composition model load time in the analyzer.

The *Generator* is the builder of Glue and consequently is specific to the platform on which the applications run. We currently provide a generator for EJB 2.0 platform and another for JMX platform. A generator consists of an API and its implementation. The API should allow Controller to create/read/modify the models based on the specific platform. The *Controller* is the processor of GGT. It manages the generation of Glue using the API of the Generator. It parses the merge tree and triggers the generation of glue according to a generation mechanism. Since the Glue depends on the kind of platforms, the generation of the controller also depends on the platforms.

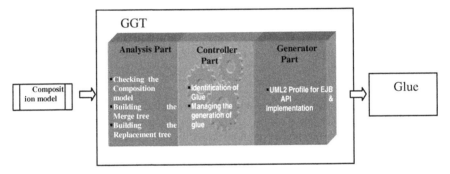

Fig. 3. Architecture of GGT

2.3 Epsilon Merging Language

The Epsilon Merging Language (EML) is a metamodel agnostic language for expressing model compositions. It includes a model comparison and model transformation language as subsets, and is built atop a generic model management language called the Epsilon Object Language (EOL) [6], which is inspired by OCL. An EML specification consists of a set of rules describing how model compositions should be carried out. Rules in EML are of three types: match rules, merge rules, and transform rules. Match rules can be further subdivided into comparison and conformance rules (examples to follow). Each match rule has a unique name and two metaclass names as parameters. The rule itself is composed of a *compare* part and a *conform* part. The rule is executed for all pairs of instances of the metaclasses that appear in the source models. The compare part of a match rule determines whether two instances match, using a minimum set of (syntactic) criteria. The conform part applies only to instances that satisfy the compare part of a rule; the conformance rule part refines this match. If the conformance part of the rule fails, then an exception is raised. An example is shown in Figure 4:

```
abstract rule ModelElements
    match l: Left!ModelElement
    with r: Right!ModelElement
    extends Elements {

    compare {
            return l.name = r.name
            and l.namespace.matches(r.namespace);
    }
}

rule Classes
    match l: Left!Class
    with r: Right!Class
    extends ModelElements {

    conform { return l.isAbstract = r.isAbstract; }
}
```

Fig. 4. Matching rules in EML

The rule on ModelElements is abstract and provides basic behaviour that is used by rules that *extend* it; EML supports rule reuse via inheritance. The behaviour of this abstract rule is to match model elements that have identical names (*l.name=r.name*) and matching namespaces. A similar match rule is used for classes. Classes match when they obey the rules declared in their parent and when the *conform* part of the rule holds, i.e., when classes are either both abstract or both not abstract.

2.3.1 EML Model Element Categorisation

After the execution of all match rules in an EML specification, all model elements are categorised in four groups: those that match and conform; those that match but do not conform; those that do not match; and those to which no match rule has applied (the last category of element produces warnings). The results of this matching process are used in the merging process. In particular, elements that match and conform will be merged with their identified opposite. The specification of merging is captured in *merge rules*. Elements that do not match will be *transformed* into model elements compatible with the target metamodel. This is captured using *transformation rules*.

2.3.2 EML Merge Rules

Merge rules in EML are used to specify the behaviour necessary to compose two instances of model elements that match and conform. Each merge rule consists of a unique name, two metaclass-typed parameters, and a list of the model elements that the rule creates in the target model.

For all pairs of matching instances of the two paramters, the rule is executed and the declared empty model element(s) are created in the target model.. The contents of the newly created model element are defined by the body of the merge rule. Two examples of merge rules are shown in Figure 5:

```
rule ModelElements {                    rule Classes {
    merge l: Left!ModelElement              merge l: Left!Class
    with r: Right!ModelElement              with r: Right!Class
    into m: Merged!ModelElement             into m: Merged!Class
                                            extends ModelElements

    m.name := l.name;                       m.feature := l.feature.
    m.namespace:=l.namespace.equivalent()       includeAll(r.feature).
}                                               equivalent();
                                        }
```

Fig. 5. EML Merge Rule

Figure 5 presents two merge rules, one for merging ModelElements and a second for merging UML classes ("Classes"). The first rule applies to all Model Elements and produces a new, merged ModelElement whose name is that of the left original model element, and whose namespace is that of the left original model element. In the second rule, the two parameters, *l:Left!Class* and *r:Right!Class*, are declared; the merge rule is also declared to produce an instance of the Merged!Class metaclass. The "Classes" rule creates a new instance of the Class metaclass, carries out all operations declared in its parent (ModelElements), and sets the feature list of the new class to be the union of all features from the left and right arguments.

There is a slight twist to the merging rule that takes the union of all features from the left and right model elements: the use of the *equivalent()* operation. This operator returns the *equivalent of the model element to which it is applied* in the target model. The equivalent of an element is the result of a merge rule if the element has a matching element in the opposite model; otherwise it is the result of a transform rule. This operator is necessary because the target and source metamodels may differ, and it ensures that all source elements are expressed in the target metamodel.

A key aspect of merging models in EML is that many merge rules can in fact be inferred from the *structure* of the metamodel itself: for example, when merging two classes, a basic merge rule can automatically be inferred that merges the contents of the classes (i.e., behavioural features and attributes). Such inferred rule sets we call *strategies*; further details on them (and on EML) can be found in [6].

3   Glossary and Common Definitions

We propose a set of definitions for a model composition framework. They are an extraction of the common points of AMW, GGT and EML. The formal definitions are intended as a starting point for a common canonical scheme.

The three frameworks follow standards of model-driven development. This means they all have models as the central concept. The models are represented as graphs. In this case it is straightforward to converge to a graph model representation.

Definition 1 (Directed graph). A directed multigraph $G = (N_G, E_G, \Gamma_G)$ consists of a finite set of nodes N_G and a finite set of edges E_G and a mapping function $\Gamma_G : E_G \rightarrow N_G \times N_G$.

Definition 2 (Model). A model $M = (G, \omega, \mu)$ is a triple where:

- $G = (N_G, E_G, \Gamma_G)$ is a directed multigraph,
- ω is itself a model (called the reference model of M) associated to a graph $G_\omega = (N_\omega, E_\omega, \Gamma_\omega)$,
- $\mu : N_G \cup E_G \rightarrow N_\omega$ is a function associating elements (nodes and edges) of G to nodes of G_ω. This means both nodes and edges of G are constrained by nodes from G_ω.

The relation between a model and its reference model is called conformance. This definition allows an indefinite number of levels. However we observe from different domains that usually only three levels are sufficient. We call these three levels metametamodel (M3), metamodel (M2) and terminal model (M1).

We illustrate the three levels with different technical spaces:

- relational database (RDBMS): the instances (M1), the relational schemas (M2) and the relational data model (M3).
- XML: the XML documents (M1), XML schemas (M2) and the XML schema definition (M3).

Definition 3 (Metametamodel). A metametamodel is a model that is its own reference model.

A metametamodel is self-defined. This allows using the same set of composition tools for the three levels in a uniform way.

Definition 4 (Metamodel). A metamodel is a model such that its reference model is a metametamodel.

Definition 5 (Terminal model). A terminal model is a model such that its reference model is a metamodel.

The three approaches provide a way to capture the correspondences between the models to compose. In AMW, the weaving model has matching and composition links. In GGT, the expression of composition (EC) is a model with correspondence, composition and override rules. EML provides comparison rules (ECL) that produce a weaving model that contains the relationships between the model elements. Differently from the previous two approaches, the composition rules are not specified within the same model. They specify merge rules that take as input the result of the comparison rules.

We thus define a correspondence model that captures links between different models. The metamodel of the correspondence model (correspondence metamodel) is extensible, because different matching and composition links are defined (match, override, correspondence, equality, merge, JoinClasses).

Definition 6 (Correspondence model). A correspondence model $C = (G_C, \omega, \mu)$ represents links between elements of different models, such that:

- $S = \{M_i = (G_i, \omega_i, \mu); i = [1..n]\}$ is a set of models,
- G_C has two types of nodes: *links* and *link endpoints*,
- for each *link endpoint*, there is an edge coming from a *link*,

- each *link endpoint* refers to an element e of a model M_i from the set S by the means of identification functions. An identification function ρ takes a *link endpoint* as input and returns an element of a model from the set S.

Consider two models M_A and M_B and a correspondence model C. M_A contains classes *FirstName* and *LastName*, M_B contains class *Name*. The correspondence model C contains three link endpoints; each endpoint refers to elements *FirstName*, *LastName* and *Name*, respectively. There is one link element with outgoing edges to all the three end points.

The correspondence model is created by different procedures. In AMW, the weaving model is created by a user interface and pluggable match algorithms (in Java code). In GGT, the expression of composition is created by a user interface based on EMF. In EML, a match operation is defined using comparison rules (ECL). These rules search for relationships between the models elements. The process of creating the correspondence model is encapsulated in a match operation. The matching rules produce a weaving model as result.

Definition 7 (Match operation). Match is an operation C = Match (S) that takes a set of models S = $\{M_i = (G_i, \omega_i, \mu_i); i = [1..n]\}$ as input, searches for equivalences between their elements and produces a correspondence model C as output.

The match operator does not have fixed semantics. The semantic is defined with comparison and conformance rules. Comparison rules determine syntactic similarities between model elements. Conformance rules identify if a subset of syntactically similar elements are semantically compatible.

In all solutions there are translation and generation procedures. In AMW, transformations are used for executing the composition. The composition operation is generated using HOTs. In GGT, a Glue is automatically produced from the expression of composition. In EML, transformations are used as part of composition rules to add elements that do not match in the input models. This generation procedures are subsumed in the notion of model transformations. AMW uses metamodel extension to extend the basic weaving metamodel before generating a transformation. The definitions of metamodel extension and model transformation are given below.

Definition 8 (Metamodel extension operation). The operation MM_A = Extend (MM_A, MM_B) takes two metamodels $MM_A = (G_A, \omega, \mu)$ and $MM_B = (G_B, \omega, \mu)$ as input and extends G_A with all nodes and edges of G_B. The operation main requirement is to create at least one new edge in the resulting metamodel from an element $m_A \in N_{GA} \cup E_{GA}$ to an element $m_B \in N_{GB} \cup E_{GB}$. We assume that there are no conflicts between the two metamodels.

Consider two class-based metamodels MM_A and MM_B. MM_A contain classes *Person* and *Address*. One person refers to many addresses. MM_B contain classes *Teacher* and *Student*. MM_A is extended with the elements of MM_B. The class *Professor*, classes *Teacher* and *Student* are copied to MM_A and they is an inheritance relation with *Person*.

Definition 9 (Model transformation). A model transformation is an operation that takes a set of models as input, executes a set of rules over the model(s) elements and produces a set of models as output.

A transformation has the following signature OUT = T(IN) where T is the transformation name, IN is a set of input models and OUT a set of output models. The transformation T translates the input models IN into the output models OUT. A transformation is a model. This means that all general operations on models may be applied to transformations (including transformations).

In AMW, the weaving model is a high-level specification for the composition. It produces a transformation that is the executable composition operation. This transformation receives two or more models as input and produces the composed model as output. In GGT, the compose operation is a Glue. A Glue is a domain specific structure to compose models. A Glue does not create a new composed model, but an intermediary structure (for example a Bean for composing EJBs) that virtually compose two input models. In EML, there are a set of merge rules to execute the composition. Model elements that are not explicitly referenced in the merge rules are composed by the means of merge strategies.

Finally we define the compose operation on two models:

Definition 10 (Compose operation). The compose operation M_{AB} = Compose (M_A, M_B, C_{AB}) takes two models M_A, M_B and a correspondence model C_{AB} between them as input and combines their elements into a new output model.

In the three approaches there are some differences in the terminology to specify what a composition is. Besides composition, the second most employed term is *merge*. However it is advisable to separate merge and composition. Composition is a more general operation. The semantic is specified in the different operations by a set of rules, and it varies from case to case. Merge, however, is a special case of model composition. Merge has information preservation constraints, i.e., all the information from the input models should be present in the output models, and no duplicate information.

Definition 11 (Merge operation). The merge operation M_{AB} = Merge (M_A, M_B, C_{AB}) takes two models M_A, M_B and a correspondence model C_{AB} between them as input, and returns a model M_{AB} including all the information from M_A and M_B, without duplicate information. The correspondence model is created by the match operation. It specifies the elements that are going to be merged.

4   Requirements for Model Composition Frameworks

We now identify a core set of requirements for a model composition framework. By doing so we attempt to complement the canonical definitions for model composition presented in Section 3 with a concrete set of minimal requirements for a model composition framework. Obviously, this is an initial set of requirements and it will likely need refinement after more practical experience and experiments with the frameworks have been carried out.

4.1   Requirements for a Model Composition Framework

A model composition framework *must* provide at least the following operations:

- means to identify *corresponding* elements in the models that are to be composed (e.g., MOF classes with the same MOF identifier may be said to correspond, e.g., a weaving model or a set of rules).

- means to define how corresponding elements are to be *merged* and *composed* in producing the target model;
- means to define how elements that do not correspond can be *transformed* to the target metamodel, in order to, e.g., not lose information.
- means to manage and *reuse* correspondences, merges, and compose operations. In AMW this is supported via metamodel extension (e.g., by extending a weaving model), whereas in EML this is supported via rule inheritance.

Thus, a model composition framework should also provide the means to carry out transformations (e.g., via MOF 2.0 QVT or ATL) to satisfy the fourth requirement. In order to satisfy the first two requirements, a model composition framework should include the means to *compare models*.

Two *desirable*, practical requirements can be identified from the previous sections:

- A model composition framework should provide the means for minimising the effort expended by the developer to write composition or merge operations, e.g., by allowing rules to be inferred by metamodel structure (e.g., merging strategies in EML) or by allowing expressions of composition or weaving models to be reused.
- A model composition framework should be metamodel independent to support backwards compatibility, future extension, and a wide suite of modelling tools.

4.2 Requirements on Model Composition Tools

Tool support for model composition must provide at least the following:

- validation and verification of model composition operations, i.e., syntax and type checking of rules, merging models, etc.
- a virtual machine (or similar means) for executing composition operations;
- a debugger, for analysing failures and inconsistencies that arise during the composition process
- a serialisation mechanism for loading and saving models.

4.3 Comparison of AMW, GGT, and EML

We summarise the three previously described model composition frameworks against the requirements identified in Section 4.1 and 4.2. The results of the comparison are in Table 1; columns represent a particular framework, whereas rows represent a model composition framework operation or feature. We note that all three frameworks provide reasonably comprehensive coverage of tool requirements (though only AMW provides debugging support via its integration with ATL).

We can observe from the summary in Table 1 that already we are seeing a convergence of functionality in several of the existing frameworks: all three frameworks support most, if not all of the operations described in the canonical set of definitions, and it is already possible to loosely couple some of the frameworks (AMW and EML) together via weaving models.

Table 1. Comparison of model composition frameworks

	GGT	AMW	EML
Compose	Glue	Weaving model	Merge rules
Merge	Glue	Weaving model	Merge rules that are information lossless.
Transform	Automatically carried out.	ATL transformations	Transform rules
Match	Expression of correspondence (EC), via EMF GUI	Weaving model via EMF GUI	Comparison rules which produce weaving models.
Correspondence	EC	Weaving model	Comparison rules
Metamodel extn.	No	Yes	Indirectly, via generation of weaving model imported by AMW.
Tool support	No debugger.	All.	No debugger.

5 Conclusions

The main contributions of this paper are a canonical set of definitions regarding model composition, and set of requirements for model composition frameworks. The intent is that the canonical scheme, definitions, and requirements will be helpful for comparing different model composition solutions, building new solutions, and assessing the completeness and coherency of existing solutions. The contributions of this paper may also be helpful in any future standardisation efforts – within or without of the OMG – on model composition. We expect to work further on more closely aligning the three frameworks described in this paper, and to explore additional operations that engineers find helpful in model composition scenarios.

The fact that three different solutions for model composition have been developed in the same project is not the mere result of hazard. It shows that the problem is of practical importance and takes multiple forms. There is an obvious need for unification and conceptualization in the field. As discussed in [15], the QVT OMG model transformation proposal [2] only marginally addresses the composition issues. What we have done in this paper is to gather some experimental material that may help giving first class status to model composition as has been done previously with model transformation techniques.

Acknowledgement

The work in this paper was supported by the European Commission via the MODELWARE project. The MODELWARE project is co-funded by the European Commission under the "Information Society Technologies" Sixth Framework

Programme (2002-2006). Information included in this document reflects only the authors' views. The European Commission is not liable for any use that may be made of the information contained herein.

References

1. Object Management Group. Model Driven Architecture official web-site. Internet resource. http://www.omg.org/mda/.
2. Meta Object Facility Queries-Views-Transformations. Internet resource. http:// neptune. irit.fr/ Biblio/ qvt specification.shtml.
3. Object Management Group. XMI specification. Internet resource. http://www.omg.org/ technology/documents/formal/xmi.htm.
4. Object Management Group. Meta Object Facility official web-site. Internet resource. http://www.omg.org/mof/.
5. Modelware IST Project. Internet resource. http://www.modelware-ist.org.
6. D.S. Kolovos, Epsilon Project Page, http://www.cs.york.ac.uk/~dkolovos
7. S. Bouzitouna and M. P. Gervais, *Composition rules for PIM reuse*, Proceedings of the Second European Workshop on Model Driven Architecture with Emphasis on Methodologies and Transformations (EWMDA'04), Canterbury, UK, September 2004, pp36-43
8. S. Bouzitouna, M. P. Gervais and X. Blanc, *Model Reuse in MDA*, Proceedings of the International Conference on Software Engineering Research and Practice (SERP'05), Las Vegas, USA, June 2005.
9. M Lenzerini Data integration: a theoretical perspective, Proceedings of the twenty-first ACM SIGMOD-SIGACT-SIGART Symposium on Principles of database systems, June 03-05, 2002, Madison, Wisconsin
10. Atlas Model Weaver Project Web Page. http://www.eclipse.org/gmt/amw/, 2005.
11. R. Pottinger and P. Bernstein. Towards Model Composition, in *Proc. VLDB 2003*, ACM, 2003.
12. C. Batini and M. Lenzerini. A Comparative Analysis of Methodologies for Database Schema Integration. *ACM Computing Surveys* 18(4), December 1986.
13. R. Reddy, R. France, S. Ghosh, F. Fleurey, B. Baudry. Model Composition: a Signature Based Approach. In *Proc. Workshop on Aspect-Oriented Modelling,* co-located with MODELS 2005, October 2005.
14. T. Cottenier, A. van den Berg and T. Elrad. Modelling Aspect-Oriented Compositions. In *Proc. Workshop on Aspect-Oriented Modelling,* co-located with MODELS 2005, October 2005.
15. F. Jouault and I. Kurtev. On the Architectural Alignment of ATL and QVT. *Proc. Symposium on Applied Computing (SAC 06)*, ACM Press, April 2006.
16. M. Didonet Del Fabro, J. Bézivin,, F. Jouault, and P. Valduriez. Applying Generic Model Management to Data Mapping. *Proc. Journées Bases de Données Avancées (BDA05)*, Saint Malo, France.

MOFLON: A Standard-Compliant Metamodeling Framework with Graph Transformations[*]

C. Amelunxen, A. Königs, T. Rötschke, and A. Schürr

Real-Time Systems Lab
Darmstadt University of Technology
{amelunx, koenigs, rotschke, schuerr}@es.tu-darmstadt.de

Abstract. The crucial point in Model Driven Architecture (MDA[1]) is that software and system development are based on abstract models that are successively transformed into more specific models, ideally resulting in the desired system. To this end, developers must be enabled to model different aspects like structure, behavior, consistency constraints of the system. This results in a variety of related models, which in turn need tool support on the metalevel. However, there is a lack of tools offering uniform support for metamodel definition, analysis, transformation, and integration. In this paper we present the metamodeling framework MOFLON that addresses these issues by bringing together the latest OMG standards with graph transformations and their formal semantics. MOFLON provides a combination of visual and textual notations and offers powerful modularization concepts. Using MOFLON, developers can generate code for specific tools needed to perform the desired modeling tasks.

1 Introduction

Implementing the Model Driven Architecture (MDA) paradigm in software and system development means that the developers start with modeling the structure and behavior of the desired system on an abstract level using their favorite modeling tools. These abstract models will then successively be transformed into more specific models ideally resulting in the desired system. Thus, developers have to deal with lots of different models, and need domain- and project-specific tool support in defining, analyzing, transforming, and integrating them.

Metatools provide assistance with the realization of the required tool support. Current solutions either are limited to a subset of model-related tasks, lack a proper formal foundation, are not compliant to common standards, or make use of not standard compliant or unfortunate notations. Therefore, they do not

---

[*] Work supported in part by the European Community's Human Potential Programme under contract HPRN-CT-2002-00275, SegraVis.
[1] "Model Driven Architecture" and "MDA" are registered trademarks of the Object Management Group (OMG).

A. Rensink and J. Warmer (Eds.): ECMDA-FA 2006, LNCS 4066, pp. 361–375, 2006.

provide full support for the realization of MDA-enabling tools, make it hard to validate such tools, cannot easily be integrated with related approaches, or are difficult to use and understand.

In this paper we present our metamodeling framework MOFLON[2] that addresses these deficiencies. MOFLON aims at compliance to the latest OMG standards, and integrates them with the well-known formalism of graph transformations.

Section 2 presents some industrial case studies that motivate our efforts. In Section 3 we provide a running example that will be used in Section 4 in order to illustrate the application of MOFLON. In Section 5, we present the architecture of our metamodeling framework. We compare our solution with related ones in Section 6. In Section 7, we summarize our results and discuss further steps.

2   Case Studies

To begin with, we use MOFLON in its own development process. Initially, we created a simplified MOF 2.0 [1] metametamodel in Rational Rose, exported it as XMI and generated the resulting Java representation using an existing code generator [2]. This Java code forms the core of the schema editor and the code generator. Meanwhile, we are able to generate this core from a metametamodel, which consists of the complete UML 2.0 Infrastructure Library and MOF 2.0 specification with a small number of deviations. During this bootstrapping process, we gained a very deep insight in the advantages and shortcomings of the latest OMG specifications and were able to improve the MOFLON machinery.

Several industrial partners from various domains (medical imaging, multi purpose industrial printers and enterprise storage solutions) have faced the task of restructuring their software architectures to deal with increased complexity and adopt new technologies. As business needs demand continuous output of new releases, all projects require an evolutionary analysis approach to monitor restructuring progress during the ongoing development of "normal" features. MOFLON is used to support these efforts by generating individual reverse engineering and architecture monitoring tools from project-specific metamodels, metrics, and consistency rules [3].

Our industrial partner from the automotive sector develops integrated systems such as adaptive cruise control or windscreen wipers with rain sensors. The development processes involve quite a number of different tools each specialized in certain tasks (e.g. requirements engineering, modeling of software and hardware functionality, test case maintenance). Thus, the data of a project as a whole is distributed over different tools. Typically, these tools are commercial-of-the-shelf (COTS) that are rarely designed to integrate with each other. Nevertheless, the data stored in the separate tools is related. Our running example (cf. Section 3) demonstrates how these relationships can be detected automatically and utilized for integration purposes. Our integration approach is part of the tool integration framework Toolnet [4].

---

[2] http://gforge.echtzeitsysteme.org/projects/moflon/

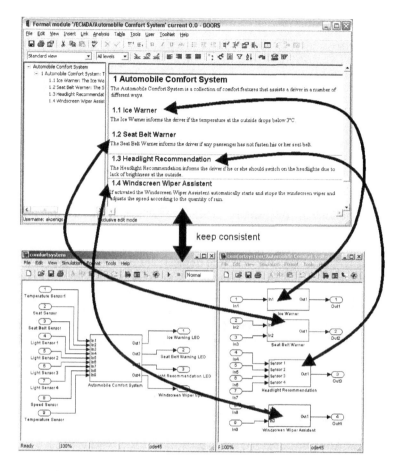

Fig. 1. Consistency between DOORS and Matlab/Simulink

From industrial case studies we have learned, that we need metamodel-based support for repositories, standard-compliant tool interfaces, constraint- and design rule-checking, as well as intra- and inter-model transformations. In our case however, it turned out that unlike classical meta-CASE tools, that we need no support for generating diagram editors.

3 Example: Automobile Comfort System

In this section, we introduce an illustrative toy example that describes a very small system development project motivated by a real world scenario from the automotive domain. We present tasks that a developer is confronted with, and demonstrate what kind of support he needs. The project deals with the development of an integrated automobile comfort system. The comfort system is a collection of several subsystems that assists the driver in a number of different

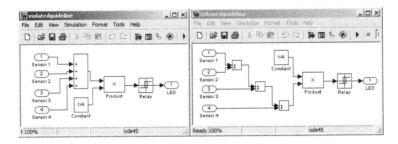

Fig. 2. Example of the application of design guidelines in Matlab/Simulink

ways. In the following we primarily turn our attention to the *Headlight Recommendation Subsystem (HRS)*. According to these requirements the developer chooses to design the system using the system modeling tool Matlab/Simulink (cf. Fig. 1 at the bottom). The left side depicts the *Automobile Comfort System* that is connected to a number of sensors. These sensors internally are connected to the corresponding subsystems as shown on the right side.

The developer is provided with a requirements document stored in the requirements management tool DOORS as shown in Fig. 1 at the top. The requirements state that the Automobile Comfort System consists of four subsystems including the HRS. He models the HRS as depicted in Fig. 2 at the left-hand side, providing the HRS with a number of light sensors. It calculates the average of all measured values by using a Sum and a Product block. If the Relay block calculates that the average is below a certain threshold, the HRS informs the driver by activating the LED.

As the developer is designing the system another developer is still working on the requirements refining, changing, and maintaining them. The system designer has to merge these changes into his system in order to keep it consistent with the requirements document. In particular, the requirements correspond to the subsystems of the Automobile Comfort System. Finally, the system designer has to ensure that he has implemented all requirements. Besides the requirements document the system designer is provided with modeling guidelines to which he must adhere to. Among others, the guidelines demand that the designer should not use Sum blocks with more than two Input Ports[3]. As a matter of fact this is not enforced by Matlab/Simulink itself. Nevertheless, the guidelines force the developer to change his model into another model that might look like the one depicted in Fig. 2 on the right-hand side. The Sum block has been replaced by an equivalent cascade of Sum blocks that only have two Input Ports each. Without any tool support the system designer has to fulfill the tasks of consistency preserving, traceability maintenance, and guideline constraint checking by hand. Although this is not impossible for rather small projects it is very time consuming and error prone in medium or large scale projects. The situation becomes even worse if the number of developers, involved tools, and documents increase.

---

[3] A code generator produces erroneous code for blocks with more than two inputs.

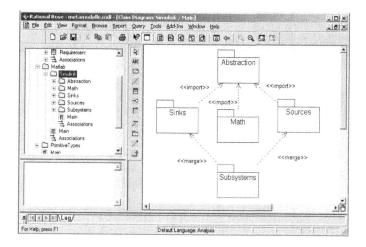

Fig. 3. Metamodel of Matlab/Simulink in Rational Rose

In the following we present how developers can specify their tasks on an abstract level. From these specifications we can then generate the needed tool support.

4   Generating Tool Support with MOFLON

In the following sections we describe how tool support for the outlined scenario can be generated with MOFLON. The scenario as described before is clearly a matter of metamodeling. For the application of transformations of Matlab/Simulink models as well as for the application of the integration between DOORS requirements and Matlab/Simulink models, the metamodels of both tools have to be defined. Based on these metamodels, the transformations, analysis, and integration operations can be specified.

4.1   Specifying Metamodels

MOFLON uses MOF 2.0, the latest OMG metamodeling-standard, as metametamodel. MOF 2.0 is characterized by powerful concepts for modularization, abstraction, and refinement of large metamodels. In the following the new concepts of MOF 2.0 are demonstrated on the metamodel of Matlab/Simulink which is introduced in detail. Fig. 3 depicts a screenshot of Rational Rose that shows a very simplified part of the Matlab/Simulink metamodel. The metamodel could have been modeled in MOFLON directly as well. But since COTS modeling tools are very popular among our industrial partners, MOFLON offers an XMI import to allow the users to retain their established modeling customs. The imported metamodel is shown as screenshot of MOFLON in Fig. 4. It shows the packages `Abstraction`, `Sources`, and `Subsystems` from Fig. 3 in detail. The metamodel

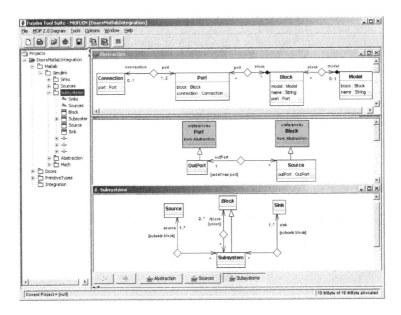

Fig. 4. Imported Metamodel of Matlab/Simulink in MOFLON

is decomposed in several packages. The package `Abstraction` describes the general dependencies between the most general elements `Model`, `Block`, `Port`, and `Connection`.

Those general concepts are reused and refined in the packages `Sources` and `Sinks` by importing `Abstraction`. In package `Sources` for instance, the relationship between the special block `Source` and the special port `outPort` is redefined in such a way that a `Source` always has exactly one `outPort`. The concepts, namely the classes, of the `Sinks` and `Sources` are extended in `Subsystems` by the application of package merges, the metamodel refinement concept of MOF 2.0. In `Subsystems` the class `Source` is extended by a navigable association end because each subsystem has at least one source. Due to the package merge to `Sources` the attributes (and association ends) of the classes `Source` in the packages `Sources` and `Subsystems` are merged in the class `Source` in package `Subsystems`.

Beside the redefinition of association ends in MOF 2.0, another very helpful feature is the subsetting of assocation ends as demonstrated by the association ends `block` and `source`. A subsystem contains an arbitrary number of blocks but at least one sink and one source. The mandatory sinks and sources are also blocks and should, therefore, be available through the association end `block`. Thus `source` is declared as subset of `block` which means that all instances of `Source` that are linked with an instance of `Subsystem` are available via `source` as well as via `block`. The declaration of `block` as union of its subsets causes the collection of `Block`-instances which is represented by `block` to be composed from all subsets of `block`.

Fig. 5. Design guideline as OCL 2.0 constraint in MOFLON

From such a description of the abstract semantics of Matlab/Simulink it is possible to generate Java code with JMI-compliant (Java Metadata Interface [5]) interfaces. The code can be used to create, query, destroy, and serialize instances of the specified metamodel according to the static semantics specified in MOF 2.0. It can easily be integrated based upon an event mechanism which is compatible with the Netbeans Metadata Repository (MDR) [6]. Regarding the outlined example, the metamodels of DOORS and Matlab/Simulink act as basis on which design guidelines and transformation can be defined. They also provide the basis for the integration of DOORS and Matlab/Simulink models as instances of the generated metamodel representations.

4.2 Adding Constraints

With MOF 2.0 as metamodeling language, we are able to specify the abstract syntax of a modeling language, but to specify its static semantics, we need constraints as discussed in this section. For instance, it is not possible to express that a block's name has to be unique within a subsystem. In such cases, additional constraints are needed. The Object Constraint Language (OCL) [7] as the textual constraint language within the OMG standardization scenario is the appropriate choice to fill this gap. On the one hand OCL can be used to express the static semantics of a metamodel more precisely, on the other hand it is also possible to specify additional information about the usage and application of the metamodel, like for instance design guidelines. Concerning the outlined example, the design guideline stating that a Sum-block should not have more than two input ports can be expressed in OCL. Fig. 5 shows the appropriate constraint. OCL constraints can only be evaluated on instances of the associated metamodel. Thus, the evaluation of OCL constraints is a matter of the generated code. MOFLON integrates the Dresden OCL compiler framework [8] consisting of a parser and a code generator which generates code for the evaluation of invariants in a first version. In the long run, support for body constraints as well as pre- and postconditions is also planned. The generated code checks the compliance of the metamodel instances to the specified invariants.

Currently, we are working on the implementation of several (incremental) constraint evaluation strategies as well as on the integration of constraint checking with the execution of appropriate repair actions. A repair action in form of a transformation has to be triggered if a constraint is broken.

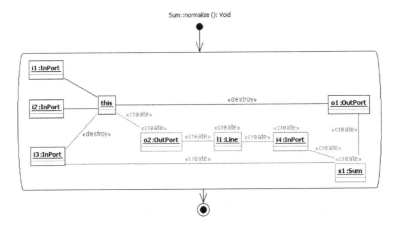

Fig. 6. Repair action as example of a graph transformation rule

4.3 Defining Model Transformation

Until now, we are only able to describe the syntax and static semantics of a modeling language. Still missing are means to specify queries and transformations on models. We also need to define actions that can be invoked if constraint violations are detected. Object-oriented graph transformation languages provide an intuitive means to implement such queries and transformations. When we designed MOFLON, we decided to adopt the graph transformation engine of the Fujaba Toolsuite [9], as it uses UML-like graph schemata and generates Java code from specifications. The transformation language is called Story Driven Modeling (SDM). In [10], we discussed the necessary modifications to adopt the SDM machinery for MOF 2.0 and JMI code generation.

The graph transformation Sum::normalize() in Fig. 6 can be used as repair action, until the constraint discussed in section 4.2 is no longer violated. The rule reads as follows: The given Sum block, that we try to normalize, is called this. If it is associated with at least three different Inputs and one Output, the rule matches. The links to the third matched Input i3 and the Output o1 are removed. As a replacement, this is connected to a new Output o2. Input i3 is connected to a new Sum block s1. Output o2 is connected to a new Input i4 through a new Line l1. Input i4 is then connected to s1, which finally is connected to the original Output o1 to preserve the context. Currently, Fujaba is being equipped with a new template-based code generator [11] that allows developers to generate code for various target languages and interfaces. While the core developers are creating the templates for the proprietary Fujaba interface, we are busy with completing alternative templates to generate JMI-compliant code for transformations that works directly with the Java representation generated by the MOFLON code generator for the schema part. As a result, the code generated by MOFLON includes executable transformations that can be executed manually or triggered as repair actions of violated constraints.

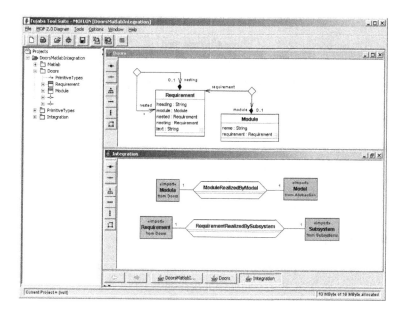

Fig. 7. Schema for the specification of TGG rules

Considering the outlined example, the surveillance of design guidelines can already be realized until this point.

4.4   Specifying Model Integration

Finally, the model of the Automobile Comfort System should be kept consistent with the requirements document and vice versa[4]. To this end the developer must identify which model elements in Matlab/Simulink correspond to which requirements in DOORS. Since the correspondences should be used for traceability purposes as well as for consistency checking, consistency recovery, and change propagations it is preferable to have a declarative model integration approach. Using a declarative approach means that the developer has to specify only a single rule from which all needed operational rules for the desired integration tasks can be derived automatically. As we are using SDM which is based on graph transformations in Section 4.3 on the one hand and we want to provide a declarative approach on the other hand it is reasonable to rely on *triple graph grammars* [12] for that purpose. For a more detailed discussion on this decision the reader is referred to [13].

Triple Graph Grammars are based on a schema as common graph grammars do [14]. In our approach the schema is a metamodel that declares types for correspondences and links classes from the corresponding tools' metamodels. Fig. 7 shows the schema specified with MOFLON we use in our toy example. The schema declares a correspondence type `ModuleRealizedByModel`.

---

[4] For a more realistic integration scenario the reader is referred to [12].

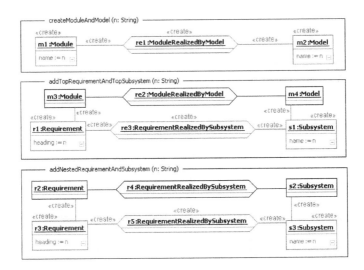

Fig. 8. Example of a declarative TGG rule

This type expresses that each `Module` from DOORS corresponds to one `Model` from Matlab/Simulink and vice versa. Accordingly, the schema declares a type `RequirementRealizedBySubsystem`. Besides the schema a Triple Graph Grammar provides a set of declarative rules. Generally speaking, the rules describe the simultaneous evolution of the tools' models and the correspondence model. Rule 8 at the top states that a DOORS `Module` m1 is created simultaneously with a Matlab/Simulink `Model` m2 which correspond to each other. The `name` attributes of m1 and m2 respectively are set to the value of the rule's parameter n. Rule 8 in the middle describes the simultaneous addition of a `Requirement` r1 to a `Module` m3 and a `Subsystem` s1 to a `Model` m4 that corresponds to m3. Again, the rule sets the `heading` of r1 as well as the `name` of s1 to the value of the parameter n. Accordingly, rule 8 at the bottom specifies the simultaneous addition of a (Sub-)`Requirement` r3 to a `Requirement` r2 and a `Subsystem` s3 to a `Subsystem` s2 that corresponds to r2. From these declarative rules we can automatically derive a number of operational graph rewriting rules. Fig. 9 gives an example of such an rule. This rule is used to transform the given `Requirement` r into a corresponding `Subsystem` s5. s5 will be added to a `Subsystem` s4 which corresponds to a `Requirement` r4 that contains r. The value of the `name` attribute of s5 will be set to the `name` of r. Furthermore, a correspondence link between r and s5 will be created. For additional operational rules that can be derived from each declarative integration rule automatically the reader is referred to [12].

4.5   Applying the Generated Code

As we have shown above, MOFLON generates Java code from all specifications. In particular, MOFLON generates JMI interfaces from the tools' metamodels. In order to access the tools' data in our running example the implementations of

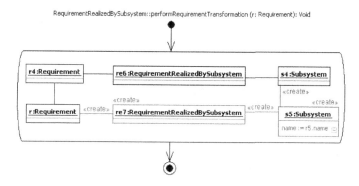

Fig. 9. Example of an operational integration rule

these interfaces have to realize adapters on the tools' APIs. These implementations can either be written manually or generated from templates. The Java code generated from the constraints, model transformations, and model integration operations complies to the JMI interfaces, and can, therefore, be mapped onto tool operations by the adapters. Thereby, using MOFLON we are able to realize the needed tool support for model-driven development related tasks which a developer is confronted with. Note that our case studies does not force us to deal with concrete syntax. Nevertheless, the integration of metamodels generated with MOFLON into graphical editor frameworks is possible as well.

5   MOFLON Architecture

In this section, we provide an overview of the internal MOFLON architecture. When we started to design MOFLON in 2003, our goal was to reuse existing technology where possible and focus on conceptual improvements. Back then, there were no MOF 2.0-editors and code generators available, but there were several graph transformation tools. After comparing different approaches, we decided to realize MOFLON on top of the Fujaba Toolsuite which already featured graph transformations for UML-like graph schemata.

Fig. 10 provides an overview of MOFLON and Fujaba parts working together. Note that the large MOFLON block is divided into three layers: On top are various editor components to manipulate data. In the center, repositories symbolize metamodels, constraints and transformation rules. The bottom layer consists of several code generators working together in MOFLON. Domain-specific metamodels and tool representations can be created either using a commercial *CASE tool* such as Rational Rose or directly using the new *MOF 2.0 Editor* plugin for Fujaba. Metamodels from external tools are exported as XMI and imported by MOFLON using an *XMI interchange* plugin. As most commercial tools do not yet support MOF 2.0, new features must be entered using certain conventions with respect to stereotypes or comments. We would like to mention that we have been able to import the complete UML 2.0 Infrastructure + Superstructure as

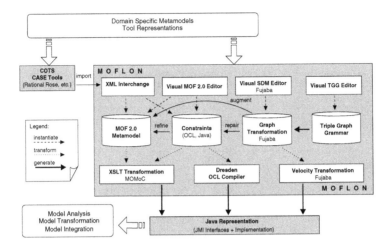

Fig. 10. MOFLON architecture overview

provided by the OMG[5], apart from some specification errors, which had to be fixed manually. The *metamodel* is kept in memory, as instance of a JMI-compliant Java representation of the MOF 2.0 metametamodel.

Graph transformation rules are edited using the *SDM editor* that already exists in Fujaba. These rules are also kept in memory and augment the MOF 2.0 metamodel instance conceptually, by providing visually specified implementations of methods defined in the schema. In our current implementation, we use the object adapter pattern ([15], p. 141) to map each MOF element to one or more Fujaba metamodel interfaces, which the SDM rules actually are built on. As most adapters are generated from XML descriptions, we could adopt the Fujaba graph rewriting engine with reasonable effort rather than writing our own.

The *TGG editor*, which actually consists of a schema and a rule editor has also been adopted from Fujaba. The *Triple Graph Grammar*, i.e. TGG schema and rules are also stored in memory. Upon user request, ordinary SDM rules are generated from these TGG rules using a MOFLON-specific translation.

The metamodel can be refined using *OCL constraints*. They are used to define invariants and derived attributes as well as pre- and postconditions and body constraints for methods implemented by graph transformations. Opposed to that, assertions are used to express application conditions in graph transformations. While constraints have been factored out in Fig. 10 to be discussed separately, they are actually stored as strings within the metamodel. Graph transformations are used to define *repair actions* for constraint violations. We also allow to directly enter Java code for constraint expressions as preliminary alternative for OCL constraints.

From the MOF metamodel, JMI-compliant Java code is generated by *XSLT transformation* with an descendant of the MOMoC code generator [2]. This gen-

---

[5] http://www.omg.org/cgi-bin/apps/doc?ptc/04-10-05.zip

erator also deals with constraints provided as Java code. We are currently working on the integration of the Dresden OCL compiler [8] to generate Java code for OCL 2.0 constraints. Java code for graph transformations is generated using Fujaba's latest *Velocity-based code generator* [11].

According to the JMI standard, the resulting Java representation features tailored and reflective interfaces, XMI import and export. Besides, the generated code features an event mechanism that makes our approach interface-compatible with MDR [6]. Depending on the requirement of the concrete task, we combine the generated code with suitable parsers, tool adapters and user interfaces to create a specific solution for model analysis, transformation, and integration.

6 Related Work

Like MOFLON, there are a number of approaches for metamodeling and model transformation, for an extensive overview, cf. [16]. In this section we focus on tools that are specifically interesting for our approach.

Some tools like GReAT [17], MoTMoT [18], and MDR [6] value OMG *standard-compliant schemata* like MOF and UML, while Microsoft Domain Specific Language Tools [19], GME [17], *MetaEdit+* [20], PROGRES [21], prefer proprietary metametalanguages. Fujaba [9] mixes standard and proprietary elements, EMF Transformation Engine / GMF [22,23] only implements EMOF, a small subset of the current standard, and tools like AToM³[24] use ER-Diagrams that could be considered "standard" some time ago.

Only MOFLON puts a strong emphasis on complete standard compliance with MOF 2.0 to benefit from its new features. Among these are strong *modularization and refinement* possibilities. Tools like [19,24] provide no schema modularization at all, others like [9,17,20,21] provide either hierarchies or view mechanism to structure data. MOFLON uses package imports, package merges, element imports, redefinition of association ends etc. with full effect on identifier visibility not only in schemata but also constraints and graph transformations.

Many tools [19,24,17,23,25,26], often meta-CASE tools, deal with the *concrete syntax* of modeling languages to create diagram editors. MOFLON is more about model analysis, transformation and integration and hence, does not support concrete syntax.

MOFLON provides *local model transformations* through graph transformations, which is also true for [21,9,17,24,18]. Other tools [22,27] only provide textual model transformations or none at all [19,6]. Like MOFLON, only some of these tools [21,9,17,18] use visual *rule application strategies* to compose large transformations. While Fujaba and hence MOFLON use a proprietary syntax embedding Story Patterns inside UML Activity Diagrams, MoTMoT is truely standard-compliant by providing an adequate UML profile, but at the cost of defining story patterns as class diagrams, which appears quite unnatural to us.

MOFLON and Tefkat[22] provide declarative model-to-model transformations that are QVT-like. Opposed to that, GReAT only provides the possibility to define operational model-to-model transformations.

7   Conclusion

MOFLON is an integrated, standard-compliant metamodeling environment that provides full support for the new MOF 2.0 modularization and refinement concepts. Due to JMI-compliance and the event mechanism, the model repository can either exist in main memory or in a NetBeans Metadata Repository [6]. Besides, MOFLON features constraint checking based on the Dresden OCL compiler [8]. A visual graph transformation language with control flow diagrams for rule-application strategies has been adopted from Fujaba [9] to perform local model transformations. For model-to-model-integration, we use a declarative QVT-like approach based on Triple Graph Grammars. Finally, MOFLON has a template-based code generator supporting XSLT and Velocity technology.

We are currently completing the first public MOFLON-release. In the near future, we will work on an incremental constraint checking algorithm adapted from PROGRES [28]. Finally, we plan to merge MOFLON with DiaGen II [25] to be able to generate support for both syntax-directed and free-hand diagram editing, constraint-based layout, and parsing of diagrams, thus making MOFLON also a meta-CASE tool.

References

1. Object Management Group: Meta Object Facility (MOF) Core Specification. (2006) formal/06-01-01.
2. Amelunxen, Bichler, Schürr: Codegenerierung für Assoziationen in MOF 2.0. In: Proc. Modellierung 2004, Marburg, Germany. (2004) 149–168 In German.
3. Rötschke, T.: Re-engineering a Medical Imaging System Using Graph Transformations. In: Applications of Graph Transformations with Industrial Relevance. Volume 3062 of LNCS., Springer (2003) 185–201
4. Altheide, F., et al.: An Architecture for a Sustainable Tool Integration. In Dörr, Schürr, eds.: TIS 2003 Workshop on Tool Integration in System Development. (2003) 29–32
5. Dirckze, R.: Java^{TM} Metadata Interface (JMI) Specification, Version 1.0. Unisys. (2002)
6. Matula, M.: NetBeans Metadata Repository. SUN Microsystems. (2003)
7. Object Management Group: OCL 2.0 Specification. (2005) ptc/2005-06-06.
8. Löcher, S., Ocke, S.: A Metamodel-Based OCL-Compiler for UML and MOF. In Schmitt, P., ed.: Workshop Proc. OCL 2.0 - Industry standard or scientific playground? Volume 102 of Electronic Notes in Theoretical Computer Science., Elsevier (2004) 43–61
9. Zündorf, A.: Rigorous Object Oriented Software Development. University of Paderborn (2001) Habilitation Thesis.
10. Amelunxen, C., Rötschke, T., Schürr, A.: Graph Transformations with MOF 2.0. In Giese, H., Zündorf, A., eds.: Proc. 3rd International Fujaba Days 2005. Volume tr-ri-05-259., Universität Paderborn (2005) 25–31
11. Geiger, L., Schneider, C., Reckord, C.: Template- and Modelbased Code Generation for MDA-Tools. In: 3rd International Fujaba Days 2005, Paderborn, Germany (2005)

12. Königs, A., Schürr, A.: Tool Integration with Triple Graph Grammars - A Survey. In Heckel, R., ed.: Proc. SegraVis School on Foundations of Visual Modelling Techniques. Volume 148 of Electronic Notes in Theoretical Computer Science., Amsterdam, Elsevier Science Publ. (2006) 113–150

13. Amelunxen, C., Königs, A., Rötschke, T., Schürr, A.: MOSL: Composing a Visual Language for a Metamodeling Framework. Submitted to IEEE Symposium on Visual Languages and Human-Centric Computing 2006 (2006)

14. Nagl, M.: Graph-Grammatiken. Vieweg Press (1979) German.

15. Gamma, E., Helm, R., Johnson, R., Vlissides, J.: Design Patterns: Elements of Reusable Object-Oriented Software. Addison-Wesley (1995)

16. Czarnecki, Helsen: Classification Of Model Transformation Approaches. In: 2nd OOPSLA Workshop on Generative Techniques in the context of Model Driven Architecture. (2003) http://www.softmetaware.com/oopsla2003/czarnecki.pdf.

17. Agrawal, A., Levendovszky, T., Sprinkle, J., Shi, F., Karsai, G.: Generative Programming via Graph Transformations in the Model Driven Architecture. In: Proc. Workshop on Generative Techniques in the Context of Model Driven Architecture. (2002)

18. Schippers, H., Van Gorp, P., Janssens, D.: Levering UML Profiles to Generate Plugins from Visual Model Transformations. In: Proc. Software Evolution through Transformations. (2004) 7–17

19. Microsoft Corporation: Visual Studio 2005: Domain-Specific Language Tools. http://msdn.microsoft.com/vstudio/DSLTools/ (2006)

20. MetaCase: MetaEdit+®metaCASE tool. http://www.metacase.com (2006)

21. Schürr, A., Winter, A., Zündorf, A. In: PROGRES: Language and Environment. Volume 2. World Scientific (1999) 487–550

22. Lawley, M., Steel, J.: Practical Declarative Model Transformation With Tefkat. In Bézivin, J., Rumpe, B., Schürr, A., Tratt, L., eds.: Proc. Workshop on Model Transformations in Practice. (2005) http://sosym.dcs.kcl.ac.uk/events/mtip05/.

23. The Eclipse Foundation: Eclipse Graphical Modeling Framework. http://www.eclipse.org/gmf/ (2006)

24. De Lara Jaramillo, J., Vangheluwe, H., Moreno, M.A.: Meta-modelling and Graph Grammars for Multi-Paradigm Modelling in AToM^3. Software & Systems Modeling **3**(3) (2004) 194–209

25. Minas, M.: Concepts and Realization of a Diagram Editor Generator-based on Hypergraph Transformation. Science of Computer Programming **44** (2002) 157–180

26. Böhlen, B., Jäger, D., Schleicher, A., Westfechtel, B.: UPGRADE: A Framework for Building Graph-Based Interactive Tools. In Mens, T., Schürr, A., Taentzer, G., eds.: Proc. International Workshop on Graph-Based Tools. Volume 72(2) of Electronic Notes in Theoretical Computer Science. (2002)

27. Jouault, F., Kurtev, I.: Transforming Models with ATL. In: Proc. Workshop on Model Transformations in Practice. (2005)

28. Münch, M.: Generic Modelling with Graph Rewriting Systems. PhD thesis, RWTH Aachen (2002)

Mutation Analysis Testing for Model Transformations

Jean-Marie Mottu[1], Benoit Baudry[1], and Yves Le Traon[2]

[1] IRISA, Campus Universitaire de Beaulieu, 35042 Rennes Cedex, France
{jean-marie.mottu, bbaudry}@irisa.fr
[2] France Télécom R&D, 2 av. Pierre Marzin 22307 Lannion Cedex, France
yves.letraon@francetelecom.com

Abstract. In MDE, model transformations should be efficiently tested so that it may be used and reused safely. Mutation analysis is an efficient technique to evaluate the quality of test data, and has been extensively studied both for procedural and object-oriented languages. In this paper, we study how it can be adapted to model oriented programming. Since no model transformation language has been widely accepted today, we propose generic fault models that are related to the model transformation process. First, we identify abstract operations that constitute this process: model navigation, model's elements filtering, output model creation and input model modification. Then, we propose a set of specific mutation operators which are directly inspired from these operations. We believe that these operators are meaningful since a large part of the errors in a transformation are due to the manipulation of complex models regardless of the concrete implementation language.

1 Introduction

Validation refers to a process that aims at increasing our confidence that software meets its requirements. It usually relies on a combination of reasoning and testing, and encompasses unit, integration, and acceptance testing. Testing is thus a key aspect of software development, because of its cost and impact on final product reliability.

In the case of model-driven development, classical views on testing and their associated testing models are not well-suited to the significant changes this software paradigm has induced to the development process. The standardization of a model transformation language (QVT) reveals the need of a systematic way for specifying and implementing the model transformations. However, as for any other program, faults may occur in a model transformation program which must be detected through testing. Programming a model transformation is a very specific task which implies operations a classical programmer does not usually manipulate, such as navigating the input/output metamodels or filtering model elements in collections. If a skilled programmer of a model transformation can still introduce classical faults in the program, specific faults appear. These specific faults are more at a semantic level than classical programming faults. For instance, the programmer may have navigated a wrong association from class A to class B, thus manipulating class incorrect instances of the expected type. He may also be wrong in the criteria used to select some class instances (e.g. selecting all classes while he should have selected only persistent ones). Such faults are related to new fault categories we introduce in this paper.

A. Rensink and J. Warmer (Eds.): ECMDA-FA 2006, LNCS 4066, pp. 376–390, 2006.

A fundamental step in the elaboration of a test environment for a given software programming paradigm consists of defining criteria to estimate the quality of a test dataset. Structural coverage criteria are a classical way to have such an estimate. However, they are not directly related to the capacity of a test dataset to reveal faults (e.g. a faulty statement can be executed and covered several times without provoking the error).

In this paper, we focus on mutation analysis as a convincing way to check the efficiency of a test dataset for detecting faults in the program under test. Mutation analysis consists of systematically creating faulty versions of a program (called mutants) and of checking the efficiency of a test dataset to reveal the faults in these erroneous programs. The main interest of mutation analysis is to provide an estimate of the quality of a test dataset with the proportion of faulty programs it detects. Instead of structural test adequacy criteria, this estimate really reflects the "fault revealing power" [1] of the test dataset. To be effective, the mutation analysis must create mutant programs which correspond to realistic faults. In this paper, we first study the limitations of classical mutation operators for seeding model transformation programs. Then, we analyze the main activities involved in a model transformation, independently of a specific model transformation language. This analysis of model transformation leads to its decomposition in four main activities, which are fault-prone. Mutation operators are then proposed at this generic level of decomposition, which correspond to faults a programmer may (realistically) introduce into his code. The contribution of this paper is thus two-fold:

- a study of the specific faults a programmer may do in a model transformation,
- a definition of specific mutation operators for applying mutation analysis to model transformations and asses the quality of a test dataset.

The paper is structured as follows. Section 2 recalls the general process of mutation analysis. Section 3 explains the limitations of classical fault categories (classical mutation operators); studies the fault-prone activities involved in model transformations and introduce the notion of semantic mutation operators. Section 4 details the mutation operators dedicated to model transformations while Section 5 illustrates the application of two operators on several implementations of a same model transformation.

2 Mutation Testing

Mutation analysis is a testing technique that was first designed to evaluate a test dataset. It also allows to improve their effectiveness and fault revealing power [1, 2]. It has been originally proposed in 1978 [3], and consists in creating a set of faulty versions or *mutants* of a program with the ultimate goal of designing a test set that distinguishes the program from all its mutants. A mutant is the program modified by the injection of a single fault. In practice, faults are modelled as a set of *mutation operators* where each operator represents a class of software faults. To create a mutant, it is sufficient to apply its associated mutation operator to the original program.

A test set is relatively adequate if it distinguishes the original program from all its non-equivalent mutants. Otherwise, a *mutation score* is associated with the test set to measure its effectiveness in terms of percentage of the revealed non-equivalent mutants.

It is to be noted that a mutant is considered *equivalent* to the original program if it does not exist any input data on which the mutant and the original program produce a different output. A benefit of the mutation score is that even if no error is found, it still measures how well the software has been tested giving the user information about the program test quality. It can be viewed as a kind of reliability assessment for the tested software. The value of the mutation analysis is based on one assumption: if the test dataset can detect that all the mutants contain fault, then this set is able to detect real involuntary errors.

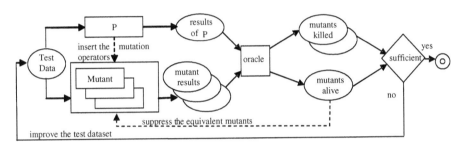

Fig. 1. Mutation process

The process of mutation analysis is presented in Figure 1 with the execution of each test datum against all the mutants of the program. An oracle function is used to determine if the failure is detected. This function compares each mutant's result with the result of the program P; the latter being considered as correct. If the results differ, it means that the test data exhibit the fault; the test data kill the mutant. During the test selection process, a mutant program is said to be *killed* if at least one test data detects the fault injected into the mutant. Conversely, a mutant is said to be *alive* if no test data detects the injected fault. If a mutant is alive, there are two possibilities:

- the mutant is equivalent,
- actual test data are not able to highlight this fault: the mutant is still alive and the test dataset must be involved. New test data may be generated or existing ones can be modified.

The equivalent mutants are suppressed from the set of mutants and a list of killed mutants is obtained. The mutation score for the test dataset is computed, which is the proportion of killed mutants compared to the total number of non-equivalent mutants; this score quantifies the quality of the test dataset.

$$MutationScore = \frac{\#KilledMutants}{\#Mutants-\#EquivalentMutants}$$

If the score is insufficient, we have to improve the test set, which could be done with new test data or actual data involving.

The relevance of mutation analysis is based on the mutants' relevance, which itself strongly depends on the mutation operators relevance. Classical mutation testing is related to a set of faults specified by mutation operators which define syntactic patterns which are identified in the program in order to inject a fault. Classical mutation operators include relational and arithmetic operator replacement (for example replacing a '+' with a '-'), variable and method calls replacements, statement deletion. Some operators dedicated to OO programs, and especially to Java, have been introduced by Ma et al. in [4], (method redefinition, inherited attributes etc.). These faults are related to the notions of classes, generalization, and polymorphism. These operators take into consideration specificities related to the semantics of OO languages, but remain simple faults which can be introduced by a syntactic analysis of the program. To execute mutation testing with these operators, the faults are inserted systematically everywhere the pattern is found in the code.

In the next part 3, we explain why we don't want to transpose this classical mutation process to the model oriented development.

3   Adapting Mutation Analysis to Model Driven Development

This section studies the application of mutation to model transformation programs, and shows that the classical mutation operators are not suitable for these specific programs. Faults at this level are related to the main activities involved in a model transformation.

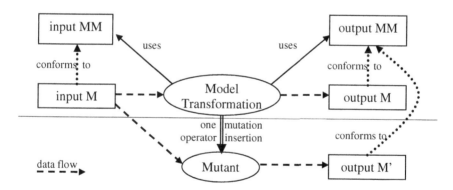

Fig. 2. Model transformation process and a model transformation mutant creation

3.1   Mutation Analysis in a Model Development Context

Before proposing fault models specific to the model transformations, we need to analyze the activities involved in development which may be fault-prone. The Figure 2 illustrates the general model transformation process. An input model is transformed and an output model is returned. Each one has its own metamodel, the transformation uses these metamodels to know which action it can process on the input and the output models. The mutants produced by the mutation operator insertions has to preserve this conformity with the metamodels, they must be able to process the input models and must not create output models that do not conform to output metamodels. Thus mutation operators must be directly connected to the metamodel notion.

3.2 Limitations of Classical Mutation Operators

All the classical and OO operators can be applied to model transformations programs, but their relevance to this very particular context is limited due to the following reasons:

- *Mutant significance*: seeded faults are far from the specific faults a transformation programmer may do if he is competent. Indeed, the transformation programmer will make an incorrect model transformation, which seems correct from his point of view, and not only a classical programming fault. He may forget some particular cases (e.g. forget to deal with the case of multiple inheritances in an input model), manipulate the wrong model elements etc. An incorrect model transformation will differ from the correct one by complicated modification in the transformation program, and not necessarily by a single faulty statement, as in classical approaches to mutation. A semantic fault, defined to represent fault in the transformation, produces viable mutants, which are not detected simply at compilation, execution or during the rest of the programming.
- *Mutant viability*: a simple fault has a high probability to generate a non viable mutant program (that does not compile or run correctly). Since a transformation program navigates both the input and the output metamodels, most simple faults will disturb this navigation in a non-consistent way (e.g. trying to navigate non-existing association due to a syntactic replacement). Thus, these faults will be detected either during programming, at compilation or at runtime. This approach generates many mutants which are not viable candidates for mutation analysis.
- *Implementation language independency*: The semantic operators have to reflect the type of fault which may appear during the implementation of a transformation. The first constraint to define these operators is that they can not take advantage of a transformation language's syntax. Indeed, today there are lots of model transformation languages which all have their specificities and which are very heterogeneous (object oriented, declarative, functional, mixed). To be independent from a given implementation language is an important issue. That leads us to choose to focus on the semantic part of the transformation instead of the syntactic one imposed by a language, that's studied next part (3.3).

Classical mutation operators (object oriented or not) are still useful, to check code or predicate coverage, for example. However they depend on the language which is used in the implementation, thus they have to be completed by injecting faults which make sense, in terms of erroneous model transformations. These new operators that we propose in the section 4 try to capture specific faults that take into account the semantics of a particular type of program: model transformations. Such mutation operators are called semantic operators.

3.3 Semantic Faults for Model Transformations Activities

The operators introduced have to be defined based on an abstract view of the transformation program, by answering the question: which type of fault could be done during a model transformation implementation? For example, if a transformation traverses the input model to find the elements to be transformed then a fault can consist of the navigation of the wrong association in the metamodel, or of selecting the incorrect elements in a collection. During a transformation, output model elements have to be created; a fault can consist of creating elements with the wrong type or wrong initialization. The analysis of these possible faults for a model transformation leads to distinguish 4 abstract operations linked to the main treatments composing a model transformation:

- **navigation:** the model is navigated thanks to the relations defined on its input/output metamodels, and a set of elements is obtained.

- **filtering:** after a navigation, a set of elements is available, but a treatment may be applied only on a subset of this set. The selection of this subset is done according to a filtering property.

- **output model creation:** output model elements are created from extracted element(s).

- **input model modification:** when the output model is a modification of the input model, elements are created, deleted or modified.

These operations define a very abstract specification of transformations, which highlights the fault-prone steps of programming a model transformation. However, we believe they explore the most frequent important model manipulations for transformations. Operators defined at this level will have to be wrapped to real languages.

Any model transformation combines and mixes these 4 operations of navigation/filtering (read mode) and output/input model modification (write mode). Let us consider the transformation UML to RDBMS to illustrate this decomposition (see Fig. 3). In the class diagram of the input model, the persistent classes are selected and correspondent tables are created with columns corresponding to the attributes. First the input model (a) is navigated to find the classes (b) which are filtered to keep the persistent ones (c). A table is created for each one (d). Then the navigation covers the persistent classes to find their attributes (e) (inherited attributes too) and corresponding columns are created (f). Finally columns are filtered (g) to find an appropriate key which is created (h).

Navigation, filtering, creation, modification are fault-prone operations which are sequentially dependent: while the navigation returns elements, these elements are often filtered before being used for model creation (or modification). We obtain a basic cycle which is repeated to compose a complete model transformation. The decomposition of a model transformation into such basic cycles provides an abstract view useful to inject faults. So, we define mutation operators which are applied on these basic cycles, by injecting faulty navigation/filtering/creation/modification operations.

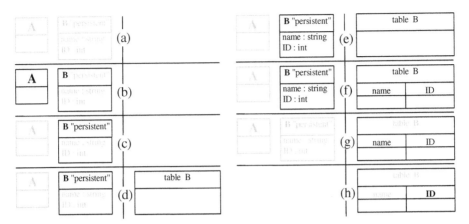

Fig. 3. Process of the transformation studied

4 Mutation Operators Dedicated to Model Transformations

Based on the analysis of the fault-prone operations which constitute a model transformation, we propose several new mutation operators. They act on the navigation and the filtering processed by the transformation on input or output models and the creation of the output model.

We present our operators starting with there names and abbreviations. Then we give a concise explanation of their functionality. The UML to RDBMS transformation and the Figure 4 (which represents a simple metamodel) will help us to illustrate our operators in a third time. Finally, we explain when these operators are the most pertinent.

4.1 Mutation Operators Related to the *Navigation*

Relation to the same class change (RSCC): This operator replaces the navigation of one association towards a class with the navigation of another association to the same class (when the metamodel allows it).

Example: the class A has three relations b1, b2, and b3 to the class B: if the original transformation navigates A.b1 then the operator replaces b1 with b2 and b3, making two mutants.

Different cases could occur when a wrong relation is navigated towards the same class, depending on the cardinality. To replace A.b1 with A.b2 leads to a cardinality difference. The results are respectively a variable and a collection, so the compilation will fail. On another hand, replacing b2 with b3 leads to a relevant fault (complex to detect): both returning a collection of instances of B. Thus the rest of the transformation being not affected, the fault is harder to detect.

Relation to another class change (ROCC): This operator replaces the navigation of an association towards a class with the navigation of another association to another class.

Example: the class A has several outgoing relations: b1, b2, b3 (to B) and c (to C), if the transformation navigates A.b1 then the operator creates one mutant, replacing b1 with c.

This operator is really relevant when the expected class and the unwanted one have same properties used in the rest of the transformation (same attribute, method or outgoing relation). Due to inheritance, this case is very common because it directly makes direct use of the generalization process. If the wrong navigation leads to a class which has a common parent with the wanted class, the parent's attributes, methods and relations are inherited by both classes. As a consequence the rest of the transformation should not be affected by this fault. In our example, the classes B and C have a common parent E, so they inherited of the same attribute name.

Relation sequence modification with deletion (RSMD): During the navigation, the transformation can navigate many relations successively. This operator removes the last step off from the composed navigation.

Example: from an instance of A, we can obtain a collection of instances of F with the composed navigation A.b1.f. In the generated mutant, the navigation becomes A.b1 and the result is not a collection of instances of F but of instances of B.

This operator leads to the same cases than the ROCC operator, which justifies its relevance.

Relation sequence modification with addition (RSMA): This operator does the opposite of RSMD. The number of mutants created depends on the number of outgoing relations of the class obtained with the original transformation.

Example: a relation is added: A.c becomes A.c.d for example. Only one mutant is created because the class C has a single outgoing relation.

This operator leads to the same cases than the ROCC operator, which justifies its relevance.

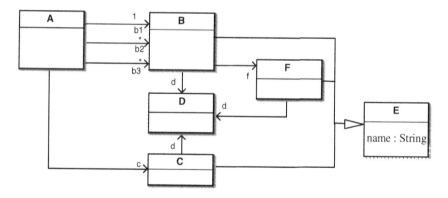

Fig. 4. Metamodel example

Mutation operators related to the *filtering*

Filtering manipulates collections to select only the elements useful for the transformation. In a general way, a filter may be considered as a guard on a collection, depending on specific criteria. Two types of filtering are considered. First, instances of a given class may be selected in function of their properties (attributes...). That's the property filtering. The second one can select some instances among a collection of instances of generic classes. That's the type filtering.

Collection filtering change with perturbation (CFCP): This operator aims at modifying an existing filtering, by influencing its parameters. One criterion could be a property of a class or the type of a class; this operator will disturb this criterion.

Example: in our transformation UML to RDBMS, this operator generates a mutant which filters depending on a wrong stereotype instead of the "persistent" one. Filtering depending on the type of the classes could also be disturbed in the Figure 4 example. The transformation could act on a collection of the generic class E. The instances in this collection are of type E, B, C or F (the classes of its children). If a filtering on this collection selects only the instances of B, this operator creates three mutants: one selects the instances of C, another the instances of E and the last the instances of F.

Two kinds of filtering are considered. In the simplest case, the filtering acts on a collection of instances of the same class, and depends on one of its properties. Then it is viable because the rest of the transformation won't be influenced. Indeed, the expected erroneous collections just have a different size. Secondly, we can consider the filtering depending on the type. To filter a collection of a generic class depending on this class or any of the classes of its children makes no difference. All these classes share the same inherited properties (attributes, methods, relations), so the fault injected by this operator will not be discovered.

Collection filtering change with deletion (CFCD): This operator deletes a filter on a collection; the mutant returns the collection it was supposed to filter.

Example: in the UML to RDBMS example, only persistent classes are used. The navigation provides all the classes and the filtering selects the persistent ones to create correspondent tables. The operator suppresses the filtering and the transformations will create tables for all classes, even the ones that are not persistent. It could be a filtering depending on the class types: the filtering of a collection of classes of type E and its specialization classes could be useful to select only the A instances. The mutant will kept all the instances without type consideration.

This operator leads to the same cases than the CFCP operator, which justifies its relevance.

Collection filtering change with addition (CFCA): This operator does the opposite of CFCD. It uses a collection and processes a useless filtering on it. This operator could return an infinite number of mutants, we have to restrict it. We choose to take a collection and to return a single element arbitrarily chosen.

Example: we do not need to illustrate this one because of its clearness.

This operator leads to the same cases than the CFCP operator, which justifies its relevance.

Mutation operators related to the *creation*

These operators are based on two abstract operations: the creation of the output model elements and the creation part of the modification operation.

Class' compatible creation replacement (CCCR): This operator replaces the creation of an object by the creation of an object of a compatible type. It could be an instance of a child class, of a parent class or of a class with a common parent.

Example: if the transformation creates an instance of B (one child of E), then the operator creates three mutants: one creating an instance of C, one an instance of F, the last an instance of E.

This operator is really interesting because the wrong created class and the right one have common inherited properties (relations, methods and attributes), then the rest of the transformation could be not affected and the fault is not detected.

Classes' association creation deletion (CACD): This operator deletes the creation of an association between two instances.

Example: when the transformation creates the relation b1 between an instance of A and an instance of B, the corresponding mutant does not create this relation.

If the relation not created has the cardinality 1 in the metamodel (or a bigger one fixed) then its absence can affect the rest of the transformation. But if the cardinality is n, then the transformation will not much be affected. The model can have an instance of A connected towards several instances of B with relations b1. If one relation is not created, the navigation A.b1 will just return a collection deprived of one element, without detectable consequence.

Classes' association creation addition (CACA): This operator adds a useless creation of a relation between two class instances of the output model, when the metamodel allows it.

In our example, the metamodel (Figure 4) allows three different relations between A and B. Then if the transformation manipulates instances of A and B then the operator generates three mutants, each one creating one of the relations b1, b2, b3 between A and B, even if one of them already exists (then overwritten relation could point to a different instance that the original one).

The errors injected by this operator are not easily detectable: collections will just have one item added and relations of cardinality 1 will just be created or overwritten.

These faults are directly linked to the way we design model transformations which are divided following the four abstract operations (navigation, filtering, creation, modification). These operators aim to generate viable mutants with pertinent faults to improve the value of the mutation analysis. This allows improving test dataset capacity to detect the faults of the programmer.

5 Examples

In this section, we present how two of our mutation operators are implemented in different languages. This reveals that the distance between the specification of a semantic mutation operator and its implementation varies with the model transformation language. This also emphasizes the need to present a semantic vision of the mutation analysis in model oriented programming instead of a syntactic one directly associated to specific languages.

We use samples of a model transformation written for the workshop MTIP (part of the MoDELS 2005 Conference). We selected three different languages to illustrate the different implementations of two mutation operators (CFCP and CFCD). The model transformation studied is quite similar to the UML to RDBMS transformation used in this paper: we study the filtering operation which selects the persistent classes to create correspondent tables.

The mutation operator CFCP will perturb the filter. In this example, the mutation operator takes the negation of the filtering condition: the non persistent classes are selected. More complex perturbations may be implemented (e.g. replacing is_ persistent with any other Boolean attribute of the class). The mutation operator CFCD will delete the filtering, tables are created for all the classes. Due to the fact the example is very simple, the seeded faults would be easily detected with a simple oracle function.

5.1 Operator Implementation with an Imperative Model Transformation Written in *Kermeta*

The transformation written in *Kermeta* is published in [5]. The excerpt is:

```
getAllClasses(inputModel)
    .select{c|c.is_persistent}
    .each { c | var table:Table init Table.new
                Table.name:=c.name
                Class2table.storeTrace(c,table)
                Result.table.add(table)
          }
```

In this example, the filtering (on the collection elts) is just a conditional expression, line 2. If we apply the CFCP operator, a mutant is generated with the code:

```
getAllClasses(inputModel)
    .select{c|not c.is_persistent}
    .each { c | var table:Table init Table.new
                Table.name:=c.name
                Class2table.storeTrace(c,table)
                Result.table.add(table)
          }
```

If we apply the CFCD operator, a mutant is generated with the code:

```
getAllClasses(inputModel)
    .each { c | var table:Table init Table.new
                Table.name:=c.name
                Class2table.storeTrace(c,table)
                Result.table.add(table)
          }
```

In *Kermeta*, filtering a collection is really simple because the operation `select` has this role. So mutation operators related to the filtering are quite simple to implement.

5.2 Operator Implementation with a Declarative Model Transformation Written in *Tefkat*

The transformation written in *Tefkat* is published in [6]. The sample is:

```
RULE ClassAndTable(C, T)
  FORALL Class C {
    is_persistent: true;
```

```
      name: N;
    }
    MAKE Table T {
      name: N;
    }
    LINKING ClsToTbl WITH class = C, table = T
  ;
```

In this example the filtering (on the collection elts) is just a conditional expression, line 3. If we apply the CFCP operator, a mutant is generated with the code:

```
RULE ClassAndTable(C, T)
    FORALL Class C {
      is_persistent: false;
      name: N;
    }
    MAKE Table T {
      name: N;
    }
    LINKING ClsToTbl WITH class = C, table = T
  ;
```

If we apply the CFCD operator, a mutant is generated with the code:

```
RULE ClassAndTable(C, T)
    FORALL Class C {
      name: N;
    }
    MAKE Table T {
      name: N;
    }
    LINKING ClsToTbl WITH class = C, table = T
  ;
```

With this declarative language, code modifications are also relatively simple. The rules are written close to the transformation design. Mutation operator implementation does not affect many statements of code.

5.3 Operator Implementation with a Language Not Devoted to the MDE, *Java*

We wrote the entire transformation using *Eclipse Modeling Framework* (EMF). The sample we are interested in is:

```
Vector cls = getClasses(modelUse);
Iterator itCls = cls.iterator();
while (itCls.hasNext()){
  Class c = (Class)(itCls.next());
  if (not c.is_persistent){
      cls.remove(c);
  }
}
createTables(cls);
```

In this example the filtering (on the collection `cls`) is implemented from line 2 to 9.

If we apply the CFCP operator, a mutant is generated with the code:

```
Vector cls = getClasses(modelUse);
Iterator itCls = cls.iterator();
while (itCls.hasNext()){
  Class c = (Class)(itCls.next());
  if (c.is_persistent){
      cls.remove(c);
  }
}
createTables(cls);
```

If we apply the CFCD operator, a mutant is generated with the code:

```
Vector cls = getClasses(modelUse);
createTables(cls);
```

If the CFCP operator modifies only one statement, the CFCD one affects a larger part of the program. In Java, the distance between the specification of the mutation operator and their implementation can be higher.

5.4 Implementing Semantic Mutation Operators

The feasibility of the implementation depends on the operators and the language. To have a comparison basis with existing mutation tools (*MuJava* [4]), we applied manually the operators on the *Java* implementation and we get the following results:

	RSCC	ROCC	RSMD	RSMA	CFCD	CFCP	CFCA	CACD	CACA	CCCR	Total
#mutants	5	13	2	7	2	6	7	3	1	0	46
implementation difficulty	A	A	A	A	A	B	B	A	C	B	

The first line presents the number of generated mutants for each operator (46 mutants were generated), and the second line gives a qualitative estimate of the difficulty for seeding the program per operator. An "A" means that the operator is easy to implement, a "B" that it is difficult and a "C" that it forces a very careful analysis of the code. Depending on the target language, this difficulty may be different, but we believe that it still corresponds to the difficulty to automate the fault injection with a dedicated tool.

With *MuJava*, 96 mutants were generated and 19 were not viable (detected at compile or runtime). With the specific mutants, 2 were not viable among the 46. Combining classical and dedicated mutants would allow a more complete verification of the quality of a test dataset. Classical mutant operators capture simple programming faults which still exists in any programming language, but the semantic operators go further and improve the level of confidence in the dataset by capturing fault related to the MDD.

6   Related Work

Several works consider model transformations as an essential feature in model driven development (MDD) [7, 8]. However, there are few works concerned with the validation of these particular programs.

As stated earlier, the validation of model transformations has not been studied much yet. In [9], the authors present the testing issues they have encountered when developing a model transformation engine, and what solutions they have adopted. They note the similarity between this task and that of testing transformations themselves, and address a number of mainly technical issues associated with using models as test data. In [10], Lin et al., identify all the core challenges for model transformation testing, and propose a framework that relates the different activities. The authors focus more particularly on the problem of model comparison which is necessary for the comparison of models produced by the original program and the mutants. They give a first algorithm inspired by graph matching algorithms. In [11], Küster considers rule-based transformations and addresses the problem of the validation of the rules that define the model transformation, i.e. syntactic correctness and termination of the set of rules. In [12], we looked at the problem of test data generation for model transformation and proposed to adapt partition testing to define test criteria to cover the input metamodel (that describes the input domain for a transformation).

Mutation analysis has often been studied in classical and object oriented programs, like *Java* [2, 4]. In [13], authors studied how to apply mutation to components' interfaces. They do not base their analysis at the code implementation level of a component, but at its interface level. In [14], mutation analysis is studied in a UML context. The idea is to propose a taxonomy of faults when designing UML class diagrams. The work presented in this paper focuses on the specific faults related to model transformations and not on the way models may be faulty.

7   Conclusion and Future Work

The approach presented in this paper aims at adapting mutation analysis for building trust into model transformation programs using this technique. By measuring the quality of a test dataset with mutation, we seek to build trust in a model transformation passing those tests. To adapt mutation analysis, we first studied the main activities involved in a model transformation and deduced some categories of faults a programmer may do. Mutation operators have been proposed for the specific paradigm of model transformation and illustrated on several implementations of the same model transformation.

Further work will consist in addressing the issue of the operators implementation in a tool (for a well-chosen model transformation language) and in conducing experi-mental studies for validating the relevance of mutation operators to the MDD context.

References

1. Voas, J.M. and K. Miller, *The Revealing Power of a Test Case*. Software Testing, Verification and Reliability, 1992. **2**(1): p. 25 - 42.
2. Offutt, A.J., J. Pan, K. Tewary, and T. Zhang, *An experimental evaluation of data flow and mutation testing*. Software Practice and Experience, 1996. **26**(2).
3. DeMillo, R., R. Lipton, and F. Sayward, *Hints on Test Data Selection : Help For The Practicing Programmer*. IEEE Computer, 1978. **11**(4): p. 34 - 41.
4. Ma, Y.-S., J. Offutt, and Y.R. Kwon, *MuJava : An Automated Class Mutation System*. Software Testing, Verification and Reliability, 2005. **15**(2): p. 97-133.
5. Muller, P.-A., F. Fleurey, D. Vojtisek, Z. Drey, D. Pollet, F. Fondement, P. Studer, and J.-M. Jézéquel. *On Executable Meta-Languages applied to Model Transformations*. in *Model Transformation in Practice Workshop, part of the MoDELS 2005 Conference*. 2005. Montego Bay, Jamaica.
6. Lawley, M. and J. Steel. *Practical Declarative Model Transformation With Tefkat*. in *Model Transformation in Practice Workshop, part of the MoDELS 2005 Conference*. 2005. Montego Bay, Jamaica.
7. Bézivin, J., N. Farcet, J.-M. Jézéquel, B. Langlois, and D. Pollet. *Reflective model driven engineering*. in *UML'03*. 2003. San Francisco, CA, USA.
8. Judson, S.R., R. France, and D.L. Carver. *Model Transformations at the Metamodel Level*. in *Workshop in Software Model Engineering (in conjunction with UML'03)*. 2003. San Francisco, CA, USA.
9. Steel, J. and M. Lawley. *Model-Based Test Driven Development of the Tefkat Model-Transformation Engine*. in *ISSRE'04 (Int. Symposium on Software Reliability Engineering)*. 2004. Saint-Malo, France.
10. Lin, Y., J. Zhang, and J. Gray, *A Testing Framework for Model Transformations*, in *Model-Driven Software Development - Research and Practice in Software Engineering*. 2005, Springer.
11. Küster, J.M. *Systematic Validation of Model Transformations*. in *WiSME'04(associated to UML'04)*. 2004. Lisbon, Portugal.
12. Fleurey, F., J. Steel, and B. Baudry. *Validation in Model-Driven Engineering: Testing Model Transformations*. in *MoDeVa*. 2004. Rennes, France.
13. Ghosh, S. and A. Mathur, *Interface mutation*. Software Testing, Verification and Reliability, 2001. **11**(4): p. 227-247.
14. Trung, D.-T., S. Ghosh, F. Robert, B. Baudry, and F. Fleurey. *A Taxonomy of Faults for UML Designs*. in *2nd MoDeVa workshop - Model design and Validation, in conjunction with MoDELS05*. 2005. Montego Bay, Jamaica.

Author Index

Lecture Notes in Computer Science

For information about Vols. 1–3977

please contact your bookseller or Springer

Vol. 4024: S. Donatelli, P. S. Thiagarajan (Eds.), Petri Nets and Other Models of Concurrency - ICATPN 2006. XI, 441 pages. 2006.

Vol. 4021: E. André, L. Dybkjær, W. Minker, H. Neumann, M. Weber (Eds.), Perception and Interactive Technologies. XI, 217 pages. 2006. (Sublibrary LNAI).

Vol. 4020: A. Bredenfeld, A. Jacoff, I. Noda, Y. Takahashi (Eds.), RoboCup 2005: Robot Soccer World Cup IX. XVII, 727 pages. 2006. (Sublibrary LNAI).

Vol. 4019: M. Johnson, V. Vene (Eds.), Algebraic Methodology and Software Technology. XI, 389 pages. 2006.

Vol. 4018: V. Wade, H. Ashman, B. Smyth (Eds.), Adaptive Hypermedia and Adaptive Web-Based Systems. XVI, 474 pages. 2006.

Vol. 4016: J.X. Yu, M. Kitsuregawa, H.V. Leong (Eds.), Advances in Web-Age Information Management. XVII, 606 pages. 2006.

Vol. 4014: T. Uustalu (Ed.), Mathematics of Program Construction. X, 455 pages. 2006.

Vol. 4013: L. Lamontagne, M. Marchand (Eds.), Advances in Artificial Intelligence. XIII, 564 pages. 2006. (Sublibrary LNAI).

Vol. 4012: T. Washio, A. Sakurai, K. Nakajima, H. Takeda, S. Tojo, M. Yokoo (Eds.), New Frontiers in Artificial Intelligence. XIII, 484 pages. 2006. (Sublibrary LNAI).

Vol. 4011: Y. Sure, J. Domingue (Eds.), The Semantic Web: Research and Applications. XIX, 726 pages. 2006.

Vol. 4010: S. Dunne, B. Stoddart (Eds.), Unifying Theories of Programming. VIII, 257 pages. 2006.

Vol. 4009: M. Lewenstein, G. Valiente (Eds.), Combinatorial Pattern Matching. XII, 414 pages. 2006.

Vol. 4008: J.C. Augusto, C.D. Nugent (Eds.), Designing Smart Homes. XI, 183 pages. 2006. (Sublibrary LNAI).

Vol. 4007: C. Àlvarez, M. Serna (Eds.), Experimental Algorithms. XI, 329 pages. 2006.

Vol. 4006: L.M. Pinho, M. González Harbour (Eds.), Reliable Software Technologies – Ada-Europe 2006. XII, 241 pages. 2006.

Vol. 4005: G. Lugosi, H.U. Simon (Eds.), Learning Theory. XI, 656 pages. 2006. (Sublibrary LNAI).

Vol. 4004: S. Vaudenay (Ed.), Advances in Cryptology - EUROCRYPT 2006. XIV, 613 pages. 2006.

Vol. 4003: Y. Koucheryavy, J. Harju, V.B. Iversen (Eds.), Next Generation Teletraffic and Wired/Wireless Advanced Networking. XVI, 582 pages. 2006.

Vol. 4001: E. Dubois, K. Pohl (Eds.), Advanced Information Systems Engineering. XVI, 560 pages. 2006.

Vol. 3999: C. Kop, G. Fliedl, H.C. Mayr, E. Métais (Eds.), Natural Language Processing and Information Systems. XIII, 227 pages. 2006.

Vol. 3998: T. Calamoneri, I. Finocchi, G.F. Italiano (Eds.), Algorithms and Complexity. XII, 394 pages. 2006.

Vol. 3997: W. Grieskamp, C. Weise (Eds.), Formal Approaches to Software Testing. XII, 219 pages. 2006.

Vol. 3996: A. Keller, J.-P. Martin-Flatin (Eds.), Self-Managed Networks, Systems, and Services. X, 185 pages. 2006.

Vol. 3995: G. Müller (Ed.), Emerging Trends in Information and Communication Security. XX, 524 pages. 2006.

Vol. 3994: V.N. Alexandrov, G.D. van Albada, P.M.A. Sloot, J. Dongarra (Eds.), Computational Science – ICCS 2006, Part IV. XXXV, 1096 pages. 2006.

Vol. 3993: V.N. Alexandrov, G.D. van Albada, P.M.A. Sloot, J. Dongarra (Eds.), Computational Science – ICCS 2006, Part III. XXXVI, 1136 pages. 2006.

Vol. 3992: V.N. Alexandrov, G.D. van Albada, P.M.A. Sloot, J. Dongarra (Eds.), Computational Science – ICCS 2006, Part II. XXXV, 1122 pages. 2006.

Vol. 3991: V.N. Alexandrov, G.D. van Albada, P.M.A. Sloot, J. Dongarra (Eds.), Computational Science – ICCS 2006, Part I. LXXXI, 1096 pages. 2006.

Vol. 3990: J. C. Beck, B.M. Smith (Eds.), Integration of AI and OR Techniques in Constraint Programming for Combinatorial Optimization Problems. X, 301 pages. 2006.

Vol. 3989: J. Zhou, M. Yung, F. Bao, Applied Cryptography and Network Security. XIV, 488 pages. 2006.

Vol. 3988: A. Beckmann, U. Berger, B. Löwe, J.V. Tucker (Eds.), Logical Approaches to Computational Barriers. XV, 608 pages. 2006.

Vol. 3987: M. Hazas, J. Krumm, T. Strang (Eds.), Location- and Context-Awareness. X, 289 pages. 2006.

Vol. 3986: K. Stølen, W.H. Winsborough, F. Martinelli, F. Massacci (Eds.), Trust Management. XIV, 474 pages. 2006.

Vol. 3984: M. Gavrilova, O. Gervasi, V. Kumar, C.J. K. Tan, D. Taniar, A. Laganà, Y. Mun, H. Choo (Eds.), Computational Science and Its Applications - ICCSA 2006, Part V. XXV, 1045 pages. 2006.

Vol. 3983: M. Gavrilova, O. Gervasi, V. Kumar, C.J. K. Tan, D. Taniar, A. Laganà, Y. Mun, H. Choo (Eds.), Computational Science and Its Applications - ICCSA 2006, Part IV. XXVI, 1191 pages. 2006.

Vol. 3982: M. Gavrilova, O. Gervasi, V. Kumar, C.J. K. Tan, D. Taniar, A. Laganà, Y. Mun, H. Choo (Eds.), Computational Science and Its Applications - ICCSA 2006, Part III. XXV, 1243 pages. 2006.

Vol. 3981: M. Gavrilova, O. Gervasi, V. Kumar, C.J. K. Tan, D. Taniar, A. Laganà, Y. Mun, H. Choo (Eds.), Computational Science and Its Applications - ICCSA 2006, Part II. XXVI, 1255 pages. 2006.

Vol. 3980: M. Gavrilova, O. Gervasi, V. Kumar, C.J. K. Tan, D. Taniar, A. Laganà, Y. Mun, H. Choo (Eds.), Computational Science and Its Applications - ICCSA 2006, Part I. LXXV, 1199 pages. 2006.

Vol. 3979: T.S. Huang, N. Sebe, M.S. Lew, V. Pavlović, M. Kölsch, A. Galata, B. Kisačanin (Eds.), Computer Vision in Human-Computer Interaction. XII, 121 pages. 2006.

Vol. 3978: B. Hnich, M. Carlsson, F. Fages, F. Rossi (Eds.), Recent Advances in Constraints. VIII, 179 pages. 2006. (Sublibrary LNAI).